REEF FISH
Identification

FLORIDA CARIBBEAN BAHAMAS

PAUL HUMANN

EDITED BY
NED DELOACH

NEW WORLD PUBLICATIONS, INC.

Printed by
Paramount Miller Graphics, Inc.
Jacksonville, Florida U.S.A.

Acknowledgments

The concept, design and information found in both the first and second editions of this book were the result of considerable encouragement, help, and advice from many friends and acquaintances. Both editions became much larger undertakings and involved many more people than expected. I wish to express my sincere gratitude to everyone involved. Naturally, the names of a few who played especially significant roles come to mind.

Copy Editor, friend and confidant, Patricia Reilly-Collins, spent untold hours making sure what I wrote was phrased in comprehensible English. Wonderful friends, John and Marion Bacon gave generously of their time, assistance and boat, helping me photograph many Florida fish; and son Mike Bacon's photographs helped fill many remaining gaps. Mark Ullmann was an indispensable resource in photographing fish of northeast Florida. Danny Grizzard of Panama City Marine Institute gave freely of his time and facilities assuring a comprehensive collection of pictures from the Florida Panhandle. Peter Hull and Neill Faulman, with Mote Marine Laboratory, Sarasota, FL, took us 40 miles offshore to photograph deep-water, west coast Florida species. Dan Wagner of P & B Productions was most helpful with his knowledge of east coast Florida species. Ken Marks' enthusiastic advice proved invaluable. I also wish to thank Guy Beard for his help in design and marketing concepts and Mary DeLoach and Jackie Jones for their editing skills. Finally, I must mention my collaborator, editor and best friend, Ned DeLoach. Without his help, this project would have never been completed.

Numerous individuals, resorts and dive operations have assisted in finding and photographing elusive species, and provided dive services and accommodations. We wish to thank them all; their help was invaluable. They include: Neal Watson of Neal Watson's Undersea Adventures; Gary Adkison and Walker's Cay Hotel and Marina; Jene Kruger and Fraizer Nivens of Nassau Scuba Centre; Orange Hill Resort, Nassau; Mike & Sandra Seale of Exploresub Barbados; Sandy Beach Hotel, Barbados; Michael and Karin Allard of Scuba St. Lucia; Anse Chastanet Resort, St. Lucia; Thomas Peabody & Iain Grummitt and Tamariain Water Sports, Anguilla; Jack Strickland of Aquaventures Culebra, P.R.; Adrien and Bonnie Briggs of Sunset House, Grand Cayman; Jon Tromm of the Isla Mia, Roatan; Cathy Church & Herb Rafael of Grand Cayman; Dr. J.R. Wilcox, Dr. Jonathan Gorham and Dr. Gary Bouska of Florida Power and Light; Anna O'Donnell and Capt. John Norwood and Scuba Bimini; Spencer Slate, Laddie Akins, Nestor Morales and Gloria Teague of Atlantis Dive Center, Key Largo; Rick Smith of Undersea Miami.

PHOTO CREDITS

All species photographs in this book were taken underwater in their natural habitat. Many underwater photographers added their work to this collection. I appreciate their efforts and assistance in making this book as comprehensive as possible. They include: **Laddie Akins**, 253t, 285t; **Mike Bacon**, 277t, 297tm, 307m, 311b, 313t, 387b; **Marjorie Bank**, 115b, 151m; **Steve Bennett**, 295m; **Dr. James Bohnsack**, 299b; **Carl Campbell**, 319t; **Rosemond Clery**, 373t; **Ned DeLoach**, 20m, 21m, 22m, 25t, 33t, 40m, 41tm, 43b, 47m, 51tmb, 53m, 57b, 59m, 63b, 65tb, 71m, 75b, 77tmb, 88m, 91b, 93b, 96b, 99b, 101m, 105m, 109tm, 120b, 121b, 123t, 125t, 126m, 131b, 133m, 139b, 140t, 144b, 145m, 152b, 153b, 154m, 158m 163m, 165b, 171b, 175m, 177m, 184m, 185t, 187b, 188b, 193mb, 205b, 206b, 207mb, 209b, 210m, 211b, 215b, 221m, 225tm, 226m, 227m, 231m, 243m, 245m, 251mb, 253m, 255m, 260m, 263b, 264br, 266bl, 267m, 268mlr, 269tb, 270b, 271b, 273tb, 275m, 276b, 277b, 281t, 283b, 284m, 301m, 303m, 315b, 325m, 333b, 335m, 337m, 352m, 354bl, 357b, 365b, 367b, 369b, 374m, 375b; **Joshua Feingold**, 317t; **A&A Ferrari/Innerspace Visions**, 81m; **Dr. David Hall**, 295b; **Howard Hall**, 385b; **Wayne Hasson**, 389m; **Mike Kelly**, 241c; **Michael Lawrence**, 169t, 303b; **Larry Lipski**, 273m; **Ken Marks**, 57m, 207t, 333m, 361t; **Fred McConnaughey**, 85m, 94t, 103m, 107b, 149m, 150m, 154bl, 219t, 307b; **Scott Michael**, 275b, 301b, 311m, 165m, 369m; **Christopher Newbert**, 48m; **Fraizer Nivens**, 383b; **Doug Perrine/Innerspace Visions**, 63m, 65m, 79b, 104m, 345t, 359t, 379b, 381mb, 387m; **Carl Roessler**, 381t; **Mike Seale**, 25b, 308bl, 311t; **Wayne Shoemake**, 359b; **David Snyder**, 67t, 93t, 209t, 259b, 267t, 327m, 339m, 357m; **Tom Stack/Tom Stack Associates**, 385t; **Walt Stearns**, 192m, 237t, 241m, 315m; **Mark Strickland**, 167t, 369m; **Graeme Teague**, 4, 261t, 299t, 309t, 319b; **Mark Ullmann**, 79m; **Louis Usie**, 301t; **Jeff Utt**, 331t; **James Watt/Innerspace Visions**, 385m; **Clay Wiseman**, 317b; the remaining 494 photographs were taken by the author, **Paul Humann**.

CREDITS

Editor: Ned DeLoach
Copy Editor: Patricia Reilly-Collins
Layout & Design: Paul Humann & Ned DeLoach
Art Director & Drawings: Michael O'Connell
Color Separations: Ben Vernon of Lithographic Services, Inc., Jacksonville, FL;
Buddy Waggoner & Kit Keating of Paramount Miller Graphics, Jacksonville, FL
First Edition, First Printing 1989; Second 1991; Third 1992; Fourth 1993; Fifth 1994.
Second Edition, First Printing 1994, Second Printing 1996, Third Printing (Revised) 1997, Fourth Printing 1999.
ISBN 1-878348-07-8, Library Edition ISBN 1-878348-14-0, Library of Congress # 94-068594
First Edition Copyright, © 1989; Second Edition, Copyright, © 1994 by Paul Humann.
Publisher: New World Publications, Inc., 1861 Cornell Road, Jacksonville, FL 32207, (904) 737-6558

Scientific Acknowledgments

Special recognition must be given to the numerous ichthyologists who gave freely of their time, advice and knowledge in confirming or providing identifications and supplemental information. Without this most generous assistance, the value of this book as a reference source would be greatly diminished and the number of included species reduced. Every attempt has been made to keep this text and the identifications as accurate as possible; however, I'm sure a few errors crept in, and they are my sole responsibility.

The ichthyologist's name is followed by their institution, and the fish family/families with which they assisted.

Dr. James Bohnsack, National Marine Fisheries Service, Miami - general reference
Dr. Margaret Bradbury, California Academy of Sciences, San Francisco - Batfishes
Mr. Lew Bullock, Florida Marine Research Institute, St. Petersburg - Seabasses
Dr. Jose I. Castro, National Marine Fisheries Service, Miami - Sharks
Dr. Ileana E. Clavijo, University of North Carolina, Wilmington - Parrotfishes, Wrasses
Dr. Kathleen S. Cole, Bishop's University, Lennoxville, Quebec - Gobies
Dr. Michael L. Domeier, Seabass/Hamlets
Dr. William Eschmeyer, California Academy of Sciences, San Francisco - Scorpionfishes
Mr. Brian Farm, Tanzania Wildlife Conservation Monitoring - Parrotfishes, Wrasses
Dr. David Greenfield, University of Hawaii, Honolulu - Gobies, Blennies, Clingfishes, Cardinalfishes
Dr. Dannie Hensley, University of Puerto Rico, Mayaguez - Damselfishes
Dr. Joseph Kimmel, National Marine Fisheries Service, St. Petersburg - Seabasses, general reference
Mr. Mark Leiby, Florida Marine Research Institute, St. Petersburg - Flounders
Mr. Kenneth Lindeman, Coastal Research & Education, Miami - Grunts, Snappers, general reference
Dr. Edward Matheson, Florida Marine Research Institute, St. Petersburg - Mojarras
Dr. John McCosker, California Academy of Sciences, San Francisco - Eels, general reference
Dr. Jack Randall, Bishop Museum, Honolulu - Porgies, Blennies, general reference
Dr. Richard Rosenblatt, Scripps Institution Of Oceanography, La Jolla - Triplefin Blennies
Dr. William Smith-Vaniz, National Fish & Wildlife Service, Gainesville - Jacks, Jawfishes, general reference
Dr. Victor G. Springer, Smithsonian, National Museum of Natural History, Washington, D.C. - Blennies
Dr. James Tyler, Smithsonian, National Museum of Natural History, Washington, D.C. - Boxfishes
Dr. Jeffrey T. Williams, Smithsonian, National Museum of Natural History, Washington D.C. - Blennies
Dr. Richard Winterbottom, Royal Ontario Museum, Toronto - Filefishes

Over the years, several ichthyologists listed above have been especially helpful and deserve additional comment.

Dr. William Smith-Vaniz was my wild dive buddy as we searched well below safe diving limits, at night and without lights, for the first living specimens of *Kryptophanaron alfredi* in 1977. Bill continues to be a friend and important source of information. He was the primary scientific reference for the First Edition of *Reef Fish Identification*.

Dr. John McCosker is another madman who went well below safe limits with me to capture the second living specimens of *Kryptophanaron alfredi* - an expedition dubbed the "Krypto Caper." John and I continue our friendship and enjoy research expeditions together. He opened many doors to the scientific community, and was my primary scientific reference for *Reef Fish Identification - Galapagos*.

Ken Lindeman developed simplified techniques for the visual identification of the exceedingly similar appearing juvenile grunts and kindly shared his methodology. Grunts are among the most abundant, diverse and important reef fish families of the western Atlantic. Enabling laymen to identify these juveniles is an important addition to this book. Ken works with Coastal Research and Education, a nonprofit organization that initiates innovative fusions of scientific research and education through ongoing applied habitat research, ichthyology, and coastal education programs.

Dr. James Bohnsack has become a friend and regular source of assistance and information. Many of his identification tips and methodology have been incorporated into this book. Jim's guidance, encouragement and influential status within the scientific community continues to be extremely valuable in the development of REEF (Reef Environmental Education Foundation) - an organization of recreational divers that regularly monitors marine fish populations and coral reef health in Florida, the Bahamas and Caribbean.

Editor's Note

No adventure on earth inspires our innate thrill of discovery more than a swim in an underwater wilderness. Here, hidden just below the ocean's surface, lies a beautiful, exotic, and enchanting realm rife with mystery. Today's divers are the pioneers who will witness and chronicle this last great undocumented natural history.

Paul Humann's *Reef Fish Identification,* 1989, and its companion text *Reef Creature Identification,* 1992, and *Reef Coral Identification*, 1993, have revolutionized marine life identification. The comprehensive, three-volume *Reef Set,* with its user-friendly, quick-reference format and unparalleled collection of photographs, provides recreational divers with the tools necessary to become underwater naturalists.

The enlarged and updated 2nd edition of *Reef Fish Identification,* with 124 new fish species (several photographed for the first time), and 325 additional color plates, was published in response to the ever-growing number of divers and marine scientists who require an even more sophisticated visual identification reference. Most significant is the incorporation of fish species found in marine habitats neighboring the reef — sand flats, rubble fields, grass beds, open-water, coral caves, and surf zones — as well as many temperate-water species from central and northeast Florida and the eastern Gulf of Mexico. These additions, coupled with the use of multiple plates showing marked visual differences within the same species are intended to greatly expand the scope and accuracy of visual identification of marine fish in Florida, the Caribbean and Bahamas.

About The Author

Paul Humann lay motionless on white sand 15 feet below the surface. For over an hour he patiently squinted into the tiny viewfinder of his reflex camera. All this time the lens remained focused on the exposed head of a small fish hiding in a hole just inches away. Without warning, the male Sailfin Blenny shot out of its burrow and rapidly fluttered its dramatic dorsal fin in an attempt to attract a nearby female. In the same instant the shutter was triggered. This was only the third exposure of the afternoon and just the 14th taken since the colony of Sailfins was discovered on the outer fringe of a patch reef the week before. The diminutive Sailfin is not a cooperative subject. Its spirited courtship display occurs rarely and without warning, but Paul was determined to capture the image he wanted.

Two weeks later, on his seventh visit to the colony and after ten hours of patiently waiting in the sand, everything came together. The fish popped out from the hole, stayed within the one-inch field of focus, spread its fin and became one more species in what has become the most extensive collection of reef fish ever photographed.

What wonderful things are accomplished by those few individuals who somehow muster the courage to leave the security of a domestic life in pursuit of a dream. Paul Humann falls easily into their ranks.

He began documenting marine life in the Caribbean in 1964. At that time he was an attorney in Wichita, Kansas; his dream of becoming an experienced underwater photographer was severely limited by the demands of a work-a-day world. At best he could only finagle a month each year to dive. Even with this limited time underwater, many of his pictures were published, including several that appeared as the "Fish of the Month" in *Skin Diver* magazine.

In a bold move, at the beginning of 1972, he left his established law practice to follow his dream. He became owner/captain of the *Cayman Diver*, the Caribbean's first successful live-aboard diving cruiser. This new way of life offered the unique opportunity to photograph and study marine life nearly every day for the next eight years. Many of the photographs in *Reef Fish Identification* were taken in the Cayman Islands during this period.

In 1979 he sold the *Cayman Diver* to photograph and write full time. His fish collection continued to grow as he traveled throughout the Caribbean, Bahamas and Florida searching for new species. His photographs and articles have appeared in nearly every major diving and wildlife publication. Untiring efforts have produced ten marine life books including *Reef Fish Identification - Galapagos*, and the two companion volumes to this text, *Reef Creature Identification* and *Reef Coral Identification,* which together complete his popular marine life trilogy.

Each of the 670 photographs in this book has it own story, but possibly the most exciting is Paul's discovery of an Atlantic Flashlight Fish, *Kryptophanaron alfredi*, in 1977. Prior to his find this elusive species was only known from two dead specimens collected by marine biologists: one from a fish trap at 600 feet; the other, a dead specimen found floating on the surface years earlier.

On the moonless night of his first sighting, Paul was leading a night dive on Cayman's West Bay Wall. During descent, one of the party had a light failure. Paul exchanged lights and swam toward the wall. In the darkness he noticed a flickering glow moving across a cave entrance. Intrigued, he moved closer and was met by what appeared to be two illuminated eyes. Retrieving his light he returned to the cave and waited until the "eyes" appeared once again. Switching on the light, a small, dark fish with glowing patches below each eye was caught in the beam.

Word about the strange sighting spread. A few months later Paul led an expedition organized by underwater photographer Fred McConnaughey and Bill Smith-Vaniz, an ichthyologist from the Academy of Natural Sciences of Philadelphia. Theorizing the fish to be primarily a deep-water dweller that only approached the surface on moonless nights, the team dived deep along the wall, well below the moon's illumination and without lights. After five nights the first Atlantic Flashlight Fish was photographed in its natural habitat and a living specimen was captured.

Today, Paul continues to actively dive the world's reefs in search of new species. Without his lifelong dedication to a dream, such an exceptional work as *Reef Fish Identification* would have never become reality.

Contents

How To Use This Book

Twelve Identification Groups

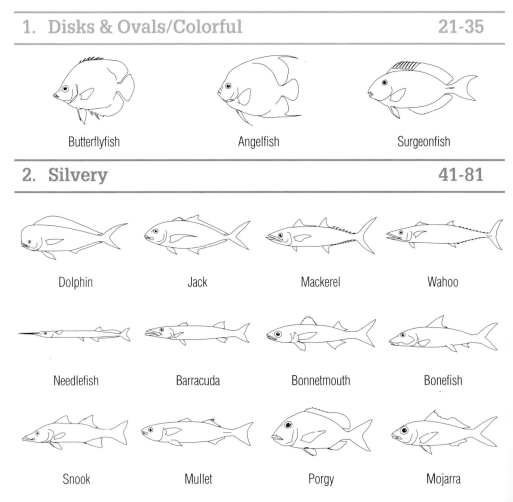

1. Disks & Ovals/Colorful   21-35

Butterflyfish   Angelfish   Surgeonfish

2. Silvery   41-81

Dolphin   Jack   Mackerel   Wahoo

Needlefish   Barracuda   Bonnetmouth   Bonefish

Snook   Mullet   Porgy   Mojarra

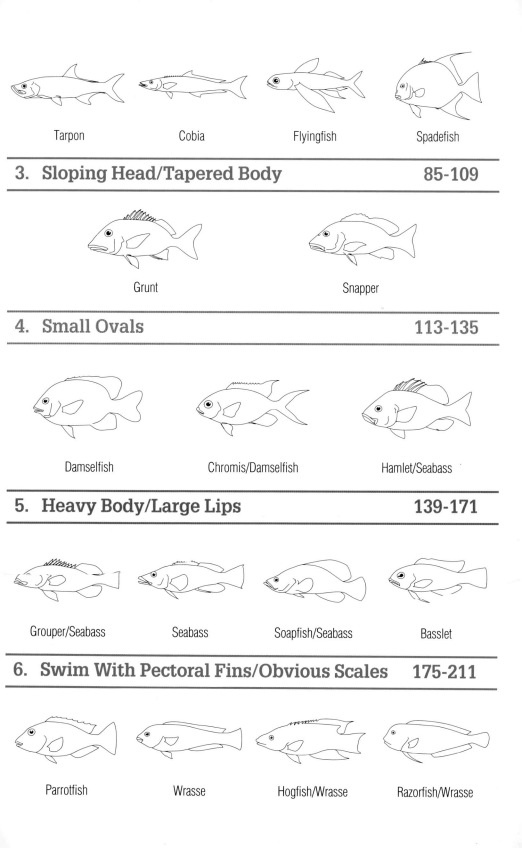

Tarpon Cobia Flyingfish Spadefish

3. Sloping Head/Tapered Body 85-109

Grunt Snapper

4. Small Ovals 113-135

Damselfish Chromis/Damselfish Hamlet/Seabass

5. Heavy Body/Large Lips 139-171

Grouper/Seabass Seabass Soapfish/Seabass Basslet

6. Swim With Pectoral Fins/Obvious Scales 175-211

Parrotfish Wrasse Hogfish/Wrasse Razorfish/Wrasse

7. Reddish/Big Eyes   215-231

Squirrelfish   Bigeye   Cardinalfish

8. Small, Elongated Bottom-Dwellers   235-287

Goby   Blenny   Dragonet   Jawfish

9. Odd-Shaped Bottom Dwellers   293-321

Flounder   Clingfish   Batfish   Toadfish

Scorpionfish   Frogfish   Stargazer   Searobin

Flying Gurnard   Lizardfish   Seahorse

Pipefish   Hawkfish   Cod

10. Odd-Shaped Swimmers 325-361

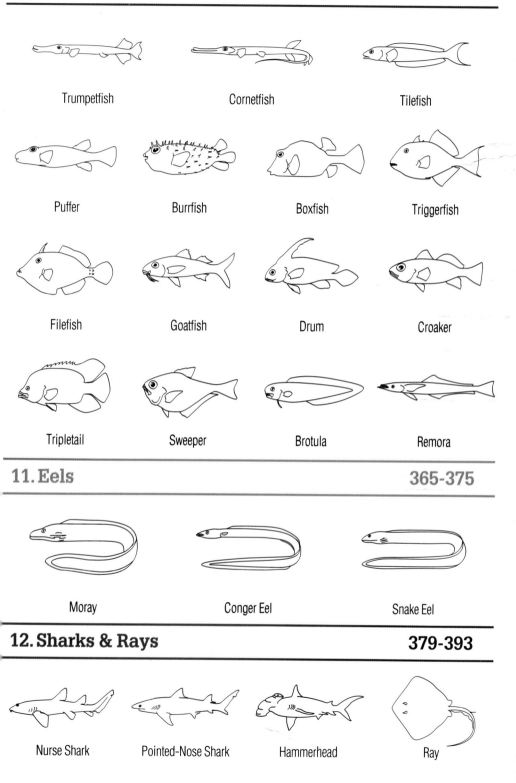

Trumpetfish

Cornetfish

Tilefish

Puffer

Burrfish

Boxfish

Triggerfish

Filefish

Goatfish

Drum

Croaker

Tripletail

Sweeper

Brotula

Remora

11. Eels 365-375

Moray

Conger Eel

Snake Eel

12. Sharks & Rays 379-393

Nurse Shark

Pointed-Nose Shark

Hammerhead

Ray

How To Use This Book

Identification Groups

Trying to identify a specific fish from the more than 500 species that inhabit the reefs of Florida, the Caribbean and the Bahamas can be a perplexing task. To help simplify the process, families are arranged into 12 color-coded and numbered ID Groups. Each group is distinguished by similar physical or behavioral characteristics that can be recognized underwater. Although there are a few anomalies, most species integrate easily into this system.

The ID Groups and their families are displayed on the Contents pages. Each group's similar characteristics are listed at the beginning of its chapter. It is important for beginning fish-watchers to become familiar with the make-up of each ID Group, so they can go quickly to the correct chapter to start the identification process.

The next step is to learn to recognize the major families that comprise each ID Group. Families are scientific groupings based on evolutionary sequence and consequently, typically have similar physical characteristics. An overview of the family's behavioral and physical characteristics (that are observable by divers) is presented at the beginning of each chapter. The total number of species included in this book, along with diagrams of representative family body shapes, is also given.

Names

Information about each fish begins with the common name (that used by the general public). In the past, using common names for identification was impractical because several fish were known by more than one name. For example, Mangrove Snapper and Gray Snapper referred to the same fish. In 1948, The American Fisheries Society helped to standardize common names by publishing a preferred list that is updated every ten years. Their recommendations are used in this book. Common names are capitalized in this book to help them stand out, although this practice is not considered grammatically correct.

Below the common name, in italics, is the two-part scientific name. The first word (always capitalized) is the genus. The genus name is given to a group of species which share a common ancestor, and usually have similar anatomical and physiological characteristics. (For example, about half of the gobies in the Caribbean are in the genus *Gobiosoma* and look and behave much the same). The second word (never capitalized) is the species. A species includes only animals that are sexually compatible and produce fertile offspring. (Continuing our example of gobies, the Spotlight Goby is *Gobiosoma louisae*, while the Yellowline Goby is *Gobiosoma horsti*, and so on.) Each usually has a combination of visually distinctive features that separates them from all others. Genus and species names, rooted in Latin and Greek, are used by scientists throughout the world.

The common and scientific family names are listed next. Because of its importance in identification, the common family name is also printed at the top of the left page.

Phases

Many species are exhibited in more than one photograph. This is necessary to demonstrate the variations in color, markings and shape that occur within the species.

Occasionally, the maturation phases of certain fish are so dramatic that they may be confused as a different species altogether. These phases can include JUVENILE, INTERMEDIATE and ADULT. Parrotfish and wrasse are somewhat different; the adult stage is called the INITIAL PHASE (IP); and an additional stage, not present in other families, the TERMINAL PHASE (TP), includes only sexually mature males which are the largest and most colorful of the species. When the maturation phase is not given, the photograph is that of an adult. No attempt has been made to include juveniles that resemble the adults, or that live in habitats not frequented by divers.

Many fishes are able to alter both color and markings, either for camouflage or with mood changes. If these changes confuse identification, they may also be pictured. (Examples are the Yellowfin Grouper, pg. 141 and Longlure Frogfish, pg. 309. In a few species, the appearance of the MALE and FEMALE also differs. (An example is the Rosy Blenny, pg. 265).

Size

The general size range of the fish that divers are most likely to observe, followed by the maximum recorded size.

Depth

The depth range within which this species is generally reported. This range is not absolute; on occasion, the species may be found shallower or deeper.

Distinctive Features

Colors, markings and anatomical differences that distinguish the fish from similar appearing species. In most cases, these features are readily apparent to divers, but occasionally they are quite subtle. When practical, the locations of these features are indicated by numbered arrows on the drawing next to the photograph. The numbers are keyed to the DISTINCTIVE FEATURES explanation in bold type on the left page.

Description

A general description of colors, markings and anatomical features. The information given in "DISTINCTIVE FEATURES" (above) is not repeated in this section unless it is qualified or expanded upon.

Colors — The colors of many species vary considerably from individual to individual. In such situations, the DESCRIPTION might read: "Vary from reddish brown to olive-brown or gray." This means that the fish could be any of the colors and shades between. Many fish also have an ability to pale, darken, and change color. Because of this, color alone is rarely used for identification. (An exception is the Fairy Basslet, pg. 171, whose colors are distinctive and never change.).

Markings — The terminology used to describe fish markings is defined in the following drawings.

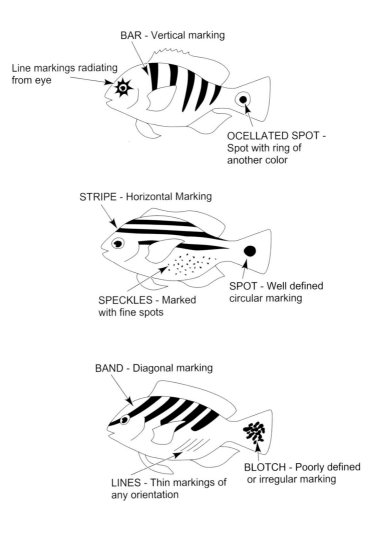

BAR - Vertical marking

Line markings radiating from eye

OCELLATED SPOT - Spot with ring of another color

STRIPE - Horizontal Marking

SPECKLES - Marked with fine spots

SPOT - Well defined circular marking

BAND - Diagonal marking

LINES - Thin markings of any orientation

BLOTCH - Poorly defined or irregular marking

Anatomy — Anatomical features are often referred to as part of the identification process. The features used in this text are pinpointed in the following drawings.

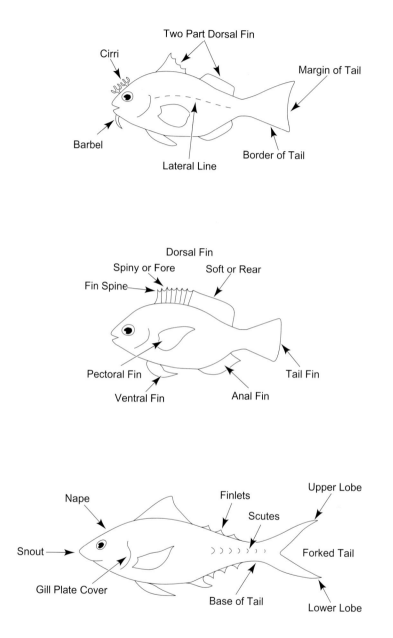

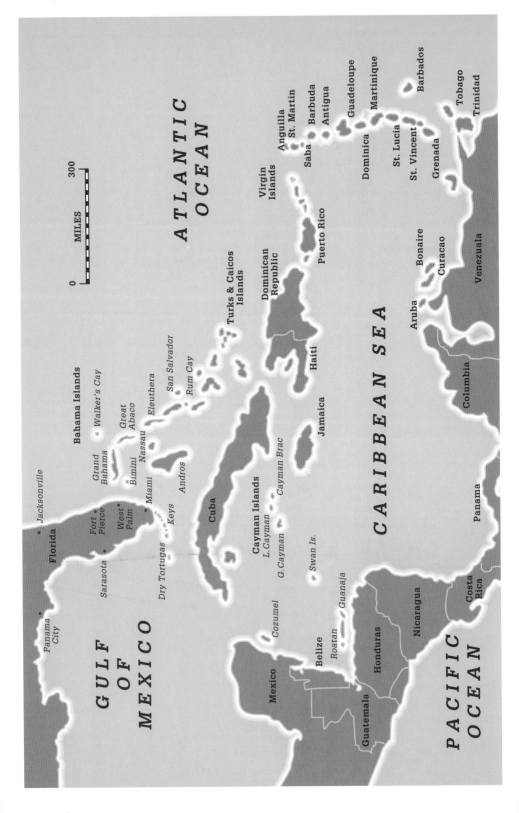

14

Abundance & Distribution

Abundance refers to a diver's likelihood of observing a species in its normal habitat and depth range on any given dive. Because of reclusive habits and other factors, this does not always present an accurate portrait of actual populations. (Abundance information is not given, however, for areas outside Florida, Bahamas or the Caribbean.) Definitions are as follows:

Abundant — At least several sightings can be expected on nearly every dive.

Common — Sightings are frequent, but not necessarily expected on every dive.

Occasional — Sightings are not unusual, but are not expected on a regular basis.

Uncommon — Sightings are unusual.

Rare — Sightings are exceptional.

Not reported — The species has not been reported from the indicated area.

Distribution describes where the species is found geographically. Its distribution within Florida, Bahamas and the Caribbean is given first. If the abundance within this range varies, the locations are listed in sequence from areas of most sightings to those of least sightings. Additional distribution outside Florida, Bahamas and the Caribbean follows. Concluding this section is a listing of areas within Florida, the Bahamas and/or the Caribbean where the species has not been reported (if any). Below each picture is the location where the photograph was taken.

Habitat & Behavior

Habitat is the type of underwater terrain where a particular species is likely to be found. Habitats frequented by divers, such as reefs, adjacent areas of sand and rubble, sea grass beds and walls have been emphasized.

Behavior is the fish's normal activities that may be observed by a diver that helps in identification. Two distinctive behaviors, schooling and cleaner stations, are detailed below.

Schooling — Many fish congregate in groups commonly called schools. The two primary reasons for this behavior are predator protection and cooperative hunting. It is theorized that hunted species pack together and move in unison so that predators have a difficult time picking out and attacking a single target. In the confusion of numbers, all members of the school may survive the attack. If, however, a fish becomes separated from the school, the predator can concentrate on the lone fish and the attack is often successful. Some predators also school. They facilitate hunting by cooperating with each other in separating and confusing potential victims. The advantage of schooling also extends to algae-grazing fish such as Blue Tangs who, by sheer force of numbers, may overcome the territorial defenses of damselfish.

There are several types of congregations. Polarized schools are those in which all fish swim together in the same direction, at the same speed, keeping the same relative distance between one another. Non-polarized schools, or simply "schools," are those where the fish stay well together,

Polarized school of Silversides attacked by Barracuda [left].

Non-polarized school of juvenile Blueheads [right].

but do not display the rigid uniformity of movement seen in polarized schools. Fish may also come together for reasons other than protection or hunting. These types of gatherings often include a mixing of species and should, more properly, be called aggregations, rather than schools. For example, they may drift together in the shade of a coral head, or be attracted to the same area because of food. There is considerable gradation between the three types of congregations, making clear-cut categorizations difficult at times.

Aggregations of several species often congregate while feeding in the plankton stream above the reef [left].

Aggregation of several species on the reef [right].

Cleaner Stations — Several species of fish and marine invertebrates feed by cleaning parasites and organic debris from other fish. Best known for this behavior are several of the gobies, juvenile Spotfin and Spanish Hogfish, juvenile Bluehead Wrasse, and several species of shrimp. "Cleaners" often gather on and around a single coral head and wait for the arrival of fish wanting to be cleaned. These established areas are called "cleaner stations." Groupers are the most common visitors to cleaner stations, but numerous other species are occasionally cleaned. Fish wanting to be cleaned arrive at the station and go into a distinctively relaxed position, often resting on the bottom and listing from side to side. The cleaners then swim out and scour the fish, including the insides of their mouths and between the gills. When satisfied, the cleaned fish gives a distinctive shake and the cleaners depart.

Cleaning Gobies stream out from reef to clean a Yellowmouth Grouper [left].

Juvenile Spanish Hogfish cleans a Tiger Grouper [opposite top].

16

Reaction To Divers

This information relates to the fish's normal reaction to divers, and what a diver can do to try to get a closer look.

Similar Species

Occasionally there are similar appearing species that are not pictured. Usually they are fish that are rarely observed by divers. Characteristics and information are given that distinguish them from the pictured species.

Note

Includes any supplementary information that may help in the identification process or be of general interest. Also included are other (but not preferred) common names, and recent changes in scientific classification.

Disks & Ovals/Colorful
Butterflyfish– Angelfish – Surgeonfish

This ID Group consists of fish that are thin-bodied and have round or oval profiles. All have small mouths and are generally quite colorful.

FAMILY: Butterflyfish—Chaetodontidae
5 Species Included

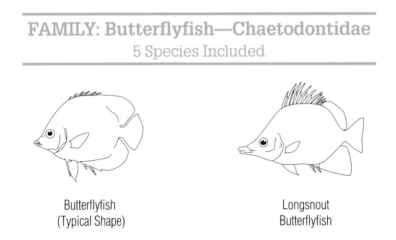

Butterflyfish
(Typical Shape)

Longsnout
Butterflyfish

Reminiscent of their butterfly namesake, these small, colorful fish flit about the reefs in search of food. They travel alone, or often in pairs, using keen eyesight to spot tiny worms, exposed polyps and other marine invertebrates.

These round, thin-bodied fish are easy to recognize. Their small size (usually less than six inches) and slightly concave foreheads make them easy to distinguish from the larger, similar-shaped angelfish which have rounded foreheads. Only the Longsnout differ somewhat from the family in that they are somewhat smaller, generally inhabit deeper reefs, and are usually solitary and secretive.

Butterflyfish are silver to white, with yellow tints and dark markings. Their eyes are concealed by dark bars on the head. This, and the false eyespots found on juveniles and two adult species, are characteristics thought to confuse predators. At night they become inactive, and may change color and markings.

The colors and markings of juveniles are somewhat different from those of adults, though their body shapes are nearly identical. Identifying adults is not difficult; however, learning to differentiate these similar-appearing juveniles is more of a challenge.

FAMILY: Angelfish—Pomacanthidae
7 Species Included

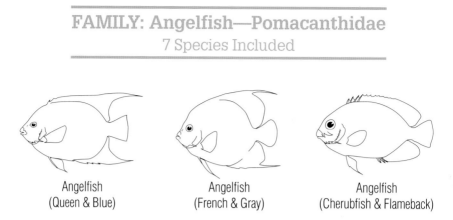

Angelfish
(Queen & Blue)

Angelfish
(French & Gray)

Angelfish
(Cherubfish & Flameback)

Beautiful, disk-shaped angelfish are similar in habits and shape to butterflyfish; in fact, they were included in the same family for many years. Angelfish swim more gracefully, and generally grow to more than one foot in length (exceptions are the Cherubfish and Flameback, which grow to only three inches). Adult angelfish have long dorsal and anal fins, and rounded foreheads. A spine extending from the rear cheek over the lower gill cover conclusively distinguishes them from Butterflyfish.

Adults are easily distinguished from one another; however, most juveniles differ significantly in both markings and color, and are more difficult to identify. The Queen and Blue Angelfish, like the Gray and French, have similar body shapes and markings both as adults and juveniles; however, each has distinctive features that make underwater identification possible. The Cherubfish, primarily found on Florida's deeper reefs, and the rare Flameback from the southern Caribbean, are the only family members that do not resemble the others in shape and size.

FAMILY: Surgeonfish—Acanthuridae
4 Species Included

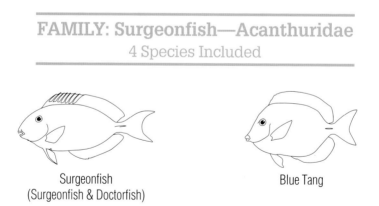

Surgeonfish
(Surgeonfish & Doctorfish)

Blue Tang

A spine as sharp as a surgeon's scalpel, located on each side of the body at the base of the tail, is the origin of this family's common name. They use these spines as defensive weapons by slashing their tails from side to side. When not in use, they fold forward against the body. Surgeonfish are thin-bodied and oval, with relatively long dorsal and anal fins, and a crescent tail. Their scales are not as conspicuous as those of butterfly and angelfish. All are frequently seen reef inhabitants that often mix in loose aggregations as they move about the reefs, feeding on algae.

Surgeonfish and doctorfish are easy to confuse, but can be distinguished underwater by careful observation. Except for size, the juveniles are like the adults. Blue Tangs are rounder, usually seen in large groups; juveniles are yellow.

DISTINCTIVE FEATURES: 1. Two wide, black midbody bands. JUVENILE: 2. Black spot ringed in white on rear dorsal fin (easily distinguished from similar juveniles by lack of any yellowish fins).

DESCRIPTION: Silver to white. Black bar on head runs across eye; blackish border on rear of body, base of rear dorsal and anal fins.

ABUNDANCE & DISTRIBUTION: Common to occasional Florida, Bahamas, Caribbean; also north to New Jersey, Bermuda, Gulf of Mexico and south to Brazil.

HABITAT & BEHAVIOR: Flit about reef tops, usually in pairs.

REACTION TO DIVERS: Tend to ignore divers, but move away when approached.Often the best way to get a close look is to wait quietly in a concealed position near their course of travel.

**Foureye Butterflyfish
Juvenile**

SIZE: 1¹/₂-2¹/₂ in.

DRY TORTUGAS, FL

DISTINCTIVE FEATURES: 1. Black spot, ringed in white, on rear body near upper base of tail. JUVENILE: 2. Two wide, dusky body bars. 3. Very young have second, smaller black spot ocellated in white on rear dorsal above larger spot.

DESCRIPTION: Silver-gray. Marked with numerous dark, thin lines that radiate at a diagonal from midbody; black bar on head runs across eye; yellowish submarginal band on rear dorsal, tail and anal fins.

ABUNDANCE & DISTRIBUTION: Common to occasional Florida, Bahamas, Caribbean; also north to Massachusetts, Bermuda, and Gulf of Mexico.

HABITAT & BEHAVIOR: Flit about reef tops; often in pairs.

REACTION TO DIVERS: Tend to ignore divers, but move away when approached. Often the best way to get a close look is to wait quietly in a concealed position near their course of travel.

BANDED BUTTERFLYFISH
Chaetodon striatus
FAMILY:
Butterflyfish –
Chaetodontidae

SIZE: 3-5 in., max. 6 in.
DEPTH: 10-60 ft.

ROATAN

Banded Butterflyfish
Juvenile

SIZE: 1¹/₂-3 in.

BIMINI

FOUREYE BUTTERFLYFISH
Chaetodon capistratus
FAMILY:
Butterflyfish –
Chaetodontidae

SIZE: 3-4 in., max. 6 in.
DEPTH: 10-60 ft.

CAYMAN

DISTINCTIVE FEATURES: 1. Fins (except pectoral) bright yellow. 2. Black dot on outer edge of rear dorsal fin. **JUVENILE:** 3. Very young have a black spot on the rear dorsal, anal and base tail fins which, with maturity, join to form a rear body bar.

DESCRIPTION: Silver-white. Black bar on head runs across eye; may have darkish spot on rear dorsal fin below distinctive black dot noted above. **JUVENILE:** Tail translucent.

ABUNDANCE & DISTRIBUTION: Common to occasional Florida, Bahamas, Caribbean; also north to Massachusetts, Gulf of Mexico and south to Brazil.

HABITAT & BEHAVIOR: Flit about reef tops, often in pairs.

REACTION TO DIVERS: Tend to ignore divers, but move away when approached. Often the best way to get a close look is to wait quietly in a concealed position near their course of travel.

Reef Butterflyfish
Juvenile

SIZE: 1¹/₂-3 in.

CULEBRA, PR

DISTINCTIVE FEATURES: 1. Broad, dark, bar-like area on rear body, including the rear portions of dorsal and anal fins. **JUVENILE:** 2. Black bar on rear anal fin and base of tail. 3. Very young have small black spot on rear dorsal fin.

DESCRIPTION: Yellowish back and dorsal fin; silver-white lower body; yellow to reddish yellow tail. Black bar on head runs across eye.

ABUNDANCE & DISTRIBUTION: Common to occasional South Florida, Bahamas, eastern and southern Caribbean; rare to absent balance of Caribbean; also northern Gulf of Mexico.

HABITAT & BEHAVIOR: Flit about reef tops, often in pairs.

REACTION TO DIVERS: Tend to ignore divers, but move away when approached. Often the best way to get a close look is to wait quietly in a concealed position near their course of travel.

SIMILAR SPECIES: Bank Butterflyfish, *C. aya*, distinguished by black bar running from rear spinous dorsal fin to anal fin. Rare shallower than 100 feet; Florida, also Gulf of Mexico and north to North Carolina.

SPOTFIN BUTTERFLYFISH
Chaetodon ocellatus
FAMILY:
Butterflyfish –
Chaetodontidae

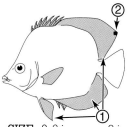

SIZE: 3-6 in., max. 8 in.
DEPTH: 10-60 ft.

ROATAN

Spotfin Butterflyfish
Older Juvenile

Size 1$^1/_2$-3 in.

DRY TORTUGAS, FL

REEF BUTTERFLYFISH
Chaetodon sedentarius
FAMILY:
Butterflyfish –
Chaetodontidae

SIZE: 3-4 in., max. 6 in.
DEPTH: 20-120 feet.

WEST PALM BEACH, FL

DISTINCTIVE FEATURES: 1. Long, pointed snout. 2. Dusky to yellow bar runs from upper head across eye, but not below eye as in other butterflies.

DESCRIPTION: Upper half of body yellowish changing to orange, and darkening to orangish brown and black on dorsal fin; lower body white.

ABUNDANCE & DISTRIBUTION: Common to occasional South Florida, Bahamas, Caribbean; also Gulf of Mexico.

HABITAT & BEHAVIOR: Usually solitary; generally inhabit deeper reefs and walls. Tend to be more secretive than other family members; often forage in dark recesses for marine invertebrates.

REACTION TO DIVERS: Shy; dart into dark recesses when closely approached. Sometimes curious, occasionally peer out entrance.

DISTINCTIVE FEATURES: 1. Yellow to orange face and chest. (Compare similar Flameback, *C. aurantonotus*, [next] where orange to yellow extends onto back and dorsal fin.) **2. Dark blue body.**

DESCRIPTION: Thin blue ring around eye; outer edge of dorsal and anal fins iridescent blue.

ABUNDANCE & DISTRIBUTION: Common Florida; occasional to rare Bahamas and Caribbean; also Bermuda.

HABITAT & BEHAVIOR: Inhabit deep reefs and occasionally walls, usually deeper than 80 feet, except southern Caribbean where they are often on shallow reef tops. Dart in and out of holes in rocks and coral. Swim in pairs or small groups.

REACTION TO DIVERS: Quite wary; usually hide when approached.

DISTINCTIVE FEATURES: 1. Yellow to orange face and nape continuing onto back and dorsal fin. 2. Dark blue body.

DESCRIPTION: Outer edge of dorsal and anal fins iridescent blue. Yellow to orange area on back extends to soft dorsal fin on young and recedes to spinous dorsal fin with age.

ABUNDANCE & DISTRIBUTION: Occasional southeastern islands of Caribbean; absent balance of Caribbean, Florida and Bahamas.

HABITAT & BEHAVIOR: Inhabit deep reefs and occasionally walls, usually deeper than 75 feet. Dart in and out of holes in rocks and coral. Swim in pairs or small groups, often mix with Cherubfish, *C. argi*, [previous].

REACTION TO DIVERS: Quite wary; usually hide when approached.

LONGSNOUT BUTTERFLYFISH
Chaetodon aculeatus
FAMILY:
Butterflyfish –
Chaetodontidae

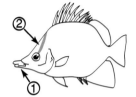

SIZE: 2-3 in., max. 3½ in.
DEPTH: 30-200 feet.

BIMINI

CHERUBFISH
Centropyge argi
FAMILY:
Angelfish –
Pomacanthidae

SIZE: 1½-2½ in.,
max. 3 in.
DEPTH: 30-350 ft.

CAYMAN

FLAMEBACK ANGELFISH
Centropyge aurantonotus
FAMILY:
Angelfish –
Pomacanthidae

SIZE: 1½-2½ in.,
max. 3 in.
DEPTH: 50-600 ft.

BARBADOS

DISTINCTIVE FEATURES: 1. Dark blue spot on forehead, speckled and ringed with brilliant blue, forms the "crown." 2. Tail yellow. **JUVENILE:** 3. Second blue body bar is curved.

DESCRIPTION: Blue to greenish blue, with yellow rims on scales; yellow ventral and pectoral fins; deep blue lips and markings on gill cover; yellowish face. A rare color variety is yellow to orange with blue markings only on the head, dorsal and anal fin borders. **JUVENILE:** Dark blue body with three brilliant blue to white bars; dark blue bar bordered in brilliant blue across eye; yellow lips; yellow area from around pectoral to ventral fins; yellow tail.

ABUNDANCE & DISTRIBUTION: Common to occasional Florida, Bahamas, Caribbean; also Bermuda, Gulf of Mexico, and south to Brazil.

HABITAT & BEHAVIOR: Often blend into background of sea whips, sea fans and corals as they swim slowly about reefs. Juveniles prefer offshore reefs; often act as cleaners.

REACTION TO DIVERS: Somewhat shy, but occasionally curious. After retreating a short distance often turn to observe diver.

**Blue Angelfish
Juvenile**

SIZE: 1-5 in.

DRY TORTUGAS, FL

DISTINCTIVE FEATURES: 1. Tail and pectoral fins bordered in yellow (Queen Angelfish, *H. ciliaris*, [previous] the entire tail and pectoral fins are yellow; also has "crown.") **JUVENILE:** 2. Middle blue body bar is straight. (Compare Queen Angelfish, *H. ciliaris*, distinguished by curved bar.)

DESCRIPTION: Purplish to blue-green often with pronounced gray cast; rims of scales pale. Ventral fins yellow; dorsal and tail fins covered with yellowish to brown dots. **JUVENILE:** Dark blue body with three brilliant blue to white bars; blue bar bordered in brilliant blue across eye; yellow lips; yellow area from around pectoral to ventral fins; yellow tail.

ABUNDANCE & DISTRIBUTION: Common Florida; occasional to uncommon Bahamas; also Bermuda and Gulf of Mexico. Not reported Caribbean.

HABITAT & BEHAVIOR: Swim about reef tops. Juveniles prefer bays, channels and inshore reefs.

REACTION TO DIVERS: Somewhat shy, but can be curious. After retreating a short distance, often turn to observe diver.

QUEEN ANGELFISH
Holacanthus ciliaris
FAMILY:
Angelfish –
Pomacanthidae

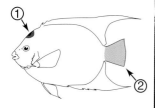

SIZE: 8-14 in., max. 18 in.
DEPTH: 20-80 ft.

ANGUILLA

Queen Angelfish Juvenile

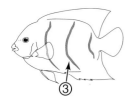

SIZE: 1-5 in.

L. CAYMAN

BLUE ANGELFISH
Holacanthus bermudensis
FAMILY:
Angelfish –
Pomacanthidae

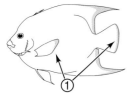

SIZE: 8-14 in.,
max. 18 in.
DEPTH: 20-80 ft.

WEST PALM BEACH, FL

27

DISTINCTIVE FEATURES: None, see below.

DESCRIPTION: Queen and Blue Angelfish [previous page] occasionally interbreed, resulting in fish that share some distinctive markings from both species. For example: may have blue crown without central specks and/or half yellow tail, etc.

ABUNDANCE & DISTRIBUTION: Uncommon to rare Florida, Bahamas, also Bermuda and Gulf of Mexico. Not reported Caribbean.

HABITAT & BEHAVIOR: Swim about reef tops of inshore reefs.

REACTION TO DIVERS: Somewhat shy, but can be curious. After retreating a short distance, often turn to observe diver.

NOTE: These hybrids were once incorrectly described as a separate species, *Holacanthus townsendi*.

DISTINCTIVE FEATURES: Black with bright yellow rims on scales. **1. Tail rounded. JUVENILE: 2. Rounded tail with yellow border forms an oval.**

DESCRIPTION: Bright yellow ring around eye. All fins black except base of pectoral which is yellow. **JUVENILE:** Black with three yellow body bars; yellow band extends down from forehead, stops at base of upper lip, splits and goes around mouth.

ABUNDANCE & DISTRIBUTION: Common to occasional Florida, Bahamas and Gulf of Mexico to Brazil.

HABITAT & BEHAVIOR: Swim about reefs, often in pairs. Juveniles inhabit reefs and sandy areas, often around holes or protective crevices in hard bottoms. Actively clean parasites and debris from larger fish. Swim with distinctive fluttering motion.

REACTION TO DIVERS: Relatively unafraid. Can be closely approached.

**French Angelfish
Intermediate**

ROATAN

TOWNSEND ANGELFISH
Hybrid
FAMILY:
Angelfish –
Pomacanthidae

SIZE: 8-14 in., max. 18 in.
DEPTH: 20-80 ft.

DRY TORTUGAS, FL

FRENCH ANGELFISH
Pomacanthus paru
FAMILY:
Angelfish –
Pomacanthidae

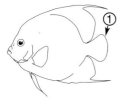

SIZE: 10-14 in.,
max. 18 in.
DEPTH: 15-80 ft.

COZUMEL

French Angelfish
Juvenile

SIZE: 1-5 in.

CAYMAN

29

DISTINCTIVE FEATURES: Gray body. **1. Yellow inner face of pectoral fin. 2. Square-cut tail. JUVENILE: 3. Square-cut tail with white to transparent margin.**

DESCRIPTION: Uniformly gray to grayish brown with light-edged scales. Intermediate phase has three pale body bars and one on base of tail. **JUVENILE:** Black with three yellow bars on body and one on foretail. Yellow band extends down from forehead and across lips to chin; there is also a yellow ring around border of lips.

ABUNDANCE & DISTRIBUTION: Common to occasional Florida, Bahamas, North and Central Caribbean; uncommon southern Caribbean; also north to New York, Bermuda, Gulf of Mexico and south to Brazil.

HABITAT & BEHAVIOR: Swim about reefs, often in pairs. Juveniles inhabit shallow patch reefs and grassy areas. May engage in cleaning parasites and debris from larger fish. Swim with short, straight motions.

REACTION TO DIVERS: Relatively unafraid; often approach divers.

Gray Angelfish Intermediate

DRY TORTUGAS, FL

DISTINCTIVE FEATURES: 1. Yellow to yellow-orange forebody and tail. 2. Mid and rear body black. JUVENILE: 3. Very young have a black spot ringed in brilliant blue on rear body. The blue ring is lost and the spot increases in size with maturity until it covers the body.

DESCRIPTION: Face and lips occasionally navy blue. Individuals along North and South American coasts less brilliantly colored.

ABUNDANCE & DISTRIBUTION: Common to occasional Caribbean; occasional to uncommon Florida, Bahamas; also north to Georgia, Bermuda, Gulf of Mexico and south to Brazil.

HABITAT & BEHAVIOR: Establish and patrol defined territories on reefs. Juveniles are secretive and hide in shells and recesses in the reef.

REACTION TO DIVERS: Somewhat shy, but can be curious. After retreating a short distance, often turn to observe diver.

SIMILAR JUVENILE: Threespot Damselfish, *Stegastes planifrons*, [pg. 115] distinguished by an additional black spot on upper base of tail.

GRAY ANGELFISH
Pomacanthus arcuatus
FAMILY:
Angelfish –
Pomacanthidae

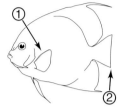

SIZE: 10-18 in., max. 2 ft.
DEPTH: 10-80 ft.

COZUMEL

**Gray Angelfish
Juvenile**

SIZE: 2-5 in.

BELIZE

ROCK BEAUTY
Holacanthus tricolor
FAMILY:
Angelfish –
Pomacanthidae

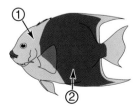

SIZE: 5-8 in., max. 12 in.
DEPTH: 10-80 ft.

WEST PALM BEACH, FL

continued next page 31

Rock Beauty
Juvenile/Intermediate

SIZE: 2-4 in.

CAYMAN

DISTINCTIVE FEATURES: Blue overall. **1. White or yellow spine on base of tail. JUVENILE:** Bright yellow overall. **INTERMEDIATE:** Blue head and body. **2. Yellow tail.**

DESCRIPTION: Can change from powder blue to deep purple, and pale or darken. Dorsal and anal fins edged in bright blue. More circular than other surgeonfishes. Changes from juvenile to intermediate and adult color phase do not depend on size, and occasionally a yellow-phase juvenile may be larger than a blue-phase adult.

ABUNDANCE & DISTRIBUTION: Abundant to common Florida, Bahamas, Caribbean; also north to New York, Bermuda, Gulf of Mexico and south to Brazil.

HABITAT & BEHAVIOR: Can be solitary, but more often in large aggregations foraging about shallow reef tops, grazing on algae. Schools can include Surgeonfish and Doctorfish.

REACTION TO DIVERS: Seem unconcerned, but tend to keep their distance and slowly move away when approached.

CAYMAN

ANGUILLA

Rock Beauty Juvenile

continued from previous page

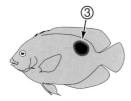

SIZE: 1-2 in.

BIMINI

BLUE TANG
Acanthurus coeruleus

FAMILY:
Surgeonfish –
Acanthuridae

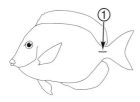

SIZE: 5-10 in., max. 15 in.
DEPTH: 10-60 ft.

CAYMAN

Blue Tang Juvenile

Bright yellow overall.

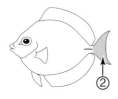

Intermediate phases
[left]

CAYMAN

DISTINCTIVE FEATURES: Uniform color with no body bars. **1. Pectoral fin clearish, often with yellow tints.** (Similar Doctorfish, *A. chirurgus*, [next] always has bars; base and leading edge of pectoral fin dark.)

DESCRIPTION: Can change from bluish gray to dark brown, and pale or darken dramatically. Markings radiate from eye. Blue or white edging on dorsal, anal and tail fins. May have pale band on base of tail [right].

ABUNDANCE & DISTRIBUTION: Common to occasional Florida, Bahamas, Caribbean; also north to Massachusetts, Bermuda, Gulf of Mexico and south to Brazil.

HABITAT & BEHAVIOR: Inhabit reefs. May swim in loose aggregations that can include Blue Tangs and look-alike Doctorfish. Often stop, head down, to pick at algae.

REACTION TO DIVERS: Seem unconcerned, but tend to keep their distance and slowly move away when approached.

Doctorfish

Obscure bars; dark color phase; no band base of tail. Note dark area extending outward from base of pectoral fin.

CAYMAN

DISTINCTIVE FEATURES: 1. Always have body bars (10-12), although they may be quite faint. 2. Dark area extends from base of pectoral fin outward along leading edge.

DESCRIPTION: Can change from bluish gray to dark brown, and pale or darken dramatically. Several markings radiate from eye. Blue or white edging on dorsal, anal and tail fins. May have pale band on base of tail [right].

ABUNDANCE & DISTRIBUTION: Abundant to common Florida, Bahamas; common to occasional Caribbean; also north to Massachusetts, Bermuda, Gulf of Mexico, south to Brazil and tropical West Africa.

HABITAT & BEHAVIOR: Inhabit reefs. May swim in loose aggregations that can include Blue Tangs and look-alike Ocean Surgeonfish. Often stop, head down, to pick at algae.

REACTION TO DIVERS: Seem unconcerned, but tend to keep their distance and slowly move away when approached.

OCEAN SURGEONFISH
Acanthurus bahianus

FAMILY:
Surgeonfish –
Acanthuridae

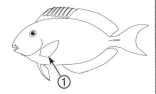

SIZE: 6-12 in., max. 15 in.
DEPTH: 15-80 ft.

ROATAN

Ocean Surgeonfish
*Dark color phase;
no band base of tail.*

KEY LARGO, FL

DOCTORFISH
Acanthurus chirurgus

FAMILY:
Surgeonfish –
Acanthuridae

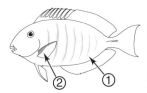

SIZE: 6-12 in., max. 14 in.
DEPTH: 15-80 ft.

CAYMAN

Silvery
Jack – Porgy – Others

This ID Group consists of fish that are silver to gray in color, and are generally unpatterned; however, several species have bluish, yellowish or greenish tints and occasional markings. All have forked tails.

FAMILY: Jack—Carangidae
19 Species Included

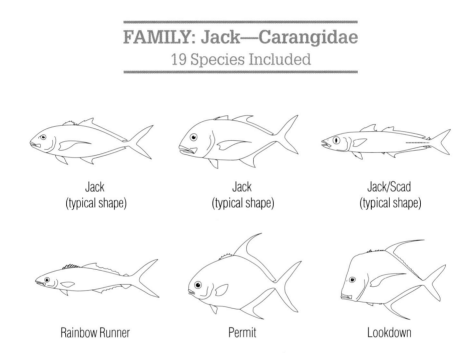

Jack (typical shape)	Jack (typical shape)	Jack/Scad (typical shape)
Rainbow Runner	Permit	Lookdown

Jacks are strong-swimming predators of the open sea. Though schools occasionally pass over reefs in search of small fish and crustaceans, only a few species are seen about reefs on a regular basis.

Most jacks have silvery sides, darkish backs and large eyes. They are thin, and have small tail bases that reduce drag. All have deeply forked tails that facilitate speed, and two-part dorsal fins (high in the front, low in the rear) that extend to the tail. As a family, jacks are easy to recognize, but it takes a sharp eye to distinguish between similar-appearing species such as the Almaco and Greater Amberjack, or the Crevalle and Horse-eye Jack. Body shape, tail fin color, and inconspicuous markings are the keys to correct identification.

Permit, Palometa and Lookdown are also in the family, but generally have higher head profiles than their relatives, and remain inshore where they feed on mollusks and crustaceans.

Jacks spawn at sea where the young, generally patterned with a series of broad, dusky bars, seek protection under floating objects such as sargassum. With maturity they lose their barred pattern, move inshore and begin to school.

Scad are smaller, generally cigar-shaped members of the jack family that swim in small to large schools and often mix with other silvery fish species.

FAMILY: Mackerel — Scombridae
4 Species Included

Mackerel
(typical shape)

Mackerels are long, silvery, strong, fast-swimming predators of the open sea and only occasionally pass over reefs. They have two dorsal fins that fold into grooves. A series of small fins, called finlets, are between the second dorsal fin, the anal fin and the tail. Base of tail is slender with two or more keels on each side. The tail is widely forked. Scales are small and not obvious. Keys to identification are subtle markings that can fade or intensify. Tunas are also members of this family.

FAMILY: Needlefish & Halfbeak — Belonidae & Exocoetidae
9 Species Included

Needlefish
(typical shape)

Halfbeak
(typical shape)

Although needlefishes and halfbeaks are classified in two separate families, they are discussed together in this text because of their similar appearance and habitat. Halfbeaks are actually members of the flyingfish family. Both are highly reflective, silvery fish with thin, elongate bodies and long, narrow, pointed jaws, and forked tails. They hover or swim just below the surface just outside the surf zone, in shallow bays, and occasionally above reefs and open water. The two families are easily separated; needlefishes have upper and lower jaws of nearly equal length, while halfbeaks have short upper and long lower jaws. Distinguishing between species within the families, however, can be quite difficult and requires careful attention to details.

Great Barracuda   Southern Sennet

The Great Barracuda is a relatively large, silvery, elongate fish with long jaws and numerous, visible pointed teeth. They have two, low, widely separated dorsal fins and large forked tails. Because they constantly work their formidable jaws to help circulate water through their gills, these voracious predators appear quite threatening. In actuality they pose no threat to divers. The few substantiated reports of attack involved spearfishing.

Unlike the Great Barracuda that is usually solitary the two smaller members of the family, Southern Sennet and Guaguanche, are usually sighted in small to large schools. Both species are more difficult to distinguish than their larger relative although attention to color shading and the habitat where they are sighted easily identifies them.

FAMILY: Porgy—Sparidae
13 Species Included

Porgy (typical shape)

Porgies are silvery, with high back profiles, large, steep heads, and mouths set well below the eyes. Their silvery color is often tinted with shades of blue and/or yellow, and many have head and/or body markings. Species are generally distinguished underwater by the line markings on the head. Juveniles are similar to the adults.

Porgies are solitary, and stay near the bottom where they feed on shellfish and crabs.

Mojarra

Mojarras are bright, reflective silver fish with compressed bodies, obvious scales, highly protrusible mouths and deeply forked tails. Rarely on reefs, they inhabit shallow, flat, open areas of sand, rubble, grass or mud where they feed on small invertebrates. Many species run in small schools; while others are solitary. Several species are very difficult to distinguish, but careful attention to subtle detail usually allows identification.

FAMILY: Others
14 Species Included

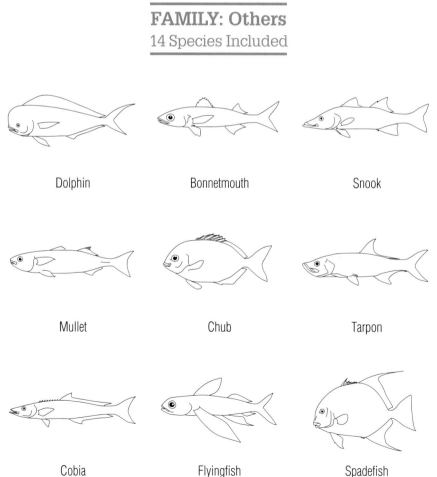

Dolphin

Bonnetmouth

Snook

Mullet

Chub

Tarpon

Cobia

Flyingfish

Spadefish

DISTINCTIVE FEATURES: 1. Long, continuous dorsal fin extends from above eye to base of tail. 2. Pectoral fin long — about length of head. 3. MALE (bull): Very blunt head. 4. FEMALE: Rounded, torpedo-shaped head.

DESCRIPTION: Brilliant silver. Males display bright yellow, yellow-green and blue iridescent spots and washes. Females display brilliant blue iridescence and washes with blue markings on head.

ABUNDANCE & DISTRIBUTION: Common Florida, Bahamas; occasional Caribbean; also north to Nova Scotia, Bermuda, Gulf of Mexico and south to Brazil; circumtropical and subtropical.

HABITAT & BEHAVIOR: Swim rapidly in open water, often under sargassum floats, rarely over shallow reefs. Usually in small aggregations of one or two bulls and numerous females.

REACTION TO DIVERS: Apparently curious; often make several rapid, close passes.

NOTE: Also commonly known as "Mahi mahi."

SIMILAR SPECIES: Pompano Dolphin, *C. equisietis*, distinguished by smaller size (usually less than 2½ ft.), deeper, less elongate body and short pectoral fins (less than half the head length).

Male

Profile with dorsal fin folded.

NASSAU

DISTINCTIVE FEATURES: 1. Two blue stripes run length of body with pale to brilliant yellow or gold stripe between. 2. Dorsal and anal finlet.

DESCRIPTION: Silvery yellow to blue; tail fins yellowish. Head more pointed and body more elongated compared to most jacks; rear dorsal and anal fins often appear to be serrated.

ABUNDANCE & DISTRIBUTION: Uncommon to rare Florida, Bahamas, Caribbean; also circumtropical.

HABITAT & BEHAVIOR: Open water fish, rarely over reefs; occasionally swim along walls. Form small, somewhat polarized groups to large schools. Prefer areas with current.

REACTION TO DIVERS: Often make rapid, single close pass (apparently attracted to bubbles) and depart.

DOLPHIN
Coryphaena hippurus
FAMILY:
Dolphin - Coryphaenidae

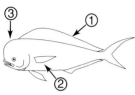

SIZE: 2-4 ft., max. 5¼ ft.
DEPTH: 0-20 ft.

NASSAU

Female
Dorsal fin erect.

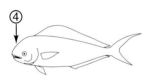

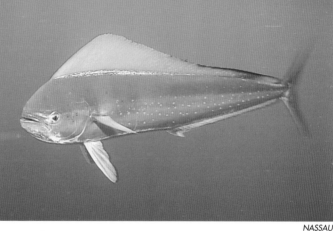

NASSAU

RAINBOW RUNNER
Elagatis bipinnulata
FAMILY:
Jack - Carangidae

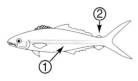

SIZE: 2-3 ft., max. 4 ft.
DEPTH: 0-120 ft.

L. CAYMAN

41

DISTINCTIVE FEATURES: 1. Bright blue-and-black border on back runs along dorsal fin and onto lower tail fin.

DESCRIPTION: Silvery. Can darken almost to black, especially when feeding near bottom.

ABUNDANCE & DISTRIBUTION: Common Florida, Bahamas, Caribbean; also north to New Jersey, Bermuda, Gulf of Mexico and south to Brazil.

HABITAT & BEHAVIOR: Swim in open water over reefs in small groups to large schools. Opportunistic feeders, they often follow or mix with goatfish and stingrays as they dig in the sand.

REACTION TO DIVERS: Often make a rapid, close pass (apparently attracted by bubbles); occasionally an entire school will swirl around a diver.

NOTE: Also commonly known as "Skipjack."

DISTINCTIVE FEATURES: 1. Tips of tail fins dark.

DESCRIPTION: Bluish silver to brassy or olive. Somewhat elongated black spot near upper end of gill cover; may have faint bluish bars on body. Breeding males become blackish.

ABUNDANCE & DISTRIBUTION: Common Florida; occasional Bahamas; uncommon to rare Caribbean; also north to Nova Scotia, Bermuda, Gulf of Mexico, south to Brazil and eastern Atlantic.

HABITAT & BEHAVIOR: Travel in large schools in offshore waters. Rarely visit reef areas and then, usually in pairs or solitary.

REACTION TO DIVERS: Often make a rapid, close pass (apparently attracted by bubbles) and depart.

NOTE: Also commonly known as "Hard-tailed Jack."

DISTINCTIVE FEATURES: 1. Yellow tail fins. No spot near gill cover. (Similar Horse-eye Jack, *C. latus,* [next] distinguished by large eye, high back profile and often a small black spot at upper end of gill cover.)

DESCRIPTION: Silvery, often with yellow cast. Fins yellowish, especially tail.

ABUNDANCE & DISTRIBUTION: Occasional to uncommon Florida, Bahamas, Caribbean; also north to Massachusetts, Gulf of Mexico and south to Brazil.

HABITAT & BEHAVIOR: Seldom swim over inshore reefs, more often over outer reefs. Usually solitary or in small groups.

REACTION TO DIVERS: Often make a rapid, close pass (apparently attracted by bubbles) and depart.

BAR JACK
Caranx ruber
FAMILY:
Jack - Carangidae

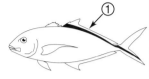

SIZE: 8-14 in., max. 2 ft.
DEPTH: 0-60 ft.

COZUMEL

BLUE RUNNER
Caranx crysos
FAMILY:
Jack - Carangidae

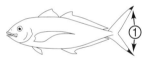

SIZE: 1-2 ft., max. 2½ ft.
DEPTH: 0-130 ft.

WALKER'S CAY, BAHAMAS

YELLOW JACK
Caranx bartholomaei
FAMILY:
Jack - Carangidae

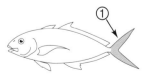

SIZE: 1-2 ft., max. 3 ft.
DEPTH: 0-130 ft.

BIIMINI

DISTINCTIVE FEATURES: 1. Yellow tail fins. 2. Pectoral fin clear. (Similar Crevalle Jack, *C. hippos*, [next] has dark blotch on base of pectoral fin.)

DESCRIPTION: Silvery. Usually have dark tips on dorsal and upper tail fin; often a small black spot at upper end of gill cover; usually have blackish scutes.

ABUNDANCE & DISTRIBUTION: Common to occasional Florida, Bahamas, Caribbean; also north to New Jersey, Bermuda, Gulf of Mexico and south to Brazil.

HABITAT & BEHAVIOR: Swim in open water over reefs, usually in small groups to large schools. May mix with similar Crevalle Jacks [next]. Occasionally a school will reside in one area.

REACTION TO DIVERS: Wary; tend to move away slowly when approached, but occasionally (apparently attracted by bubbles) schools will rapidly approach and swirl around a diver.

NOTE: Also commonly known as "Bigeye Jack."

DISTINCTIVE FEATURES: 1. Blackish blotch on pectoral fin. (Similar Horse-eye Jack, *C. latus*, [previous] lacks this blotch.)

DESCRIPTION: Silvery. Tail may be yellowish. Black spot near top of gill cover; tips of dorsal and upper tail occasionally black.

ABUNDANCE & DISTRIBUTION: Common Florida; uncommon to rare Bahamas, Caribbean; also north to Nova Scotia, Gulf of Mexico and south to Uruguay.

HABITAT & BEHAVIOR: Prefer clear, open water and rarely swim over reefs. Young adults tend to school while older fish are often solitary. May school with similar Horse-eye Jack.

REACTION TO DIVERS: Wary; tend to move away slowly when approached, but occasionally (apparently attracted by bubbles) schools will rapidly approach and swirl around a diver.

NOTE: Also commonly known as "Common Jack" or "Crevally."

DISTINCTIVE FEATURES: Dark gray or brown to black. **1. Forehead (nape) steep. 2. Dorsal and anal fins long.**

DESCRIPTION: Often have silvery to olive sheen. Black dorsal, anal and tail fins, and scutes.

ABUNDANCE & DISTRIBUTION: Uncommon to rare Florida, Bahamas, Caribbean, but locally common in a few areas; also circumtropical.

HABITAT & BEHAVIOR: Considered deep-water fish, they are often along steep drop-offs and walls. Travel alone, in pairs or small groups, in open water.

REACTION TO DIVERS: Wary; tend to move away slowly when approached, but occasionally (apparently attracted by bubbles) will rapidly approach, make a single close pass and depart.

HORSE-EYE JACK
Caranx latus
FAMILY:
Jack - Carangidae

SIZE: 1-2 ft., max. 2½ ft.
DEPTH: 0-60 ft.

BELIZE

CREVALLE JACK
Caranx hippos
FAMILY:
Jack - Carangidae

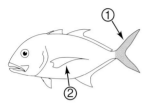

SIZE: 1-2½ ft.,
max. 3½ ft.
DEPTH: 0-130 ft.

BONAIRE

BLACK JACK
Caranx lugubris
FAMILY:
Jack - Carangidae

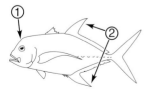

SIZE: 1-2 ft., max. 3 ft.
DEPTH: 50-1,200 ft.

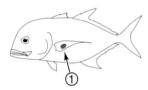

L. CAYMAN

DISTINCTIVE FEATURES: 1. Dark diagonal band runs from lip, across eye, to beginning of dorsal fin. 2. Foredorsal fin unusually long. High back profile. (Compare to similar Greater Amberjack, *S. dumerili*, [next] with more elongated body, lighter band and shorter foredorsal fin.)

DESCRIPTION: Silvery. Fins dusky.

ABUNDANCE & DISTRIBUTION: Uncommon to rare Florida, Bahamas, Caribbean; also circumtropical.

HABITAT & BEHAVIOR: Deep, open-water fish; rarely swim over reefs or near shore. Often travel alone, but occasionally in schools.

REACTION TO DIVERS: Often make rapid, close pass (apparently attracted to bubbles) and depart.

DISTINCTIVE FEATURES: 1. Diagonal band runs from lip, across eye to beginning of dorsal fin. 2. Foredorsal fin short. Sleek, elongated body. (Compare similar Almaco Jack, *S. rivoliana*, [previous] with high back profile, darker band and longer foredorsal fin.)

DESCRIPTION: Silvery; fins may have yellow cast. Often have diffuse, yellowish or amber stripe along midbody.

ABUNDANCE & DISTRIBUTION: Occasional to uncommon Florida, Bahamas, Caribbean; also circumtropical.

HABITAT & BEHAVIOR: Open-water fish; rarely swim over reefs. Often in large schools, occasionally solitary.

REACTION TO DIVERS: Often make rapid, close pass (apparently attracted to bubbles) and depart.

DISTINCTIVE FEATURES: Silvery, oval body. No distinctive markings.

DESCRIPTION: Often darkish; dorsal, anal and tail fins dark. Pectoral fins long; spinous dorsal fin low. Occasionally display four or five whitish body bars. Tongue, roof and floor of mouth white (origin of common name), the sides and throat are black.

ABUNDANCE & DISTRIBUTION: Rare Florida, Bahamas, Caribbean; also circumtropical.

HABITAT & BEHAVIOR: Pelagic; form large schools in open water. Occasionally sweep by steep slopes and walls, especially around offshore rocks and islets.

REACTION TO DIVERS: Tend to ignore divers, but move away when approached. Occasionally appear somewhat curious (apparently attracted by bubbles) and may make a single close pass and depart.

ALMACO JACK
Seriola rivoliana
FAMILY:
Jack - Carangidae

SIZE: 1-2 ft., max. 3 ft.
DEPTH: 50-180 ft.

NASSAU

GREATER AMBERJACK
Seriola dumerili
FAMILY:
Jack - Carangidae

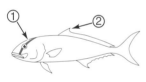

SIZE: 2-4 ft., max. 5 1/2 ft.
DEPTH: 0-140 ft.

JACKSONVILLE, FL

COTTONMOUTH JACK
Uraspis secunda
FAMILY:
Jack - Carangidae

SIZE: 8-14 in.,
max. 1 1/2 ft.
DEPTH: 0-120 ft.

SWAN ISLAND

47

DISTINCTIVE FEATURES: Crinkly, burnished silver; deep body. **1. Steep, blunt forehead.**

DESCRIPTION: Often have bluish or greenish tints; scales not obvious. Compressed body, deeply forked tail. Diamond-shaped juveniles trail long thread-like filaments from dorsal and anal fins; as fish mature, filaments usually become progressively shorter, disappearing in large adults.

ABUNDANCE & DISTRIBUTION: Uncommon Florida, Bahamas, Caribbean; also circumtropical.

HABITAT & BEHAVIOR: Open-water fish, rarely over reefs; occasionally swim along walls. May be solitary or form small, somewhat polarized schools.

REACTION TO DIVERS: Often make rapid, close pass (apparently attracted to bubbles) and depart.

NOTE: Also (especially juveniles) commonly called "Threadfin" or "Threadfish."

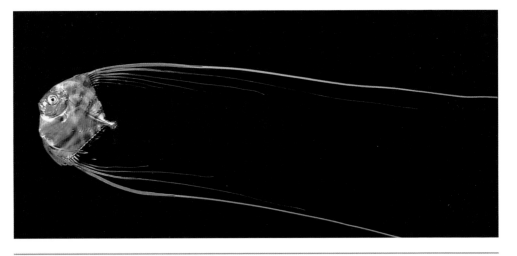

DISTINCTIVE FEATURES: 1. High back profile. 2. Orangish area at start of anal fin.

DESCRIPTION: Brilliantly silver; often have shades of iridescent blue or blue-green on head and back; belly often yellowish. Tip of dorsal fin dark; occasionally dark circular area behind base of pectoral fin; infrequently has dusky midbody blotch.

ABUNDANCE & DISTRIBUTION: Uncommon Florida, Bahamas, Caribbean; also north to Massachusetts and south to Brazil.

HABITAT & BEHAVIOR: Often swim over sand where they feed on mollusks. Occasionally swim over reefs to feed on urchins and crustaceans. Normally solitary.

REACTION TO DIVERS: May make one rapid, close approach (apparently attracted to bubbles) and depart.

NOTE: Juvenile has a nearly circular profile with elongated dorsal and anal fins. It is sometimes commonly known as the "Round Pompano."

SIMILAR SPECIES: Florida Pompano, *T. carolinus*, not easily distinguished underwater, but not over reefs and consequently rarely observed by divers. Body profile not as high; lack orangish area at anal fin. Common Florida; not reported balance of range.

AFRICAN POMPANO
Alectis ciliaris
FAMILY:
Jack - Carangidae

SIZE: 1-2 ft., max. 3½ ft.
DEPTH: 0-325 ft.

WALKER'S CAY, BAHAMAS

African Pompano Young Adult

With thread-like filaments from dorsal fin.
[right]

African Pompano Juvenile

[left]

WALKER'S CAY, BAHAMAS

PERMIT
Trachinotus falcatus
FAMILY:
Jack - Carangidae

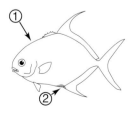

SIZE: 1-3 ft., max. 3¾ ft.
DEPTH: 0-100 ft.

CAYMAN

DISTINCTIVE FEATURES: 1. Four dark body bars. 2. Extremely long dorsal and anal fins.
DESCRIPTION: Silvery. Dorsal, anal and tail fins bordered in black.
ABUNDANCE & DISTRIBUTION: Common eastern and southern Caribbean; occasional Bahamas and Florida; uncommon to rare northwest Caribbean; also north to Massachusetts and south to Argentina.
HABITAT & BEHAVIOR: School in shallow water over sand and near shallow patch reefs. Young frequent surge zone near beaches.
REACTION TO DIVERS: Apparently attracted by bubbles; an entire school will occasionally swirl around a diver.
NOTE: Also commonly known as "Gafftopsail Pompano" and "Longfin Pompano."

DISTINCTIVE FEATURES: Very thin body. **1. Extremely blunt head.**
DESCRIPTION: Bright silver, occasionally goldish, greenish, bluish or purplish highlights. May display three or four pale body bars. Fore part of dorsal and anal fins elongated.
ABUNDANCE & DISTRIBUTION: Common Florida; uncommon to rare Bahamas, Caribbean; also north to Maine, south to Uruguay and eastern Atlantic.
HABITAT & BEHAVIOR: Prefer shallow, often murky water. Hover over bottom in somewhat forward-tilted position, appearing to "look down." Occasionally school.
REACTION TO DIVERS: Allow close approach with slow, nonthreatening movements.
NOTE ABOUT JUVENILE: Two extremely long, thread-like extensions trail from dorsal fin.

DISTINCTIVE FEATURES: 1. Black saddle on base of tail. 2. Upper lobe of tail longer than lower.
DESCRIPTION: Bright silver, with occasional greenish or yellowish highlights; yellowish tail. Usually black to dusky spot at upper edge of gill cover. Very thin body; extended belly; fore part of lateral line highly arched.
ABUNDANCE & DISTRIBUTION: Common Florida, Caribbean continental coastlines; also north to Massachusetts, Bermuda, Gulf of Mexico and south to Uruguay. Not reported Bahamas or Caribbean islands.
HABITAT & BEHAVIOR: Inhabit shallow coastal waters, including bays and estuaries.
REACTION TO DIVERS: Allow close approach with slow, nonthreatening movements.
SIMILAR SPECIES: Leatherjack, *Oligoplites saurus*, has bright yellow to yellowish tail, but is easily distinguished by lack of spot on base of tail and straight lateral line.

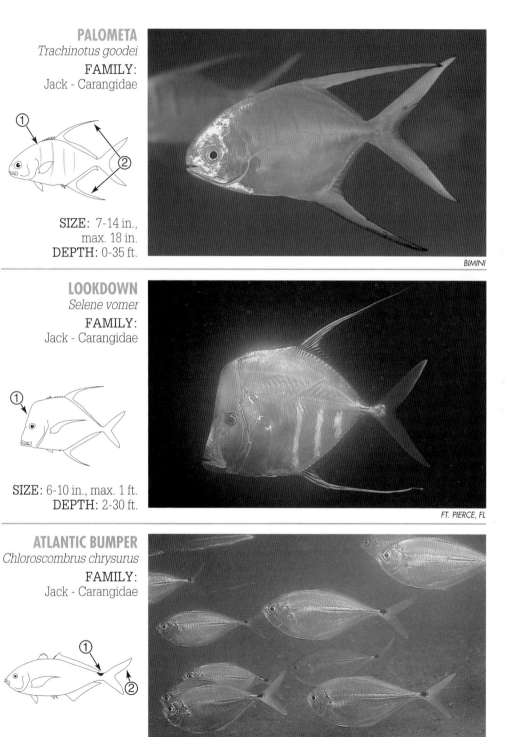

PALOMETA
Trachinotus goodei
FAMILY:
Jack - Carangidae

SIZE: 7-14 in.,
max. 18 in.
DEPTH: 0-35 ft.

BIMINI

LOOKDOWN
Selene vomer
FAMILY:
Jack - Carangidae

SIZE: 6-10 in., max. 1 ft.
DEPTH: 2-30 ft.

FT. PIERCE, FL

ATLANTIC BUMPER
Chloroscombrus chrysurus
FAMILY:
Jack - Carangidae

SIZE: 2-7 in., max. 1 ft.
DEPTH: 0-30 ft.

FT. PIERCE, FL

DISTINCTIVE FEATURES: 1. Large eye (diameter greater than snout length). 2. Scutes only on rear lateral line.

DESCRIPTION: Bright reflective silver. Deeply forked tail.

ABUNDANCE & DISTRIBUTION: Occasional Florida, Bahamas, Caribbean; also circumtropical and subtropical.

HABITAT & BEHAVIOR: Form small to large, rapidly swimming, polarized schools. Often sweep over reefs, shallow bays, along walls and past shipwrecks.

REACTION TO DIVERS: Tend to ignore divers, but keep their distance, moving away if approached. Occasionally make one or two rapid passes (apparently attracted by bubbles).

SIMILAR SPECIES: Rough Scad, *Trachurus lathami*, distinguished by very large scutes running full length of lateral line and slightly smaller eyes.

DISTINCTIVE FEATURES: 1. Black spot at upper edge of gill plate. 2. Slightly enlarged scutes on rear lateral line. (Similar Round Scad, *D. punctatus*, [next] may also have a black spot at upper edge of gill cover, but can be distinguished by enlarged scutes on base of tail.)

DESCRIPTION: Bright reflective silver often with bluish or greenish sheen. Occasionally display yellow midbody stripe. Slender, elongated body; lateral line very slightly arched; single dorsal and anal finlet.

ABUNDANCE & DISTRIBUTION: Occasional Bahamas, Caribbean; uncommon Florida; also north to Nova Scotia, Bermuda, Gulf of Mexico and south to Brazil; circumtropical and subtropical.

HABITAT & BEHAVIOR: Form large, rapidly swimming, polarized schools. Often sweep over reefs, shallow bays, along walls and past shipwrecks.

REACTION TO DIVERS: Tend to ignore divers, but keep their distance, moving away if approached. Occasionally make one or two rapid passes (apparently attracted by bubbles).

SIMILAR SPECIES: Redtail Scad, *Decapterus tabl*, distinguished by bright red tail; enlarged scutes on base of tail.

DISTINCTIVE FEATURES: 1. Series of widely spaced small black spots along forward half of lateral line. 2. Substantially enlarged scutes on base of tail. Often display a dark spot at upper edge of gill cover. (Similar to Mackerel Scad, *D. macarellus*, [previous], but can be distinguished by its thin scutes.)

DESCRIPTION: Bright reflective silver, occasionally with greenish sheen. Occasionally display yellow midbody stripe. Slender, elongated body; lateral line arched; single dorsal and anal finlet.

ABUNDANCE & DISTRIBUTION: Occasional Florida, Bahamas, Caribbean; also north to Nova Scotia, Bermuda, Gulf of Mexico and south to Brazil.

HABITAT & BEHAVIOR: Form small groups to large, rapidly swimming, polarized schools. Often sweep over reefs, shallow bays, along walls and past shipwrecks.

REACTION TO DIVERS: Tend to ignore divers, but keep their distance, moving away if approached. Occasionally make one or two rapid passes (apparently attracted by bubbles).

BIGEYE SCAD
Selar crumenophthalmus
FAMILY:
Jack - Carangidae

SIZE: 6-12 in., max. 2 ft.
DEPTH: 0-500 ft.

WEST PALM BEACH, FL

MACKEREL SCAD
Decapterus macarellus
FAMILY:
Jack - Carangidae

SIZE: 6-10 in., max. 1 ft.
DEPTH: 0-130 ft.

BARBADOS

ROUND SCAD
Decapterus punctatus
FAMILY:
Jack - Carangidae

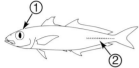

SIZE: 6-8 in., max. 10 in.
DEPTH: 0-130 ft.

PANAMA CITY, FL

DISTINCTIVE FEATURES: 1. Series of yellow-gold streaks along midline from pectoral fin to tail. (Similar Spanish Mackerel, *S. maculatus,* [next] has only spots.)

DESCRIPTION: Silvery. Small yellow-gold body spots on either side of streaks. Elongated body. Lateral line slopes gently downward below second dorsal fin.

ABUNDANCE & DISTRIBUTION: Abundant to common Bahamas, Florida, Antilles; common balance of Caribbean; also north to Massachusetts, Gulf of Mexico and south to Brazil.

HABITAT & BEHAVIOR: Open-water fish. Often swim over reefs and along drop-offs. Usually solitary, occasionally travel in pairs or small groups.

REACTION TO DIVERS: Often swim toward diver, but rarely come close.

DISTINCTIVE FEATURES: 1. Yellow-gold spots on sides. (Similar Cero, *S. regalis* [previous] has midline streaks.)

DESCRIPTION: Silvery; back often darker with bluish or olive cast. Elongated body. Lateral line slopes gently downward below second dorsal fin.

ABUNDANCE & DISTRIBUTION: Abundant Florida; rare to absent Bahamas, Caribbean; also north to Virginia and Gulf of Mexico.

HABITAT & BEHAVIOR: Primarily an open-water fish and almost never over reefs; may enter shallow water estuaries. Occasionally encountered while making open-water drifts or safety stops. Usually form large schools.

REACTION TO DIVERS: Apparently somewhat curious; often swim toward diver, but rarely come close.

SIMILAR SPECIES: Reports of this species off Bahamas and Caribbean islands are usually mis-identifications of juvenile King Mackerel [next] that have similar spots. Atlantic Sierra, *S. brasiliensis*, along continental coastlines from Yucatan to Brazil.

DISTINCTIVE FEATURES: 1. Lateral line drops abruptly below second dorsal fin. (Compare similar Spanish Mackerel, *S. maculatus* and Cero, *S. regalis* [previous].)

DESCRIPTION: Silvery with no markings; back often darker with bluish or olive cast. Elongated body. Juveniles have small dark to gold spots on sides. (Around islands often confused with Spanish Mackerel [previous].)

ABUNDANCE & DISTRIBUTION: Occasional Florida, Bahamas, Caribbean; also north to Massachusetts, Gulf of Mexico and south to Brazil.

HABITAT & BEHAVIOR: Primarily an open-water fish, but occasionally over reefs. Travel solitary or in small groups. Occasionally encountered while making open-water drifts or safety stops.

REACTION TO DIVERS: Apparently somewhat curious; often swim toward diver, making a single close pass.

CERO
Scomberomorus regalis
FAMILY:
Mackerel - Scombridae

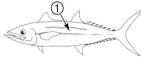

SIZE: 1¹/₂-3 ft., max. 4 ft.
DEPTH: 0-60 ft.

CAYMAN

SPANISH MACKEREL
Scomberomorus maculatus
FAMILY:
Mackerel - Scombridae

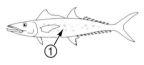

SIZE: 1¹/₂-3 ft., max. 4 ft.
DEPTH: 0-60 ft.

HOLLYWOOD, FL

KING MACKEREL
Scomberomorus cavalla
FAMILY:
Mackerel - Scombridae

SIZE: 2-4 ft., max. 5¹/₂ ft.
DEPTH: 0-60 ft.

GRAND BAHAMA

DISTINCTIVE FEATURES: Long, cigar-shaped body. **1. Sharply pointed snout.**

DESCRIPTION: Bright silver to silvery gray; back may have dark bluish cast. May display numerous dark bars, especially when stressed. Nine dorsal finlets and widely forked tail.

ABUNDANCE & DISTRIBUTION: Occasional Florida, Bahamas, Caribbean; also circumtropical and subtropical.

HABITAT & BEHAVIOR: Primarily an open-water fish, but may swim over deeper reefs. Travel solitary or in pairs. Occasionally encountered while making open-water drifts or safety stops.

REACTION TO DIVERS: Apparently somewhat curious; often swim toward diver making several close passes.

DISTINCTIVE FEATURES: (Lower specimen only, see note.) Body laterally compressed. **1. Numerous dark bars on body. 2. Rear portion of dorsal fin dusky to black.**

DESCRIPTION: Back greenish silver gradually changing to silver belly. Elongated "needle-like" body. Beak short and only slightly longer than length of head; lower lobe of tail larger than upper.

ABUNDANCE & DISTRIBUTION: Occasional Florida, Bahamas, Caribbean; also north to New Jersey and south to Brazil; circumtropical and subtropical.

HABITAT & BEHAVIOR: Considered oceanic, but occasionally may come near shore in clear water, especially near islands. Generally drift and feed just below surface.

REACTION TO DIVERS: Relatively shy; generally move away when approached.

NOTE: Upper specimen is a Houndfish, *Tylosurus crocodilus*, [next page]. Needlefish rarely on reef tops; these were apparently attracted by the juvenile angelfish that was acting as a cleaner.

DISTINCTIVE FEATURES: 1. Wide, flattened, lateral keel on each side of base of tail.

DESCRIPTION: Silver. Elongated "needle-like" body. Beak long and slender, upper jaw slightly shorter than lower; lobes of tail nearly equal in size.

ABUNDANCE & DISTRIBUTION: Occasional Florida, Bahamas, Caribbean; also north to New Jersey and south to Brazil; circumtropical and subtropical.

HABITAT & BEHAVIOR: Considered oceanic, but occasionally may come near shore in clear water, especially near islands. Generally drift and feed just below surface.

REACTION TO DIVERS: Relatively shy; generally move away when diver approaches.

SIMILAR SPECIES: Redfin Needlefish, *Strongylura notata*, distinguished by red to reddish dorsal, anal fins and lobes of tail, especially the tips; black bar on gill cover; tail lobes of nearly equal size.

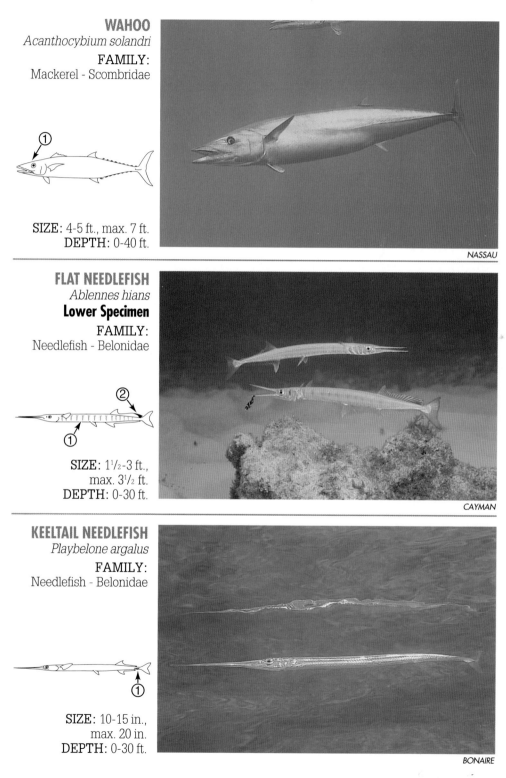

WAHOO
Acanthocybium solandri
FAMILY:
Mackerel - Scombridae

SIZE: 4-5 ft., max. 7 ft.
DEPTH: 0-40 ft.

NASSAU

FLAT NEEDLEFISH
Ablennes hians
Lower Specimen
FAMILY:
Needlefish - Belonidae

SIZE: 1 1/2-3 ft.,
max. 3 1/2 ft.
DEPTH: 0-30 ft.

CAYMAN

KEELTAIL NEEDLEFISH
Playbelone argalus
FAMILY:
Needlefish - Belonidae

SIZE: 10-15 in.,
max. 20 in.
DEPTH: 0-30 ft.

BONAIRE

DISTINCTIVE FEATURES: Largest needlefish. **1. Black lateral keel on each side of base of tail.**

DESCRIPTION: Silver. May have darkish bar or bars on gill cover. Elongated "needle-like" body. Beak short compared to most other needlefishes, about one and a half times the length of the head; lower lobe of tail larger than upper.

ABUNDANCE & DISTRIBUTION: Occasional Florida, Bahamas, Caribbean; also north to New Jersey and south to Brazil; circumtropical and subtropical.

HABITAT & BEHAVIOR: Inhabit all shallow inshore waters; most common over flats with coral heads, small patch reefs and sea grasses between and around islands. Generally drift and feed just below surface.

REACTION TO DIVERS: Relatively shy and will generally move away when approached.

SIMILAR SPECIES: Timucu, *Strongylura timucu*, distinguished by dark head and body stripe; dorsal fin further back than anal. Atlantic Needlefish, *S. marina*, distinguished by bluish tail.

DISTINCTIVE FEATURES: 1. Upper lobe of tail yellow to orange. 2. Upper jaw extremely short, lower jaw long with yellow to orange or red tip.

DESCRIPTION: Silver; back often has greenish sheen. Leading edge of dorsal fin often yellow to orange. Tail deeply forked; lower lobe largest.

ABUNDANCE & DISTRIBUTION: Occasional Florida, Bahamas, Caribbean; also north to Massachusetts, Gulf of Mexico and south to Brazil; also eastern Atlantic.

HABITAT & BEHAVIOR: Inhabit shallow inshore waters. May be over reefs, but more often in calm bays and lagoons, and especially over manatee grass beds. Generally drift and feed in schools just below surface.

REACTION TO DIVERS: Shy; move away upon approach. Best tactic for close view is to move into direction of travel.

DISTINCTIVE FEATURES: 1. Lobes of tail violet to blue (on rare occasion, upper lobe is reddish and/or red tipped). 2. Upper jaw extremely short, lower jaw long with orange to red tip.

DESCRIPTION: Silver; often with violet to blue sheen, especially on back. Leading edge of dorsal fin often violet to blue. Tail deeply forked; lower lobe largest.

ABUNDANCE & DISTRIBUTION: Occasional Florida, Bahamas, Caribbean; also north to New York, Bermuda, Gulf of Mexico and south to Brazil; circumtropical and subtropical.

HABITAT & BEHAVIOR: Inhabit both oceanic and shallow inshore waters. May be near reefs, in calm bays and lagoons, or over sea grass beds. Generally drift and feed in schools just below surface.

REACTION TO DIVERS: Shy; move away upon approach. Best tactic for close view is to move into direction of travel.

SIMILAR SPECIES: Halfbeak, *Hyporhamphus unifasciatus*, distinguished by only slightly forked tail with lobes of equal size; usually has greenish sheen.

HOUNDFISH
Tylosurus crocodilus
FAMILY:
Needlefish - Belonidae

SIZE: 2-3½ ft., max. 5 ft.
DEPTH: 0-30 ft.

CAYMAN

BALLYHOO
Hemiramphus brasiliensis
FAMILY:
Flyingfish/Halfbeak -
Exocoetidae

SIZE: 8-12 in., max. 16 in.
DEPTH: 0-30 ft.

ST. LUCIA

BALAO
Hemiramphus balao
FAMILY:
Flyingfish/Halfbeak -
Exocoetidae

SIZE: 8-12 in., max. 15 in.
DEPTH: 0-30 ft.

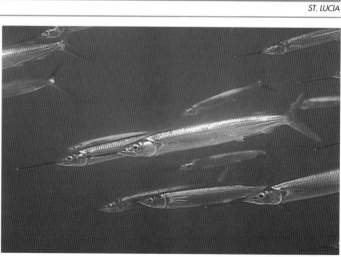

CONCEPTION IS., BAHAMAS

Barracuda

DISTINCTIVE FEATURES: Silver. Long, cylindrical body. **1. Large underslung jaw, pointed teeth often obvious.**

DESCRIPTION: Usually has scattered, dark blotches. Can darken showing side bands. Dorsal fins widely separated.

ABUNDANCE & DISTRIBUTION: Common Florida, Bahamas, Caribbean; also north to Massachusetts, Bermuda, Gulf of Mexico, south to Brazil and almost circumtropical.

HABITAT & BEHAVIOR: Drift around reefs and other habitats. Solitary or in small groups. Open and close mouth to assist respiration.

REACTION TO DIVERS: Have the unnerving habit of approaching divers and following them about the reef. This appears to be nothing more than curiosity, as there are no reports of unprovoked attacks (The only substantiated incidents involved spearfishing.) Normally move away if closely approached.

DISTINCTIVE FEATURES: Long, slender and silver with no obvious markings. (Similar Barracuda, *S. barracuda*, [previous] is heavier bodied and usually shows some dark markings.)

DESCRIPTION: May have two faint yellowish body stripes. Widely separated dorsal fins.

ABUNDANCE & DISTRIBUTION: Uncommon Florida, Bahamas, Caribbean; also Bermuda and south to Uruguay.

HABITAT & BEHAVIOR: Inhabit reefs and sandy areas between patch reefs. Form loosely polarized schools. (Similar Great Barracuda [previous] rarely school.)

REACTION TO DIVERS: When approached, schools slowly move away. Will encircle diver on rare occasion.

DISTINCTIVE FEATURES: Long, slender and silvery. **1. Yellowish to yellow or gold midbody stripe.**

DESCRIPTION: Sides silvery; back silvery brown to olive. Widely separated dorsal fins.

ABUNDANCE & DISTRIBUTION: Occasional Florida, Bahamas, Caribbean; also north to Massachusetts, Gulf of Mexico and south to Brazil.

HABITAT & BEHAVIOR: Inhabit shallow inshore waters including sand flats, grass beds, mud bottoms, bays and estuaries; rare around reefs. Form loosely polarized schools. (Similar Great Barracuda, *S. barracuda*, [previous] rarely school.)

REACTION TO DIVERS: When approached, schools slowly move away.

GREAT BARRACUDA
Sphyraena barracuda
FAMILY:
Barracuda - Sphyraenidae

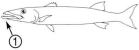

SIZE: 1¹/₂-3 ft., max. 6 ft.
DEPTH: 0-60 ft.

BELIZE

SOUTHERN SENNET
Sphyraena picudilla
FAMILY:
Barracuda - Sphyraenidae

SIZE: 8-14 in., max. 18 in.
DEPTH: 5-60 ft.

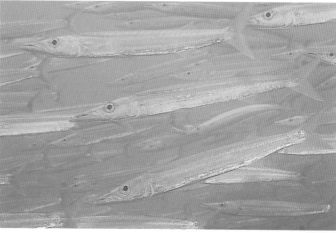

ROATAN

GUAGUANCHE
Sphyraena guachancho
FAMILY:
Barracuda - Sphyraenidae

SIZE: 6-14 in., max. 2 ft.
DEPTH: 3-40 ft.

FT. PIERCE, FL

DISTINCTIVE FEATURES: Silvery blue with thin stripes. **1. Rear base of foredorsal fin connects with front base of second dorsal fin.** (Similar Bonnetmouth, *Emmelichthyops atlanticus*, [next] is distinguished by two widely separated dorsal fins.)

DESCRIPTION: Thin body stripes in a variety of colors, including yellow, blue and black. Body is occasionally brownish; snout often yellowish. Cylindrical body.

ABUNDANCE & DISTRIBUTION: Occasional to common South Florida, Bahamas, Caribbean; also Bermuda.

HABITAT & BEHAVIOR: Schooling open-water fish. Occasionally swim over deeper reefs and along edges of walls, most often between 50 and 90 feet. Often mix with schools of Creole Wrasse, *Clepticus parrae*, [pg.193].

REACTION TO DIVERS: Can be closely approached with slow, nonthreatening movements.

DISTINCTIVE FEATURES: Silvery green to yellow with thin stripes above midbody. **1. Brown stripe at midbody. 2. Two dorsal fins widely separated.** (Similar Boga, *Inermia vittata*, [previous] distinguished by dorsal fins connected at base.)

DESCRIPTION: Pale belly. Cylindrical body. Deeply forked tail can fold in scissor-like manner.

ABUNDANCE & DISTRIBUTION: Uncommon to rare South Florida, Bahamas, Caribbean.

HABITAT & BEHAVIOR: Schooling, rapid-swimming fish. Most commonly observed at night in reef pockets, around patch reefs and over sand.

REACTION TO DIVERS: Apparently attracted by divers' lights at night, they often make several close passes.

DISTINCTIVE FEATURES: 1. Short, underslung mouth that ends before eye. 2. Single dorsal fin. 3. Deeply forked tail.

DESCRIPTION: Silver. No obvious markings; darkish area at tip of snout and base of pectoral fin; may display faint bars.

ABUNDANCE & DISTRIBUTION: Abundant to occasional South Florida, Bahamas, Caribbean; rare North Florida; also south to Brazil and circumtropical.

HABITAT & BEHAVIOR: Feed over shallow flats on a rising tide, often near mangroves. When not feeding may be observed on sand and coral rubble flats between shallow patch reefs or in passes between fringe reefs.

REACTION TO DIVERS: Extremely shy. Difficult to approach.

SIMILAR SPECIES: Ladyfish, *Elops saurus*, distinguished by long, upturned mouth that extends beyond eye. Ventral fins are directly below dorsal fin.

BOGA
Inermia vittata
FAMILY:
Bonnetmouth -
Inermiidae

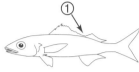

SIZE: 5-7 in., max. 9 in.
DEPTH: 30-150 ft.

CAYMAN

BONNETMOUTH
*Emmelichthyops
atlanticus*
FAMILY:
Bonnetmouth -
Inermiidae

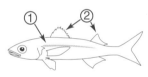

SIZE: 5-7 in., max. 9 in.
DEPTH: 10-300 ft.

KEY LARGO, FL

BONEFISH
Albula vulpes
FAMILY:
Bonefish - Albulidae

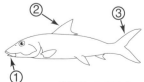

SIZE: 1-2$\frac{1}{2}$ ft.,
max. 3$\frac{1}{4}$ ft.
DEPTH: 0-30 ft.

BONAIRE

DISTINCTIVE FEATURES: 1. Obvious black lateral line. 2. Forehead depressed.

DESCRIPTION: Silvery olive.

ABUNDANCE & DISTRIBUTION: Common Florida, central and northern South American continental coastlines; rare or absent Bahamas and islands of Caribbean; also north to South Carolina, Gulf of Mexico and south to Brazil.

HABITAT & BEHAVIOR: Prefer areas near mangroves. Hover in secluded spots. Occasionally swim in small groups over grassy flats and shallow patch reefs.

REACTION TO DIVERS: Wary of divers, but tend to ignore them unless closely approached.

DISTINCTIVE FEATURES: 1. Dark spots on base of each scale form stripes on side. 2. Base of pectoral fin dark.

DESCRIPTION: Silvery, often with greenish, bluish or brownish tints; back appears dark because of large spot on each scale; belly silvery white; second dorsal fin and tail dusky. Second dorsal and anal fins line up, directly opposite one another.

ABUNDANCE & DISTRIBUTION: Occasional Florida; rare or absent Caribbean; also north to Nova Scotia and south to Brazil; circumtropical. Not reported Bahamas.

HABITAT & BEHAVIOR: Inhabit shallow inshore waters; occasionally enter fresh water. Often travel in huge schools.

REACTION TO DIVERS: Wary of divers, but tend to ignore them unless closely approached.

DISTINCTIVE FEATURES: 1. Large, semicircular or oval spot on base of pectoral fin is bluish black to dusky. 2. Dark to dusky margin on tip of rear dorsal fin and tail.

DESCRIPTION: Silvery; back is often shades of olive; sides and belly have bluish tints. Often have one or two goldish blotches on each side of head. Obvious scales.

ABUNDANCE & DISTRIBUTION: Common Florida, Bahamas, Caribbean; also north to Massachusetts, Bermuda, Gulf of Mexico and south to Brazil; tropical eastern Atlantic and Pacific.

HABITAT & BEHAVIOR: Inhabit areas of sand, sea grasses and algae, mud and other soft bottoms. Often swim around inlets, bays and estuaries. May enter fresh water. Feed on organic material and tiny organisms found on plants and algae, in surface scum and bottom material.

REACTION TO DIVERS: Wary, but tend to ignore divers unless closely approached.

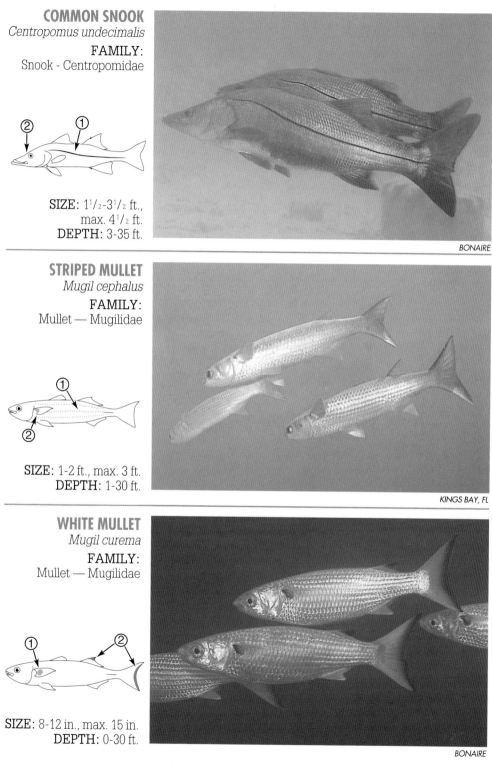

COMMON SNOOK
Centropomus undecimalis
FAMILY:
Snook - Centropomidae

SIZE: $1^1/_2$-$3^1/_2$ ft.,
max. $4^1/_2$ ft.
DEPTH: 3-35 ft.

BONAIRE

STRIPED MULLET
Mugil cephalus
FAMILY:
Mullet — Mugilidae

SIZE: 1-2 ft., max. 3 ft.
DEPTH: 1-30 ft.

KINGS BAY, FL

WHITE MULLET
Mugil curema
FAMILY:
Mullet — Mugilidae

SIZE: 8-12 in., max. 15 in.
DEPTH: 0-30 ft.

BONAIRE

DISTINCTIVE FEATURES: 1. Black spot on upper base of tail (occasionally forming saddle over top which, on rare occasion, may extend nearly to underside). (Similar Spottail Pinfish, *D. holbrooki*, [next] usually distinguished by large black spot or band encircling base of tail.) **2. Ventral fins bluish silver, other fins yellowish.**

DESCRIPTION: Silvery with thin, pale yellow stripes along scale rows. Occasionally have faint dusky vertical bars on body; black edge on gill cover. In Florida, when black spot on tail is large (as the specimen pictured), identification can be confirmed only by counting the scales along the lateral line which vary from 62 to 65 (Spottail Pinfish has 56 and is absent in the Bahamas and Caribbean).

ABUNDANCE & DISTRIBUTION: Uncommon Bahamas, Caribbean; rare Florida; also south to Argentina.

HABITAT & BEHAVIOR: Inhabit clear, turbulent inshore waters, usually along rocky coasts or on shallow reefs; often in surf.

REACTION TO DIVERS: Shy; keep their distance and move away upon approach.

DISTINCTIVE FEATURES: 1. Large black spot or, often, a band, encircles base of tail. (Similar Silver Porgy, *D. argenteus*, [previous] usually distinguished by black spot only on upper base of tail.) **2. All fins dusky to silver.**

DESCRIPTION: Silvery with thin, pale yellow stripes along scale rows. Occasionally have faint dusky vertical bars on body; black edge on gill cover. Identification can be confirmed only by counting the scales along the lateral line which number 56 (Silver Porgy has 62 to 65).

ABUNDANCE & DISTRIBUTION: Occasional Florida; also north to Chesapeake Bay and Gulf of Mexico. Not reported Bahamas or Caribbean.

HABITAT & BEHAVIOR: Inhabit inshore sea grass beds and, occasionally, inshore reefs and areas of rocky rubble.

REACTION TO DIVERS: Shy; keep their distance and move away upon approach.

DISTINCTIVE FEATURES: 1. Large dusky spot behind gill cover and below lateral line. (Similar Pinfish, *Lagodon rhomboides* [next], has spot centered on lateral line.) **2. Narrow bronze stripes on body.**

DESCRIPTION: Bluish silver; ventral and anal fins orangish. Body disk-like (compare with more elongated Pinfish [next]).

ABUNDANCE & DISTRIBUTION: Occasional Florida, Caribbean; also north to New Jersey and south to Brazil. Not reported Bahamas.

HABITAT & BEHAVIOR: Inhabit grass beds and mangrove areas; occasionally on shallow reefs.

REACTION TO DIVERS: Shy; keep their distance and move away upon approach.

SILVER PORGY
Diplodus argenteus
FAMILY:
Porgy - Sparidae

SIZE: 4-8 in., max. 12 in.
DEPTH: 0-80 ft.

FT. PIERCE, FL

SPOTTAIL PINFISH
Diplodus holbrooki
FAMILY:
Porgy - Sparidae

SIZE: 4-8 in., max. 18 in.
DEPTH: 0-40 ft.

HOLLYWOOD, FL

SEA BREAM
Archosargus rhomboidalis
FAMILY:
Porgy - Sparidae

SIZE: 5-8 in., max. 13 in.
DEPTH: 1-35 ft.

HOLLYWOOD, FL

DISTINCTIVE FEATURES: 1. Large dusky spot behind gill cover centered on lateral line. (Similar Sea Bream, *Archosargus rhomboidalis*, [previous] has spot below lateral line.) **2. Narrow bronze and blue stripes on body.**

DESCRIPTION: Bluish to greenish silver. May have four dusky cross bars. Body somewhat elongated (compare with more disk-like Sea Bream).

ABUNDANCE & DISTRIBUTION: Occasional eastern Florida; common to abundant western Florida and Gulf of Mexico; also north to Massachusetts. Not reported Bahamas, Caribbean.

HABITAT & BEHAVIOR: Wide range of habitats from rocky shoals to reefs and shipwrecks. Active swimmer.

REACTION TO DIVERS: Tend to ignore divers.

DISTINCTIVE FEATURES: Reddish silver. **1. Pinkish tail with darker reddish margin.**

DESCRIPTION: Numerous blue spots on scales occasionally form blue stripes on body; often reddish spot at rear base of dorsal fin.

ABUNDANCE & DISTRIBUTION: Common both coasts of Florida; also north to New York, south along continental coasts to Argentina and eastern Atlantic. Not reported Bahamas or Caribbean islands.

HABITAT & BEHAVIOR: Swim and hover around reefs, rocky outcroppings, ledges and adjacent sand areas. Adults inhabit deeper parts of the continental shelf; young prefer shallower water to 60 feet.

REACTION TO DIVERS: Not shy; usually allow a slow, nonthreatening approach. Curious; if diver remains still, apparently doing something, fish may come over to watch.

NOTE: Former species classification was *sedecim*.

DISTINCTIVE FEATURES: 1. Five to six dark, somewhat diagonal, body bars.

DESCRIPTION: Whitish to yellowish silver; back may be somewhat olive to brown.

ABUNDANCE & DISTRIBUTION: Common to occasional Florida and continental coastline, including Gulf of Mexico, to Brazil; also north to Nova Scotia. Not reported Bahamas or Caribbean islands.

HABITAT & BEHAVIOR: Inhabit rocky areas, shipwrecks and areas around dock pilings; occasionally enter brackish bays, lagoons and Florida spring basins.

REACTION TO DIVERS: Not shy; usually allow a slow, nonthreatening approach. Curious; if diver stays still, apparently doing something, fish may come over to watch.

PINFISH
Lagodon rhomboides
FAMILY:
Porgy - Sparidae

SIZE: 4-8 in., max. 14 in.
DEPTH: 3-65 ft.

PANAMA CITY, FL

RED PORGY
Pagrus pagrus
FAMILY:
Porgy - Sparidae

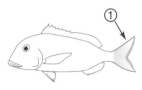

SIZE: 1-2½ ft., max. 3 ft.
DEPTH: 60-600 ft.

PANAMA CITY, FL

SHEEPSHEAD
Archosargus probatocephalus
FAMILY:
Porgy - Sparidae

SIZE: 1-1½ ft., max. 3 ft.
DEPTH: 3-40 ft.

JACKSONVILLE, FL

DISTINCTIVE FEATURES: 1. Black spot on upper base of pectoral fin.

DESCRIPTION: Silvery with bluish, lavender or yellow iridescent sheen. Usually pale gray or blue line around underside of eye; often display dark body bars when near bottom, especially when feeding; occasionally have dark margin on tail.

ABUNDANCE & DISTRIBUTION: Occasional Florida, Bahamas, Caribbean; also Gulf of Mexico and south to Brazil.

HABITAT & BEHAVIOR: Swim and hover above reefs and adjacent sand areas.

REACTION TO DIVERS: Not shy; usually allow a slow, nonthreatening approach. If diver remains still, apparently doing something, or digs in sand, fish may come near to watch.

Saucereye Porgy
Yellow wash over head and forebody.

NASSAU

DISTINCTIVE FEATURES: 1. Short, bluish, saucer-shaped line below eye. 2. Small, bluish blotch at upper base of pectoral fin. 3. Corners of mouth yellow.

DESCRIPTION: Silvery with bluish, yellowish and/or brassy cast; often yellow wash over head and forebody. Can change coloration rapidly and show a striped or blotched pattern, especially when feeding.

ABUNDANCE & DISTRIBUTION: Occasional Florida, Bahamas, Caribbean; also north to North Carolina, Bermuda, Gulf of Mexico and south to Brazil.

HABITAT & BEHAVIOR: Swim and hover above reefs and adjacent sand areas.

REACTION TO DIVERS: Not shy; usually allow a slow, nonthreatening approach. If diver remains still, apparently doing something, or digs in sand, fish may come near to watch.

SHEEPSHEAD PORGY
Calamus penna
FAMILY:
Porgy - Sparidae

SIZE: 8-14 in., max. 18 in.
DEPTH: 10-250 ft.

PANAMA CITY, FL

Sheepshead Porgy
Displaying dark body bars.

BIMINI

SAUCEREYE PORGY
Calamus calamus
FAMILY:
Porgy - Sparidae

SIZE: 8-14 in., max. 16 in.
DEPTH: 4-70 ft.

CAYMAN

71

Porgy

DISTINCTIVE FEATURES: 1. **Large eye, long sloping snout and large mouth with thick lips.** (Similar Saucereye Porgy, *C. calamus*, [previous] distinguished by blunter snout, and small mouth with thin lips.) 2. **Yellowish orange at corner of mouth.**

DESCRIPTION: Silver; may have faint iridescent blue, blue-green, lavender and/or brassy cast. Usually two large, silvery, horizontal markings under eye and on gill cover; a blue line directly under the eye is normally visible. Can change coloration rapidly and show a striped or blotched pattern, especially when feeding.

ABUNDANCE & DISTRIBUTION: Occasional Florida, Bahamas, Caribbean; also north to Rhode Island, Bermuda, Gulf of Mexico and south to Brazil.

HABITAT & BEHAVIOR: Swim and hover above reefs and adjacent sand areas.

REACTION TO DIVERS: Not shy; usually allow a slow, nonthreatening approach. If diver stays still, apparently doing something, fish may come near to watch.

SIMILAR SPECIES: Whitebone Porgy, *C. leucosteus*, distinguished by blue line above and below eye; usually has small blotches. Florida only.

DISTINCTIVE FEATURES: 1. **Short, blue rectangular stripe behind eye.** 2. **Bluish and brassy irregular lines and markings below eye.** (Similar Littlehead Porgy, *C. proridens*, [next] has lines that tend to be more regular and distinct, but is easily distinguished by location — only in Florida and Gulf of Mexico.)

DESCRIPTION: Silvery; commonly with yellow and/or brassy cast; snout above lip, nape and back often yellow. Bluish semicircular marking below eye. Can change coloration rapidly and show a striped or blotched pattern, especially when feeding.

ABUNDANCE & DISTRIBUTION: Occasional Bahamas, Caribbean; also south to Brazil. Not reported Florida.

HABITAT & BEHAVIOR: Inhabit reefs, grass beds and adjacent areas of sand and coral rubble.

REACTION TO DIVERS: Not shy; usually allow a slow, nonthreatening approach. If diver stops to dig or disturb bottom material, fish may come near to watch.

DISTINCTIVE FEATURES: 1. **Short blue stripe behind eye.** 2. **Numerous thin, horizontal blue lines over yellow background on cheek between mouth and eye.** (Similar Pluma, *C. pennatula*, [previous] tends to have less distinct and more irregular lines and markings, but is easily distinguished by its range — only in Bahamas and Caribbean.)

DESCRIPTION: Silvery, commonly with yellow and/or brassy cast; snout above lip, nape and back often yellow. Bluish semicircular marking below eye. Can change coloration rapidly and show a striped or blotched pattern, especially when feeding. With age, adults develop a pronounced or humped forehead. (Similar adult Pluma does not develop this hump.)

ABUNDANCE & DISTRIBUTION: Common northeastern Florida and Panhandle; occasional both coasts of South Florida and Keys; also Gulf of Mexico. Not reported Bahamas or Caribbean.

HABITAT & BEHAVIOR: Swim and hover above reefs and adjacent sand areas.

REACTION TO DIVERS: Not shy; usually allow a slow, nonthreatening approach. If diver stops to dig or disturb bottom material, fish may come near to watch.

SIMILAR SPECIES: Knobbed Porgy, *C. nodosus*, distinguished by bronze spots on cheek between mouth and eye, instead of lines. Florida, including Gulf of Mexico.

JOLTHEAD PORGY
Calamus bajonado
FAMILY:
Porgy - Sparidae

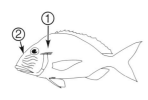

SIZE: 1-1½ ft., max. 2 ft.
DEPTH: 15-150 ft.

CAYMAN

PLUMA
Calamus pennatula
FAMILY:
Porgy - Sparidae

SIZE: 8-12 in., max. 15 in.
DEPTH: 3-275 ft.

NASSAU

LITTLEHEAD PORGY
Calamus proridens
FAMILY:
Porgy - Sparidae

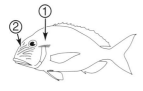

SIZE: 8-14 in., max. 18 in.
DEPTH: 30-200 ft.

PANAMA CITY, FL

73

DISTINCTIVE FEATURES: Gray to silver. "Football-shaped" body. (Note: Reliably distinguishing between these two species visually while underwater is considered impossible — fin ray and gill raker counts are required for confirmed identification.)

DESCRIPTION: Initially appear uniformly gray to silver; occasionally display whitish blotches. A close look reveals thin yellow to bronze stripes on body and a stripe, bordered in white, under eye from mouth to gill cover. (The Bermuda Chub is said to have "straw-yellow" markings, while the Yellow Chub markings are reported to be more bronze or gold, but this difference is not regarded as a dependable distinction.)

ABUNDANCE & DISTRIBUTION: Common to occasional Florida, Bahamas, Caribbean; also north to Massachusetts, Bermuda and south to Brazil.

HABITAT & BEHAVIOR: Medium-sized schools swim about rapidly, over reefs and along walls; occasionally form loose feeding aggregations near the surface. The two species often mix in schools and aggregations.

REACTION TO DIVERS: Often make one rapid, close pass, then continue down reef.

DISTINCTIVE FEATURES: 1. Yellow ventral fins. 2. Usually show several indistinct vertical bars on body.

DESCRIPTION: Bright silver; pectoral fins may be yellowish.

ABUNDANCE & DISTRIBUTION: Occasional to common Florida, Bahamas, Caribbean; also Bermuda, Gulf of Mexico, south to Brazil; also eastern Pacific from Mexico to Peru.

HABITAT & BEHAVIOR: Swim and hover over sand near reefs, stopping occasionally to dig for small invertebrates.

REACTION TO DIVERS: Unafraid; often allow a slow, nonthreatening approach. If diver stops and digs in sand, fish will often come near to watch.

DISTINCTIVE FEATURES: 1. Spinous dorsal fin has black tip with white stripe below.

DESCRIPTION: Bright silver; back may have greenish or brownish cast.

ABUNDANCE & DISTRIBUTION: Occasional Florida, Caribbean, more common along continental coastlines; also Bermuda, Gulf of Mexico, south to Brazil; also eastern Pacific from Mexico to Peru. Not reported Bahamas.

HABITAT & BEHAVIOR: Inhabit shallow bays, lagoons and estuaries, may enter fresh water. Often just below surf zone along sandy beach areas. Swim and hover over sand and grass beds. Move quickly from spot to spot on sand, stopping to feed; occasionally stop and raise dorsal fins for a split second.

REACTION TO DIVERS: Shy; usually move away upon approach. Occasionally allow a slow, nonthreatening approach. If diver stops and digs in sand, fish may come near to watch.

CHUB
(BERMUDA/YELLOW)
Kyphosus sectatrix/incisor
FAMILY:
Chub - Kyphosidae

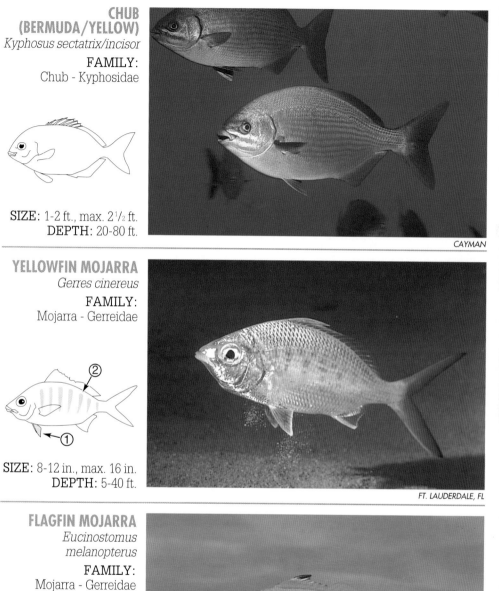

CAYMAN

SIZE: 1-2 ft., max. 2½ ft.
DEPTH: 20-80 ft.

YELLOWFIN MOJARRA
Gerres cinereus
FAMILY:
Mojarra - Gerreidae

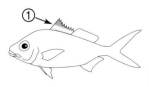

SIZE: 8-12 in., max. 16 in.
DEPTH: 5-40 ft.

FT. LAUDERDALE, FL

FLAGFIN MOJARRA
Eucinostomus melanopterus
FAMILY:
Mojarra - Gerreidae

SIZE: 4-6 in., max. 7 in.
DEPTH: 0-30 ft.

ST. LUCIA

DISTINCTIVE FEATURES: Slender body (body depth divides into length [tip of snout to start of tail] 3.0 to 3.4 times).

DESCRIPTION: Usually bright silver without other markings, but occasionally may display some dusky bars or mottling on back. May have dusky oval marking in front upper part of iris.

ABUNDANCE & DISTRIBUTION: Occasional Florida, Bahamas, Caribbean; also north to Massachusetts, Bermuda, Gulf of Mexico and south to Brazil.

HABITAT & BEHAVIOR: Inhabit shallow bays, grass beds, sandy beach areas and sands around shallow patch reefs and coral heads. Move quickly from spot to spot on sand, stopping to feed; occasionally stop and hover, raising dorsal fins for a split second.

REACTION TO DIVERS: Shy; usually move away upon approach. Occasionally allow a slow, nonthreatening approach. If diver stops and digs in sand, fish may come near to watch.

DISTINCTIVE FEATURES: 1. Dusky rectangular to roundish spot on central upper iris.

DESCRIPTION: Bright silver body, usually with some dusky bars or mottling on back. Foredorsal and tail often dusky and/or with darkish borders. Only mojarra to have two anal fin spines, others have three.

ABUNDANCE & DISTRIBUTION: Occasional Florida, Bahamas, Caribbean; also north to North Carolina, Bermuda, Gulf of Mexico and south to Brazil.

HABITAT & BEHAVIOR: Inhabit shallow sandy shorelines, occasionally tidal creeks and bays (especially young). Often swim and hover just below surf line.

REACTION TO DIVERS: Shy; usually move away upon approach. Occasionally allow a slow, nonthreatening approach. If a diver stops and digs in sand, fish may come near to watch.

DISTINCTIVE FEATURES: Deep body. **1. Usually have dusky tip on dorsal fin.**

DESCRIPTION: Bright silver body; may have dusky diagonal bands or blotches on sides, especially when young.

ABUNDANCE & DISTRIBUTION: Occasional Florida, Bahamas, Caribbean; also north to Massachusetts, Bermuda, Gulf of Mexico and south to Brazil.

HABITAT & BEHAVIOR: Inhabit a variety of shallow-water zones including grass beds, areas of gravel and coral rubble, fresh water coastal inlets, and sandy shorelines. Do not inhabit coral reefs.

REACTION TO DIVERS: Shy; usually move away upon approach. Occasionally allow a slow, nonthreatening approach. If a diver stops and digs in sand, fish will often come near to watch.

SIMILAR SPECIES: Bigeye Mojarra, *E. havana*, distinguished by larger eye and somewhat slimmer body.

SLENDER MOJARRA
Eucinostomus jonesi
FAMILY:
Mojarra - Gerreidae

SIZE: 4-6 in., max. 8 in.
DEPTH: 0-30 ft.

BIMINI

MOTTLED MOJARRA
Eucinostomus lefroyi
FAMILY:
Mojarra - Gerreidae

SIZE: 4-7 in., max. 9 in.
DEPTH: 0-20 ft.

BONAIRE

SILVER JENNY
Eucinostomus gula
FAMILY:
Mojarra - Gerreidae

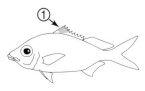

SIZE: 3-5 in., max. 7 in.
DEPTH: 0-20 ft.

BIMINI

77

DISTINCTIVE FEATURES: Shiny, large "stainless steel" scales. **1. Upturned mouth.**
DESCRIPTION: Stout body with no markings. Long filament trails from rear base of dorsal fin.
ABUNDANCE & DISTRIBUTION: Occasional Florida, Bahamas, Caribbean; also north to Virginia, Bermuda, Gulf of Mexico and south to Brazil.
HABITAT & BEHAVIOR: Drift in canyons and secluded areas. Normally school during the day. Large schools may inhabit a specific area on a reef for years, where they can reliably be observed. Actively feed at night.
REACTION TO DIVERS: Apparently unafraid, a nonthreatening diver can slowly swim through a school. Schools will slowly move away when diver activity becomes a nuisance.

DISTINCTIVE FEATURES: Long "torpedo-shaped" body.
DESCRIPTION: Silver to dark brown. Often have dusky midbody stripe. Lower jaw protrudes; tail forked.
ABUNDANCE & DISTRIBUTION: Occasional Florida; uncommon to rare Bahamas, Caribbean; also north to Massachusetts, Bermuda, Gulf of Mexico and south to Argentina; circumtropical and subtropical.
HABITAT & BEHAVIOR: Coastal to open-water fish; often hover below anchored ships and floating buoys; occasionally swim over reefs. Swim with pectoral fins stiffly extended.
REACTION TO DIVERS: Unafraid. Can be closely approached.
NOTE ABOUT JUVENILE: Very similar to adult Sharksucker, *Echeneis naucrates*, [pg. 361] distinguished by dark tail borders with white in between. (Sharksucker has white tail borders with dark in between.)

DISTINCTIVE FEATURES: 1. Wide white border on trailing edge of pectoral fins is noticeable when extended. 2. Blunt snout.
DESCRIPTION: Silvery blue to green above, pale below. A pale triangle extends from base of pectoral fins.
ABUNDANCE & DISTRIBUTION: Uncommon Bahamas and eastern Caribbean. Not reported Florida and balance of Caribbean.
HABITAT & BEHAVIOR: Considered oceanic; inhabit water near surface. Rapid swimmers; when frightened, they can break the surface and glide great distances on extended pectoral fins. Rarely come over reefs during the day; may feed above deep reefs at night.
REACTION TO DIVERS: Shy; rapidly retreat. At night they may be attracted by divers' lights near the surface, where they can be closely observed.
SIMILAR SPECIES: There are over a dozen species of flyingfish in the waters of Florida, Bahamas and Caribbean. All are oceanic, rarely observed underwater and difficult to distinguish.

TARPON
Megalops atlanticus
FAMILY:
Tarpon - Elopidae

SIZE: 2-4 ft., max. 8 ft.
DEPTH: 0-40 ft.

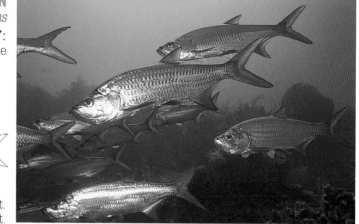

CAYMAN

COBIA
Rachycentron canadum
FAMILY:
Cobia - Rachycentridae

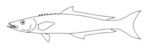

SIZE: 2-4 ft., max. 6 ft.
DEPTH: 0-60 ft.

JACKSONVILLE, FL

MIRRORWING FLYINGFISH
Hirundichthys speculiger
FAMILY:
Flyingfish - Exocoetidae

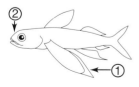

SIZE: 6-8 in., max. 10 in.
DEPTH: 0-10 ft.

BIMINI

DISTINCTIVE FEATURES: Silver body. **1. Several dark bars.**

DESCRIPTION: Silver may turn gray. Bars can pale dramatically. Body shape resembles a "spade" on playing cards.

ABUNDANCE & DISTRIBUTION: Common Florida and Bahamas; occasional to uncommon Caribbean; also north to Massachusetts, Bermuda, Gulf of Mexico and south to Brazil.

HABITAT & BEHAVIOR: Usually swim in small schools in open water, although occasionally in huge schools (especially along the coasts of Florida and western Bahamas).

REACTION TO DIVERS: Often circle a diver closely, apparently attracted by the bubbles.

DISTINCTIVE FEATURES: 1. Five to seven bold dark bars encircle body.

DESCRIPTION: Silvery white to gray. Long, torpedo-shaped body and forked tail.

ABUNDANCE & DISTRIBUTION: Occasional Florida, Bahamas, Caribbean; circumtropical and warm, temperate waters.

HABITAT & BEHAVIOR: Accompany large fish, including sharks, rays, whales and occasionally ships.

REACTION TO DIVERS: Ignore divers.

DISTINCTIVE FEATURES: Tiny silver, fork-tailed schooling fish.

DESCRIPTION: There are about 10 different species of similar fish that are virtually impossible to distinguish underwater. Many species mix together in a single school, making identification even more difficult; consequently, they are grouped here as one.

ABUNDANCE & DISTRIBUTION: Occasional throughout Florida, Bahamas, Caribbean.

HABITAT & BEHAVIOR: Densely packed polarized schools flow and drift in caves, deep-cut canyons and other sheltered areas of reefs. Often congregate in the interiors of shipwrecks.

REACTION TO DIVERS: The silvery fish will part, flow and contour around divers as they pass through the schools.

ATLANTIC SPADEFISH
Chaetodipterus faber
FAMILY:
Spadefish - Ephippidae

SIZE: 1-1½ ft., max. 3 ft.
DEPTH: 10-70 ft.

GRAND BAHAMA

PILOT FISH
Naucrates ductor
FAMILY:
Jack - Carangidae

SIZE: 6-15 in., max. 2 ft.
DEPTH: 3-100 ft.

NASSAU

SILVERSIDES, HERRINGS, ANCHOVIES

FAMILIES:
Atherinidae, Clupeidae,
Engraulididae

SIZE: 1-3 in., max. 6 in.
DEPTH: 10-60 ft.

CAYMAN

Sloping Head/Tapered Body
Grunt – Snapper

This ID Group consists of fish that have what can best be described as a basic, "fish-like" shape, relatively large mouths and notched tails.

FAMILY: Grunt – Haemulidae
14 Species Included

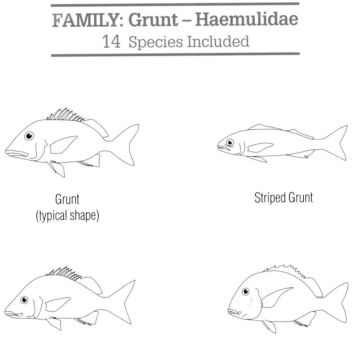

Grunt
(typical shape)

Striped Grunt

Margate

Porkfish

The common family name is derived from the unusual "grunt" sound produced when teeth grinding deep within their throats is amplified by the air bladder. Grunts are closely related to snapper, but are generally smaller (normally between 12 and 18 inches), with more deeply notched tails. They also lack the snapper's sharp canine teeth. Most are colorful, and congregate during the day in small groups to large schools that drift in the shadows of reefs. At night, the nocturnal feeders scavenge the sand flats and grass beds near reefs for crustaceans. Grunts often make up the largest biomass on reefs in continental or insular shelf areas that have large expanses of grass beds and sand flats. Grunt populations are less prominent around islands lacking these habitats.

Differences in color, body stripes and tail markings are keys to identifying grunts. Adults all have distinctive features and are fairly easy to distinguish. Those which may cause confusion are the Bluestripe and White Grunt; the Sailor's Choice and Black Grunt;

and the more elongated Small Mouth and Striped Grunt. Identifying early juvenile grunts (one to two inches) is difficult. Most are silver-white with similar dark body stripes, and have a dot on the tail base. Careful attention to subtle differences, however, makes identification possible.

Margate (white), Black Margate and Porkfish are also family members. All three have higher back profiles than other grunts. The margates are also larger than other family members (up to 27 inches).

FAMILY: Snapper—Lutjanidae
12 Species Included

Snapper
(typical shape)

Yellowtail Snapper

The behavior of snapping their jaws when hooked gives snappers their name. They are medium-sized (usually one to two feet), oblong-shaped fish with triangular heads. All have a single, continuous dorsal fin that is often higher in the front, and shallow, notched tail. They have slightly upturned snouts, large mouths, and prominent canine teeth near the front of the jaw. Similar-appearing grunts lack these canine teeth.

Snappers are nocturnal predators that feed on crustaceans and small fish. When seen on the reef in daytime, Dog, Cubera and Mutton Snappers tend to be solitary; Mahogany, Gray and Lane Snappers often gather in small groups; Yellowtail Snappers swim in loose aggregations well above the reefs; while Schoolmasters often form schools, though larger individuals may be solitary. Deep-water species, such as the Red, Vermilion, Silk and Blackfin Snapper, have a reddish tint. They are seldom seen, however, because of the great depths at which they congregate.

Dog, Cubera and Gray Snappers are difficult to differentiate because they are generally all gray with only subtle markings. Lane, Mahogany and Mutton Snappers are also easily confused because of the distinctive dark body spot found on all three, but it is not always present making identification even more difficult. Subtle differences between all these species, however, make underwater identification possible.

Grunt

DISTINCTIVE FEATURES: 1. Yellow stripes below lateral line set on diagonal.
DESCRIPTION: Yellow stripes on a white to bluish or yellowish silver background. Stripes above lateral line are horizontal. Fins yellow.
ABUNDANCE & DISTRIBUTION: Abundant Florida Keys; common Florida, Bahamas, Caribbean; also north to South Carolina, Bermuda, Gulf of Mexico and south to Brazil.
HABITAT & BEHAVIOR: Prefer coral reefs. Drift in small to large schools that may number in the thousands. Often in shade of formations.
REACTION TO DIVERS: Wary; generally keep their distance. Patient, slow maneuvers are required for a close view.

DISTINCTIVE FEATURES: Elongated, cylindrical body. **1. Normally have five yellow to brown stripes on upper body (no stripes on belly). 2. Short snout; eyes near mouth.**
DESCRIPTION: Silver to white; head and back occasionally dusky; tail may be dark.
ABUNDANCE & DISTRIBUTION: Occasional to uncommon Florida and Caribbean; rare Bahamas; also Gulf of Mexico and south to Brazil.
HABITAT & BEHAVIOR: Inhabit deep reefs; become more abundant with depth.
REACTION TO DIVERS: Wary; generally keep their distance. Patient, slow maneuvers are required for a close view.

DISTINCTIVE FEATURES: Elongated, cylindrical body. **1. Five or six yellow stripes. 2. Fins yellow.**
DESCRIPTION: Stripes over bluish silver to silvery-white background. Have pale phase. Noticeably smaller mouth than other grunts.
ABUNDANCE & DISTRIBUTION: Common South Florida and Keys; occasional Bahamas and Caribbean; also south to Brazil.
HABITAT & BEHAVIOR: Prefer shallow reefs. Drift in small schools, near bottom, in the shelter of coral formations, often around elkhorn and staghorn.
REACTION TO DIVERS: Wary; generally keep their distance. Patient, slow maneuvers are required for a close view.

FRENCH GRUNT
Haemulon flavolineatum
FAMILY:
Grunt - Haemulidae

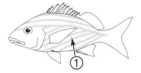

SIZE: 6-10 in., max. 1 ft.
DEPTH: 12-60 ft.

DRY TORTUGAS, FL

STRIPED GRUNT
Haemulon striatum
FAMILY:
Grunt - Haemulidae

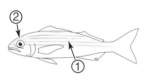

SIZE: 6-9 in., max. 11 in.
DEPTH: 40-100 ft.

WEST PALM BEACH, FL

SMALLMOUTH GRUNT
Haemulon chrysargyreum
FAMILY:
Grunt - Haemulidae

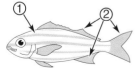

SIZE: 7-9 in., max. 10 in.
DEPTH: 8-50 ft.

CAYMAN

DISTINCTIVE FEATURES: 1. Stripes only on head.

DESCRIPTION: Head stripes yellow and bluish silver. Large scales on body form checkered pattern of yellow and bluish silver, often with a pearly iridescence.

ABUNDANCE & DISTRIBUTION: Common Florida, Bahamas, Caribbean; also north to Maryland, Bermuda, Gulf of Mexico and south to Brazil.

HABITAT & BEHAVIOR: Drift in small to large schools, often along edges of shallow patch reefs or in shade of large coral formations.

REACTION TO DIVERS: Wary; generally keep their distance. Patient, slow maneuvers are required for a close view.

DISTINCTIVE FEATURES: 1. Dark tail and rear dorsal fin. 2. Blue stripes.

DESCRIPTION: Blue stripes over yellow-gold. Dark tail and dorsal fins have light margins; other fins yellow.

ABUNDANCE & DISTRIBUTION: Common Florida, Bahamas, Caribbean; also north to South Carolina, Bermuda, Gulf of Mexico and south to Brazil.

HABITAT & BEHAVIOR: Drift in small to midsized schools on reef, especially near drop-offs.

REACTION TO DIVERS: Tend to be more wary than most grunts. Schools often flow away when divers approach. Patient, slow maneuvers are required for a close view.

DISTINCTIVE FEATURES: 1. Yellow to dark copper/bronze stripes. 2. Dusky rear dorsal, anal and tail fins.

DESCRIPTION: Stripes over white to silver-blue or silver-gray background. Tail has pale margin. Eyes often bright blue.

ABUNDANCE & DISTRIBUTION: Occasional to uncommon South Florida, Bahamas, Caribbean; also Bermuda and south to Brazil.

HABITAT & BEHAVIOR: Drift in small schools near coral formations.

REACTION TO DIVERS: Tend to be more wary than most grunts. Schools often flow away when divers approach. Patient, slow maneuvers are required for a close view.

WHITE GRUNT
Haemulon plumieri
FAMILY:
Grunt - Haemulidae

SIZE: 8-14 in.,
max. 18 in.
DEPTH: 12-40 ft.

CAYMAN

BLUESTRIPED GRUNT
Haemulon sciurus
FAMILY:
Grunt - Haemulidae

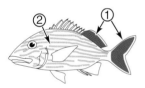

SIZE: 8-14 in.,
max. 18 in.
DEPTH: 12-50 ft.

ROATAN

CAESAR GRUNT
Haemulon carbonarium
FAMILY:
Grunt - Haemulidae

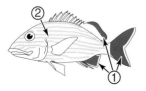

SIZE: 7-12 in.,
max. 15 in.
DEPTH: 10-50 ft.

CAYMAN

Grunt

DISTINCTIVE FEATURES: 1. Prominent yellow to bronze stripe runs from snout through eye to base of tail; another thinner stripe on back. 2. Fins pale. 3. Black spot on base of tail (not always present).

DESCRIPTION: Silvery-white to tan body. May have additional thin stripes on body. One of the smaller grunts.

ABUNDANCE & DISTRIBUTION: Common to uncommon Florida, Bahamas, Caribbean; also north to Massachusetts, Bermuda, Gulf of Mexico and south to Brazil.

HABITAT & BEHAVIOR: Inhabit reefs, sea grass beds and sand flats. Tend to be more common on shallow reefs where they often mix with other grunts.

REACTION TO DIVERS: Wary; generally keep their distance. Patient, slow maneuvers are required for a close view.

Cottonwick

Displaying incomplete dorsal stripe and entirely black midbody stripe.

KEY LARGO, FL

DISTINCTIVE FEATURES: 1. Bold, black stripe on dorsal fin continues to form a "V" on tail (absent in pale phase). 2. Black stripe begins on snout, runs across eye and continues to tail; color may change to yellow behind eye.

DESCRIPTION: Narrow, pale yellow horizontal stripes over white to silver background. Dark body stripe may run to base of tail.

ABUNDANCE & DISTRIBUTION: Uncommon to occasional Florida, Bahamas, Caribbean; also Bermuda and south to Brazil.

HABITAT & BEHAVIOR: Inhabit clear water reefs. Drift near bottom in small groups.

REACTION TO DIVERS: Wary; generally keep their distance. Patient, slow maneuvers are required for a close view.

TOMTATE
Haemulon aurolineatum
FAMILY:
Grunt - Haemulidae

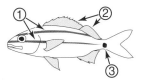

SIZE: 5-8 in., max. 10 in.
DEPTH: 5-65 ft.

ANGUILLA

Tomtate
*Phase without
black spot on tail.*

ANGUILLA

COTTONWICK
Haemulon melanurum
FAMILY:
Grunt - Haemulidae

SIZE: 7-10 in., max. 13 in.
DEPTH: 10-50 ft.

CAYMAN

89

Grunt

DISTINCTIVE FEATURES: 1. Bold black stripes on upper body. 2. Yellow-green dorsal hump. 3. Yellow saddle or spot on base of tail.

DESCRIPTION: Silver-gray; yellow pectoral fin; yellow borders on rear dorsal, anal and tail fins. Black stripe running from eye to tail is especially noticeable.

ABUNDANCE & DISTRIBUTION: Common Florida Keys; occasional South Florida, Bahamas; occasional to uncommon Caribbean; also Bermuda and south to Brazil.

HABITAT & BEHAVIOR: Drift alone or in small groups over reefs, often in secluded areas. Prefer clear water.

REACTION TO DIVERS: Wary; generally keep their distance. Patient, slow maneuvers are required for a close view.

DISTINCTIVE FEATURES: Distinct scale pattern accentuated by black spots forms lines over body. 1. Fins dusky to dark (except pectoral which may be light).

DESCRIPTION: Silvery to pearly gray.

ABUNDANCE & DISTRIBUTION: Common to occasional Florida, Bahamas and continental coasts of Central and South America; occasional to rare in islands of Caribbean; also Gulf of Mexico and south to Brazil.

HABITAT & BEHAVIOR: Inhabit open areas of reefs. Normally drift in small schools, but occasionally solitary.

REACTION TO DIVERS: Wary, generally keep their distance. Patient, slow maneuvers are required for a close view.

SIMILAR SPECIES: Black Grunt, *H. bonariense*, distinguished by pale fins (except tail which is dark). Only reported from southern Caribbean, especially along coasts of Central and South America.

DISTINCTIVE FEATURES: 1. High back profile. 2. Light pectoral fins.

DESCRIPTION: Normally pearl gray and unmarked, but may have dusky spots over the body and three faint stripes at and above lateral line. Dorsal and tail fins are usually dusky. Largest of grunts.

ABUNDANCE & DISTRIBUTION: Occasional Florida, Bahamas, Caribbean; also Bermuda and south to Brazil.

HABITAT & BEHAVIOR: Inhabit sand flats between patch reefs; also swim over sea grass beds and rocky areas. Drift alone or in small schools. Prefer clear water.

REACTION TO DIVERS: Wary; generally keep their distance, but on occasion are curious and approach diver.

SPANISH GRUNT
Haemulon macrostomum

FAMILY:
Grunt - Haemulidae

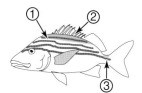

SIZE: 10-15 in.,
max. 17 in.
DEPTH: 15-60 ft.

KEY LARGO, FL

SAILORS CHOICE
Haemulon parra

FAMILY:
Grunt - Haemulidae

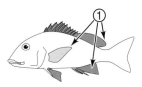

SIZE: 8-12 in.,
max. 17 in.
DEPTH: 10-60 ft.

CAYMAN

MARGATE (WHITE)
Haemulon album

FAMILY:
Grunt - Haemulidae

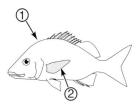

SIZE: 10-20 in.,
max. 27 in.
DEPTH: 6-50 ft.

KEY LARGO, FL

Grunt

IDENTIFICATION OF EARLY JUVENILE GRUNTS

Early juveniles (one to two inches in length) of grunts in the genus *Haemulon* are quite similar in appearance. They inhabit both reef and vegetated habitats and often occur in great abundance. Prior to, and during, the onset of adult coloration, easily distinguished categories exist: 1. Species with short upper eye stripe; 2. Species with a long upper eye stripe running parallel to the midlateral stripe (ML); 3. Species with a long upper eye stripe curving toward the midlateral stripe. In each of these categories, the shape of a spot on the base of the tail (caudal spot), in combination with other features, often makes species identification possible.

FRENCH GRUNT
Haemulon flavolineatum

Short upper eye stripe.
Caudal spot like Tomtate,
ID via diagonal scale rows
below ML & diagonal yellow
stripes in larger stages.

KEY LARGO, FL

SMALLMOUTH GRUNT
Haemulon chrysargyreum

Long, parallel upper eye
stripe. ML continuous with
upward bent caudal spot.
Elongate body.

KEY LARGO, FL

STRIPED GRUNT
Haemulon striatum

Short upper eye stripe.
Pale, narrow caudal spot.
Elongate body.

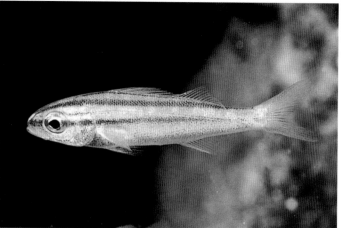

JUPITER, FL

TOMTATE
Haemulon aurolineatum

Short upper eye stripe.
Caudal spot like French,
ID via parallel scale
rows below ML.

ANGUILLA

CAESAR GRUNT
Haemulon carbonarium

Long, parallel upper eye
stripe. Caudal spot is oval/
rectangular and large. Upper
eye stripe often bronze and
lengthens with age, unlike
other grunts. Stripe curves
downward in larger stages.

KEY LARGO, FL

93

Grunt

BLUESTRIPED GRUNT
Haemulon sciurus

Long, parallel upper eye stripe. Parallel yellow stripes below ML. ML more distinct than similar White Grunt.

SAILORS CHOICE
Haemulon parra

Long, downward curving upper eye stripe. ID via distinct contrast between black stripes and white background. Similar Bluestriped and White Grunts have darker undercolor.

WHITE GRUNT
Haemulon plumieri

Long, downward curving upper eye stripe. ML frequently indistinct or absent, region below is often shaded dark or has diagonal yellow stripes.

ROATAN

SPANISH GRUNT
Haemulon macrostomum

Long, downward curving upper eye stripe. Caudal spot is distinctive, large and wedge-shaped. Yellow/green back and nape in larger stages.

ANGUILLA

COTTONWICK
Haemulon melanurum

Long, downward curving upper eye stripe. ML continuous with straight caudal spot.

NASSAU

DISTINCTIVE FEATURES: Numerous yellow to bronze spots, dashes and line markings. **1. Small mouth.**

DESCRIPTION: Gray, often with bluish highlights and tint.

ABUNDANCE & DISTRIBUTION: Occasional to common northern Florida; also north to New York, Bermuda and Gulf of Mexico. Not reported Bahamas or Caribbean.

HABITAT & BEHAVIOR: Inhabit murky coastal waters and muddy bays. Attracted to artificial reefs and shipwrecks.

REACTION TO DIVERS: Wary; tend to keep their distance and move away upon approach. May make several close passes if diver remains still.

DISTINCTIVE FEATURES: Bright yellow-gold. **1. Two bold black diagonal bands on head. 2. High back profile. JUVENILE: 3. Brilliant yellow head. 4. Black stripe on back and midbody. 5. Spot at base of tail.**

DESCRIPTION: Yellow-gold and silver body stripes. **JUVENILE:** Translucent to pearly white.

ABUNDANCE & DISTRIBUTION: Abundant Florida, especially Keys; occasional to rare Caribbean; rare Bahamas; also Bermuda and south to Brazil.

HABITAT & BEHAVIOR: Drift in large schools over reefs in Florida Keys; usually solitary or in small groups over balance of range.

REACTION TO DIVERS: Relatively unafraid. Can often be closely approached.

Porkfish
Very Young Juvenile

HOLLYWOOD, FL

PIGFISH
Orthopristis chrysoptera
FAMILY:
Grunt - Haemulidae

SIZE: 7-10 in., max. 15 in.
DEPTH: 10-70 ft.

PANAMA CITY, FL

PORKFISH
Anisotremus virginicus
FAMILY:
Grunt - Haemulidae

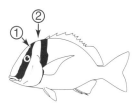

SIZE: 6-10 in., max. 14 in.
DEPTH: 10-60 ft.

KEY LARGO, FL

Porkfish Juvenile

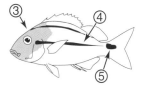

SIZE: 2-3$^1/_2$ in.

HOLLYWOOD, FL

97

DISTINCTIVE FEATURES: 1. High back profile. 2. Dark patch behind pectoral fin.

DESCRIPTION: Silvery-gray. Scales on back have dark centers. Fins dusky.

ABUNDANCE & DISTRIBUTION: Occasional Florida, Bahamas, Caribbean; also Gulf of Mexico and south to Brazil.

HABITAT & BEHAVIOR: Inhabit rocky inshore areas and reefs. Drift alone or in small groups near caves, ledge overhangs and other dark recesses.

REACTION TO DIVERS: Shy; move into caves or recesses when approached. Often remain near entrance where they can be closely observed.

DISTINCTIVE FEATURES: 1. Fine blue lines below eye. 2. Pointed anal fin. 3. Black spot on midbody line below rear dorsal fin (absent on rare occasion). (Compare juvenile Mahogany Snapper, [pg. 105] which may display a similar spot.)

DESCRIPTION: Silver to gray, reddish brown and maroon; fins have reddish tint. May lighten or darken dramatically. Occasionally display dark bars. Adults develop a high back.

ABUNDANCE & DISTRIBUTION: Occasional Florida, Bahamas, Caribbean; also north to Massachusetts, Bermuda, Gulf of Mexico and south to Brazil.

HABITAT & BEHAVIOR: Drift above bottom, most commonly over sand, but also reefs and sea grass beds.

REACTION TO DIVERS: Very curious. If diver remains still, fish may make a close approach.

Mutton Snapper
Barred gray phase.

L. CAYMAN

BLACK MARGATE

Anisotremus surinamensis

FAMILY:
Grunt - Haemulidae

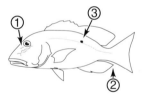

SIZE: 1-1¹/₂ ft., max. 2 ft.
DEPTH: 10-60 ft.

CAYMAN

MUTTON SNAPPER

Lutjanus analis

FAMILY:
Snapper - Lutjanidae

SIZE: 1-2 ft., max. 2¹/₂ ft.
DEPTH: 5-60 ft.

KEY LARGO, FL

Mutton Snapper

Reddish brown phase with bars on back.

ST. LUCIA

99

Snapper

DISTINCTIVE FEATURES: Often no distinguishing features; identification can be by process of elimination. (Similar Cubera Snapper, *L. cyanopterus*, [next] distinguished by large size, blunter head and more pronounced lips.) **1. Darkish band occasionally runs from lip across eye.**

DESCRIPTION: Vary from pale gray to dark gray or reddish brown; often tinged with olive, bronze or red; may lighten or darken dramatically. Occasionally have faint body bars or blotches; tail may have dark margin. Anal fin rounded.

ABUNDANCE & DISTRIBUTION: Occasional to common Florida, Bahamas, Caribbean; also north to Massachusetts, Bermuda, Gulf of Mexico, south to Brazil and eastern Atlantic.

HABITAT & BEHAVIOR: Drift in small schools. Inhabit shallow inshore areas, especially near mangrove sloughs, rocky outcroppings and under docks; also encountered on reefs. (Similar Cubera Snapper usually on reefs more than 60 feet deep.)

REACTION TO DIVERS: Not shy. Can generally be approached with slow, nonthreatening movements.

NOTE: Also commonly known as "Mangrove Snapper."

Gray Snapper
Dark reddish brown phase.

JUPITER, FL

DISTINCTIVE FEATURES: Often no distinguishing features; identification can be by process of elimination. (Similar Gray Snapper, *L. griseus*, [previous] distinguished by smaller size, more elongated head and smaller lips.) **1. Thick lips. 2. Occasionally have pale bars on back.** (Never have band across eye like similar Gray Snapper, or triangular patch like Dog Snapper, *L. jocu*, [next].)

DESCRIPTION: Vary from silvery steel gray to dark brown, occasionally with purplish sheen; may lighten or darken dramatically. Anal fin rounded.

ABUNDANCE & DISTRIBUTION: Occasional South Florida, Bahamas, Caribbean; also north to New Jersey, Bermuda, Gulf of Mexico, south to Brazil and eastern Atlantic.

HABITAT & BEHAVIOR: Solitary, deep-reef dweller (usually deeper than 60 feet), normally inhabit secluded areas of rocky ledges and overhangs. (Similar Gray Snapper usually in shallower water, less than 60 feet.)

REACTION TO DIVERS: Very shy. Difficult to approach; normally observed only at a distance.

GRAY SNAPPER
Lutjanus griseus

FAMILY:
Snapper - Lutjanidae

SIZE: 10-18 in., max. 2 ft.
DEPTH: 2-60 ft.

GRAND TURK

Gray Snapper
*Displaying dark band
across eye.*

DRY TORTUGAS, FL

CUBERA SNAPPER
Lutjanus cyanopterus

FAMILY:
Snapper - Lutjanidae

SIZE: 1 1/2 -3 ft., max. 5 ft.
DEPTH: 60 -180 ft.

BONAIRE

101

DISTINCTIVE FEATURES: 1. Pale triangular patch under eye.

DESCRIPTION: Pale gray to reddish brown; may lighten or darken dramatically. Line of blue dots under eye. Two large, fang-like teeth at front of upper jaw (source of common name).

ABUNDANCE & DISTRIBUTION: Occasional Florida, Bahamas, Caribbean; also north to Massachusetts, Bermuda, Gulf of Mexico and south to Brazil.

HABITAT & BEHAVIOR: Prefer mid-range reefs; also found around wrecks and rocky inshore areas. Drift alone in shaded, secluded areas of reefs.

REACTION TO DIVERS: Very wary. Difficult to approach; normally observed only at a distance.

Mahogany Snapper
Young adult displaying dark body spot.

CAYMAN

DISTINCTIVE FEATURES: 1. Reddish margin on tail (may be quite narrow and pale).

DESCRIPTION: Silver to white, often with reddish tinge. Reddish border on dorsal and anal fins. Often have dark spot below rear dorsal fin.

ABUNDANCE & DISTRIBUTION: Occasional to common Bahamas and Caribbean; uncommon Florida; also north to North Carolina and south to Guianas.

HABITAT & BEHAVIOR: Drift alone or in small groups over coral reefs, often in the shadows of gorgonians and coral heads.

REACTION TO DIVERS: Usually wary; generally move away upon approach. Close observation may require repeated, nonthreatening approaches.

DOG SNAPPER
Lutjanus jocu
FAMILY:
Snapper - Lutjanidae

SIZE: 1¹/₂-2¹/₂ ft.,
max. 3 ft.
DEPTH: 30-100 ft.

CAYMAN

Dog Snapper
Reddish brown phase.

KEY LARGO, FL

MAHOGANY SNAPPER
Lutjanus mahogoni
FAMILY:
Snapper - Lutjanidae

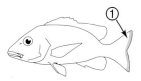

SIZE: 7-12 in., max. 15 in.
DEPTH: 20-60 ft.

CAYMAN

DISTINCTIVE FEATURES: 1. Fins yellow. JUVENILE: 2. Bars on back.

DESCRIPTION: Silver to copper. Blue line under eye. Often have pale bars.

ABUNDANCE & DISTRIBUTION: Abundant Caribbean; common Bahamas, Florida; also north to Massachusetts, Bermuda, Gulf of Mexico, south to Brazil and eastern Atlantic.

HABITAT & BEHAVIOR: Drift in small to medium groups just above reefs, in shade of large coral structures, especially elkhorn and large gorgonians. Juveniles often inhabit shallow bays, inlets and mangrove lagoons.

REACTION TO DIVERS: Usually wary; tend to keep their distance. Close observation may require repeated, nonthreatening approaches.

Lane Snapper

Phase with reddish tail, yellow ventral and anal fins, and without a dark body spot.

GRAND BAHAMA

DISTINCTIVE FEATURES: 1. Several faint yellow to pink body stripes.

DESCRIPTION: Silvery. Pectoral, ventral and anal fins often yellow; dorsal and tail fins often reddish. Black spot just below rear dorsal fin (absent on rare occasion); occasionally have light olive bars.

ABUNDANCE & DISTRIBUTION: Common to abundant Florida; occasional Bahamas, Caribbean; also north to North Carolina, Bermuda, Gulf of Mexico and south to Brazil.

HABITAT & BEHAVIOR: Commonly inhabit shallow reefs and other inshore areas where they drift in schools. Occasionally venture over deeper reefs.

REACTION TO DIVERS: Usually wary; tend to keep their distance. Close observation may require repeated, nonthreatening approaches.

SCHOOLMASTER
Lutjanus apodus
FAMILY:
Snapper - Lutjanidae

SIZE: 10-18 in., max. 2 ft.
DEPTH: 10-80 ft.

CAYMAN

Schoolmaster
Juvenile

DRY TORTUGAS, FL

LANE SNAPPER
Lutjanus synagris
FAMILY:
Snapper - Lutjanidae

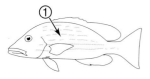

SIZE: 8-12 in., max. 15 in.
DEPTH: 5-130 ft.

CAYMAN

105

DISTINCTIVE FEATURES: 1. Brilliant yellow midbody stripe and tail.

DESCRIPTION: Silvery to white, often tinged with blue. May have yellow spots on upper body. Tail deeply forked.

ABUNDANCE & DISTRIBUTION: Abundant Caribbean; common Bahamas and Florida; also north to Massachusetts, Bermuda, Gulf of Mexico, south to Brazil and eastern Atlantic.

HABITAT & BEHAVIOR: Swim alone or in loose schools or aggregations, well above reefs.

REACTION TO DIVERS: Unafraid; often closely approach diver.

Blackfin Snapper Juvenile

SIZE: 1 1/2 - 4 in.

CAYMAN

DISTINCTIVE FEATURES: Red. 1. Dark blotch at base of pectoral fin. 2. Iris orange or bronze. JUVENILE: 3. Brilliant yellow below rear dorsal fin, upper base of tail and both lobes of tail.

DESCRIPTION: Dusky below rear dorsal fin on upper base of tail and both lobes tail. **JUVENILE:** Bluish white to pale brown. May have faint bars. With maturity become red and yellow areas becomes dusky red.

ABUNDANCE & DISTRIBUTION: Occasional Florida, Bahamas, Caribbean; also north to Massachusetts, Gulf of Mexico and south to Brazil.

HABITAT & BEHAVIOR: Inhabit rocky ledges generally between 200 and 300 feet. **JUVENILE:** Inhabit rocky outcroppings near reefs, generally from 20-60 feet. The intermediates (like the pictured specimen) inhabit depths between those of the juveniles and adults.

REACTION TO DIVERS: Appear unafraid. Allow close approach with slow, nonthreatening movements.

YELLOWTAIL SNAPPER
Ocyurus chrysurus
FAMILY:
Snapper - Lutjanidae

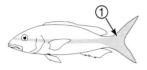

SIZE: 1-2 ft., max. 2¹/₂ ft.
DEPTH: 10-60 ft.

CAYMAN

Yellowtail Snapper Juvenile

NASSAU

BLACKFIN SNAPPER
Lutjanus buccanella
Intermediate
FAMILY:
Snapper - Lutjanidae

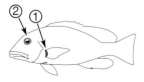

SIZE: 1-2 ft., max. 2¹/₂ ft.
DEPTH: 20-300 ft.

KEY LARGO, FL

DISTINCTIVE FEATURES: Pinkish red upper head and body. **1. Red iris. 2. Pointed anal fin.**

DESCRIPTION: Lower body fades to silvery white. Young (one to ten inches) have a dusky spot below soft dorsal fin at and above midline.

ABUNDANCE & DISTRIBUTION: Occasional Florida; also north to North Carolina and Gulf of Mexico. Can be locally abundant. Not reported Bahamas or Caribbean.

HABITAT & BEHAVIOR: Inhabit deep reefs, banks and rocky outcroppings. Often mix with schools or aggregations of grunts and other snappers. Larger individuals are more common below safe diving limits.

REACTION TO DIVERS: Relatively unafraid. Allow close approach with slow, nonthreatening movements.

SIMILAR SPECIES: Caribbean Red Snapper, *L. purpureus*, is visually indistinguishable; differences are in fin ray and scale counts. Primarily northwest and central Caribbean.

DISTINCTIVE FEATURES: Light red to salmon upper head, body, dorsal and tail fins. **1. Protruding lower jaw. 2. Shallow forked tail.**

DESCRIPTION: Lower body fades to silver; thin diagonal lines on upper body are formed by rows of tiny blue dots; midbody occasionally has yellow streaks.

ABUNDANCE & DISTRIBUTION: Occasional Florida, Bahamas, Caribbean; also north to South Carolina, Bermuda, Gulf of Mexico and south to Brazil.

HABITAT & BEHAVIOR: Inhabit deep reefs, banks and rocky outcroppings. Often mix with schools or aggregations of grunts and other snappers. More common below safe diving limits.

REACTION TO DIVERS: Relatively unafraid. Allow close approach with slow, nonthreatening movements.

NOTE: Also commonly known as "B-Liner."

RED SNAPPER
Lutjanus campechanus
FAMILY:
Snapper - Lutjanidae

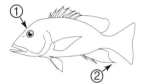

SIZE: 1-2 ft., max. 3 ft.
DEPTH: 60-400 ft.

JACKSONVILLE, FL

VERMILLION SNAPPER
Rhomboplites aurorubens
FAMILY:
Snapper - Lutjanidae

SIZE: 1-2 ft., max. 2 ½ ft.
DEPTH: 90-200 ft.

JACKSONVILLE, FL

Small Ovals
Damselfish – Chromis/Damselfish – Hamlet/Seabass

This ID Group consists of small fish (generally three to six inches) that have a "perch-like" or oval profile.

FAMILY: Damselfish—Pomacentridae
9 Species Included

Damselfish
(typical shape)

These energetic little fish are an evident part of the coral reef community. The most distinctive (but difficult to observe) family characteristic is a single nostril on each side of the snout, rather than the usual two. Although most of the adults are drab, the juveniles are quite colorful.

Several species spend their days busily tending and patrolling a private algae patch that is pugnaciously defended from intruders. When the domain of the Cocoa, Dusky, Longfin or Three Spot is threatened, the fish dart back and forth with fins erect, ready to attack. Even divers are not immune to the aggressive assaults of these feisty fish. If divers linger, they may receive a sharp nip on any exposed skin. Egg clusters are also defended in this manner by some males. The Yellowtail, Beaugregory and Bicolor Damselfish are territorial, but much less aggressive.

Distinguishing between the dark-bodied Longfin, Dusky, Beaugregory, Cocoa and Three Spot Damselfish is a bit confusing; however, subtle differences make underwater identification possible. Except for the two sergeants, juvenile damselfish differ dramatically from adults both in color and markings, and although similar, are easily distinguished.

Although the American Fisheries Society classifies most members of this family in the genus *Pomacentrus*, most ichthyologists dealing with this family believe they should be classified as *Stegastes*, which is used in this text.

FAMILY: Chromis/Damselfish—Pomacentridae
5 Species Included

Chromis
(Blue & Brown)

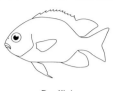

Reeffish
(typical shape)

Members of the genus *Chromis* are part of the damselfish family, but are discussed separately because the group carries its own common name, and its members are somewhat different in appearance. The Blue and Brown Chromis are the most frequently seen species. Both are somewhat elongated, and have deeply forked tails. During the day they swim in small to large aggregations well above the reefs, feeding on plankton. They often feed together and, occasionally, mix with the slightly larger Creole Wrasse [pg. 193].

Sunshinefish, Purple Reeffish and Yellow Reeffish are also in the genus. They are quite colorful, and more closely resemble other damselfish in shape. All three inhabit deeper reefs, and live in small groups near the bottom.

FAMILY: Hamlet/Seabass—Serranidae
11 Species Included

Hamlet

Hamlets of the genus *Hypoplectrus* are members of the seabass family, but are discussed here because, in appearance and size, they more closely resemble damselfish. Their relatives, grouper and bass, are discussed in the next ID Group—Heavy Body/Large Lips. The hamlets' flat head profile easily distinguishes them from damselfish, which have rounded heads. Most are quite colorful, small (generally three to five inches), and have nearly identical body shapes; however, there are several distinctive color patterns and markings, generally making identification simple.

Within the scientific community, there is a long-running debate whether hamlets are different species or simply a single species, *Hypoplectrus unicolor*, with different color and marking phases. Aquarium-based observations and experiments indicate individuals of like color patterns and markings usually mate together. On rare occasion, however, especially when a similar appearing mate is not present, different appearing individuals will mate producing offspring that do not easily fit into the dozen or so common color patterns and markings. These "mixed" hamlets make up about three percent of the hamlet population. Although the American Fisheries Society lists them as one species, for convenience in identifying their common distinct color phases, they are listed here as different species.

DISTINCTIVE FEATURES: 1. **Dorsal and anal fins elongated and pointed, extending well beyond base of tail.** (Difficult to distinguish from other similar adult damselfish, especially the Dusky Damselfish, *S. fuscus*, [next] with shorter rounded fins.) **JUVENILE:** Yellow-gold. 2. **Brilliant blue lines run from snout across nape and down back.** (Similar Cocoa, *S. variabilis*, [pg. 115] and Beaugregory, *S. leucostictus*, [pg. 117] have a blue wash instead of distinct lines.)

DESCRIPTION: Dark brown to almost black. No distinctive markings, except occasional light blue outline on rear dorsal and anal fins. **JUVENILE:** Black dot ringed in blue on dorsal fin.

ABUNDANCE & DISTRIBUTION: Occasional South Florida, Bahamas, Caribbean.

HABITAT & BEHAVIOR: Inhabit rocky areas. Territorial; pugnaciously chase away intruders.

REACTION TO DIVERS: Unafraid. Aggressively attempt to move divers from their territory.

NOTE: Juvenile formerly classified as a separate species, "Honey Damselfish," *P. mellis*. *See chapter introduction concerning genus name.

Dusky Damselfish Juvenile

ROATAN

DISTINCTIVE FEATURES: 1. **Dorsal and anal fins rounded and rarely extend beyond base of tail.** (Difficult to distinguish from other similar adult damselfish, especially the Longfin Damselfish, *E. diencaeus*, [previous] with longer pointed fins.) **JUVENILE:** 2. **Brilliant orange wash from snout across nape and about halfway down dorsal fin.**

DESCRIPTION: Dark olive-brown to almost black. Nape area often pale olive. Faint dark bands on body. Normally have darkish area at upper edge of pectoral fin base. May have light blue outline on rear dorsal and anal fins. **JUVENILE:** Bluish silver-gray. Blue dot/dash markings on head and back. Dark spot on dorsal fin and another on base of tail, both ringed in white to pale blue.

ABUNDANCE & DISTRIBUTION: Occasional Florida, Bahamas, Caribbean; also Bermuda, Gulf of Mexico and south to Brazil.

HABITAT & BEHAVIOR: Inhabit rocky areas. Territorial; pugnaciously chase away intruders.

REACTION TO DIVERS: Unafraid. Aggressively attempt to move divers from their territory.

NOTE: Many ichthyologists consider the Brazilian population to be a separate species, *S. fuscus*, in this case, the correct name for populations to the north would be *S.dorsopunicans*.

LONGFIN DAMSELFISH
Stegastes diencaeus
FAMILY:
Damselfish -
Pomacentridae

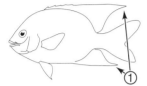

SIZE: 3-4 in., max. 5 in.
DEPTH: 15-80 ft.

CAYMAN

Longfin Damselfish
Juvenile

CAYMAN

DUSKY DAMSELFISH
Stegastes fuscus
FAMILY:
Damselfish -
Pomacentridae

SIZE: 3-5 in., max. 6 in.
DEPTH: 5-40 ft.

ROATAN

113

Damselfish

DISTINCTIVE FEATURES: 1. Yellow-gold crescent above eyes. 2. Dark spot on base of pectoral fin. 3. Black saddle on upper base of tail. JUVENILE: 4. Black saddle on upper base of tail is retained into adulthood. 5. Larger second dot on back and dorsal fin is lost with maturity. (Similar juvenile Rock Beauty, *Holocanthus tricolor* [pg. 31], lacks dot on base of tail.)

DESCRIPTION: Vary from yellowish brown to tan and gray; become darker with age. Head profile of nape and snout is straight. (Similar adult Cocoa Damselfish, *S. variabilis*, [next] has a slightly convex head profile.)

ABUNDANCE & DISTRIBUTION: Abundant to common Caribbean; common Bahamas, South Florida; also Bermuda and Gulf of Mexico.

HABITAT & BEHAVIOR: Inhabit reef tops in areas of algae growth. Territorial; pugnaciously guard relatively large areas, and rapidly dart about, nipping and chasing away intruders, regardless of size.

REACTION TO DIVERS: Unafraid. Attempt to chase divers from their territory, nipping at fingers, ears and other exposed areas.

CAYMAN   ANGUILLA

DISTINCTIVE FEATURES: 1. Area around eyes dark. (Similar Threespot Damselfish, *S. planifrons*, [previous] has yellow-gold crescent above eyes.) **2. Dark spot on base of pectoral fin. 3. Dark spot usually present on upper base of tail. JUVENILE: 4. Blue wash from snout across nape, down the back and dorsal fin. 5. Dark spot on upper base of tail.** (Similar juvenile Beaugregory, *S. leucostictus,* [next] lacks this spot.)

DESCRIPTION: Dark grayish brown, lighter below. May show faint, dark vertical lines on body. Head profile of nape and snout is slightly convex. (Similar adult Threespot Damselfish, [previous] has a straight head profile.) **JUVENILE:** Yellow body. Dark spot on rear portion of dorsal fin; in very young this spot is ringed with brilliant blue.

ABUNDANCE & DISTRIBUTION: Common South Florida; occasional to uncommon Bahamas, Caribbean; also south to Brazil.

HABITAT & BEHAVIOR: Found on reefs. Territorial, but not always aggressive, except during spawning season.

REACTION TO DIVERS: Not shy. Can be approached with nonthreatening movements.

THREESPOT DAMSELFISH
Stegastes planifrons
FAMILY:
Damselfish -
Pomacentridae

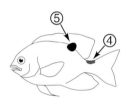

SIZE: 3-4 in., max. 5 in.
DEPTH: 0-130 ft.

ROATAN

Threespot Damselfish Juvenile
[right]

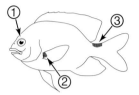

Young Adult [far left]

**Intermediate
Juvenile/Adult** [left]

CAYMAN

COCOA DAMSELFISH
Stegastes variabilis
FAMILY:
Damselfish -
Pomacentridae

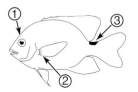

SIZE: 3-4 in., max. 5 in.
DEPTH: 15-60 ft.

DRY TORTUGAS, FL

continued next page **115**

**Cocoa Damselfish
Intermediate**

DRY TORTUGAS, FL

DISTINCTIVE FEATURES: 1. Pale to yellowish tail. No spot on upper base of tail. (Distinguished from similar Cocoa Damselfish, *S. variabilis*, [previous] which has spot.) **JUVENILE: 2. Blue wash from snout across nape, down back and dorsal fin.** No spot on upper base of tail. (Similar juvenile Cocoa [previous] has a spot.)

DESCRIPTION: Olive-brown; become darker with age until all juvenile markings are lost (young adult pictured); light dots on nape, back and dorsal fin may persist for some time. Body more slender than other similar Damselfish. **JUVENILE:** Yellow. Dark spot near rear of dorsal fin.

ABUNDANCE & DISTRIBUTION: Common Florida, Bahamas, Caribbean; also north to Maine, Bermuda, Gulf of Mexico, south to Brazil and eastern Atlantic.

HABITAT & BEHAVIOR: Inhabit sand, grass and rocky coral rubble areas, occasionally reef tops. Territorial, but not as aggressive as other damselfish.

REACTION TO DIVERS: Not shy. Can be closely approached.

ROATAN

CAYMAN

Cocoa Damselfish Juvenile

continued from previous page

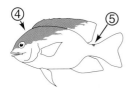

DRY TORTUGAS, FL

BEAUGREGORY

Stegastes leucostictus

FAMILY
Damselfish -
Pomacentridae

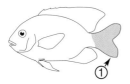

SIZE: 2½-3½ in.,
max. 4 in.
DEPTH: 3-35 ft.

ST. LUCIA

Beaugregory Juvenile
[right]

Young Adults [left]

CAYMAN

DISTINCTIVE FEATURES: Black and white. **1. Forebody is usually black.**

DESCRIPTION: Location of boundary between dark and pale area varies greatly (examples below); dark area may cover only upper head or extend past midbody to base of tail; pale area often yellowish near boundary, especially toward belly. Pale fins may have bluish cast. On rare occasion, there is a reverse color phase.

ABUNDANCE & DISTRIBUTION: Common South Florida, Bahamas, Caribbean; also Gulf of Mexico.

HABITAT & BEHAVIOR: Inhabit reef tops. Aggressively territorial, but tend to guard only a small area, and chase off only small fish.

REACTION TO DIVERS: Unafraid. Allow close approach.

ST. LUCIA   BARBADOS

DISTINCTIVE FEATURES: Dark body. **1. Yellow tail. JUVENILE: 2. Brilliant blue dots on dark blue.** (Occasionally called Jewelfish because of these gem-like dots.) **3. Translucent to whitish tail, changes to yellow with maturity.**

DESCRIPTION: Vary from brown to bluish black. Bright blue speckles on head, back and dorsal fin.

ABUNDANCE & DISTRIBUTION: Common Florida, Bahamas, Caribbean; also Bermuda and Gulf of Mexico.

HABITAT & BEHAVIOR: Inhabit reef tops. Maintain a small territory, but do not aggressively defend their domain. **JUVENILE:** Inhabit areas around fire coral.

REACTION TO DIVERS: Unafraid. Can be closely approached. **JUVENILE:** Shy; hide in blades of fire coral.

BICOLOR DAMSELFISH
Stegastes partitus

FAMILY:
Damselfish -
Pomacentridae

SIZE: 2-3¹/₂ in., max. 4 in.
DEPTH: 20-80 ft.

ANGUILLA

Bicolor Damselfish
Color morphs.

ROATAN

YELLOWTAIL DAMSELFISH
Microspathodon chrysurus

FAMILY:
Damselfish -
Pomacentridae

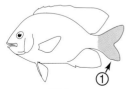

SIZE: 4-6¹/₂ in.,
max. 7¹/₂ in.
DEPTH: 10-40 ft.

CAYMAN

continued next page **119**

Damselfish

Yellowtail Damselfish
Juvenile/Intermediate

DISTINCTIVE FEATURES: 1. Five black body bars. 2. Upper lip does not overhang lower.

DESCRIPTION: Upper body usually yellow, occasionally with shades of green to blue, and white to bluish silver or light gray below. Male becomes dark blue to purple during mating season when guarding reddish purple egg patches. (Similar Night Sergeant, *A. taurus*, [next] has shades of brown only.)

ABUNDANCE & DISTRIBUTION: Abundant Florida, Bahamas, Caribbean; also north to Rhode Island, Bermuda, Gulf of Mexico and south to Uruguay.

HABITAT & BEHAVIOR: Swim in all habitats; most often in midwater. Usually in loose aggregations.

REACTION TO DIVERS: Unafraid. Often approach divers.

Sergeant Major
Juvenile

Yellowtail Damselfish Juvenile
continued from previous page

BELIZE

SERGEANT MAJOR
Abudefduf saxatilis
FAMILY:
Damselfish -
Pomacentridae

SIZE: 4-6 in., max. 7 in.
DEPTH: 1-40 ft.

CAYMAN

Sergeant Major
Color of male guarding eggs.

BIMINI

121

DISTINCTIVE FEATURES: 1. Five dark brown body bars. 2. Upper lip slightly overhangs lower.

DESCRIPTION: Hues of brown; may have a blue-green tint. (Similar Sergeant Major, *A. saxatilis*, [previous] not brown.)

ABUNDANCE & DISTRIBUTION: Occasional South Florida, Bahamas, Caribbean.

HABITAT & BEHAVIOR: Prefer shallow, rocky inshore surge areas, often around wave-cut shelves and overhangs. Stay near bottom close to dark recesses; venture out at night.

REACTION TO DIVERS: Shy and evasive. Difficult to approach.

DISTINCTIVE FEATURES: 1. Yellow to clear tail. 2. Bright, iridescent blue "V" on snout continues across upper eyes.

DESCRIPTION: Blue upper body; blue or white underside; rear of dorsal and anal fins yellow to clear.

ABUNDANCE & DISTRIBUTION: Occasional Florida; uncommon to rare Bahamas, Caribbean; also Bermuda and Gulf of Mexico.

HABITAT & BEHAVIOR: Inhabit deep reef tops and nearby sand patches. Tend to cluster in small groups near any bottom obstruction that offers protection.

REACTION TO DIVERS: Not shy; slowly retreat and hide upon close approach.

DISTINCTIVE FEATURES: Brilliant blue. 1. Slender, deeply forked tail with dark borders.

DESCRIPTION: Often dark on nape and along back.

ABUNDANCE & DISTRIBUTION: Abundant Caribbean; common Florida, Bahamas; also Bermuda.

HABITAT & BEHAVIOR: Swim in midwater above reefs, feeding on plankton. Often in large, loose aggregations. May mix with Brown Chromis, *C. multilineatus* [next].

REACTION TO DIVERS: Not shy, but move toward bottom cover when closely approached.

NIGHT SERGEANT
Abudefduf taurus
FAMILY:
Damselfish -
Pomacentridae

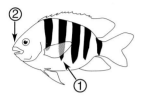

SIZE: 5-8 in., max. 10 in.
DEPTH: 1-15 ft.

BIMINI

YELLOWTAIL REEFFISH
Chromis enchrysurus
FAMILY:
Chromis/Damselfish -
Pomacentridae

SIZE: 2¹/₂-3¹/₂ in.,
max. 4 in.
DEPTH: 80-160 ft.

WEST PALM BEACH, FL

BLUE CHROMIS
Chromis cyanea
FAMILY:
Chromis/Damselfish -
Pomacentridae

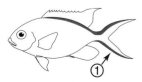

SIZE: 3-4 in., max. 5 in.
DEPTH: 35-80 ft.

CAYMAN

123

DISTINCTIVE FEATURES: Brown. **1. Border of dorsal fin and tips of tail fin yellow. 2. Dark spot around base of pectoral fin.**

DESCRIPTION: Vary from brownish gray to olive-brown. Usually a white or pale yellow spot located just below last dorsal fin ray; may have black borders on tail, primarily in southern Caribbean. Slender, deeply forked tail.

ABUNDANCE & DISTRIBUTION: Common Florida, Bahamas, Caribbean; can be abundant in localized areas; also south to Brazil.

HABITAT & BEHAVIOR: Swim in midwater above reefs, feeding on plankton. Often in large, loose aggregations. May mix with Blue Chromis, *C. cyanea* [previous].

REACTION TO DIVERS: Not shy, but move toward bottom cover when closely approached.

**Purple Reeffish
Juvenile**

WEST PALM BEACH, FL

DISTINCTIVE FEATURES: Slate blue to dark blue. **1. Bright blue crescent around upper part of eyes (disappears with age). JUVENILE:** Brilliant blue.

DESCRIPTION: Often have bright blue markings on head and back. **JUVENILE:** Brilliant blue "V" on snout.

ABUNDANCE & DISTRIBUTION: Occasional Florida; also Gulf of Mexico. Not reported Bahamas or Caribbean.

HABITAT & BEHAVIOR: Prefer deep reefs. Tend to cluster in small groups near bottom, remaining in one area.

REACTION TO DIVERS: Not shy, but move away or hide when closely approached.

BROWN CHROMIS
Chromis multilineata
FAMILY:
Chromis/Damselfish -
Pomacentridae

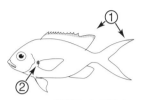

SIZE: 3-5 ½ in.,
max. 6 ½ in.
DEPTH: 35-80 ft.

CAYMAN

Brown Chromis

*Note typical white spot
at rear base of dorsal
fin and unusual black
borders on tail.*

CULEBRA, PR

PURPLE REEFFISH
Chromis scotti
FAMILY:
Chromis/Damselfish
Pomacentridae

SIZE: 2 ½-3 ½ in.,
max. 4 in.
DEPTH: 80-160 ft.

KEY LARGO, FL

DISTINCTIVE FEATURES: 1. Yellow or transparent rear soft dorsal fin and wide margin on tail. JUVENILE: 2. Brilliant yellow to chartreuse upper body; brilliant blue to purple, lavender or dull olive below.

DESCRIPTION: Green to olive, brown and dark brown upper body; belly may be same, but often paler color to silvery gray; anal and pectoral fins often clear. Often have an iridescent blue line that runs from snout across upper eye (whether this is a regional or other variation is unknown).

ABUNDANCE & DISTRIBUTION: Common Florida, Bahamas, Caribbean; also north to North Carolina, Bermuda and Gulf of Mexico.

HABITAT & BEHAVIOR: Inhabit deep reefs and walls. Tend to cluster in small groups close to bottom, remaining around a single small coral head. Adults and juveniles often mix. Become more abundant with depth.

REACTION TO DIVERS: Not shy; slowly retreat and hide upon close approach.

BIMINI

ST. LUCIA

DISTINCTIVE FEATURES: 1. Large black saddle blotch on base of tail.

DESCRIPTION: Grayish white to yellow. Blue markings on head and gill cover; often have black dot on snout that is outlined in blue. Can pale or darken.

ABUNDANCE & DISTRIBUTION: Most common hamlet in Florida Keys; occasional balance of Florida, Bahamas and Caribbean.

HABITAT & BEHAVIOR: Swim about reefs, near bottom.

REACTION TO DIVERS: Shy, but curious. Can often be approached with slow, nonthreatening movements.

NOTE: Some ichthyologists consider all hamlets to be variations of this species. See family introduction for more information.

SUNSHINEFISH
Chromis insolata
FAMILY:
Chromis/Damselfish -
Pomacentridae

SIZE: 2-3¹/₂ in., max. 4 in.
DEPTH: 50-180 ft.

CAYMAN

Sunshinefish Juvenile
[right]

*Note brilliant blue line
from snout to above eye.*

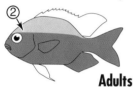

Adults

*Without brilliant blue
line on head. Olive with
pale belly.* [left]

*Dark brown overall with yellow
rear dorsal and tail fins.* [far left]

ROATAN

BUTTER HAMLET
Hypoplectrus unicolor
FAMILY:
Hamlet/Seabass -
Serranidae

SIZE: 3-4¹/₂ in., max. 5 in.
DEPTH: 10-50 ft.

CAYMAN

DISTINCTIVE FEATURES: 1. Broad V-shaped bar on midbody.

DESCRIPTION: Brown body bars over pale white to yellowish background. Bright blue vertical lines on head and around eyes, and spots on snout.

ABUNDANCE & DISTRIBUTION: Most common hamlet in Caribbean; occasional Florida and Bahamas.

HABITAT & BEHAVIOR: Swim about reefs, near bottom.

REACTION TO DIVERS: Shy, but curious. Can often be approached with slow, nonthreatening movements.

NOTE: Some ichthyologists consider all hamlets to be variations of one species, *H. unicolor*. See family introduction for more information.

DISTINCTIVE FEATURES: 1. Blue and white bars.

DESCRIPTION: Wide medium blue to indigo bars separated by narrower white bars. Blue ventral fins; pectoral fins white or clear.

ABUNDANCE & DISTRIBUTION: Common Cayman Islands; occasional Bay Islands, Belize and Bahamas; rare balance of Caribbean and Florida.

HABITAT & BEHAVIOR: Swim about reefs, near bottom.

REACTION TO DIVERS: Somewhat shy, but can be curious. After retreating a short distance, often turn to observe, and may approach if diver remains still.

NOTE: Some ichthyologists consider all hamlets to be variations of one species, *H. unicolor*. See family introduction for more information.

DISTINCTIVE FEATURES: 1. All fins are bright yellow. 2. Yellow on face and chest. (Yellow area does not extend over base of tail as on similar Yellowbelly Hamlet [next].)

DESCRIPTION: Yellow to gold, with dark area under dorsal fin that extends to cover entire base of tail. Bright blue markings on snout and head.

ABUNDANCE & DISTRIBUTION: Occasional Cayman Islands; rare to absent Florida, Bahamas and balance of Caribbean.

HABITAT & BEHAVIOR: Swim about reefs, near bottom, often in areas of staghorn coral.

REACTION TO DIVERS: Shy and reclusive, but can be curious. Occasionally approachable with slow, nonthreatening movements.

NOTE: Some ichthyologists consider all hamlets to be variations of one species, *H. unicolor*. See family introduction for more information.

BARRED HAMLET
*Hypoplectrus puella**
FAMILY:
Hamlet/Seabass -
Serranidae

SIZE: 3¹/₂-4¹/₂ in.,
max. 6 in.
DEPTH: 10-50 ft.

CAYMAN

INDIGO HAMLET
*Hypoplectrus indigo**
FAMILY:
Hamlet/Seabass -
Serranidae

SIZE: 3-4¹/₂ in.,
max. 5¹/₂ in.
DEPTH: 30-130 ft.

ROATAN

SHY HAMLET
*Hypoplectrus guttavarius**
FAMILY:
Hamlet/Seabass -
Serranidae

SIZE: 3-4¹/₂ in., max. 5 in.
DEPTH: 10-50 ft.

CAYMAN

129

DISTINCTIVE FEATURES: 1. Yellow underside extends to tail.

DESCRIPTION: Dark brown to slate blue upper body. Dorsal fin yellowish brown lightening toward rear; other fins yellow. Head may have bluish cast and extensive bright blue markings. May have dark saddle dot on upper base of tail.

ABUNDANCE & DISTRIBUTION: Uncommon South Florida and Caribbean; not reported Bahamas.

HABITAT & BEHAVIOR: Swim about reefs, near bottom.

REACTION TO DIVERS: Shy and wary.

NOTE: Some ichthyologists consider all hamlets to be variations of one species, *H. unicolor*. See family introduction for more information.

DISTINCTIVE FEATURES: Gold to yellow.

DESCRIPTION: Iridescent blue and black markings on face.

ABUNDANCE & DISTRIBUTION: Occasional northwest Caribbean including Cuba; uncommon Bahamas, South Florida, central Caribbean; can be common in localized areas. Not reported southern Caribbean.

HABITAT & BEHAVIOR: Swim about reef tops. Generally found deeper than other hamlets.

REACTION TO DIVERS: Somewhat shy, but can be curious. After retreating a short distance, often turn to observe, and may approach if diver remains still.

NOTE: Some ichthyologists consider all hamlets to be variations of one species, *H. unicolor*. See family introduction for more information.

DISTINCTIVE FEATURES: Dark body. 1. Yellow tail.

DESCRIPTION: Body and fins vary from dark brown to dark blue, navy blue and black.

ABUNDANCE & DISTRIBUTION: Occasional to uncommon southern and southeastern Caribbean; rare balance of Caribbean. Not reported Florida or Bahamas.

HABITAT & BEHAVIOR: Swim about reefs, near bottom.

REACTION TO DIVERS: Shy and reclusive.

NOTE: Some ichthyologists consider all hamlets to be variations of one species, *H. unicolor*. See family introduction for more information.

YELLOWBELLY HAMLET
*Hypoplectrus aberrans**

FAMILY:
Hamlet/Seabass -
Serranidae

SIZE: 3-4$\frac{1}{2}$ in., max. 5 in.
DEPTH: 10-40 ft.

CAYMAN

GOLDEN HAMLET
*Hypoplectrus
gummigutta**

FAMILY:
Hamlet/Seabass -
Serranidae

SIZE: 3-4$\frac{1}{2}$ in., max. 5 in.
DEPTH: 30-130 ft.

CAYMAN

YELLOWTAIL HAMLET
*Hypoplectrus chlorurus**

FAMILY:
Hamlet/Seabass -
Serranidae

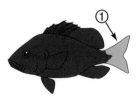

SIZE: 3-4$\frac{1}{2}$ in., max. 5 in.
DEPTH: 10-40 ft.

BONAIRE

131

DISTINCTIVE FEATURES: Solid dark color. **1. Pelvic fins unusually long.**
DESCRIPTION: Entire body dark bluish brown to black.
ABUNDANCE & DISTRIBUTION: Occasional Caribbean, Bahamas; uncommon Florida.
HABITAT & BEHAVIOR: Swim about reef tops. Prefer shallow water.
REACTION TO DIVERS: Not shy. Easily approached.
NOTE: Some ichthyologists consider all hamlets to be variations of one species, *H. unicolor*. See family introduction for more information.

DISTINCTIVE FEATURES: Bright iridescent blue.
DESCRIPTION: Thin, dark borders on tail. Can pale or darken.
ABUNDANCE & DISTRIBUTION: Common to occasional South Florida and Keys; rare Bahamas. Not reported Caribbean.
HABITAT & BEHAVIOR: Swim about reefs, near bottom.
REACTION TO DIVERS: Somewhat shy, but can be curious. After retreating a short distance, often turn to observe, and may approach if diver remains still.
NOTE: Some ichthyologists consider all hamlets to be variations of one species, *H. unicolor*. See family introduction for more information.

DISTINCTIVE FEATURES: 1. Black mask extends triangularly down from eyes.
DESCRIPTION: Pale with bluish or brownish cast. Ventral fins dark with bluish cast; black borders on tail and upper pectoral fin; tail may be dark. Black blotch on upper base of tail. May have light blue lines and dots around face.
ABUNDANCE & DISTRIBUTION: Uncommon Cayman Islands, Belize, Honduras and Providencia Island. Not reported balance of Caribbean, Florida, Bahamas.
HABITAT & BEHAVIOR: Swim about reefs, near bottom.
REACTION TO DIVERS: Shy, but quite curious. May be approached with slow, non-threatening movements.
NOTE: If uniquely marked and colored hamlets are determined to be separate species, then this form which has consistent coloration and markings over a broad geographical area probably should be scientifically described.

BLACK HAMLET
Hypoplectrus nigricans*
FAMILY:
Hamlet/Seabass -
Serranidae

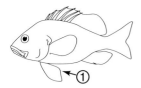

SIZE: 3-4 1/2 in., max. 6 in.
DEPTH: 10-40 ft.

BELIZE

BLUE HAMLET
Hypoplectrus gemma*
FAMILY:
Hamlet/Seabass -
Serranidae

SIZE: 3-4 1/2 in., max. 5 in.
DEPTH: 10-40 ft.

KEY LARGO, FL

MASKED HAMLET
Hypoplectrus sp.
FAMILY:
Hamlet/Seabass -
Serranidae

SIZE: 3-4 1/2 in., max. 5 in.
DEPTH: 20-50 ft.

BELIZE

133

DISTINCTIVE FEATURES: Shades of golden brown overall. **1. First spine of ventral fins blue.**

DESCRIPTION: Usually without any other markings; may have darkish spot on snout.

ABUNDANCE & DISTRIBUTION: Occasional South Florida, southern Bahamas and south to Puerto Rico and Anguilla. Not reported balance of Caribbean, Florida, Bahamas.

HABITAT & BEHAVIOR: Swim about reefs, near bottom.

REACTION TO DIVERS: Shy, but quite curious. May be approached with slow, nonthreatening movements.

NOTE: If uniquely marked and colored hamlets are determined to be separate species, then this form which has consistent coloration and markings over a broad geographical area probably should be scientifically described.

Hamlet

Possibly hybrid of Blue and Barred.

DRY TORTUGAS

Hamlet Juvenile

Prominent black and white markings on tail base are typical of all juvenile hamlets. Body occasionally golden. With maturity acquire adult color and markings.

SIZE: 1½ - 2 in.

CAYMAN

TAN HAMLET
Hypoplectrus sp.
FAMILY:
Hamlet/Seabass -
Serranidae

SIZE: 3-4 ½ in., max. 5 in.
DEPTH: 20-50 ft.

CULEBRA, PR

Hamlet
*Possibly hybrid of
Yellowbelly and Shy.*

ANGUILLA

Hamlet
*Possibly hybrid of
Yellowtail and Yellowbelly.*

ST. LUCIA

135

Heavy Body/Large Lips
Grouper/Seabass – Seabass – Basslet

This ID Group consists of fish with strong, well-built, "bass-like" bodies. They have large mouths and lips, and a jutting lower jaw. The long, continuous dorsal fin is noticeably divided into two parts. The fore portion is constructed of sharp spines that can be held erect or lowered; the rear is soft and quite flexible.

FAMILY: Grouper/Seabass—Serranidae
21 Species Included

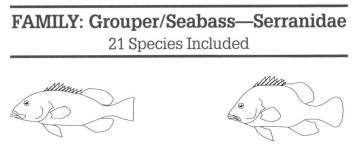

Grouper (typical shape)   Marble Grouper

Groupers are the best known members of the seabass family. All have strong, stout bodies and large mouths. They vary in size from the giant Jewfish that grows to seven feet to the one-foot Coney. They are solitary carnivores that live near the bottom. Most of their days are spent lurking in the shadows of reefs, ledges and wrecks where larger species blend with the background.

Although awkward in appearance, these fish can cover short distances quickly. Fish or crustaceans are drawn into their gullets by the powerful suction created when they open their large mouths. Held securely by thousands of small, rasp-like teeth that cover the jaws, tongue and palate, the prey is swallowed whole. Grouper are hermaphroditic, beginning life as females but changing to males with maturity.

Many of the larger groupers are difficult to distinguish because of their ability to radically change both colors and markings. Examples are the Yellowfin [pg. 141] and Yellowmouth [pg. 147]. The smaller groupers (Red Hind, Rock Hind, Graysby and Coney) are commonly confused. However, each has distinctive features that are easy to recognize underwater.

FAMILY: Seabass—Serranidae
18 Species Included

Bass (typical shape)   Peppermint Bass   Creolefish

Often called bass, these members of the seabass family are generally more colorful than grouper. Most are small, two to four inches, with the exceptions of Mutton Hamlet, Creolefish and Sand Perch, which grow to nearly a foot. All are stocky like grouper, but tend to be more cylindrical and elongated. All stay near the bottom or inhabit dark recesses, except the Creolefish that is often in open water above the reef. Generally, their color and markings make them easy to distinguish on the reef.

Note: Hamlets of the genus *Hypoplectrus* are also members of the seabass family, but because of their oval shape, they are discussed in the previous ID Group—Small Ovals.

FAMILY: Soapfish/Seabass—Serranidae
3 Species Included

Soapfish

Soapfish were formerly classified as a separate family, Grammistidae, but are now considered a part of the seabass family. Their bodies are covered with mucus that produces soapsuds-like bubbles when they are caught or handled. Typically soapfishes have elongated, pointed heads with an upturned mouth, protruding lower jaw, and rounded tail fin. Most grow to less than one foot. The size, color and distribution of body spots are keys to identification. They generally inhabit shallower waters, are solitary, reclusive night-feeders that tend to lie on the bottom and often lean against the back of a protective overhang during the day.

FAMILY: Basslet — Grammatidae
3 Species Included

Basslet (typical shape)

This family of small (one to four inches) fish is closely related to the seabass, but lacks a continuous lateral line. They generally inhabit deeper reefs and walls, although Fairy Basslets are usually found in shallower water. These colorful fish are frequently spotted near undercuts and small recesses in reefs.

DISTINCTIVE FEATURES: Largest fish observed on the reefs. Small dark spots over body and fins.

DESCRIPTION: Yellowish brown to olive-green. Oblique bars (more apparent in the young up to two feet). Can pale or darken. Tail fin rounded.

ABUNDANCE & DISTRIBUTION: Uncommon Florida, Bahamas, Caribbean; also Bermuda, Gulf of Mexico and south to Brazil. (Once common in Florida, but numbers greatly reduced by spearfishing.)

HABITAT & BEHAVIOR: Reclusive; hide in caves, wrecks and under ledges. Juveniles inhabit mangroves.

REACTION TO DIVERS: Often shy, but can be indifferent. On rare occasions, quite bold; have been known to charge divers.

SIMILAR SPECIES: Warsaw Grouper, *E. nigritus*, uniform brown, with no obvious markings or spots. Second spine of dorsal fin distinctly long. Tail fin square. Second in size only to Jewfish, reported to six feet. Occasional northern Gulf coast of Florida; rare northern Atlantic coast of Florida and eastern Caribbean to Brazil.

DISTINCTIVE FEATURES: 1. Black saddle spot on base of tail. 2. Dorsal fin notched between forward spines.

DESCRIPTION: Five irregular, olive-brown bars over light background. Diagonal bar from snout across eye to start of dorsal fin. Can change from pale to almost black.

ABUNDANCE & DISTRIBUTION: Occasional Florida, Bahamas, Caribbean; also Bermuda, Gulf of Mexico and south to Brazil. (Once common in many locations, but numbers greatly reduced by spearfishing.)

HABITAT & BEHAVIOR: Inhabit shallow to mid-range coral reefs, rarely deeper than 90 feet. Often rest on bottom, blending with surroundings.

REACTION TO DIVERS: Tend to be curious; can often be closely approached with slow, nonthreatening movements.

DISTINCTIVE FEATURES: 1. Foredorsal fin has smooth, straight edge (not notched). No saddle spot at base of tail. (Compare to similar Nassau Grouper, *E. striatus*, [previous] which has saddle spot and notched dorsal fin.) **JUVENILE: 2. Pale bluish borders on rear dorsal, anal and tail fins.**

DESCRIPTION: Variable earthtones, usually reddish brown with small, scattered whitish blotches. May have bars and blotches similar to Nassau Grouper. Can change color, pale or darken.

ABUNDANCE & DISTRIBUTION: Occasional Florida and Bahamas; rare Caribbean; also north to Massachusetts, Bermuda, Gulf of Mexico and south to Brazil. Can be locally abundant. (Populations greatly reduced by spearfishing).

HABITAT & BEHAVIOR: Inhabit reefs and margins of sea grass beds. Rest on bottom, blending with surroundings.

REACTION TO DIVERS: Apparently curious; if diver remains still and appears to be doing something, grouper will often move in to watch.

JEWFISH
Epinephelus itajara
FAMILY:
Grouper/Seabass -
Serranidae

SIZE: 4-6 ft., max. 8 ft.
DEPTH: 10-100 ft.

BELIZE

NASSAU GROUPER
Epinephelus striatus
FAMILY:
Grouper/Seabass -
Serranidae

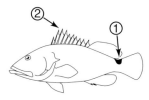

SIZE: 1-2 ft., max. 4 ft.
DEPTH: 20-100 ft.

L. CAYMAN

RED GROUPER
Epinephelus morio
FAMILY:
Grouper/Seabass -
Serranidae

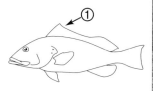

SIZE: 1-2 ft., max. 3 ft.
DEPTH: 6-400 ft.

KEY LARGO, FL

**Red Grouper
Juvenile**

DRY TORTUGAS, FL

DISTINCTIVE FEATURES: 1. Outer third of pectoral fin is pale to bright yellow. 2. Ends of rectangular body blotches rounded (can pale blotch pattern to become indistinct, showing only spots). (Compare similar Black Grouper, *M. bonaci*, [next] where ends are square.) **3. Tail has thin, dark irregular margin.**

DESCRIPTION: Rectangular blotches over light background can be black, gray, brown, olive-green or red (pictured below). Can dramatically change color, pale or darken.

ABUNDANCE & DISTRIBUTION: Occasional Florida, Bahamas, Caribbean; also Bermuda, Gulf of Mexico and south to Brazil.

HABITAT & BEHAVIOR: Inhabit reef tops and walls. Often rest on bottom in secluded spots.

REACTION TO DIVERS: Wary, but occasionally curious. Can often be approached with slow, nonthreatening movements.

Yellowfin Grouper
*Dark phase displaying
only spots.*

ROATAN

Red Grouper

continued from previous page

Displaying barred pattern similar to Nassau Grouper. Note foredorsal fin has smooth, straight edge.

DRY TORTUGAS, FL

YELLOWFIN GROUPER

Mycteroperca venenosa

FAMILY:
Grouper/Seabass - Serranidae

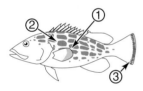

SIZE: 1-2 ft., max. 3 ft.
DEPTH: 15-120 ft.

ROATAN

Yellowfin Grouper

Red phase displaying rounded rectangular body blotches.

L. CAYMAN

DISTINCTIVE FEATURES: 1. Thin, pale to yellow margin on pectoral fins. 2. Ends of rectangular blotches on upper body are nearly square. (Compare similar Yellowfin Grouper, *M. venenosa*, [previous] where ends are rounded.) **3. Tail has wide, black margin with thin, white edge.**

DESCRIPTION: Vary from reddish brown to black. Can pale or darken until markings become indistinct.

ABUNDANCE & DISTRIBUTION: Common to occasional Florida, Bahamas, Caribbean; also north to Massachusetts, Bermuda, Gulf of Mexico and south to Brazil.

HABITAT & BEHAVIOR: Inhabit reefs. Drift near bottom, occasionally in open water well above reefs or off walls.

REACTION TO DIVERS: Shy; usually retreat and hide upon approach.

ROATAN   CAYMAN

DISTINCTIVE FEATURES: Dark body spots tend to form broken stripes and rectangular blotches. (Compare similar Gag, *M. microlepis,* [pg. 149] with markings that give marbled appearance.) **1. Dusky tail has pale margin.**

DESCRIPTION: Light tan to brown. Can pale or darken dramatically.

ABUNDANCE & DISTRIBUTION: Common to occasional Florida and continental coast to northern South America (Similar Yellowmouth Grouper, *M. interstitialis,* [pg. 147] tends to be found around islands.); also north to Massachusetts and Gulf of Mexico.

HABITAT & BEHAVIOR: Drift above reefs. Often in openings of recesses in reefs.

REACTION TO DIVERS: Appear unafraid and curious; move away only when closely approached.

NOTE: Also commonly known as "Salmon Rockfish."

BLACK GROUPER
Mycteroperca bonaci

FAMILY:
Grouper/Seabass -
Serranidae

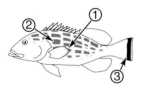

SIZE: 1¹/₂-3 ft., max. 4 ft.
DEPTH: 20-100 ft.

BELIZE

Black Grouper
*Color and
marking phases.*

NASSAU

SCAMP
Mycteroperca phenax

FAMILY:
Grouper/Seabass -
Serranidae

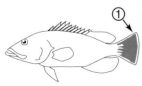

SIZE: 1-1¹/₂ ft., max. 2 ft.
DEPTH: 10-80 ft.

DRY TORTUGAS, FL

DISTINCTIVE FEATURES: 1. Dramatic "tiger-stripe" bars. **JUVENILES:** Yellow. **2. Dusky mid-body streak.**

DESCRIPTION: Nine brown-to-black diagonal bars over light background. Can dramatically change color, pale or darken. Occasionally bright red, especially in cleaning stations. **JUVENILE:** With maturity, dusky bars appear and gradually become more pronounced.

ABUNDANCE & DISTRIBUTION: Common Bahamas, Caribbean; occasional South Florida; also Bermuda, southern Gulf of Mexico and south to Brazil.

HABITAT & BEHAVIOR: Inhabit reefs and walls. Often rest on bottom in secluded spots. Often in cleaning stations.

REACTION TO DIVERS: Wary, tend to be curious. Can occasionally be approached with slow, nonthreatening movements.

CAYMAN   *CAYMAN*

**Tiger Grouper
Intermediate**

BONAIRE

TIGER GROUPER
Mycteroperca tigris
FAMILY:
Grouper/Seabass -
Serranidae

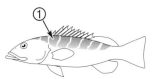

SIZE: 1-2 ft., max. 3½ ft.
DEPTH: 10-60 ft.

CAYMAN

Tiger Grouper
Color phases.

*Note individual
is being cleaned.*
[near left]

BONAIRE

Tiger Grouper
Juvenile

ANGUILLA

145

DISTINCTIVE FEATURES: 1. Eight to nine forward-sloping dark bars (adults similarly marked). 2. Dark saddle on base of tail (adults do not have this marking).

DESCRIPTION: White to shades of gray to dark brown.

ABUNDANCE & DISTRIBUTION: Rare Florida; uncommon Bahamas, Caribbean; also Bermuda and south to Brazil.

HABITAT & BEHAVIOR: Juveniles occasionally inhabit mid-range to deep reefs. Adults inhabit waters well below safe diving limits.

REACTION TO DIVERS: Wary, but often curious. Can occasionally be approached with slow, nonthreatening movements.

NOTE: Adults inhabit deep rocky ledges from 500-1000 feet.

DISTINCTIVE FEATURES: 1. **Distinct yellow around corners of mouth.** (Similar Scamp, M phenax, [pg. 143] does not have yellow around mouth.) 2. **Pectoral fins pale at base and margin. JUVENILE: 3. Bicolored; dark back, white belly. 4. Yellow spinous fin.**

DESCRIPTION: Brown to brownish gray; color may be uniform or have pattern of close-set dots and occasionally blotches. Can pale or darken dramatically.

ABUNDANCE & DISTRIBUTION: Common to occasional Bahamas and Caribbean Islands. (Similar Scamp tends to be along continental coasts.); rare Florida; also Bermuda and south to Brazil.

HABITAT & BEHAVIOR: Inhabit reefs. Drift in gorgonians and openings to recesses in reefs. Frequent cleaner stations.

REACTION TO DIVERS: Wary, but occasionally curious. Can often be approached with slow, nonthreatening movements.

**Yellowmouth Grouper
Juvenile**

PUERTO RICO

MISTY GROUPER
Juvenile
Epinephelus mystacinus
FAMILY:
Grouper/Seabass -
Serranidae

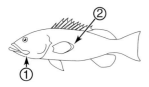

SIZE: 3-6 in.
(adults to 5 ft.)
DEPTH: 40-1000 ft.

BELIZE

YELLOWMOUTH
GROUPER
Mycteroperca interstitialis
FAMILY:
Grouper/Seabass -
Serranidae

SIZE: 1-2 ft., max. 2¹/₂ ft.
DEPTH: 10-80 ft.

CAYMAN

Yellowmouth Grouper
Blotched pattern.

CAYMAN

147

DISTINCTIVE FEATURES: 1. Lines radiate from eye. 2. Dusky tail has thin, blue margin.

DESCRIPTION: Pale to dark gray or olive-gray. Dusky scrawled or blotched markings give body a marbled appearance. (Similar Comb Grouper, *M. rubra*, [next] distinguished by whitish spots and blotches on upper body and by geographical location. Compare with similar Scamp, *M. phenax*, [pg. 143], with markings that tend to form broken stripes and rectangular blotches.)

ABUNDANCE & DISTRIBUTION: Occasional Florida; also north to Massachusetts, Bermuda, Gulf of Mexico and Brazil. Not reported Caribbean or Bahamas.

HABITAT & BEHAVIOR: Inhabit rocky outcroppings, ledges, undercuts and reefs. Drift near bottom.

REACTION TO DIVERS: Shy; retreat and often hide upon approach.

DISTINCTIVE FEATURES: 1. Three to four dark lines extend from eye and cheek to just beyond gill cover.

DESCRIPTION: Brownish to gray. Small whitish blotches over upper body and fins. (Similar Gag, *M. microlepis*, [previous] distinguished by dusky scrawled markings or blotches on body and by geographical location.) Pale scrawled markings on belly. Markings become less distinct with age. Can pale or darken.

ABUNDANCE & DISTRIBUTION: Common southern Caribbean; rare in north; also western Gulf of Mexico, south to Brazil and eastern Atlantic. Not reported Florida or Bahamas.

HABITAT & BEHAVIOR: Inhabit reefs, drifting just above bottom.

REACTION TO DIVERS: Wary, but tend to be curious. Can occasionally be approached with non-threatening movements.

DISTINCTIVE FEATURES: 1. Eyes set close to tip of snout; red iris; pupil dark, often green. 2. Several distinctive bands on pectoral fins formed by series of spots on spine rays. 3. Three faint wide bands radiate from rear of eye; top band is longest and most obvious.

DESCRIPTION: Mottled, blotched and occasionally banded in varying shades of reddish brown to orange-brown, olive and white; often have orange spots. Deep-water inhabitants tend to be more uniformly orange.

ABUNDANCE & DISTRIBUTION: Uncommon Florida, Bahamas, Caribbean; also Bermuda, south to Argentina and eastern Pacific.

HABITAT & BEHAVIOR: Prefer sea grass and coral rubble; occasionally on reefs and deep rocky slopes. Expert at camouflage.

REACTION TO DIVERS: Unafraid. Can be closely approached with slow movements.

GAG
Mycteroperca microlepis
FAMILY:
Grouper/Seabass -
Serranidae

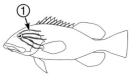

SIZE: 1 1/2-2 ft., max. 3 ft.
DEPTH: 20-100 ft.

JACKSONVILLE, FL

COMB GROUPER
Mycteroperca rubra
FAMILY:
Grouper/Seabass -
Serranidae

SIZE: 1-2 ft., max. 2 1/2 ft.
DEPTH: 10-130 ft.

BONAIRE

MUTTON HAMLET
Alphestes afer
FAMILY:
Seabass - Serranidae

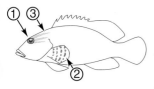

SIZE: 5-10 in., max. 1 ft.
DEPTH: 5-80 ft.

BARBADOS

149

DISTINCTIVE FEATURES: 1. Large white body blotches. 2. High back profile. JUVENILE: Dark brown to black. **3. Large, well-defined, scattered white blotches.**

DESCRIPTION: Mottled olive to brown and black. Black dots over body.

ABUNDANCE & DISTRIBUTION: Rare Florida, Bahamas, Caribbean; also Bermuda.

HABITAT & BEHAVIOR: Secretive. Occasionally hide in caves and other secluded places on reefs. Most common on deep rocky ledges well below safe diving limits.

REACTION TO DIVERS: Extremely shy. Dart into cover when approached.

NOTE: Formerly classified in genus *Dermatolepis*.

Graysby
Juvenile

BONAIRE

DISTINCTIVE FEATURES: 1. Three to five pale or dark spots along base of dorsal fin. 2. Tail more rounded than similar species. JUVENILE: 3. White band runs from nape, between eyes to lower lip.

DESCRIPTION: Light reddish brown to gray, with darker orangish brown spots over body. Can change color, pale or darken. **JUVENILE:** May have yellowish wash over head and back.

ABUNDANCE & DISTRIBUTION: Common South Florida, Bahamas, Caribbean; also Bermuda and south to Brazil.

HABITAT & BEHAVIOR: Prefer coral reefs with small ledges and caves. Rest quietly on bottom, blending with surroundings.

REACTION TO DIVERS: Somewhat wary. Can occasionally be approached with slow, non-threatening movements.

NOTE: Also commonly known as "Kitty Mitchell." Many icthyologists believe this species should be classified in the genus *Cephalopholis*.

MARBLED GROUPER
Epinephelus inermis
FAMILY:
Grouper/Seabass -
Serranidae

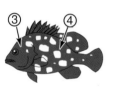

SIZE: 1-2 ft., max. 3 ft.
DEPTH: 10-700 ft.

SWAN IS.

Marbled Grouper Juvenile

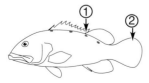

CAYMAN

GRAYSBY
Epinephelus cruentatus
FAMILY:
Grouper/Seabass -
Serranidae

SIZE: 6-10 in., max. 1 ft.
DEPTH: 10-60 ft.

CAYMAN

151

DISTINCTIVE FEATURES: 1. Tail and rear fins have black margin edged in white. (Similar Rock Hind, *E. adscensionis*, [next] distinguished by lack of black margin.)

DESCRIPTION: Reddish spots over whitish background (no spots on tail or dorsal fin). Can pale or darken.

ABUNDANCE & DISTRIBUTION: Common Caribbean; occasional Bahamas and Florida; also Bermuda, Gulf of Mexico and south to Brazil.

HABITAT & BEHAVIOR: Inhabit shallow inshore patch reefs to deep banks. Drift just above bottom or rest quietly on pectoral fins, blending with surroundings.

REACTION TO DIVERS: Appear unafraid and somewhat curious; move away only when closely approached.

NOTE: Also commonly known as "Speckled Hind" and "Strawberry Grouper."

DISTINCTIVE FEATURES: 1. Black saddle blotch on base of tail. (Similar Red Hind, *E. guttatus*, [previous] distinguished by lack of saddle blotch.)

DESCRIPTION: Reddish to dark dots cover body and all fins. One to four pale or dark blotches along back, below dorsal fin. Can pale to almost white or darken dramatically.

ABUNDANCE & DISTRIBUTION: Common Florida, Bahamas, eastern Caribbean; rare balance of Caribbean; also north to Massachusetts, Bermuda, Gulf of Mexico and south to Brazil.

HABITAT & BEHAVIOR: Inhabit shallow, rocky, often rough inshore areas, and occasionally deep reefs. Drift near bottom with tail down.

REACTION TO DIVERS: Shy, especially in shallow areas where they retreat rapidly upon approach, often hiding in dark recesses. Appear less afraid on deep reefs and often allow close view.

Rock Hind Young

FT. LAUDERDALE, FL

RED HIND
Epinephelus guttatus
FAMILY:
Grouper/Seabass -
Serranidae

SIZE: 10-15 in., max. 2 ft.
DEPTH: 10-160 ft.

L. CAYMAN

ROCK HIND
Epinephelus adscensionis
FAMILY:
Grouper/Seabass -
Serranidae

SIZE: 8-14 in., max. 2 ft.
DEPTH: 2-100 ft.

FT. LAUDERDALE, FL

Rock Hind
*Pale phase displaying
dark blotches on back.*

BONAIRE

153

Seabass

DISTINCTIVE FEATURES: 1. Two black dots on lower lip. 2. Two black dots behind dorsal fin on base of tail. **JUVENILE:** 3. White spot on middorsal fin and back, often surrounded by black. 4. Four spots on lower lip. 5. Two white spots on base of tail.

DESCRIPTION: Identification by color impractical because of several color phases. Shades of reddish brown to brown most common; also has a bicolor phase (upper dark and lower pale); and a brilliant yellow-gold phase. Body covered with small blue to pale dots (golden phase uncommon).

ABUNDANCE & DISTRIBUTION: Common Caribbean; common to occasional South Florida and Bahamas; also Bermuda, Gulf of Mexico and south to Brazil.

HABITAT & BEHAVIOR: Prefer reefs. Drift just above or rest on bottom; stay close to protected areas. Gregarious.

REACTION TO DIVERS: Somewhat wary, but often curious. Can usually be closely approached with slow, nonthreatening movements.

NOTE: Many icthyologists believe this species should be classified in the genus *Cephalopholis*.

Coney
Brown Color Phase

BELIZE

GRAND TURK

ROATAN

CONEY
Epinephelus fulvus

FAMILY:
Grouper/Seabass -
Serranidae

SIZE: 6-10 in., max. 16 in.
DEPTH: 10-60 ft.

CAYMAN

**Coney
Bicolor Phase**

CAYMAN

**Coney
Golden Phase**
[right]

Juvenile/Adult
[far left]

*Note four dark
spots on lower lip.*

Juvenile [near left]

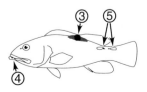

CAYMAN

155

Seabass

DISTINCTIVE FEATURES: 1. Six to seven dark bars on back. 2. Immediately below each is a rectangular blotch (may not be completely separated from the bar).

DESCRIPTION: Undercolor white to cream, tan or yellowish. Bluish line markings between eyes and on snout; often have dark spots along lateral line. Adult's tail develops three pointed extensions.

ABUNDANCE & DISTRIBUTION: Common to occasional northeastern Florida and Gulf Coast including Keys; also north to North Carolina and Gulf of Mexico. Not reported Bahamas or Caribbean.

HABITAT & BEHAVIOR: Inhabit hard bottoms and areas of rocky rubble.

REACTION TO DIVERS: Wary, but usually remain still and move only when closely approached.

DISTINCTIVE FEATURES: 1. White-edged borders on tail. 2. Pale centers of scales form numerous narrow, light body stripes.

DESCRIPTION: Shades of bluish black to gray and brown; occasionally dusky midbody stripe. Adult's tail develops three pointed extensions. **MALE:** Spines of foredorsal fin have white tips [pictured]. **FEMALE:** White area on nape.

ABUNDANCE & DISTRIBUTION: Common to occasional Northeast Florida and Gulf Coast (may reach South Florida in cold winters); also north to Maine. Not reported Bahamas and Caribbean.

HABITAT & BEHAVIOR: Inhabit rocky areas and hard bottoms, especially around jetties. More common in shallow waters.

REACTION TO DIVERS: Wary, but usually remain still and move only when closely approached.

DISTINCTIVE FEATURES: 1. Series of small dark spots along lateral line. 2. Dusky blotch below rear of spinous dorsal fin.

DESCRIPTION: Mottled shades of red-brown to dark brown; belly white. Pectoral, dorsal and tail fins clear to translucent; ventral and anal fins dark. Two to four diffuse, dusky bars often on body; dusky band frequently below eye.

ABUNDANCE & DISTRIBUTION: Common to occasional North Florida and Panhandle; uncommon South Florida and continental coast to Venezuela; rare balance of Caribbean; also north to South Carolina and Gulf of Mexico. Not reported Bahamas.

HABITAT & BEHAVIOR: Inhabit areas of rubble, gravel and sand; also in sea grass beds. Lie on bottom blending with background.

REACTION TO DIVERS: Wary, but usually remain still and move only when closely approached.

BANK SEA BASS
Centropristis ocyurus

FAMILY:
Grouper/Seabass -
Serranidae

SIZE: 5-9 in., max. 1 ft.
DEPTH: 60-250 ft.

PANAMA CITY, FL

BLACK SEA BASS
Centropristis striata

FAMILY:
Grouper/Seabass -
Serranidae

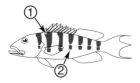

SIZE: 6-18 in., max. 2 ft.
DEPTH: 6-120 ft.

JACKSONVILLE, FL

PYGMY SEA BASS
Serraniculus pumilio

FAMILY:
Grouper/Seabass -
Serranidae

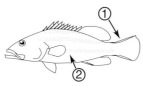

SIZE: 1$\frac{1}{2}$-2$\frac{1}{2}$ in.,
max. 3 in.
DEPTH: 1-200 ft.

PANAMA CITY, FL

DISTINCTIVE FEATURES: 1. Pale blue line markings on head. 2. Thin, blue to bluish white body stripes.

DESCRIPTION: Bars and/or stripes on body in shades of orangish or yellowish brown to tan; bars tend to be more distinct at rest, stripes more prominent when moving; midbody stripe often very dark and conspicuous ends with a dark spot on fore-tail. Can pale, darken or change stripe and bar pattern rapidly; back usually darker.

ABUNDANCE & DISTRIBUTION: Common Florida; occasional Bahamas, Cuba; rare to absent Caribbean; also north to North Carolina, Gulf of Mexico, and south to Uruguay.

HABITAT & BEHAVIOR: Inhabit grass, sand and coral rubble areas. Build burrows.

REACTION TO DIVERS: Somewhat wary; often retreat into burrow. Can occasionally be approached with slow, nonthreatening movements.

SIMILAR SPECIES: Dwarf Sand Perch, *D. bivittatum*, distinguished by small, dark triangular mark under and behind gill cover. Brown upper body, tan below, marked with stripes and short, irregular bars. Florida only. Aquavina, *D. radiale*, distinguished by orangish cheek and two blue spots on upper edge of tail. Light greenish blue. Primarily in Caribbean. Both may have blue lines on cheek.

Harlequin Bass
Juvenile

SIZE: 1-1½ in.

BIMINI

DISTINCTIVE FEATURES: 1. Dark, tiger-like bars.

DESCRIPTION: Upper body has whitish undercolor; lower body pale yellow. Series of dark dots form diffuse horizontal lines on body. Head more pointed than that of other family members.

ABUNDANCE & DISTRIBUTION: Common South Florida, Bahamas, Caribbean; also Bermuda.

HABITAT & BEHAVIOR: Inhabit areas of sea grass, coral rubble and reefs. Drift above bottom to forage for small crustaceans.

REACTION TO DIVERS: Curious. Can be closely approached with slow, nonthreatening movements.

SIMILAR SPECIES: Snow Bass, *S. chionaraia*, distinguished by a row of black dots along borders of tail, and white belly. Primarily on deep Florida reefs. Two-spot Bass, *S. flaviventris*, distinguished by two dark spots on base of tail, white belly. Inhabit grass beds and areas of rubble.

SAND PERCH
Diplectrum formosum
FAMILY:
Seabass - Serranidae

SIZE: 5-9 in., max. 1 ft.
DEPTH: 2-25 ft.

WEST PALM BEACH, FL

Sand Perch
*Displaying stripe pattern,
note darker midbody stripe
and spot on fore-tail.*

WEST PALM BEACH, FL

HARLEQUIN BASS
Serranus tigrinus
FAMILY:
Seabass - Serranidae

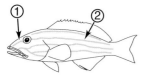

SIZE: 2½-3½ in.,
max. 4 in.
DEPTH: 2-120 ft.

ANGUILLA

159

Seabass

DISTINCTIVE FEATURES: 1. Obvious row of dark, rectangular blotches on lower side. 2. Band of four black spots on base of tail.

DESCRIPTION: Body marked with rows of dark to orange rectangular blotches and spots over white. Inhabitants of deeper water are suffused with more red to orange or yellow than those from shallow water, which tend to be paler.

ABUNDANCE & DISTRIBUTION: Occasional South Florida, Bahamas, Caribbean.

HABITAT & BEHAVIOR: Prefer coral rubble and sea grass beds. Hover just above or rest on bottom.

REACTION TO DIVERS: Wary; usually quickly retreat into protection of rubble or grass. Apparently curious, they generally reappear and can be approached with slow, nonthreatening movements.

DISTINCTIVE FEATURES: 1. Two orange to yellow squares outlined in black behind eyes.

DESCRIPTION: Orange markings on head; dark orangish brown pattern of markings on back; orange to yellow rectangular markings on the white undercolor of midbody and belly.

ABUNDANCE & DISTRIBUTION: Occasional South Florida, Bahamas, Caribbean; also Bermuda.

HABITAT & BEHAVIOR: Inhabit deep reefs and rocky areas; rare in water less than 100 feet. Rest on bottom near entrances of protective recesses.

REACTION TO DIVERS: Not shy; remain perched in open unless closely approached with rapid movements.

DISTINCTIVE FEATURES: 1. Midbody is shades of orange to brown (tobacco color). 2. Dark "U-shaped" border on tail.

DESCRIPTION: Alternating series of dark and white to yellow or salmon blotches along back. Belly white. **JUVENILE:** Markings tend to be more distinct.

ABUNDANCE & DISTRIBUTION: Common to occasional South Florida, Bahamas, Caribbean; also Bermuda and south to Brazil.

HABITAT & BEHAVIOR: Inhabit reefs and adjacent areas of sand and coral rubble. Tend to stay near bottom.

REACTION TO DIVERS: Curious; allow slow, nonthreatening approach.

SIMILAR SPECIES: School Bass, *Schultzea beta*, distinguished by dark bar below eye and yellow tail. Body orangish with no markings; may have two to four dusky blotches at base of tail. Tend to cluster in small groups on deeper reefs of Florida and Bahamas.

LANTERN BASS
Serranus baldwini
FAMILY:
Seabass - Serranidae

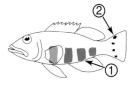

SIZE: 1½-2 in.,
max. 2½ in.
DEPTH: 2-240 ft.

CAYMAN

ORANGEBACK BASS
Serranus annularis
FAMILY:
Seabass - Serranidae

SIZE: 1½-2 in.,
max. 2½ in.
DEPTH: 50-220 ft.

WEST PALM BEACH, FL

TOBACCOFISH
Serranus tabacarius
FAMILY:
Seabass - Serranidae

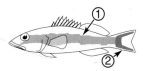

SIZE: 3-4½ in., max. 7 in.
DEPTH: 3-225 ft.

CAYMAN

161

Seabass

DISTINCTIVE FEATURES: 1. Dark wedge-shaped "belt" begins between spinous and soft dorsal fin and extends to belly. 2. Large white patch on belly.

DESCRIPTION: Shades of brown with darkish bars on body. All fins finely spotted except ventrals.

ABUNDANCE & DISTRIBUTION: Common to occasional North Florida to Palm Beach; uncommon to rare South Florida and Keys; also north to North Carolina and northern Gulf of Mexico. Not reported Bahamas or Caribbean.

HABITAT & BEHAVIOR: Inhabit rocky reefs and areas of sand mixed with rubble.

REACTION TO DIVERS: Curious; can be closely approached with slow, nonthreatening movements.

DISTINCTIVE FEATURES: 1. Black bar from foredorsal fin to belly. 2. Dark midbody stripe from behind silvery bar to tail. 3. Wide black, diagonal band below eye.

DESCRIPTION: White undercolor. Occasionally have a few additional minor brownish bars and stripes.

ABUNDANCE & DISTRIBUTION: Uncommon Florida, Caribbean; also north to South Carolina, Bermuda and Gulf of Mexico. Not reported Bahamas.

HABITAT & BEHAVIOR: Inhabit deep rocky areas and sand mixed with rubble; rarely shallower than 100 feet. Perch on bottom near entrance to recess.

REACTION TO DIVERS: Shy; usually quickly retreat into protection of recess. Apparently curious, however, they generally reappear in a few minutes and may be approached with slow, non-threatening movements.

DISTINCTIVE FEATURES: 1. Series of pale and dark bars across back.

DESCRIPTION: Usually bluish, but can be orange to brown.

ABUNDANCE & DISTRIBUTION: Occasional South Florida, Bahamas, central and northern Caribbean. Not reported southern Caribbean.

HABITAT & BEHAVIOR: Hover in small groups over sand bottoms and coral rubble.

REACTION TO DIVERS: Wary; move slowly away when approached. Persistent slow, nonthreatening approaches may allow close view.

BELTED SANDFISH
Serranus subligarius
FAMILY:
Seabass - Serranidae

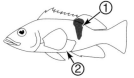

SIZE: 2¹/₂-3¹/₂ in.,
max. 4 in.
DEPTH: 1-85 ft.

JACKSONVILLE, FL

TATTLER BASS
Serranus phoebe
FAMILY:
Seabass - Serranidae

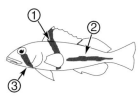

SIZE: 2¹/₂-5 in., max. 6 in.
DEPTH: 85-600 ft.

WEST PALM BEACH, FL

CHALK BASS
Serranus tortugarum
FAMILY:
Seabass - Serranidae

SIZE: 1¹/₂-3 in.,
max. 3¹/₂ in.
DEPTH: 35-300 ft.

ANGUILLA

DISTINCTIVE FEATURES: 1. Dark spot on dorsal and anal fin. 2. Two blotches on tail are joined. (Compare similar Candy Basslet, *L. mowbrayi*, [next] distinguished by lack of spot on anal fin and dark blotches on tail that do not join.)

DESCRIPTION: Boldly marked with maroon, pinkish rose and yellowish gold stripes.

ABUNDANCE & DISTRIBUTION: Common (although sightings are rare) South Florida, Bahamas, Caribbean.

HABITAT & BEHAVIOR: Inhabit coral reefs. Secretive; stay hidden in deep, dark recesses.

REACTION TO DIVERS: Reclusive; retreat from view when approached. Very slow movements and patient waiting outside recess are usually rewarded by a second or even third view.

DISTINCTIVE FEATURES: 1. Dark spot on dorsal fin. 2. Two blotches on upper and lower lobes of tail are separated. (Compare similar Peppermint Bass, *L. rubre*, [previous] distinguished by dark spot on anal fin and two blotches on tail lobes that join.)

DESCRIPTION: Boldly marked with stripes generally in shades of light brown to red-brown or yellow-brown alternating with red to maroon; stripes may be occasionally yellow to lavender or blue.

ABUNDANCE & DISTRIBUTION: Occasional (although sightings are rare) Florida Keys, Bahamas, Caribbean.

HABITAT & BEHAVIOR: Inhabit deep coral reefs. Secretive; stay hidden in deep, dark recesses. Rarely shallower than 80-90 feet.

REACTION TO DIVERS: Reclusive; retreat from view when approached. Very slow movements and patient waiting outside recess are usually rewarded by a second or even third view.

DISTINCTIVE FEATURES: Salmon to dark red. **1. Black submarginal band on tail. 2. Black spot on second dorsal fin.**

DESCRIPTION: Yellow stripe runs from tip of snout to eye. Margin of second dorsal fin and tail white to brilliant blue.

ABUNDANCE & DISTRIBUTION: Common to occasional southern, central and western Caribbean; occasional to uncommon Bahamas, northern Caribbean; rare South Florida; also Bermuda.

HABITAT & BEHAVIOR: Deep reef and wall dweller. Extremely shy; stay hidden in caves, deep undercuts and dark recesses in reefs.

REACTION TO DIVERS: Reclusive; retreat from view when approached. Very slow movements and patient waiting outside recess are usually rewarded by a second or even third view.

NOTE: Also commonly known as "Ridgeback Bass."

PEPPERMINT BASS
Liopropoma rubre
FAMILY:
Seabass - Serranidae

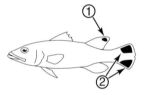

SIZE: 1 ½-3 in.,
max. 3 ½ in.
DEPTH: 10-140 ft.

L. CAYMAN

CANDY BASSLET
Liopropoma carmabi
FAMILY:
Seabass - Serranidae

SIZE: 1-1 ¾ in., max. 2 in.
DEPTH: 50-200 ft.

BIMINI

CAVE BASS
Liopropoma mowbrayi
FAMILY:
Seabass - Serranidae

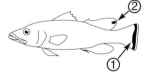

SIZE: 1 ½-3 in.,
max. 3 ½ in.
DEPTH: 80-200 ft.

BELIZE

165

DISTINCTIVE FEATURES: 1. Wide, red-brown midbody stripe, bordered in bright yellow, runs from snout to tail.

DESCRIPTION: Back and belly red to red-brown. Thin, pale bluish white edge on margin of tail.

ABUNDANCE & DISTRIBUTION: Occasional eastern Florida to Keys; also north to North Carolina. Not reported Bahamas or Caribbean.

HABITAT & BEHAVIOR: Deep rocky reef dweller. Lurk under ledges and in shaded, protective recesses.

REACTION TO DIVERS: Shy; retreat when rapidly approached. Apparently curious, however, often peer out of recess and allow a slow, close, nonthreatening approach.

DISTINCTIVE FEATURES: 1. Bright red spot at base of pectoral fin. 2. Three light or dark spots along back.

DESCRIPTION: Varies from olive to bright reddish brown, occasionally with a purplish cast; belly pale salmon. Forked tail.

ABUNDANCE & DISTRIBUTION: Common central and southern Caribbean; rare Bahamas, Florida and northern Caribbean; also Bermuda, Gulf of Mexico, south to Brazil, eastern Atlantic and eastern Pacific.

HABITAT & BEHAVIOR: Prefer deep reefs. Drift in small groups to large schools, generally well up in water column, but may hover over reef; individuals often hide on reef.

REACTION TO DIVERS: Wary; move to more protected areas of reef when approached.

DISTINCTIVE FEATURES: Mottled and covered with pale indistinct blotches and spots. (Compare with similar Whitespotted, *R. maculatus* and Spotted Soapfish, *R. subbifrenatus* [next], that have more well-defined markings.)

DESCRIPTION: Vary from drab reddish brown to gray; may have green or blue cast.

ABUNDANCE & DISTRIBUTION: Occasional Florida, Bahamas, Caribbean; Bermuda and south to Brazil.

HABITAT & BEHAVIOR: Reclusive. Solitary and inactive; often rest on bottom or lean against ledges or coral heads. Feed at night on small fishes, especially cardinals. Their common name derives from the soap-like toxic mucus they secrete.

REACTION TO DIVERS: Unafraid; generally allow a close approach and retreat only when threatened.

SIMILAR SPECIES: Freckled Soapfish, *R. bistrispinus*, distinguished by smaller size and small dark spots over brown body; noticeably darker upper body. South Florida and Bahamas to northern South America.

WRASSE BASS
Liopropoma eukrines
FAMILY:
Seabass - Serranidae

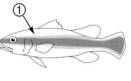

SIZE: 2-4 in., max. 5 in.
DEPTH: 80-500 ft.

CAPE CANAVERAL, FL

CREOLE-FISH
Paranthias furcifer
FAMILY:
Seabass - Serranidae

SIZE: 4-8 in.,
max. 10 ½ in.
DEPTH: 25-160 ft.

BONAIRE

GREATER SOAPFISH
Rypticus saponaceus
FAMILY:
Seabass - Serranidae
SUBFAMILY:
Soapfish - Grammistinae

SIZE: 5-9 in., max. 13 in.
DEPTH: 15-60 ft.

CAYMAN

167

DISTINCTIVE FEATURES: 1. Random white spots on body often outlined in black.

DESCRIPTION: Dark to medium brown; pale stripe often runs from lips across snout and nape, fading to dorsal fin. Pointed head with upturned mouth.

ABUNDANCE & DISTRIBUTION: Occasional North Florida to Palm Beach and Gulf Coast; also north to Rhode Island. Not reported Bahamas or Caribbean.

HABITAT & BEHAVIOR: Reclusive. Solitary and inactive; often rest on bottom or lean against ledges or coral heads. Their common name derives from the soap-like toxic mucus they secrete.

REACTION TO DIVERS: Unafraid; generally allow a close approach and retreat only when threatened.

DISTINCTIVE FEATURES: 1. Random black spots with pale borders on body.

DESCRIPTION: Olive to brown; pale stripe often runs from lips across snout and nape, fading to dorsal fin; may have occasional random white spots. Pointed head with upturned mouth.

ABUNDANCE & DISTRIBUTION: Uncommon South Florida, Bahamas, Caribbean.

HABITAT & BEHAVIOR: Reclusive. Solitary and inactive; often rest on bottom or lean against ledges or coral heads. Their common name derives from the soap-like toxic mucus they secrete.

REACTION TO DIVERS: Unafraid; generally allow a close approach and retreat only when threatened.

DISTINCTIVE FEATURES: 1. Yellow streaks run from below eye across gill cover. 2. Gold ring around eye.

DESCRIPTION: Vary from olive-green to blue, greenish blue most common. Can have faint gold dots on body.

ABUNDANCE & DISTRIBUTION: Occasional to rare Bahamas, Caribbean. Not reported Florida.

HABITAT & BEHAVIOR: Prefer deep walls and become more abundant with depth. Generally live deeper than safe diving limits except eastern Caribbean where they inhabit shallower depths. Flit about in or near recesses. May orient belly to ceiling of cave or ledge and swim "upside-down."

REACTION TO DIVERS: Wary; slowly retreat into dark recesses when closely approached.

WHITESPOTTED SOAPFISH
Rypticus maculatus
FAMILY:
Seabass - Serranidae
SUBFAMILY:
Soapfish - Grammistinae

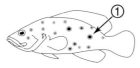

SIZE: 5-7 in., max. 8 in.
DEPTH: 15-130 ft.

PANAMA CITY, FL

SPOTTED SOAPFISH
Rypticus subbifrenatus
FAMILY:
Seabass - Serranidae
SUBFAMILY:
Soapfish - Grammistinae

SIZE: 4-6 in., max. 7 in.
DEPTH: 15-130 ft.

DOMINICA

YELLOWCHEEK BASSLET
Gramma linki
FAMILY:
Basslet - Grammatidae

SIZE: 2-3 in., max. 4 in.
DEPTH: 60-430 ft.

L. CAYMAN

DISTINCTIVE FEATURES: 1. Bicolored — purple to violet front and yellow to gold rear. **2. Dark spot on dorsal fin.**

DESCRIPTION: Several streaks on head run across eye.

ABUNDANCE & DISTRIBUTION: Abundant Caribbean and Bahamas; also Bermuda. Not reported Florida.

HABITAT & BEHAVIOR: Flit about, in or near recesses. May orient belly to ceiling of cave or ledge and swim "upside-down."

REACTION TO DIVERS: Wary; slowly retreat into dark recesses when approached. With patient waiting and nonthreatening movements, fish will often reappear and can be closely observed.

SIMILAR SPECIES: Heliotrope Basslet, *G. klayi*, distinguished by lack of dark spot on dorsal fin. Prefer deep walls. May mix with Fairy Basslets. Not reported Florida.

NOTE: Also commonly known as "Royal Gramma."

DISTINCTIVE FEATURES: 1. "Black cap" from lip to foredorsal fin.

DESCRIPTION: Tones of magenta to indigo. Faint gold lines on head, dots on body.

ABUNDANCE & DISTRIBUTION: Common northwest Caribbean and southern Caribbean; occasional to uncommon Bahamas, balance of Caribbean; Not reported Florida and some eastern Caribbean islands.

HABITAT & BEHAVIOR: Prefer deep walls and become more abundant with depth; inhabit shallow reefs in southern Caribbean. Flit about, in or near recesses. May orient belly to ceiling of cave or ledge and swim "upside-down."

REACTION TO DIVERS: Somewhat wary; slowly retreat into dark recesses when approached. With patient waiting and nonthreatening movements, fish will often reappear and can be closely observed.

DISTINCTIVE FEATURES: 1. Three, bluish to brilliant iridescent blue lines edged in black on head; one centered on snout runs to foredorsal fin and one from behind each eye runs onto back.

DESCRIPTION: Pale shades of tan; often yellowish to bright yellow wash on head and forebody and occasionally bluish rearbody.

ABUNDANCE & DISTRIBUTION: Occasional South Florida, Bahamas and Caribbean.

HABITAT & BEHAVIOR: Prefer deep walls and reefs. Inhabit caves, recesses and deep cut ledge overhangs where they often orient their belly to the ceiling and swim "upside-down." Rarely near entrance of hiding place or in open.

REACTION TO DIVERS: Reclusive; stay hidden and retreat further into recess when approached.

FAIRY BASSLET
Gramma loreto
FAMILY:
Basslet - Grammatidae

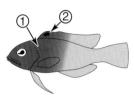

SIZE: 1 1/2-2 1/2 in.,
max. 3 in.
DEPTH: 10-200 ft.

BELIZE

BLACKCAP BASSLET
Gramma melacara
FAMILY:
Basslet - Grammatidae

SIZE: 2-3 in., max. 4 in.
DEPTH: 60-400 ft.

CAYMAN

THREELINE BASSLET
Lipogramma trilineatum
FAMILY:
Basslet – Grammatidae

SIZE: 3/4-1 1/4 in.,
max. 1 1/2 in.
DEPTH: 70- 160 ft.

BIMINI

171

Swim with Pectoral Fins/Obvious Scales

Parrotfish – Wrasse – Hogfish/Wrasse – Razorfish/Wrasse

This ID Group consists of fish that primarily use their pectoral fins to swim. (A few other fishes also use their pectoral fins, but not as conspicuously.) They have even rows of large, noticeable scales and beak-like mouths.

FAMILY: Parrotfish — Scaridae
14 Species Included

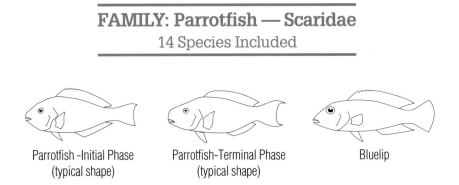

Parrotfish -Initial Phase
(typical shape)

Parrotfish-Terminal Phase
(typical shape)

Bluelip

Powerful jaws, fused teeth or "beaks," and bright colors give parrotfish their common family name. They are among the most common large fish seen on reefs. Sizes range from the four-foot Rainbow to the seven-inch Greenblotch. Many are solitary, while others join loose aggregations that often mix with other species. Their stout, scaly bodies are colored in bizarre combinations of greens and blues highlighted with reds and yellows. Several have the ability to change colors, becoming drab, mottled or pale. They swim about reefs using their pectoral fins — tails are used only for bursts of speed.

Their "beaks" are used to scrape algae and polyps from coral and rocks. In the process, large amounts of coral (limestone) are taken in and ground in their gullets to extract bits of polyp and algae. Clouds of the chalky residue are regularly excreted as the fish move about the reef. This process makes parrotfish one of the major sources of sand in tropical waters. They also graze on nearby grass, but seldom stray far from one area. A few species secrete mucus bubbles that envelop their bodies at night while they sleep.

Identification of parrotfish is made difficult due to the dramatic changes in shape, color and markings that occur in most species as they mature. The phases include JUVENILE PHASE (JP), INITIAL PHASE (IP), and TERMINAL PHASE (TP), which is the largest and most colorful. Some even have additional INTERMEDIATE color phases between the three primary phases. IP include sexually mature females and, in some species, immature and mature males. TP are always sexually mature males. Some parrotfish are hermaphroditic and go through a sex reversal to become TP, while others simply mature, never changing their sex. Learning to identify parrotfish in all their phases can be quite a challenge.

FAMILY: Wrasse — Labridae
10 Species Included

| Wrasse (typical shape) | Creole Wrasse | Puddingwife |

Wrasse are prolific reef inhabitants. They are closely related and similar to parrotfish, but are generally much smaller, and have more elongated "cigar" shapes. Sizes range from the 18-inch Puddingwife to the tiny three-inch Dwarf Wrasse. Greens, blues and yellows are their predominant colors. All are scaly and have noticeable front teeth that give them a "bucktoothed" profile. The teeth are used to obtain food by crushing the shells of invertebrates such as sea urchins.

By day, wrasse swim busily in loose, often mixed aggregations around coral heads. (The Creole Wrasse is the only species that schools in open water.) A few wrasse inhabit grass beds. At night several species bury themselves in the sand.

Like parrotfish, wrasse go through several changes in color, shape and markings during maturation. The phases include JUVENILE PHASE (JP), INITIAL PHASE (IP) and TERMINAL PHASE (TP), the largest and most colorful. Some even have additional INTERMEDIATE color phases between the three primary phases. IP include sexually mature females and, in some species, immature and mature males. TP are sexually mature males. Some wrasse are hermaphroditic and go through a sex reversal to become TP, while others simply mature, never changing their sex. Identifying wrasse in all their phases can be difficult.

FAMILY: Hogfish, Razorfish/Wrasse — Labridae
6 Species Included

| Hogfish | Hogfish (Spanish & Spotfin) | Razorfish |

Hogfish and razorfish are members of the wrasse family, but because of their unique shape have acquired separate common names. Hogfish have long snouts which they use to root for food, similar to their namesakes. They generally grow larger than other wrasse (to three feet). Their fin structure and colors make the three species easy to identify.

Razorfish are named for their blunt, highly compressed "razor-like" heads that are shaped something like the prow of a ship. All members of the Genus *Hemipteronotus*, they are small (three to six inches) and inhabit sand and grass beds. When frightened, they quickly dive headfirst into the sand using their "razor-like" foreheads and "tunnel away" using rapid body vibrations.

DISTINCTIVE FEATURES: TP & IP: All blue. **TP: 1. Squared-off head. IP: 2. Conical head. JP: 3. Yellow wash on snout extending back to foredorsal fin.**

DESCRIPTION: TP & IP: Vary from powder blue to deep blue and blue-green. **JP:** Bluish white to purplish blue. Some have yellow dorsal, ventral and anal fins.

ABUNDANCE & DISTRIBUTION: Occasional Florida, Bahamas, Caribbean; north to Maryland, Bermuda and south to Brazil. Not reported northern Gulf of Mexico.

HABITAT & BEHAVIOR: Swim about reefs; stop to scrape algae from rocks and coral.

REACTION TO DIVERS: Appear unconcerned, but shy away when closely approached.

KEY LARGO, FL   *KEY LARGO, FL*

DISTINCTIVE FEATURES: ALL PHASES: Navy blue. **1. Bright blue markings on head.**

DESCRIPTION: Body scales occasionally have light blue centers. All phases are essentially the same in appearance.

ABUNDANCE & DISTRIBUTION: Occasional Florida, Bahamas, Caribbean; north to Maryland, Bermuda and south to Brazil. Not reported Gulf of Mexico.

HABITAT & BEHAVIOR: Swim about reefs and sand areas; stop to scrape algae from rocks and coral.

REACTION TO DIVERS: Appear unconcerned, but shy away when closely approached.

BLUE PARROTFISH
Scarus coeruleus
Terminal Phase
FAMILY:
Parrotfish - Scaridae

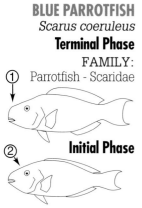

Initial Phase

SIZE: 1-2½ ft., max. 4 ft.
DEPTH: 10-80 ft.

CAYMAN

**Blue Parrotfish
Intermediate,
Juvenile/Initial Phase**
[right]

Juveniles

*With yellow dorsal, ventral
and anal fins and purplish
blue body.* [far left]
Bluish white body. [near left]

KEY LARGO, FL

MIDNIGHT PARROTFISH
Scarus coelestinus
FAMILY:
Parrotfish - Scaridae

SIZE: 1-2 ft., max. 3 ft.
DEPTH: 15-240 ft.

L. CAYMAN

175

DISTINCTIVE FEATURES: TP: 1. Orange-brown head. 2. Bright green rear body. IP: Scale centers shades of green, edges orangish. **3. Tail squared.**

DESCRIPTION: Greenish beak. With age head becomes blunter and tips of tail grow longer. The amount of orange-brown versus green on TP varies between individuals.

ABUNDANCE & DISTRIBUTION: Occasional South Florida, Bahamas, Caribbean; also Bermuda and south to Argentina. Not reported northern Gulf of Mexico.

HABITAT & BEHAVIOR: Swim about reefs; stop to scrape algae from rocks and coral. Often inhabit caves and holes.

REACTION TO DIVERS: Appear unconcerned, but shy away when closely approached.

NOTE ABOUT JUVENILE: Brown with two indistinct stripes on side, belly lighter. Rarely observed.

**Queen Parrotfish
Initial Phase**

SIZE: 2¹/₂-10 in.,
max. 12 in.

ANGUILLA

DISTINCTIVE FEATURES: TP: 1. Dramatic blue to green markings around mouth. 2. Light bar on pectoral fin. IP: Dark gray to black. **3. Broad, white stripe, with diffuse edges, down midbody.**

DESCRIPTION: Green to blue-green. May have yellow markings around mouth and stripe at base of dorsal and anal fins; tail may have light crescent marking.

ABUNDANCE & DISTRIBUTION: Common South Florida, Bahamas, Caribbean; also Bermuda.

HABITAT & BEHAVIOR: Swim about reefs; stop to scrape algae from rocks and coral.

REACTION TO DIVERS: Appear unconcerned, but shy away when closely approached.

RAINBOW PARROTFISH
Scarus guacamaia
Terminal Phase
FAMILY:
Parrotfish - Scaridae

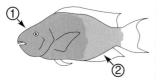

SIZE: 1½-3 ft., max. 4 ft.
DEPTH: 10-80 ft.

COZUMEL

Rainbow Parrotfish
Initial Phase

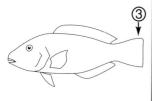

BONAIRE

QUEEN PARROTFISH
Scarus vetula
Terminal Phase
FAMILY:
Parrotfish - Scaridae

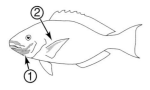

SIZE: 12-16 in., max. 2 ft.
DEPTH: 10-80 ft.

CAYMAN

Parrotfish

DISTINCTIVE FEATURES: TP: 1. Bright yellow spot at upper corner of gill cover. 2. Yellow area at base of tail. 3. Salmon to yellow crescent on tail. IP: 4. Red belly and tail. JP: 5. Three rows of widely spaced white spots run length of body.

DESCRIPTION: TP: Emerald green. Salmon to yellow markings on head and fins. Tail is crescent-shaped. IP: Upper body and head mottled reddish brown, often mixed with white scales and crescent on tail. JP: Body dark reddish brown with lighter belly. White bar on tail.

ABUNDANCE & DISTRIBUTION: Common to occasional Florida, Bahamas, Caribbean; also Bermuda, eastern Gulf of Mexico and south to Brazil.

HABITAT & BEHAVIOR: Swim about reefs; stop to scrape algae from rocks and coral.

REACTION TO DIVERS: Appear unconcerned, but shy away when closely approached.

**Stoplight Parrotfish
Initial Phase**

④

SIZE: 5 - 10 in., max. 1 ft.

CAYMAN

DISTINCTIVE FEATURES: TP: 1. Borders of tail yellow to orange or pink. 2. Yellow or orangish stripe down midbody, fading toward rear. IP & JP: 3. Borders of tail dark. (Similar Striped Parrotfish, *S. iserti*, [next] distinguished by lack of markings on borders of tail.)

DESCRIPTION: TP: Blue to green. Two blue to green stripes extend from snout and pass across eye; distinct yellow or orange or pink stripe runs length of dorsal fin. JP: Three black stripes, two white stripes and white belly, often with thin silver stripes. IP: With maturity stripes fade and become brown. Fins often become yellowish.

ABUNDANCE & DISTRIBUTION: Common to occasional South Florida, Bahamas, Caribbean; also Bermuda and south to Brazil.

HABITAT & BEHAVIOR: Swim about reefs; stop to scrape algae from rocks and coral. IP & JP often mix with similar age Striped Parrotfish [next].

REACTION TO DIVERS: Appear unconcerned, but shy away when closely approached.

STOPLIGHT PARROTFISH
Sparisoma viride
Terminal Phase
FAMILY:
Parrotfish - Scaridae

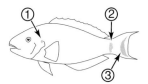

SIZE: 1-1½ ft., max. 2 ft.
DEPTH: 15-80 ft.

L. CAYMAN

Stoplight Parrotfish Juvenile

SIZE: 2-5 in., max. 6 in.

CAYMAN

PRINCESS PARROTFISH
Scarus taeniopterus
Terminal Phase
FAMILY:
Parrotfish - Scaridae

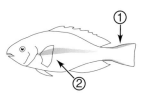

SIZE: 8-10 in., max. 13 in.
DEPTH: 10-80 ft.

ANGUILLA

continued next page **179**

Princess Parrotfish
Initial Phase

SIZE: 5 - 7 ½ in.

ST. LUCIA

DISTINCTIVE FEATURES: TP: 1. Dark blue or green tail has pink, yellow or orangish linear markings between borders. 2. Gold to yellow spot or stripe above and behind pectoral fin. IP & JP: 3. No dark marking on borders of tail. (Similar Princess Parrotfish, *S. taeniopterus*, [previous] distinguished by dark borders on tail.)

DESCRIPTION: TP: Blue to green. Dorsal fin has distinct pink, yellow or orangish stripe down the middle that is broken by blue to green linear markings. **IP & JP:** Three black stripes, two white stripes and white belly, often with thin, broken silver, yellow or dark stripes. Usually yellow smudge on nose; occasionally yellow ventral fins and/or belly and/or tail.

ABUNDANCE & DISTRIBUTION: Common Florida, Bahamas, Caribbean; also Bermuda, Gulf of Mexico.

HABITAT & BEHAVIOR: Swim about reefs; stop to scrape algae from rocks and coral. IP & JP often mix with similar age Princess Parrotfish [previous]. IP with yellow ventral fins are thought to be territorial females.

REACTION TO DIVERS: Appear unconcerned, but shy away when closely approached.

DRY TORTUGAS, FL

DRY TORTUGAS, FL

Princess Parrotfish
Juvenile

*continued from
previous page*

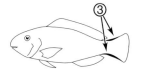

SIZE: 2-4 in.

ST. LUCIA

STRIPED PARROTFISH
Scarus croicensis
Terminal Phase
FAMILY:
Parrotfish - Scaridae

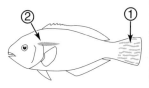

SIZE: 8-9 in., max. 10 in.
DEPTH: 10-80 ft.

ROATAN

Striped Parrotfish
Juvenile/Initial Phase
[right]
Note yellow smudge on nose.

Terminal Phase [far left]
*With gold stripe behind
pectoral fin.*

Initial Phase [left]
With yellow tail.

ROATAN

181

DISTINCTIVE FEATURES: TP: 1. Small yellow blotch with two or more small black spots on upper forebody. 2. Usually salmon to orange or yellow band from corner of mouth to below eye. **IP & JP:** 3. White spot behind dorsal fin (also often present on TP).

DESCRIPTION: TP: Greenish overall, underside lighter; anal fin usually reddish. Outer tips of tail black. Tail square-cut. **IP:** Highly variable, from solid olive to green to blue-green body with red fins to mottled browns with two white stripes. **JP:** Shades of red-brown, usually with two white stripes and black blotch behind upper gill cover. Both IP & JP can rapidly fade, intensify or change color and markings.

ABUNDANCE & DISTRIBUTION: Common to occasional Florida, Bahamas, Caribbean; also Bermuda and south to Brazil.

HABITAT & BEHAVIOR: Swim about reefs; stop to scrape algae from rocks and coral.

REACTION TO DIVERS: Appear unconcerned, but shy away when closely approached.

**Redband Parrotfish
Intermediate,
Juvenile/Initial Phase**
Displaying mottled stripes.

SIZE: 2¹/₂-6 in., max. 6 in.

CAYMAN

ROATAN

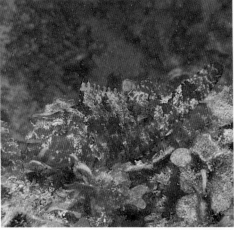
HOLLYWOOD, FL

REDBAND PARROTFISH
Sparisoma aurofrenatum
Terminal Phase
FAMILY:
Parrotfish - Scaridae

SIZE: 6-10 in., max. 11 in.
DEPTH: 10-60 ft.

ANGUILLA

Redband Parrotfish Initial Phase
Solid body color with red fins.

SIZE: 2½-6 in., max. 6 in.

CAYMAN

Redband Parrotfish
Juvenile [right]
Striped pattern with black blotch behind gill cover.

Initial Phase [far left]
Striped pattern.

Juvenile [left]
Mottled (camouflage) phase.

SIZE: 1½-2½ in., max. 3 in.

ANGUILLA

Parrotfish

DISTINCTIVE FEATURES: TP: 1. Turquoise to blue area behind pectoral fin and belly. 2. Reddish crescent on margin of tail. 3. Pectoral fins clear with black blotch at base. **IP:** Reddish overall, including tail.

DESCRIPTION: TP: Olive to green to bluish green; fins often shades of red to yellow. **IP:** Reddish gray. Can rapidly fade, intensify or change color.

ABUNDANCE & DISTRIBUTION: IP common, TP occasional South Florida, Bahamas, Caribbean; also south to Brazil.

HABITAT & BEHAVIOR: Prefer shallow areas of coral rubble and sea grass, occasionally on reefs. May lie on bottom.

REACTION TO DIVERS: Shy; tend to keep their distance. Difficult to closely approach.

Yellowtail Parrotfish
Initial Phase

SIZE: 8-12 in., max. 14 in.

KEY LARGO, FL

DISTINCTIVE FEATURES: TP: Shades of green to blue overall. **1. Basal two-thirds of pectoral fin dusky with black blotch at base. 2. Central tail yellow to white with pale translucent to transparent margin. IP: 3. Base of tail and tail pale to bright yellow. 4. Ventral and anal fins red.**

DESCRIPTION: TP: May be somewhat mottled; belly often lighter shades of green to blue-green. **IP:** Mottled gray to brown. Can rapidly fade, intensify or change color.

ABUNDANCE & DISTRIBUTION: IP common to abundant, TP uncommon Florida, Bahamas, Caribbean; also north to Massachusetts, Bermuda and south to Brazil. Not reported Gulf of Mexico.

HABITAT & BEHAVIOR: Prefer shallow areas of coral rubble and sea grass, occasionally on reefs. May lie on the bottom.

REACTION TO DIVERS: Shy; tend to keep their distance. Difficult to approach; if chased, may disappear into surf.

NOTE: Also commonly known as "Redfin Parrotfish."

REDTAIL PARROTFISH
Sparisoma chrysopterum
Terminal Phase
FAMILY:
Parrotfish - Scaridae

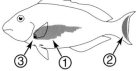

SIZE: 14-16 in.,
max. 18 in.
DEPTH: 5-40 ft.

BIMINI

Redtail Parrotfish
Initial Phase

SIZE: 8-14 in., max. 16 in.

ROATAN

YELLOWTAIL PARROTFISH
Sparisoma rubripinne
Terminal Phase
FAMILY:
Parrotfish - Scaridae

SIZE: 8-14 in, max. 1½ ft.
DEPTH: 3-35 ft.

ROATAN

DISTINCTIVE FEATURES: ALL PHASES: 1. Yellow-gold eye. TP: 2. Faint pale to dusky or dark blotch above pectoral fin. IP: Red overall. JP: 3. Lower half of body striped. 4. Faint yellowing at base of pectoral fin.

DESCRIPTION: TP: Shades of green to blue-green, may be mottled and/or have reddish tints. **IP:** Often bright red (may appear brown in ambient light at depth), occasionally dull red to yellowish red and may be somewhat mottled. **JP:** Upper head has yellow-gold wash; upper body brown to yellowish red, may be indistinctly striped; belly white. All phases can fade, intensify or change color and markings rapidly.

ABUNDANCE & DISTRIBUTION: Occasional South Florida, Bahamas, Caribbean; also Bermuda.

HABITAT & BEHAVIOR: Inhabit mid-range to deep reefs; often along steep, sloping drop-offs.

REACTION TO DIVERS: Appear unconcerned, but shy away when closely approached.

ST. LUCIA

ST. LUCIA

DISTINCTIVE FEATURES: TP: 1. Black margin on tail and anal fin. 2. Black pectoral fin base. IP: 3. Bluish pectoral fin base.

DESCRIPTION: Highly variable combinations of mottling, blotches, patches and stripes in shades of earthtones. Can change color and markings rapidly to match most backgrounds.

ABUNDANCE & DISTRIBUTION: Common to occasional Florida, Bahamas, Caribbean; also Bermuda and Gulf of Mexico.

HABITAT & BEHAVIOR: Prefer sea grass beds, occasionally in coral rubble near sea grasses, rarely on reefs. IP often lie on bottom blending with background. TP swim about rapidly, just above grass beds.

REACTION TO DIVERS: Shy when swimming; move away upon approach. Slow nonthreatening movements occasionally enable close approach. When resting on bottom they do not move, apparently relying on camouflage. Generally, IP is easy to approach, while TP is very difficult to approach.

GREENBLOTCH PARROTFISH
Sparisoma atomarium
Terminal Phase
Initial Phase
FAMILY:
Parrotfish - Scaridae

SIZE: 3 ¹/₂-4 in.,
max. 4¹/₂ in.
DEPTH: 50-180 ft.

ANGUILLA

Greenblotch Parrotfish
Juvenile [right]

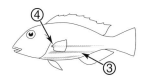

Terminal Phase [left]
Color varieties.

SIZE: 1¹/₂-2¹/₂ in.

CAYMAN

BUCKTOOTH PARROTFISH
Sparisoma radians
Terminal Phase
FAMILY:
Parrotfish - Scaridae

SIZE: 3-5 in.,
max. 7¹/₂ in.
DEPTH: 3-35 ft.

BIMINI

continued next page
187

Parrotfish

Bucktooth Parrotfish
Initial Phase
Mottled pattern to blend with background.

DISTINCTIVE FEATURES: ALL PHASES: Very slender body. **1. Stripe from eye to tail; TP rose to pink or lilac; IP dark brown to light reddish brown. TP: 2. Snout and nape green to turquoise or blue.**

DESCRIPTION: TP: Generally shades of green to blue. Display brilliant yellow or orange in area of pectoral when mating [right]. **IP:** Usually pale undercolor with stripes in shades of green-brown to reddish brown or dark brown, occasionally somewhat mottled.

ABUNDANCE & DISTRIBUTION: Occasional South Florida, Bahamas, Caribbean; also Bermuda and south to Brazil.

HABITAT & BEHAVIOR: Prefer shallow sea grass beds, occasionally in coral rubble or around stands of gorgonians, rarely deep or on reefs. Swim about rapidly, only occasionally stopping to nibble on sea grasses. IP often in pairs.

REACTION TO DIVERS: Act unconcerned, but move about at such a rapid pace they are difficult to approach.

NOTE: Also commonly called "Rosy Parrotfish" and "Slender Parrotfish."

Bucktooth Parrotfish Initial Phase
continued from previous page

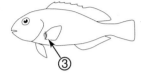

SIZE: 2-4 in.

ANGUILLA

BLUELIP PARROTFISH
Cryptotomus roseus
Terminal Phase
FAMILY:
Parrotfish - Scaridae

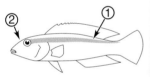

SIZE: 2¹/₂-3¹/₂ in.,
max. 5 in.
DEPTH: 3-180 ft.

ANGUILLA

Bluelip Parrotfish Initial Phase
[right and near left]

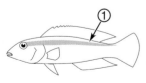

Terminal Phase [far left]
Normal coloration.

ST. LUCIA

DISTINCTIVE FEATURES: 1. First three spines of dorsal fin are long. 2. Black blotch near end of dorsal fin.

DESCRIPTION: Vary from pearl white to mottled or banded reddish brown; large, dusky to dark area covering snout and nape to foredorsal fin. Large adults develop a pronounced snout; have a wide black bar across the central tail; and tend to lose the black blotch near end of dorsal fin.

ABUNDANCE & DISTRIBUTION: Common to occasional Florida, Bahamas, Caribbean (rare in some areas because of spearfishing); also north to North Carolina, Bermuda and Gulf of Mexico.

HABITAT & BEHAVIOR: Most common on open bottoms, occasionally on reefs. Swim constantly; occasionally stop to dig in bottom material in search of food. Tend to display reddish brown mottled or banded phase when rooting in bottom.

REACTION TO DIVERS: In non-spearfishing areas, generally unafraid, and may even approach divers.

Hogfish
Intermediate displaying normal swimming coloration.

CAYMAN

DISTINCTIVE FEATURES: 1. Purple upper forebody. 2. Yellow-gold belly and tail.

DESCRIPTION: Purple may become reddish. Large adults become mottled purplish yellow.

ABUNDANCE & DISTRIBUTION: Common to occasional South Florida, Bahamas, Caribbean; also Bermuda, Gulf of Mexico and south to Brazil.

HABITAT & BEHAVIOR: Constantly swim about reefs.

REACTION TO DIVERS: Appear unafraid. Often allow a close approach.

NOTE ABOUT JUVENILE: Have purple head and forebody; as they mature, purple area becomes restricted to upper forebody. Often work as cleaners, removing parasites and debris from larger fish.

HOGFISH
Lachnolaimus maximus
FAMILY:
Hogfish/Wrasse -
Labridae

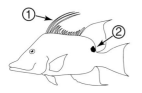

SIZE: 1-2 ft., max. 3 ft.
DEPTH: 10-100 ft.

BELIZE

Hogfish
*Young displaying
mottled phase.*

WEST PALM BEACH, FL

SPANISH HOGFISH
Bodianus rufus
FAMILY:
Hogfish/Wrasse -
Labridae

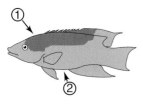

SIZE: 8-14 in., max. 2 ft.
DEPTH: 10-100 ft.

CAYMAN

191

DISTINCTIVE FEATURES: ADULT: 1. Bright yellow rear dorsal fin, upper base of tail and tail. 2. Dark area at outer tip of pectoral fin. INTERMEDIATE: 3. Bright yellow from rear dorsal anal fins to tail. 4. White stripe begins under mouth, runs across pectoral fin and onto body. (Stripe persists well into adulthood.) **JUVENILE:** Bright yellow. **5. Black blotch on foredorsal fin.**

DESCRIPTION: ADULT: Red body. **INTERMEDIATE:** Dark maroon to blackish upper and lower body. All phases have two dusky to dark bands running from eye across gill cover.

ABUNDANCE & DISTRIBUTION: Common Florida; occasional Bahamas; uncommon to rare Caribbean.

HABITAT & BEHAVIOR: Constantly swim about reefs. **JUVENILE:** Often school with juvenile Blueheads. May act as cleaners, removing parasites and debris from larger fish.

REACTION TO DIVERS: Appear unconcerned. Often allow close approach.

Spotfin Hogfish
Intermediate

SIZE: 2-4 in.

MIAMI, FL

DISTINCTIVE FEATURES: TP & IP: Dark purple to violet or lavender. **1. Snout usually dark purple. TP: 2. Older individuals develop yellow to reddish areas on lower rear body. JP: 3. Series of spots or short bands along back composed of dark and light dots.**

DESCRIPTION: Upper body often darker. Does not have the dramatic color phases of other wrasse; younger, sexually mature TP are identical in appearance to IP.

ABUNDANCE & DISTRIBUTION: Abundant Caribbean; common Florida and Bahamas; also north to North Carolina; Bermuda and Gulf of Mexico.

HABITAT & BEHAVIOR: Prefer deep, outer reefs, especially the edges of drop-offs. Swim constantly, often in open water above reefs, in small groups to large schools. Commonly form long streaming schools along drop-offs in late afternoon.

REACTION TO DIVERS: Virtually ignore divers.

SPOTFIN HOGFISH
Bodianus pulchellus
Adult
FAMILY:
Hogfish/Wrasse -
Labridae

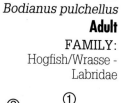

SIZE: 4½-7½ in.,
max. 9 in.
DEPTH: 60-360 ft.

MIAMI, FL

Spotfin Hogfish
Juvenile

SIZE: 1-2 in.

BIMINI

CREOLE WRASSE
Clepticus parrae
FAMILY:
Wrasse - Labridae

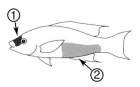

SIZE: 4-7 in., max. 1 ft.
DEPTH: 30-80 ft.

BIMINI

continued next page **193**

Creole Wrasse
Initial Phase

ROATAN

DISTINCTIVE FEATURES: TP & IP: Blue to green. **TP: 1.** Yellowish margin on tail. **2.** Dark dot at base of pectoral fin. **IP & JP: 3.** Five white bars or dots across upper back. **JP: 4.** Two yellow to gold stripes down midbody with white stripe between. **5.** Navy to blue spot on mid-back and dorsal fin.

DESCRIPTION: TP: Greenish blue scrawls on head; may have white midbody bar. **IP:** Young are yellowish green to bluish green with areas of yellow gold; one or two black rectangular areas on back.

ABUNDANCE & DISTRIBUTION: Occasional Florida, Bahamas, Caribbean; also north to North Carolina, Bermuda, Gulf of Mexico and south to Brazil.

HABITAT & BEHAVIOR: Constantly swim about reefs.

REACTION TO DIVERS: Shy; tend to keep their distance. Often the best way to get a close view is to quietly wait in a concealed position near their course of travel.

WEST PALM BEACH, FL

ROATAN

194

**Creole Wrasse
Juvenile**

*continued from
previous page*

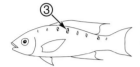

ANGUILLA

PUDDINGWIFE
Halichoeres radiatus
Terminal Phase
FAMILY:
Wrasse - Labridae

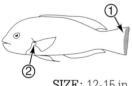

SIZE: 12-15 in.,
max. 18 in.
DEPTH: 10-50 ft.

CAYMAN

**Puddingwife
Initial Phase**
[right]

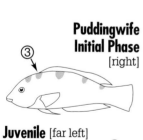

Juvenile [far left]

**Intermediate
Juvenile/Initial Phase**
[near left]

CAYMAN

195

DISTINCTIVE FEATURES: TP: 1. Yellow head and forebody. 2. Dark midbody bar. TP & IP: 3. Two wavy lines radiate from rear upper eye. IP: 4. Dark to dusky back, often shaded with blue. 5. Yellow belly. JP: Usually bright yellow; rarely shading to reddish gold. 6. Brilliant blue midbody stripe.

DESCRIPTION: TP: Head and forebody vary from bright yellow to yellowish or greenish tan; dark blue to green rear body and tail. Dark midbody bar continues as a wide border along back to tail. **IP:** Color shadings highly variable, especially intermediates between TP and JP.

ABUNDANCE & DISTRIBUTION: Common Florida, Bahamas, Caribbean; also Bermuda, Gulf of Mexico and south to Brazil.

HABITAT & BEHAVIOR: Constantly swim about reefs.

REACTION TO DIVERS: Appear unconcerned, but tend to keep their distance. Can often be approached by moving into their direction of travel.

ST. LUCIA

ROATAN

CAYMAN

ST. LUCIA

YELLOWHEAD WRASSE
Halichoeres garnoti
Terminal Phase
FAMILY:
Wrasse - Labridae

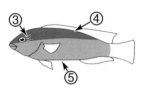

SIZE: 5-6 in., max. 8 in.
DEPTH: 10-50 ft.

ST. LUCIA

**Yellowhead Wrasse
Initial Phase**
[right]

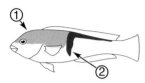

**Intermediate or Young
Terminal Phase** [far left]
**Intermediate or Older
Initial Phase** [near left]

BARBADOS

**Yellowhead Wrasse
Juvenile** [right]

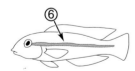

**Intermediate
Juvenile/Initial Phase**
[far left]

Juvenile
*Unique reddish gold
color phase.* [near left]

L. CAYMAN

Wrasse

DISTINCTIVE FEATURES: TP: 1. Blue head. 2. Two dark bars behind head, separated by white bar. IP & JP: 3. Black spot behind second dorsal ray extends to base of fin. (Mimic Wrasse Blenny, distinguished by spot behind third dorsal ray that does not extend to base of fin.)

DESCRIPTION: TP: Rear body is green to blue-green. **IP &JP:** Cannot be distinguished by color pattern or size. They display three basic phases, all with white belly, and can change from one to the other rapidly, with intermediate color patterns between: **a.** White bars break dark midbody stripe into series of rectangular blotches; back yellowish to greenish or bluish. **b.** Solid, dark midbody stripe runs from snout to tail; over reefs, back is usually yellow, over sand or rubble back is usually white. **c.** Yellow head and body above belly; two squarish spots behind eye; no midbody stripe.

ABUNDANCE & DISTRIBUTION: Very common Caribbean; common South Florida and Bahamas; also Bermuda and southern Gulf of Mexico.

HABITAT & BEHAVIOR: Constantly swim about reefs. **IP & JP:** In all phases, individuals as small as 1½ inches can be sexually mature females or males; however, the broken midbody stripe pattern usually occurs only in larger individuals and probably does not include juveniles. May act as cleaners, removing parasites and debris from larger fish. Often swim about reefs in schools.

REACTION TO DIVERS: Appear unconcerned; often swim within close range.

Bluehead
Initial Phase

Broken midbody stripe pattern, bluish back.

SIZE: 3-5 in.

CAYMAN

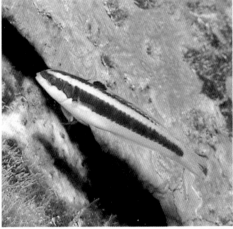

ANGUILLA

ANGUILLA

BLUEHEAD
*Thalassoma
bifasciatum*
Terminal Phase
FAMILY:
Wrasse - Labridae

SIZE: 4-5 in., max. 6 in.
DEPTH: 6-80 ft.

CAYMAN

Bluehead
Initial Phase

*Broken midbody stripe
pattern, yellowish back.*

SIZE: 3-5 in.

NASSAU

Bluehead
Juvenile/Initial Phase

All yellow pattern. [right]

*Midbody stripe pattern with
white back.* [far left]

*Midbody stripe pattern with
yellow back.* [near left]

SIZE: 1-5 in.

CAYMAN

199

DISTINCTIVE FEATURES: ALL PHASES: 1. Small green and yellow bicolored spot above pectoral fin. **2.** Darkish to black midbody stripe; a second, lower stripe is less distinct (often absent in JP). **TP: 3.** Dark triangular corners on tail.

DESCRIPTION: TP: Shades of green. **IP:** Colors and markings vary greatly, ranging from shades of green to medium brown. **JP:** Usually white. Most individuals have a small dark spot at the rear base of the pectoral fin; many JP and young IP display a small black spot or large blue dot on middorsal fin.

ABUNDANCE & DISTRIBUTION: Very common to occasional Florida, Bahamas, Caribbean; also north to North Carolina, Bermuda, Gulf of Mexico and south to Brazil.

HABITAT & BEHAVIOR: Constantly swim about reefs, adjacent sand areas and grass beds.

REACTION TO DIVERS: Appear unconcerned, but tend to keep their distance. Can often be approached by moving into their direction of travel.

ANGUILLA

CAYMAN

JACKSONVILLE, FL

SARASOTA, FL

SLIPPERY DICK
Halichoeres bivittatus
Terminal Phase
FAMILY:
Wrasse - Labridae

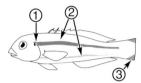

SIZE: 5¹/₂-7 in., max. 9 in.
DEPTH: 6-40 ft.

ST. LUCIA

**Slippery Dick
Initial Phase**
[right]

**Intermediate
Initial Phase/
Terminal Phase** [left]

NASSAU

**Slippery Dick
Juvenile**
[right]

**Intermediate
Juvenile/Initial Phase**
[left]

ANGUILLA

201

DISTINCTIVE FEATURES: TP & IP: 1. Three red line markings across top of head and two U-shaped lines on snout. **TP: 2.** Dark midbody blotch. **IP: 3.** Two dark spots on foredorsal fin merge to form an elongated oval in TP. **JP: 4.** Thin yellow-gold stripe runs from snout, above eye, to tail, with a wider black stripe below.

DESCRIPTION: TP & IP: A variety of markings and shadings in green, blue, violet, rose, orange and yellow; pale underside. **JP:** White underside.

ABUNDANCE & DISTRIBUTION: Common to uncommon Florida, Bahamas, Caribbean; also north to North Carolina, Bermuda and south to Brazil.

HABITAT & BEHAVIOR: Constantly swim about reefs.

REACTION TO DIVERS: Appear unconcerned, but keep their distance. Can often be approached by moving into their direction of travel.

Clown Wrasse
Intermediate,
Terminal/Initial Phase

ANGUILLA

Clown Wrasse
Intermediate,
Initial/Juvenile Phase
Note red lines
across top of head.

ANGUILLA

CLOWN WRASSE
Halichoeres maculipinna
Terminal Phase
FAMILY:
Wrasse - Labridae

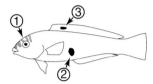

SIZE: 3-5 in., max. 6½ in.
DEPTH: 10-40 ft.

CAYMAN

Clown Wrasse Initial Phase

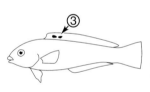

BELIZE

Clown Wrasse Juvenile

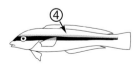

ANGUILLA

DISTINCTIVE FEATURES: ALL PHASES: 1. Small, orange to purplish red spot adjacent to upper rear of eye. **2.** Black spot at base of rear dorsal fin. **TP: 3.** Purplish red diagonal bands form "V" in tail, with stripe in center. **IP & JP:** Shades of green to chartreuse.

DESCRIPTION: TP: Shades of green to purplish brown, often with orangish shading or bands on forebody. **ALL PHASES:** Have ability to pale or darken overall color rapidly. Can quickly display or conceal a black spot between eye and edge of gill cover (source of the common name); occasionally have small black spot on middorsal fin and another on the base of the tail. There are no visual distinctions between IP and JP.

ABUNDANCE & DISTRIBUTION: Common to uncommon Florida, Bahamas, Caribbean; also south to Brazil.

HABITAT & BEHAVIOR: Inhabit grass beds and shallow reefs. Actively swim about reefs, but in grass beds may remain still, hiding among blades.

REACTION TO DIVERS: Appear unconcerned, but keep their distance. Can often be approached by moving into their direction of travel.

KEY LARGO, FL   BIMINI

DISTINCTIVE FEATURES: TP: 1. Black blotch on base of tail. **2.** Orange streak on center of tail. **3.** Blue stripes on head above and below eye. **IP: 4.** Black to dark brown stripe from snout, through eye, to tail, becomes less distinct toward tail, especially in JP. **5.** Pale brown stripe below dorsal fin. (Similar IP Bluehead, *Thalassoma bifasciatum*, [pg. 199] and Wrasse Blenny, *Hemiemblemaria simulus*, [pg. 273] distinguished by black spot on foredorsal fin.) **JP: 6.** Black stripe runs from between eyes to dorsal fin.

DESCRIPTION: TP: Shades of blue green to green on upper forebody; bluish midbody stripe; pale bluish underside; orange to red dorsal fin. **IP & JP:** Yellow-brown back; white underside.

ABUNDANCE & DISTRIBUTION: Uncommon Bahamas, Caribbean; rare South Florida; also south to Brazil.

HABITAT & BEHAVIOR: Actively swim about reefs.

REACTION TO DIVERS: Appear unconcerned, but keep their distance. Can often be approached by moving into their direction of travel.

NOTE: Also commonly known as "Painted Wrasse."

BLACKEAR WRASSE
Halichoeres poeyi
Terminal Phase
FAMILY:
Wrasse - Labridae

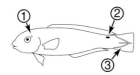

SIZE: 4 - 5½ in., max. 8 in.
DEPTH: 3-30 ft.

ANGUILLA

Blackear Wrasse
Initial Phase / Juvenile
*With black spots on dorsal
fin and base of tail.* [right]

*Without black spots on
dorsal fin and base of tail.*
[near left]

Terminal Phase [far left]
Displaying "black ear".

WEST PALM BEACH, FL

RAINBOW WRASSE
Halichoeres pictus
Terminal Phase
FAMILY:
Wrasse - Labridae

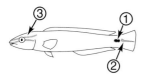

SIZE: 4 - 5½ in., max. 7 in.
DEPTH: 15 - 80 ft.

BELIZE

continued next page **205**

BELIZE

DRY TORTUGAS, FL

DISTINCTIVE FEATURES: ALL PHASES: 1. Yellow runs from mouth across nape to foredorsal fin, and brilliant blue below. **TP: 2.** Two wavy lines radiate from upper rear of eye. **JP: 3.** Deep blue spot on middorsal fin and another on base of tail.

DESCRIPTION: TP: White belly. **IP:** Have lost spots of JP and have not developed eye lines of TP. **JP:** Below the yellow head and back, young may be brown to tan rather than blue.

ABUNDANCE & DISTRIBUTION: Uncommon to rare South Florida, Bahamas, Caribbean.

HABITAT & BEHAVIOR: Continuously swim about reefs. Rarely shallower than 60 feet.

REACTION TO DIVERS: Tend to be unafraid. Often allow a close approach.

Yellowcheek Wrasse
Initial Phase

DRY TORTUGAS, FL

Rainbow Wrasse
Juvenile [right]
continued from previous page

Initial Phase [near left]

Intermediate, Initial/Terminal Phases
[far left]

CAYMAN

YELLOWCHEEK WRASSE
Halichoeres cyanocephalus
Terminal Phase
FAMILY:
Wrasse - Labridae

SIZE: 2½-4½ in.,
max. 6 in.
DEPTH: 60-130 ft.

DRY TORTUGAS, FL

Yellowcheek Wrasse
Juvenile

DRY TORTUGAS, FL

207

DISTINCTIVE FEATURES: 1. Pointed head and mouth. 2. Unlike other wrasses, fore part of dorsal fin (first three spines) is tall and distinct.

DESCRIPTION: Vary from green to tan; scattered white and yellowish to reddish brown markings. May display faint bars. Can change color and pale or darken dramatically.

ABUNDANCE & DISTRIBUTION: Uncommon Florida, Bahamas, Caribbean; also Bermuda and eastern Atlantic.

HABITAT & BEHAVIOR: Inhabit shallow water. Hide in and around sea grasses and other bottom growth. Change color to blend with background.

REACTION TO DIVERS: Remain still, apparently relying on their camouflage and allow a close approach. When aware of detection they dart away to new hiding spot.

NOTE: Pictured specimen was photographed out of water after being netted in sea grass bed.

DISTINCTIVE FEATURES: ALL PHASES: 1. Margin of tail rounded. **MALE:** 2. Dark spot (occasionally two) at midbody. **FEMALE:** No distinctive marks (may have bars). **JUVENILE:** 3. First two dorsal spines are long, with pigmented tissue between. 4. Clear dorsal fin with two or three pigmented bars, the rear two of which correspond to similar bars in the anal fin.

DESCRIPTION: ALL PHASES: Colors vary greatly, but most commonly have greenish cast. May have bars and markings ranging from reddish brown to yellow, green and white. Eyes have a bright red iris and green pupil.

ABUNDANCE & DISTRIBUTION: Occasional Florida, Bahamas, Caribbean; also Bermuda and south to Brazil.

HABITAT & BEHAVIOR: Hover above shallow, sandy bottoms, often near rocks, gorgonians or other cover. May hide in sea grasses or algae. Often curl body to blend with background. Dive into sand when alarmed.

REACTION TO DIVERS: Keep their distance by moving away; if threatened, quickly dive into the sand. If a diver waits quietly for several minutes, fish may re-emerge.

NOTE: Formerly classified in genus *Hemipteronotus*.

BELIZE

WEST PALM BEACH, FL

DWARF WRASSE
Doratonotus megalepis
FAMILY:
Wrasse - Labridae

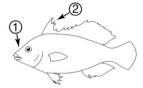

SIZE: 1½-2½ in.,
max. 3 in.
DEPTH: 4-30 ft.

JUPITER, FL

GREEN RAZORFISH
Xyrichtys splendens
Male
FAMILY:
Razorfish/Wrasse - Labridae

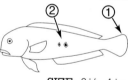

SIZE: 2½- 4 in.,
max. 5½ in.
DEPTH: 5 - 35 ft.

CAYMAN

Green Razorfish
Juvenile [right]

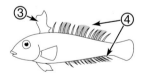

SIZE: ¾-1½ in.

Female
Without bars. [far left]
Displaying bars and curling body. [near left]

SIZE: 1½- 3½ in.

KEY LARGO, FL

Wrasse

DISTINCTIVE FEATURES: ALL PHASES: 1. Margin of tail straight. **MALE: 2.** Darkened area at base of pectoral fin. **FEMALE: 3.** White belly patch with reddish line markings. **4.** Darkish bar on gill cover.

DESCRIPTION: MALE: Mixture of pastel green, blue and yellow. Head usually pale yellow with faint bars. **FEMALE:** Pearl white head. Grayish to rosy-pearl body. Brownish body bar is lost with maturity.

ABUNDANCE & DISTRIBUTION: Common Florida, Bahamas, Caribbean.

HABITAT & BEHAVIOR: Hover above sandy areas. Often near or in sea grass patches, especially manatee grass. If alarmed, can dive into the sand and occasionally tunnel underneath for some distance.

REACTION TO DIVERS: Keep their distance by moving away; if threatened, quickly dive into the sand. If diver waits quietly for several minutes, fish may re-emerge.

NOTE: Formerly classified in genus *Hemipteronotus*.

**Pearly Razorfish
Female**

BONAIRE

DISTINCTIVE FEATURES: ALL PHASES: 1. Extremely steep snout gives head a squared-off appearance. **2.** Small eyes set high up on head. **MALE: 3.** Wide, diagonal, dusky or reddish band on side. **FEMALE: 4.** Pearly white area on upper belly.

DESCRIPTION: ALL PHASES: Commonly pearly white, often with tints of, or occasionally shaded, blue to green, rose or orange to yellow. **JUVENILES:** Have four diffuse, dark body bars.

ABUNDANCE & DISTRIBUTION: Occasional Florida, Bahamas, Caribbean; also north to North Carolina, Gulf of Mexico and south to Brazil.

HABITAT & BEHAVIOR: Hover above shallow sand and coral rubble bottoms. Build nests of coral rubble. Can dive into sand when alarmed.

REACTION TO DIVERS: Keep their distance by moving away; if threatened, quickly dive into the sand.

NOTE: Formerly classified in genus *Hemipteronotus*.

ROSY RAZORFISH
Xyrichtys
martinicensis
Male
FAMILY:
Razorfish/Wrasse -
Labridae

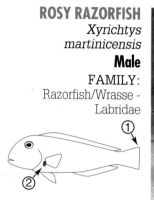

SIZE: 3 - 4 1/2 in., max. 6 in.
DEPTH: 5 - 45 ft.

BELIZE

Rosy Razorfish
Female

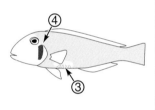

SIZE: 2 1/2 - 3 1/2 in.,
max. 4 1/2 in.

CAYMAN

PEARLY RAZORFISH
Xyrichtys
novacula
Male
FAMILY:
Razorfish/Wrasse -
Labridae

SIZE: 5 - 10 in., max. 15 in.
DEPTH: 10 - 100 ft.

BONAIRE

Reddish/Big Eyes
Cardinalfish – Squirrelfish – Bigeye

This ID Group consists of fish that range in color from pale red to reddish brown and have large eyes. They are generally nocturnal feeders, and usually hide in dark recesses during the day.

FAMILY: Squirrelfish — Holocentridae
8 Species Included

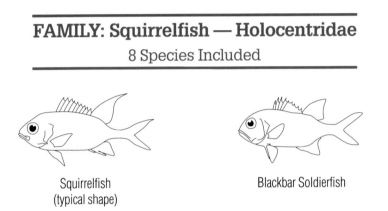

Squirrelfish
(typical shape)

Blackbar Soldierfish

This family of reddish fish, with large "squirrel-like" eyes and a long, pronounced rear dorsal fin that sticks up in a way reminiscent of a squirrel's tail, is among the most striking on the reef. Its members all have thin, white, and occasionally yellow-gold, body stripes (with the exception of soldierfish). Although nocturnally active, most are easily spotted on the reefs during the day. Exceptions are the Longjaw Squirrelfish, Blackbar and Cardinal Soldierfish that lurk during the day in dark recesses. At night, all feed in the open on invertebrates near the bottom. The species are similar in appearance, but each has distinctive features that make identification easy. Juvenile squirrelfish are thin, silvery pelagics, and are seldom seen.

FAMILY: Bigeye — Priacanthidae
3 Species Included

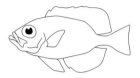

Bigeye
(typical shape)

The Bigeye and Glasseye Snapper, and occasionally the Short Bigeye, are the only members of this family found shallower than 130 feet. All are thin, reddish carnivores with large eyes and continuous dorsal fins. They grow to a foot in length.

FAMILY: Cardinalfish — Apogonidae
18 Species Included

Cardinalfish
(typical shape)

Cardinalfish are named for their reddish color. They are quite small (one-three inches), have large eyes, relatively short snouts, and two separate dorsal fins. Although common reef inhabitants, they are seldom spotted by divers because they hide during the day in protected recesses of the reef. Large groups of cardinalfish are occasionally found inside caves. A few species live in association with invertebrates such as tube sponges, anemones and queen conchs. At night they feed in the open on tiny fish and crustaceans. Black spots, dark body bars, eye markings, and their association with invertebrates are the keys to species identification.

Squirrelfish

DISTINCTIVE FEATURES: 1. Yellowish front dorsal fin.

DESCRIPTION: Reddish with light silvery stripes and occasional white patches on body. Elongated rear dorsal fin and upper lobe of tail. Largest squirrelfish.

ABUNDANCE & DISTRIBUTION: Common Florida, Bahamas, Caribbean; also north to North Carolina, Bermuda and south to Brazil.

HABITAT & BEHAVIOR: During day, drift inconspicuously in shaded areas near bottom. Most abundant on shallow patch reefs and wall tops.

REACTION TO DIVERS: Relatively unafraid. Allow close approach.

DISTINCTIVE FEATURES: 1. White triangular markings at tips of dorsal fin spines.

DESCRIPTION: Reddish with light silvery stripes and white patches on body. Elongated rear dorsal fin and upper lobe of tail.

ABUNDANCE & DISTRIBUTION: Common South Florida, Bahamas, Caribbean; also Bermuda.

HABITAT & BEHAVIOR: During day, drift inconspicuously in shaded areas near bottom.

REACTION TO DIVERS: Relatively unafraid. Allow close approach.

DISTINCTIVE FEATURES: 1. Black blotch on first dorsal fin runs from first spine to third or fourth spine.

DESCRIPTION: Reddish with light silvery body stripes (not separated by thin brown stripes as similar Deepwater Squirrelfish, *H. bullisi* [pg. 219]). Tips and base of front dorsal fin marked with white.

ABUNDANCE & DISTRIBUTION: Uncommon Florida, Bahamas, Caribbean; also Bermuda.

HABITAT & BEHAVIOR: Hide in small recesses, peeking out occasionally. Inhabit both shallow inshore and deep offshore reefs.

REACTION TO DIVERS: Shy; difficult to approach.

NOTE: Many ichthyologists believe the genus name should be *Sargocentron*.

SQUIRRELFISH
Holocentrus adscensionis

FAMILY:
Squirrelfish -
Holocentridae

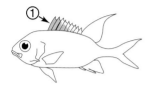

SIZE: 6-12 in., max. 16 in.
DEPTH: 4-40 ft.

CAYMAN

LONGSPINE SQUIRRELFISH
Holocentrus rufus

FAMILY:
Squirrelfish -
Holocentridae

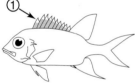

SIZE: 5-10 in.,
max. 12½ in.
DEPTH: 4-100 ft.

CAYMAN

REEF SQUIRRELFISH
Holocentrus coruscus

FAMILY:
Squirrelfish -
Holocentridae

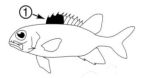

SIZE: 3½-5 in.,
max. 5½ in.
DEPTH: 5-75 ft.

ST. LUCIA

Squirrelfish

DISTINCTIVE FEATURES: 1. Anal and tail fins bordered in brownish red to bright red. 2. Red spots or markings between spines of foredorsal fin.

DESCRIPTION: Usually dusky, bronze-red (occasionally orange to gold) stripes alternate with wide silver stripes.

ABUNDANCE & DISTRIBUTION: Common to occasional Florida, Bahamas, Caribbean (more common southeastern Caribbean); also Bermuda.

HABITAT & BEHAVIOR: Inhabit shallow waters from tide pools to mid-range reefs. Hide in small recesses, peeking out only occasionally. Although common, not often observed.

REACTION TO DIVERS: Shy; usually stay well back in dark, protected areas.

NOTE: Many ichthyologists believe the genus name should be *Sargocentron*.

DISTINCTIVE FEATURES: 1. Orangish gold body stripes. 2. Unusually long anal fin spine.

DESCRIPTION: Silvery red. Gold front dorsal fin patterned with white tips and spots along base.

ABUNDANCE & DISTRIBUTION: Occasional South Florida, Bahamas, Caribbean.

HABITAT & BEHAVIOR: Hide in or near dark recesses. Rare on shallow reefs; become more abundant with depth; most abundant squirrelfish between 100-200 feet.

REACTION TO DIVERS: Somewhat wary. Usually retreat into protected recesses when approached. Can occasionally be closely observed near openings.

NOTE: Many ichthyologists believe the genus name should be *Flammeo*.

DUSKY SQUIRRELFISH
Holocentrus vexillarius

FAMILY:
Squirrelfish -
Holocentridae

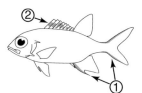

SIZE: 3-5 in., max. 7 in.
DEPTH: 1-50 ft.

CAYMAN

Dusky Squirrelfish

*Displaying bright
red borders on anal
and tail fins, and gold
to orange body stripes.*

BARBADOS

LONGJAW SQUIRRELFISH
Holocentrus marianus

FAMILY:
Squirrelfish -
Holocentridae

SIZE: 4-6 in., max. 7 in.
DEPTH: 50-200 ft.

CAYMAN

217

Squirrelfish

DISTINCTIVE FEATURES: 1. Red and white stripes on sides separated by thin brown stripes. (Similar Reef Squirrelfish, *H. coruscum* [pg. 215], distinguished by lack of the thin brown stripes.)
DESCRIPTION: Usually have spot on dorsal fin between first and second spines. (Similar Reef Squirrelfish have spot in between first and third or fourth spines.)
ABUNDANCE & DISTRIBUTION: Uncommon Florida, Bahamas, Caribbean; also north to South Carolina, Bermuda and Gulf of Mexico.
HABITAT & BEHAVIOR: Hide in small recesses, peeking out occasionally. Inhabit both shallow inshore and deep offshore reefs.
REACTION TO DIVERS: Shy; difficult to approach.

DISTINCTIVE FEATURES: Unmarked bright red to orangish red. **1. Lobes of tail rounded.**
DESCRIPTION: Fins may be pale; belly occasionally lighter shades of red.
ABUNDANCE & DISTRIBUTION: Occasional South Florida, Bahamas, Caribbean.
HABITAT & BEHAVIOR: Reclusive; hide in deep, dark recesses in reefs. Often swim upside-down, orienting themselves to ceilings of small caves and recesses.
REACTION TO DIVERS: Very shy; retreat into recess upon approach. Occasionally curious; if diver patiently waits without moving, may peer out of hiding place.

DISTINCTIVE FEATURES: 1. Black bar behind head.
DESCRIPTION: Red to silvery red. Red dorsal fin has white marks at tips and a few along base. White borders on leading edge of ventral, anal, rear dorsal and tail fins.
ABUNDANCE & DISTRIBUTION: Common to occasional Florida, Bahamas, Caribbean; also north to North Carolina, Bermuda, Gulf of Mexico, south to Brazil and eastern Atlantic.
HABITAT & BEHAVIOR: Hide in dark recesses. Often swim upside-down, orienting themselves to cave ceilings.
REACTION TO DIVERS: Curious; often peer out at divers. Seem to feel secure in reef openings, where they can be cautiously approached.

DEEPWATER SQUIRRELFISH
Holocentrus bullisi

FAMILY:
Squirrelfish -
Holocentridae

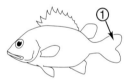

SIZE: 3¹/₂ - 4¹/₂ in.,
max. 5 in.
DEPTH: 100-250 ft.

KEY WEST, FL

CARDINAL SOLDIERFISH
Plectrypops retrospinis

FAMILY:
Squirrelfish -
Holocentridae

SIZE: 3¹/₂ - 5¹/₂ in.,
max. 8¹/₂ in.
DEPTH: 15-80 ft.

ST. LUCIA

BLACKBAR SOLDIERFISH
Myripristis jacobus

FAMILY:
Squirrelfish -
Holocentridae

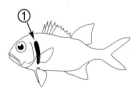

SIZE: 3¹/₂ - 5¹/₂ in.,
max. 8¹/₂ in.
DEPTH: 15-60 ft.

BONAIRE

219

Bigeye

DISTINCTIVE FEATURES: Red to salmon or orange overall. **1. Wide dark border on large ventral fins. JUVENILE: 2. Orange markings on dorsal fin.**

DESCRIPTION: Deep body with very large eye. May display three or four pale bands, especially young; adults may have red or dusky margins on anal and tail fins.

ABUNDANCE & DISTRIBUTION: Occasional to rare Florida, Bahamas, Caribbean; also north to Maine, Bermuda, Gulf of Mexico.

HABITAT & BEHAVIOR: JUVENILE: Between one and three inches, are in shallow waters during the spring and summer. Generally inhabit reefs and rocky areas where recesses afford protective cover. **ADULT:** Inhabit deep rocky bottoms, usually between 300 and 660 feet.

REACTION TO DIVERS: Juveniles are wary, staying close to protective recesses and retreat upon approach. Slow nonthreatening movements may allow close approach. Adults are easily approached.

Glasseye Snapper
Pale color phase.

CAYMAN

DISTINCTIVE FEATURES: 1. Always have silver bars on back, which may be faint. (Similar Bigeye, *P. arenatus*, [next] never has bars.)

DESCRIPTION: Vary from red to pale, silvery, mottled pink.

ABUNDANCE & DISTRIBUTION: Common to occasional Florida, Bahamas, Caribbean; also north to New Jersey, Bermuda, Gulf of Mexico, south to Brazil, and circumtropical.

HABITAT & BEHAVIOR: Generally prefer shallow reefs (a clue in distinguishing them from similar Bigeye [next] that prefer deep reef tops). Often hide in dark recesses of reefs by day, but occasionally drift in open near bottom.

REACTION TO DIVERS: Often appear unconcerned. Can usually be approached with slow, nonthreatening movements.

NOTE: Many ichthyologists believe the genus name should be *Heteropriaeanthus*.

SHORT BIGEYE
Pristigenys alta
FAMILY:
Bigeye - Priacanthidae

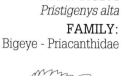

SIZE: 1 ½ - 3 ½ in.,
max. 1 ft.
DEPTH: 100-660 ft.

Short Bigeye Juvenile

GLASSEYE SNAPPER
Priacanthus cruentatus
FAMILY:
Bigeye - Priacanthidae

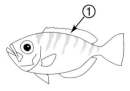

SIZE: 7-10 in, max. 1 ft.
DEPTH: 15-50 ft.

Bigeye – Cardinalfish

DISTINCTIVE FEATURES: Uniform reddish color. (Never have silver bars like similar Glasseye Snapper, *P. cruentatus* [previous].)

DESCRIPTION: Vary from bright red to salmon; often have blackish tinges. No markings other than possible duskiness along edges of rear dorsal, anal and tail fins.

ABUNDANCE & DISTRIBUTION: Common Florida, Bahamas, eastern Caribbean; occasional to uncommon balance of Caribbean; also north to Massachusetts, Bermuda, Gulf of Mexico, south to Argentina, and eastern Atlantic.

HABITAT & BEHAVIOR: Usually drift in small groups over deep reefs (a clue in distinguishing them from similar Glasseye Snapper [previous] that generally prefer shallow reefs).

REACTION TO DIVERS: Usually unafraid. Can usually be approached with slow, nonthreatening movements.

DISTINCTIVE FEATURES: 1. Dark bar from rear dorsal fin to anal fin. 2. Two bars at base of tail (may have darkish area between bars forming one wide bar with dark borders).

DESCRIPTION: Orangish red.

ABUNDANCE & DISTRIBUTION: Common South Florida, Bahamas, Caribbean.

HABITAT & BEHAVIOR: Hide by day in dark recesses and often form loose aggregations in caves. Feed in the open on reefs at night.

REACTION TO DIVERS: Normally hide; may peer out from holes. Seem to feel secure in dark places and can be cautiously approached. Frequently seen on night dives.

SIMILAR SPECIES: Broadsaddle Cardinalfish, *A. pillionatus*, has a bar at rear of dorsal fin and second wide uniform bar on base of tail (not just a darkish area between two bars).

DISTINCTIVE FEATURES: 1. Black bar from rear dorsal to anal fin. 2. Single black bar at base of tail.

DESCRIPTION: Deep orangish red or bronze to pink or salmon. Can pale dramatically.

ABUNDANCE & DISTRIBUTION: Very common Bahamas; common southeastern Florida, especially the Keys; occasional Caribbean; also Bermuda.

HABITAT & BEHAVIOR: Hide by day in dark recesses. Feed in the open on reefs at night.

REACTION TO DIVERS: Normally hide; may peer out from holes. Seem to feel secure in dark places and can be cautiously approached. Frequently seen on night dives.

BIGEYE
Priacanthus arenatus
FAMILY:
Bigeye - Priacanthidae

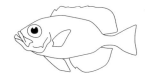

SIZE: 8-12 in., max. 16 in.
DEPTH: 50-200 ft.

WEST PALM BEACH, FL

BELTED CARDINALFISH
Apogon townsendi
FAMILY:
Cardinalfish - Apogonidae

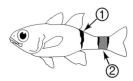

SIZE: 1 1/4 - 2 in.,
max. 2 1/2 in.
DEPTH: 5-180 ft.

CAYMAN

BARRED CARDINALFISH
Apogon binotatus
FAMILY:
Cardinalfish - Apogonidae

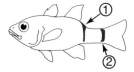

SIZE: 1 1/2 - 3 1/2 in.,
max. 4 1/2 in.
DEPTH: 2-150 ft.

L. CAYMAN

223

Cardinalfish

DISTINCTIVE FEATURES: 1. Darkish red areas along base of rear dorsal and anal fins, and on borders of tail. 2. Dusky bar extends from below rear dorsal fin to belly (never triangular). 3. Dusky bar at base of tail (wider than bar on similar Barred Cardinalfish, *A. binotatus* [previous]). (Similar Pale Cardinalfish, *A. planifrons*, [next] distinguished by pale pink coloration.)

DESCRIPTION: Shades of red; occasionally have yellow highlights, especially on back.

ABUNDANCE & DISTRIBUTION: Occasional Bahamas, northwestern Caribbean. Not reported Florida or balance of Caribbean.

HABITAT & BEHAVIOR: Inhabit reefs. Reclusive, hide in dark recesses; forage in open at night.

REACTION TO DIVERS: Normally hide; may peer out from holes. Seem to feel secure in dark places and can be cautiously approached. Frequently seen on night dives.

DISTINCTIVE FEATURES: Pale pink. 1. Dark bar extends from below rear dorsal fin to belly (never triangular). 2. Dusky bar at base of tail (wider than bar on similar Barred Cardinalfish, *A. binotatus* [previous]). (Similar Roughlip Cardinalfish, *A. robinsi*, [previous] distinguished by deeper red coloration.)

DESCRIPTION: Often have pearly highlights.

ABUNDANCE & DISTRIBUTION: Occasional South Florida, Bahamas, Caribbean.

HABITAT & BEHAVIOR: Inhabit reefs. Reclusive, hide in dark recesses; forage in open at night.

REACTION TO DIVERS: Normally hide; may peer out from holes. Seem to feel secure in dark places and can be cautiously approached. Frequently seen on night dives.

SIMILAR SPECIES: Mimic Cardinalfish, *A. phenax*, distinguished by triangular first bar below rear dorsal fin, and deeper red coloration.

DISTINCTIVE FEATURES: 1. Brilliant white spot, source of common name, just behind small, dark blotch on back, at rear dorsal fin.

DESCRIPTION: Bright red to salmon.

ABUNDANCE & DISTRIBUTION: Occasional to uncommon South Florida, Bahamas, Caribbean.

HABITAT & BEHAVIOR: Hide in dark recesses. Prefer clear water, coral reefs. Feed in the open on reefs at night.

REACTION TO DIVERS: Normally hide; may peer out from holes. Seem to feel secure in dark places and can be cautiously approached. Frequently seen on night dives.

SIMILAR SPECIES: Oddscale Cardinalfish, *A. anisolepis*, distinguished by absence of white spot.

ROUGHLIP CARDINALFISH
Apogon robinsi

FAMILY:
Cardinalfish - Apogonidae

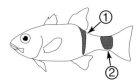

SIZE: 1 $^1/_2$ - 3 $^1/_2$ in.,
max. 4 in.
DEPTH: 10-100 ft.

BELIZE

PALE CARDINALFISH
Apogon planifrons

FAMILY:
Cardinalfish - Apogonidae

SIZE: 1 $^1/_2$ - 3 $^1/_2$ in.,
max. 4 in.
DEPTH: 10-100 ft.

BELIZE

WHITESTAR CARDINALFISH
Apogon lachneri

FAMILY:
Cardinalfish - Apogonidae

SIZE: 1 $^1/_2$ - 2 $^1/_2$ in.,
max. 3 in.
DEPTH: 15-200 ft.

L. CAYMAN

Cardinalfish

DISTINCTIVE FEATURES: 1. Two white lines across eye. 2. Dark spot behind eye. (Similar Twospot Cardinalfish, *A. pseudomaculatus*, [next] may also have these markings, but is distinguished by obvious spot on base of tail.)

DESCRIPTION: Bright red to salmon. Usually have black spot below rear dorsal fin; darkish streak may run from eye to rear of gill cover; faint bar on base of tail occasionally present.

ABUNDANCE & DISTRIBUTION: Common Florida, Bahamas, Caribbean; also Bermuda and Gulf of Mexico.

HABITAT & BEHAVIOR: Prefer shallow water. Drift in openings of dark recesses in a wide range of habitats, from dock pilings to reefs during day; forage in the open at night.

REACTION TO DIVERS: Normally hide; may peer out from holes. Seem to feel secure in dark places and can be cautiously approached. Frequently seen on night dives.

Flamefish

Pale phase without spot below rear dorsal fin or band on tail.

CAYMAN

DISTINCTIVE FEATURES: 1. Dark spot on back under rear dorsal fin. 2. Second dark spot at base of tail. (Similar Flamefish, *A. maculatus*, [previous] does not have a spot on base of tail, but may have dark bar.)

DESCRIPTION: Bright red to bronze or salmon. Often have two white lines across eyes. Fins may have dark tips; dusky spot occasionally on gill cover.

ABUNDANCE & DISTRIBUTION: Common to occasional Florida and Bahamas; occasional to uncommon Caribbean; also north to Massachusetts (possibly the only cardinalfish north of Florida), Bermuda, Gulf or Mexico and south to Brazil.

HABITAT & BEHAVIOR: Inhabit areas ranging from shallow water, bays and dock pilings to deep reefs. Hide during day in dark, secluded places. Feed in the open at night.

REACTION TO DIVERS: Normally hide; may peer out from holes. Seem to feel secure in dark places and can be cautiously approached. Frequently seen on night dives.

FLAMEFISH
Apogon maculatus
FAMILY:
Cardinalfish - Apogonidae

SIZE: 2-3½ in.,
max. 4½ in.
DEPTH: 2-60 ft.

L. CAYMAN

Flamefish
*Bright red phase
without band on tail.*

DRY TORTUGAS, FL

TWOSPOT
CARDINALFISH
Apogon pseudomaculatus
FAMILY:
Cardinalfish - Apogonidae

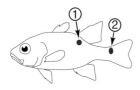

SIZE: 1½-3 in.,
max. 4½ in.
DEPTH: 2-1300 ft.

JACKSONVILLE, FL

Cardinalfish

DISTINCTIVE FEATURES: No markings. Live with anemones.

DESCRIPTION: Bright red to bronze to salmon. Two linear markings may radiate from below and behind eyes.

ABUNDANCE & DISTRIBUTION: Occasional to uncommon South Florida, Bahamas, Caribbean.

HABITAT & BEHAVIOR: Live in and around the protective zone of anemone's tentacles.

REACTION TO DIVERS: Seem to feel secure in protective zone of anemone's tentacles where they can be closely approached.

DISTINCTIVE FEATURES: 1. Dusky band at base of tail. Occasionally live with anemones. (Similar Dusky Cardinalfish, *Phaeoptyx pigmentaria*, [next page] are more speckled; do not live with anemones.)

DESCRIPTION: Bright red to bronze to salmon. Often dusky, wedge-shaped mark adjacent to lower rear eye; indistinct body stripes may run to base of tail.

ABUNDANCE & DISTRIBUTION: Occasional to uncommon South Florida, Bahamas, Caribbean.

HABITAT & BEHAVIOR: Live in and around the protective zone of anemone's tentacles.

REACTION TO DIVERS: Seem to feel secure in protective zone of anemone's tentacles where they can be closely approached.

DISTINCTIVE FEATURES: 1. Dusky stripe across eye.

DESCRIPTION: Translucent salmon to pink or bronze; clear fins.

ABUNDANCE & DISTRIBUTION: Occasional to uncommon South Florida, Bahamas, Caribbean.

HABITAT & BEHAVIOR: Prefer deep reefs and rocky outcroppings. Hide in caves and dark recesses during day. At night, drift above reefs in small groups.

REACTION TO DIVERS: Rarely seen during day. Can be closely approached at night when mesmerized by beam of bright light.

BRIDLE CARDINALFISH
Apogon aurolineatus
FAMILY:
Cardinalfish - Apogonidae

SIZE: 1 ½ - 2 ¼ in.,
max. 2 ½ in.
DEPTH: 2-250 ft.

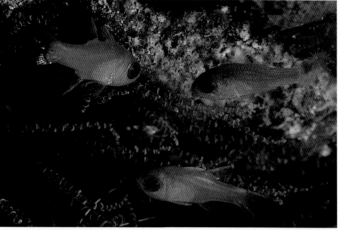

L. CAYMAN

SAWCHEEK CARDINALFISH
Apogon quadrisquamatus
FAMILY:
Cardinalfish - Apogonidae

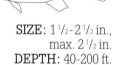

SIZE: 1 ½ - 2 ½ in.,
max. 2 ½ in.
DEPTH: 40-200 ft.

ANGUILLA

BIGTOOTH CARDINALFISH
Apogon affinis
FAMILY:
Cardinalfish - Apogonidae

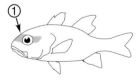

SIZE: 1 ½ - 3 in., max. 4 in.
DEPTH: 50 - 300 ft.

L. CAYMAN

Cardinalfish

DISTINCTIVE FEATURES: 1. Single dark bar at base of tail. 2. Covered with dark speckles.

DESCRIPTION: Translucent bronze to salmon. Clear, unmarked fins.

ABUNDANCE & DISTRIBUTION: Occasional to uncommon Florida, Bahamas, Caribbean; also Bermuda, Gulf of Mexico, south to Brazil and eastern Atlantic.

HABITAT & BEHAVIOR: Hide in deep caves during day. At night, drift above reefs, often near open basket stars.

REACTION TO DIVERS: Rarely seen during day. Can be closely approached at night when mesmerized by beams of bright light.

SIMILAR SPECIES: Freckled Cardinalfish, *P. conklini*, is distinguished by dark stripe on dorsal and anal fins. Sponge Cardinalfish, *P. xenus*, is distinguished by yellowish area on snout that extends under jaw. Live inside deep, cylindrical sponges.

DISTINCTIVE FEATURES: 1. Dramatic, large, dark ventral fin (if folded back, reaches beyond start of anal fin base).

DESCRIPTION: Bronze cast, with numerous black and white speckles, often with bluish, goldish or greenish highlights. Usually have pearly patch behind and below eye. Bluntish, rounded snout.

ABUNDANCE & DISTRIBUTION: Occasional South Florida, Bahamas, Caribbean; also south to Brazil.

HABITAT & BEHAVIOR: Inhabit sea grass beds in clear water. Often hide in empty shells (never in living conch). Drift in open, near bottom, close to recesses or shells, distinctively fluttering their long, ventral fins.

REACTION TO DIVERS: Retreat into shelter upon close approach, but may stay in open if approached with slow, nonthreatening movements.

SIMILAR SPECIES: Bronze Cardinalfish, *A. alutus*, distinguished by lighter bronze color and short, ventral fin that is not darkened. Never found in living conch.

DISTINCTIVE FEATURES: Mottled, pale grayish bronze to black. No distinguishing marks.

DESCRIPTION: Numerous black speckles. Often, two to four dark, broad streaks radiate from eyes, and a single row of dots runs from pectoral fin to tail. Dark, elongated ventral fin. Head somewhat pointed.

ABUNDANCE & DISTRIBUTION: Occasional Florida, Bahamas, Caribbean; also Bermuda.

HABITAT & BEHAVIOR: Inhabit mantle cavity of living queen conch (only known cardinalfish to exhibit this behavior). Come out at night to forage in open water just above reefs.

REACTION TO DIVERS: May be found during the day by carefully turning up the edge of a living conch shell. At night, may be spotted in the open on reefs.

DUSKY CARDINALFISH
Phaeoptyx pigmentaria
FAMILY:
Cardinalfish - Apogonidae

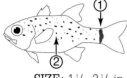

SIZE: 1 ¹/₂ - 2 ¹/₂ in.,
max. 3 ¹/₂ in.
DEPTH: 1-140 ft.

CAYMAN

BLACKFIN CARDINALFISH
Astrapogon puncticulatus
FAMILY:
Cardinalfish - Apogonidae

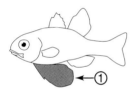

SIZE: 1-2 in., max. 2 ¹/₂ in.
DEPTH: 3-40 ft.

KEY LARGO, FL

CONCHFISH
Astrapogon stellatus
FAMILY:
Cardinalfish - Apogonidae

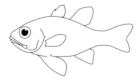

SIZE: 1-2 in., max. 3 in.
DEPTH: 3-80 ft.

BELIZE

Small, Elongated Bottom-Dwellers
Goby – Blenny – Jawfish – Dragonet

This ID Group consists of small fish that generally grow to no more than three inches. All have long, cylindrical bodies and spend most of their time perched on the bottom or in small holes with only their heads protruding. A few species drift just above the bottom.

FAMILY: Goby — Gobiidae
34 Species Included

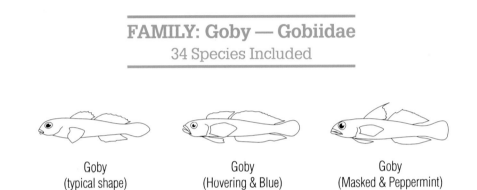

Goby	Goby	Goby
(typical shape)	(Hovering & Blue)	(Masked & Peppermint)

Gobies are the smallest members of this ID Group (generally one to two inches, with only a few species ever exceeding two and a half inches). Most rest on their pectoral and ventral fins; in surge or current, a small suction disc is formed between their ventral fins to anchor them in place. A few species drift in open water near the reef, and a few others hover just above burrows in the sand. Gobies and blennies are often confused, but can easily be distinguished by their dorsal fins — gobies have two, while most blennies have one long, continuous fin and a few have three. Another observable difference is the tendency of gobies to rest in a stiff, straight position, while blennies are more flexed and curved.

FAMILY: Blenny — Blenniidae, Clinidae & Tripterygiidae*
35 Species Included

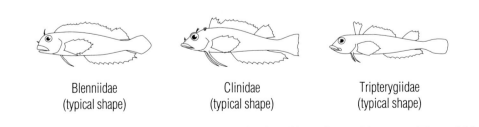

Blenniidae	Clinidae	Tripterygiidae
(typical shape)	(typical shape)	(typical shape)

Most blennies are small (one to three inches) and have long, thin ventral fins which they use to perch on the bottom. While resting and swimming, blennies tend to curve and flex their bodies in contrast to the gobies which hold their bodies stiff and straight. Most blennies have fleshy appendages, called cirri, above their eyes. There are often additional cirri on the snout and nape. Because of their small size and ability to change colors and markings to blend with the background, they often go unnoticed. Several species live in holes and are only seen with their heads exposed. Occasionally, they dart out to nab a particle of food. Many blennies are similar in appearance and difficult to distinguish. Adding to the confusion, males and females of several species are dramatically different from one another in appearance. Careful attention to detail, however, makes underwater identification possible in most cases.

*The scientific community is not in agreement as to the division of blennies. The suggested number of scientific families comprising the common group name, blenny, ranges from two to five. The most generally accepted division is three. Observable differences for the diver are: Blenniidae - no scales and a single dorsal fin; Clinidae - most species have noticeable scales and a single dorsal fin; Tripterygiidae - noticeable scales and three separate dorsal fins.

FAMILY: Jawfish — Opistognathidae
5 Species Included

Jawfish (typical shape)

Jawfish are named for their large mouths and gaping jaws. They live in holes which they construct by moving stones and sand with their mouths. Generally, they are seen with only their heads protruding, but on occasion they hover just above the bottom. When frightened, they rapidly retreat into the confines of the hole, usually tail first. Their bulbous heads are bulky in comparison to their elongated bodies. The jawfish family is easy to identify, but several species are almost impossible to distinguish with only their heads visible. Jawfish males have the curious trait of incubating eggs in their mouths.

FAMILY: Dragonet — Callionymidae
2 Species Included

Lancer Dragonet

DISTINCTIVE FEATURES: 1. Electric blue body stripe runs from front of each eye to base of tail. No markings on snout.

DESCRIPTION: Dark upper body, pale underside. Mouth located near tip of snout.

ABUNDANCE & DISTRIBUTION: Common South Florida and along continental coast and coastal islands to Honduras. Not reported Bahamas or oceanic islands of Caribbean.

HABITAT & BEHAVIOR: Cleaner fish. Congregate in cleaning stations where they perch in groups, waiting for fish requiring their services.

REACTION TO DIVERS: Unafraid. A slow extension of the hand toward fish occasionally results in fingers being cleaned.

DISTINCTIVE FEATURES: 1. Yellow or white body stripe runs from front of each eye to tail. No markings on snout.

DESCRIPTION: Bright yellow markings in Florida; often pale to white in Caribbean. Dark upper body, pale underside. Mouth located near tip of snout.

ABUNDANCE & DISTRIBUTION: Common to occasional South Florida (including Gulf Coast), Bahamas, Caribbean.

HABITAT & BEHAVIOR: Prefer medium-depth reefs. Live in and around sponges, especially tube sponges.

REACTION TO DIVERS: Shy; retreat into sponges. An extremely slow approach may enable a close view.

DISTINCTIVE FEATURES: 1. Bright yellow spot centered on snout. 2. Thin yellow body stripe runs from each eye to tail.

DESCRIPTION: Yellow markings may pale. Dark upper body, pale underside. Mouth located near tip of snout.

ABUNDANCE & DISTRIBUTION: Occasional to common Bahamas, Florida and northern Caribbean. Not reported southern Caribbean.

HABITAT & BEHAVIOR: Prefer medium to deep reefs. Live in and around sponges, especially tube sponges.

REACTION TO DIVERS: Shy; retreat into sponges. An extremely slow approach may enable a close view.

NEON GOBY
Gobiosoma oceanops
FAMILY:
Goby – Gobiidae

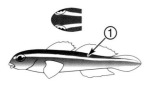

SIZE: 1-1¹/₂ in., max. 2 in.
DEPTH: 10-125 ft.

KEY LARGO, FL

YELLOWLINE GOBY
Gobiosoma horsti
FAMILY:
Goby – Gobiidae

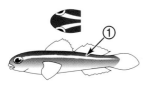

SIZE: 1-1¹/₂ in., max. 2 in.
DEPTH: 25-60 ft.

MARATHON, FL

SPOTLIGHT GOBY
Gobiosoma louisae
FAMILY:
Goby – Gobiidae

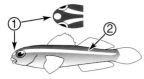

SIZE: 1-1¹/₄ in.,
max. 1¹/₂ in.
DEPTH: 40 -130 ft.

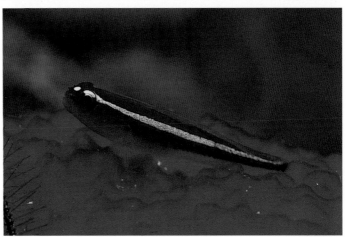

CAYMAN

DISTINCTIVE FEATURES: 1. Bright yellow or white bar on dark snout. (Compare similar Yellownose, *G. randalli*, and Barsnout, *G. illecebrosum*, [next].) **2. Bright yellow or white body stripe runs from each eye to tail.**

DESCRIPTION: The bar and body stripe are most often bright yellow, but can be white, or pale iridescent blue. Snout may be pale. Dark upper body, pale underside. Mouth is underslung, or shark-like.

ABUNDANCE & DISTRIBUTION: Occasional Florida and Jamaica to western Caribbean. Not reported balance of Caribbean or Bahamas.

HABITAT & BEHAVIOR: Prefer medium to deep reefs. Live in and around sponges, especially tube.

REACTION TO DIVERS: Shy; retreat into sponges. An extremely slow approach may enable a close view.

SIMILAR SPECIES: Slaty Goby, *G. tenox*, has yellow bar on snout and a short body stripe which stops above pectoral fin. Uncommon most of Caribbean; not reported Bahamas or Florida.

DISTINCTIVE FEATURES: 1. Bright yellow bar on pale snout. (Similar Yellowprow, *G. xanthiprora*, [previous] and Barsnout, *G. illecebrosum*, [next] have bar on dark snout.) **2. Yellow stripe runs from each eye to tail. 3. Thin bluish stripe runs from under each eye to behind pectoral fin.**

DESCRIPTION: Dark upper body, pale underside. Mouth located near tip of snout.

ABUNDANCE & DISTRIBUTION: Occasional southern Caribbean. Not reported balance of Caribbean, Florida or Bahamas.

HABITAT & BEHAVIOR: Cleaner fish. Congregate in cleaning stations where they perch in groups, waiting for fish requiring their services.

REACTION TO DIVERS: Unafraid. A slow extension of the hand toward fish occasionally results in fingers being cleaned.

DISTINCTIVE FEATURES: 1. White bar runs from upper lip to between eyes on dark upper head. 2. Blue or yellow stripe runs from each eye to tail.

DESCRIPTION: Dark upper body, pale underside. Mouth located near tip of snout.

ABUNDANCE & DISTRIBUTION: Occasional western and southern Caribbean. Not reported balance of Caribbean, Florida or Bahamas.

HABITAT & BEHAVIOR: Cleaner fish. Congregate in cleaning stations where they perch in groups, waiting for fish requiring their services.

REACTION TO DIVERS: Unafraid. A slow extension of the hand toward fish occasionally results in fingers being cleaned.

YELLOWPROW GOBY
Gobiosoma xanthiprora
FAMILY:
Goby – Gobiidae

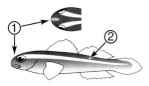

SIZE: 1 - 1 1/4 in.,
max. 1 1/2 in.
DEPTH: 30 - 90 ft.

MIAMI, FL

YELLOWNOSE GOBY
Gobiosoma randalli
FAMILY:
Goby – Gobiidae

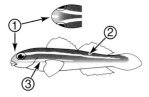

SIZE: 1 - 1 1/4 in.,
max. 1 3/4 in.
DEPTH: 20 - 80 ft.

BONAIRE

BARSNOUT GOBY
Gobiosoma illecebrosum
FAMILY:
Goby – Gobiidae

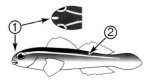

SIZE: 1 - 1 1/4 in.,
max. 1 3/4 in.
DEPTH: 30 - 90 ft.

ROATAN

DISTINCTIVE FEATURES: 1. Brilliant yellow "V" on snout fades into pale body stripes. (Compare to color phases of the very similar Sharknose Goby, *G. evelynae*, [next].)

DESCRIPTION: Dark upper body, pale underside. Mouth is underslung, or shark-like.

ABUNDANCE & DISTRIBUTION: Common Bahamas and Caribbean. Not reported Florida.

HABITAT & BEHAVIOR: Cleaner fish. Congregate in cleaning stations where they perch in groups, waiting for fish requiring their services.

REACTION TO DIVERS: Unafraid. A slow extension of the hand toward fish occasionally results in fingers being cleaned.

DISTINCTIVE FEATURES: Three distinct color phases. **(1) Bright yellow "V" on snout fades into pale or brilliant blue body stripes. (2) Narrow white "V" on snout continues into bluish white body stripes. (3) Yellow "V" on snout continues into yellow body stripes.** (Yellow "V" does not fade into white as it does on the similar Cleaning Goby, *G. genie*, [previous].)

DESCRIPTION: Mouth is underslung, or shark-like. Dark upper body, pale underside.

ABUNDANCE & DISTRIBUTION: Occasional throughout range. Color phases: (1) central Bahamas and extending south to north coast of South America; (2) mid-Caribbean; (3) central and northern Bahamas.

HABITAT & BEHAVIOR: Cleaner fish. Congregate in cleaning stations where they perch in groups, waiting for fish requiring their services.

REACTION TO DIVERS: Unafraid. A slow extension of the hand toward fish occasionally results in fingers being cleaned.

Sharknose Goby
White-stripe phase.

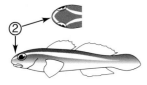

SWAN ISLAND

CLEANING GOBY
Gobiosoma genie
FAMILY:
Goby – Gobiidae

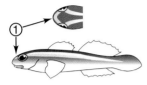

SIZE: 1-1¼ in.,
max. 1¾ in.
DEPTH: 10-50 ft.

CAYMAN

SHARKNOSE GOBY
Gobiosoma evelynae
Brilliant blue-stripe phase.
FAMILY:
Goby – Gobiidae

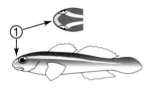

SIZE: 1-1¼ in.,
max. 1½ in.
DEPTH: 30-100 ft.

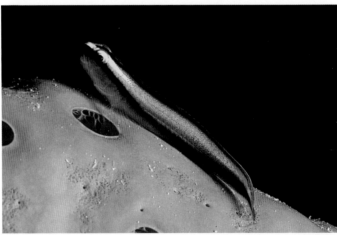

ANGUILLA

Sharknose Goby
Pale blue-stripe phase.
[top]

Yellow-stripe phase.
[below]

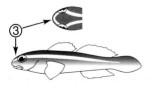

NASSAU

DISTINCTIVE FEATURES: 1. White "V" or "Y" on snout continues into white or bluish white body stripes.

DESCRIPTION: Dark upper body, pale underside. Mouth located near tip of snout. (Distinguished from similar white-stripe phase of Sharknose Goby, *G. evelynae,* [previous] whose mouth is underslung and snout marking is never "Y"-shaped.)

ABUNDANCE & DISTRIBUTION: Occasional southwest Florida and Caribbean. Not reported Bahamas.

HABITAT & BEHAVIOR: Cleaner fish. Congregate in cleaning stations where they perch in groups, waiting for fish requiring their services. Occasionally found on the outer surface of sponges, but not inside.

REACTION TO DIVERS: Unafraid. A slow extension of the hand toward fish occasionally results in fingers being cleaned.

DISTINCTIVE FEATURES: 1. A short, bright yellow stripe runs from each eye to above pectoral fin. No markings on snout.

DESCRIPTION: Dark upper body, pale underside. Snout and nape areas may be pale with yellowish or whitish cast. Mouth located near tip of snout.

ABUNDANCE & DISTRIBUTION: Occasional Bahamas and eastern Caribbean; rare western Caribbean.

HABITAT & BEHAVIOR: Live in and around sponges, especially tube sponges.

REACTION TO DIVERS: Shy; retreat into sponges. An extremely slow approach may enable a close view.

DISTINCTIVE FEATURES: Lime green body. **1. Numerous (19) light green bands ring body.**

DESCRIPTION: Red stripe starts at tip of snout and runs across eye to above pectoral fin. Fins pale green; underside of head white.

ABUNDANCE & DISTRIBUTION: Uncommon Bahamas and Caribbean. Not reported Florida.

HABITAT & BEHAVIOR: Live under rocks, sea urchins and sponges in shallow, inshore areas. Normally peer out from hiding places.

REACTION TO DIVERS: Shy; tend to hide.

SIMILAR SPECIES: Nineline Goby, *Ginsburgellus novemlineatus,* distinguished by bluish black to brownish body with nine narrow blue rings around body. No more than an inch in length.

BROADSTRIPE GOBY
Gobiosoma prochilos

FAMILY:
Goby – Gobiidae

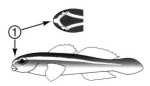

SIZE: 1-1¼ in.,
max. 1¾ in.
DEPTH: 20-80 ft.

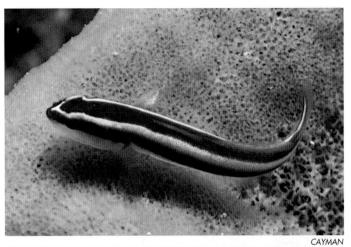

CAYMAN

SHORTSTRIPE GOBY
Gobiosoma chancei

FAMILY:
Goby – Gobiidae

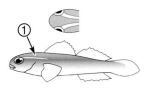

SIZE: 1-1¾ in.,
max. 1½ in.
DEPTH: 30-90 ft.

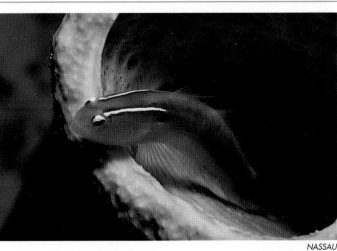

NASSAU

GREENBANDED GOBY
*Gobiosoma
multifasciatum*

FAMILY:
Goby – Gobiidae

SIZE: 1-1½ in.,
max. 1¾ in.
DEPTH: 1-15 ft.

CAYMAN

DISTINCTIVE FEATURES: Nearly transparent body. **1. Dark, narrow rings around body and head.**
DESCRIPTION: Clear fins.
ABUNDANCE & DISTRIBUTION: Occasional south Florida and southward to central Caribbean. Not reported Bahamas or southern Caribbean.
HABITAT & BEHAVIOR: Perch on shallow-water sponges and algae-covered rocks. Often hide under red algae. Occasionally found on isolated, shallow coral heads.
REACTION TO DIVERS: Shy; retreat into holes or other protected places.

DISTINCTIVE FEATURES: 1. Series of dark dashes along midbody.
DESCRIPTION: Tan to grayish translucent to transparent body; transparent fins. Dusky, somewhat indistinct, bars on body; usually darkish spot below eye.
ABUNDANCE & DISTRIBUTION: Rare Florida Gulf Coast, southeastern Florida, eastern Caribbean including Jamaica. Not reported balance of Florida and Caribbean or Bahamas.
HABITAT & BEHAVIOR: Inhabit shallow rocky areas and grass beds mixed with rubble.
REACTION TO DIVERS: Tend to ignore divers; can often be closely approached with slow, nonthreatening movements.

DISTINCTIVE FEATURES: 1. Two orangish, squared areas outlined in black behind pectoral fin and below lateral line. 2. Red and white dashes separated by black, along lateral line.
DESCRIPTION: Bright red and black markings on head. Rear body translucent.
ABUNDANCE & DISTRIBUTION: Uncommon Bahamas, Caribbean. Not reported Florida.
HABITAT & BEHAVIOR: Perch on the surface of sponges and coral heads.
REACTION TO DIVERS: Tend to ignore divers; can often be closely approached with slow, nonthreatening movements.

TIGER GOBY
Gobiosoma macrodon
FAMILY:
Goby – Gobiidae

SIZE: 1¹/₂ - 1³/₄ in.,
max. 2 in.
DEPTH: 1 - 20 ft.

KEY LARGO, FL

ROCKCUT GOBY
Gobiosoma grosvenori
FAMILY:
Goby – Gobiidae

SIZE: ³/₄ - 1 in.,
max. 1³/₄ in.
DEPTH: 1 - 35 ft.

PANAMA CITY, FL

ORANGESIDED GOBY
Gobiosoma dilepsis
FAMILY:
Goby – Gobiidae

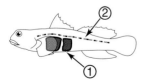

SIZE: ¹/₂ - ³/₄ in., max. 1 in.
DEPTH: 25 - 100 ft.

CAYMAN

243

DISTINCTIVE FEATURES: 1. Reddish brown spots on body. 2. One or two dark rectangular areas below midline and behind pectoral fin.

DESCRIPTION: Pale translucent to transparent background; occasionally have pinkish tints, especially on head; red to reddish brown spots and markings on head. White backbone usually visible.

ABUNDANCE & DISTRIBUTION: Uncommon Florida Keys, Caribbean. Not reported Florida coasts or Bahamas.

HABITAT & BEHAVIOR: Perch on the surface of large, rounded boulder corals.

REACTION TO DIVERS: Tend to ignore divers; can often be closely approached with slow, nonthreatening movements.

DISTINCTIVE FEATURES: 1. Black spot on first dorsal fin ringed with white. 2. Iris white.

DESCRIPTION: White to pale translucent or transparent; head often yellowish; may have yellow to orange stripes and spots on second dorsal fin. Tail long and pointed.

ABUNDANCE & DISTRIBUTION: Uncommon South Florida, Caribbean. Not reported Bahamas. Can be locally abundant.

HABITAT & BEHAVIOR: Well offshore on sand flats and in areas of gravelly rubble. Most common at depths over 100 feet.

REACTION TO DIVERS: Shy; dart away upon approach.

SIMILAR SPECIES: Spotfin Goby, *Gobionellus stigmalophius*, has dark spot in first dorsal fin not ringed in white; body usually shades of pale mottled brown. Inhabits burrows with symbiotic shrimp.

DISTINCTIVE FEATURES: 1. Dark spot in front of pectoral fin and series of dashes behind form broken stripe along midbody. 2. Dark bar runs across eye and down cheek (but not across head as Goldspot Goby, *Gnatholepis thompsoni* [next]).

DESCRIPTION: White to bluish gray, reddish brown or tan.

ABUNDANCE & DISTRIBUTION: Uncommon Florida, Bahamas, Caribbean.

HABITAT & BEHAVIOR: Inhabit sand flats mixed with coral rubble and areas of marl and sand mixed with sea grasses and algae. Perch on sand, near protective cover, and occasionally inhabit burrows. More common in water shallower than 70 feet.

REACTION TO DIVERS: Relatively unafraid; usually remain still until closely approached, then dart for cover.

LEOPARD GOBY
Gobiosoma saucrum
FAMILY:
Goby – Gobiidae

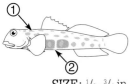

SIZE: 1/2 - 3/4 in.,
max. 1 in.
DEPTH: 15-100 ft.

DRY TORTUGAS, FL

WHITE-EYE GOBY
Bollmannia boqueronensis
FAMILY:
Goby – Gobiidae

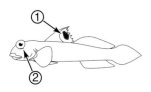

SIZE: 1 1/2 - 3 in., max. 4 in.
DEPTH: 60 - 180 ft.

KEY LARGO, FL

DASH GOBY
Gobionellus saepepallens
FAMILY:
Goby – Gobiidae

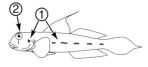

SIZE: 1-1 1/2 in., max. 2 in.
DEPTH: 0 - 150 ft.

ANGUILLA

245

DISTINCTIVE FEATURES: 1. Dark bar runs from top of head across eye and down cheek. 2. Gold spot outlined in black above pectoral fin (not obvious in some individuals).

DESCRIPTION: Whitish to tan. Dusky dots and squarish blotches along lower body.

ABUNDANCE & DISTRIBUTION: Abundant to common South Florida, Bahamas, Caribbean; also Bermuda.

HABITAT & BEHAVIOR: Prefer sandy, coral rubble areas near reefs. Perch on sand, near protective cover.

REACTION TO DIVERS: Shy; retreat quickly into small recesses when approached. Waiting motionless for several minutes often results in a close view of the fish re-emerging.

DISTINCTIVE FEATURES: White to tan translucent body. 1. Two darkish spots at base of pectoral fin (compare Spotted Goby, *C. punctipectophorus*, [next] distinguished by one spot).

DESCRIPTION: Bar at base of tail fin (may consist of two dots only lightly joined); body speckled with reddish brown spots; head may have a few dusky markings.

ABUNDANCE & DISTRIBUTION: Common to occasional South Florida, Bahamas, Caribbean.

HABITAT & BEHAVIOR: Prefer sandy, coral rubble areas, often adjacent to coral reefs. Perch on bottom, blending with background.

REACTION TO DIVERS: Relatively unafraid; retreat only when closely approached.

SIMILAR SPECIES: Bartail Goby, *C. thrix*, distinguished by large black blotch on upper half of pectoral fin base, and bar at base of tail. Inhabit mid-range waters (30-70 feet) off South Florida and Bahamas.

DISTINCTIVE FEATURES: 1. Dark spot at lower base of pectoral fin (compare Colon Goby, *C. dicrus*, [previous] distinguished by two spots). 2. Three orangish lines outlined in black extend from behind and below eye to above pectoral fin.

DESCRIPTION: White to bluish white to translucent. Series of diffuse blotches and spots on sides.

ABUNDANCE & DISTRIBUTION: Occasional Florida. Not scientifically reported Bahamas, Caribbean (however, editor has photographed this species in Bonaire).

HABITAT & BEHAVIOR: Perch on sandy bottoms near rocks and reefs, blending with background.

REACTION TO DIVERS: Relatively unafraid; retreat only when closely approached.

GOLDSPOT GOBY
Gnatholepis thompsoni
FAMILY:
Goby – Gobiidae

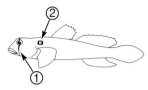

SIZE: 1¹/₂ - 2¹/₂ in.,
max. 3 in.
DEPTH: 2 - 160 ft.

CAYMAN

COLON GOBY
Coryphopterus dicrus
FAMILY:
Goby – Gobiidae

SIZE: 1¹/₄ - 1³/₄ in.,
max. 2 in.
DEPTH: 10-50 ft.

KEY LARGO, FL

SPOTTED GOBY
*Coryphopterus
punctipectophorus*
FAMILY:
Goby – Gobiidae

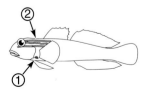

SIZE: 1 - 2 in., max. 2 in.
DEPTH: 50 - 120 ft.

WEST PALM BEACH, FL

DISTINCTIVE FEATURES: Translucent body. **1. Yellow stripe extends from rear of eye.** (Stripe may have dark outline.)

DESCRIPTION: Dusky bar on base of tail; often have faint goldish blotches or stripes on body; faint bronze to dusky spot on pectoral fin, near base.

ABUNDANCE & DISTRIBUTION: Occasional South Florida, Bahamas, Caribbean.

HABITAT & BEHAVIOR: Perch on the bottom near coral heads, blending with background.

REACTION TO DIVERS: Relatively unafraid; retreat only when closely approached.

DISTINCTIVE FEATURES: 1. White "bridle" usually runs from rear of mouth to edge of gill cover. Whitish to transparent, often without markings. (Compare similar Pallid Goby, *C. eidolon*, [previous] distinguished by yellow stripe from rear of eye; Spotted Goby, *C. punctipectophorus*, [pg. 247] distinguished by darkish spot at lower base of pectoral fin; Colon Goby, *C. dicrus* [pg. 247] distinguished by two darkish spots at base of pectoral fin.)

DESCRIPTION: Usually white (occasionally dark) spots on body; dusky bar often at base of tail fin (may consist of two dots only lightly joined); occasionally have pale yellowish to brownish "X's" on body; occasionally have dusky to dark streak running from behind eye; on rare occasions have spot above gill cover.

ABUNDANCE & DISTRIBUTION: Abundant to common Florida, Bahamas, Caribbean; also north to North Carolina, Bermuda and south to Brazil.

HABITAT & BEHAVIOR: Perch on sand near reefs, where they are usually transparent and unmarked; in grassy or rocky areas, they usually show markings.

REACTION TO DIVERS: Unafraid; do not move unless closely approached.

Bridled Goby

Dusky translucent body displaying numerous brownish "X's", dark streak behind eye and two dusky spots on base of tail; note bright white "bridle" marking from mouth to gill cover.

HOLLYWOOD, FL

PALLID GOBY
Coryphopterus eidolon
FAMILY:
Goby – Gobiidae

SIZE: 1-2 in., max. 2 in.
DEPTH: 20-90 ft.

CAYMAN

BRIDLED GOBY
Coryphopterus glaucofraenum
FAMILY:
Goby – Gobiidae

SIZE: 1¹⁄₂-2¹⁄₂ in.,
max. 3 in.
DEPTH: 5-130 ft.

CAYMAN

Bridled Goby

Almost transparent body displaying only a few pale yellowish "X's" and dusky bar on base of tail; note only an obscure white "bridle" marking is present.

CONCEPTION IS., BAHAMAS

DISTINCTIVE FEATURES: Bright orange to translucent. **1. Series of small white rectangles on lateral line.** (Note: There is no reliable way to visually distinguish between these two similar appearing species underwater — in hand examination of physical features is required.)

DESCRIPTION: Dark "mask" covers area between eyes and snout. Second spine of spinous dorsal fin of males is noticeably longer than other spines [pictured]. Generally, the Masked Goby is pale orange, has a robust body and is larger, while the Glass Goby is bright orange, has a slender body and is smaller, but this comparison is difficult to make without side by side specimens.

ABUNDANCE & DISTRIBUTION: Common to abundant Florida, Bahamas, Caribbean; also Bermuda.

HABITAT & BEHAVIOR: Hover in small to large aggregations just inside or near recesses in the reef. Generally, the Masked Goby inhabits waters between 10 and 35 feet, while the Glass Goby is 40 feet and deeper, however, the two occasionally mix, therefore depth is not a reliable indication for positive identification.

REACTION TO DIVERS: Groups tend to stay a few feet from divers.

DISTINCTIVE FEATURES: Yellow-gold to translucent body. **1. Electric blue wash on snout.**

DESCRIPTION: Several pale lines ranging from red to olive found behind eye and on forebody. Second spine of spinous dorsal fin of males noticeably longer than other spines [pictured].

ABUNDANCE & DISTRIBUTION: Common to uncommon Florida Keys and Caribbean; not reported Bahamas.

HABITAT & BEHAVIOR: Perch on coral heads.

REACTION TO DIVERS: Relatively unafraid; retreat only when closely approached.

DISTINCTIVE FEATURES: 1. Orange spots on dorsal, tail and anal fins. 2. About nine wide, dusky body bars.

DESCRIPTION: Shades of brown to red-brown to orange; iris red to gold, pupil green. Second dorsal spine elongated.

ABUNDANCE & DISTRIBUTION: Common South Florida, Bahamas, Caribbean.

HABITAT & BEHAVIOR: Inhabit reefs and areas of rocky rubble. Reclusive; often perch upside down on ceilings of small recesses in reefs or under rocks and boulders. Occasionally dart out to nab suspended particles of food.

REACTION TO DIVERS: Relatively unafraid; retreat further into recess only when closely approached.

NOTE: Formerly classified in genus *Quisquilius*.

MASKED/GLASS GOBY
*Coryphopterus
personatus/hyalinus*
FAMILY:
Goby – Gobiidae

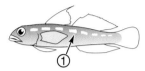

SIZE: $^3/_4$-$1^1/_4$ in.,
max. $1^1/_2$ in.
DEPTH: 10-100 ft.

CAYMAN

PEPPERMINT GOBY
Coryphopterus lipernes
FAMILY:
Goby – Gobiidae

SIZE: $^1/_4$-1 in.,
max. $1^1/_4$ in.
DEPTH: 40-130 ft.

BONAIRE

RUSTY GOBY
Priolepis hipoliti
FAMILY:
Goby – Gobiidae

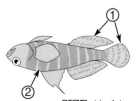

SIZE: $^1/_4$-1 in.,
max. $1^1/_2$ in.
DEPTH: 10-300 ft.

BIMINI

DISTINCTIVE FEATURES: 1. Rounded, fleshy crest on top of head.

DESCRIPTION: Shades of brown to olive-brown or red-brown. **JUVENILE & FEMALE:** Head has pale spots on gill cover and several pale lines radiate from rear of eyes; body blotched. **MALE:** First dorsal fin mostly dark, with orangish blotches; overall color relatively uniform. Breeding males dark violet to black.

ABUNDANCE & DISTRIBUTION: Occasional Florida, Bahamas, Caribbean; also Bermuda.

HABITAT & BEHAVIOR: Inhabit shallow, quiet waters; including coastlines, bays and inlets, tidal creeks and areas of mangroves.

REACTION TO DIVERS: Relatively unafraid; retreat only when closely approached.

DISTINCTIVE FEATURES: 1. Five to seven paired dark spots along midbody (often with dusky extensions that form bars). Noticeably elongated.

DESCRIPTION: Shades of tan to light gray with numerous, often orangish, spots and small blotches; orangish spots on dorsal and tail fins tend to form bands. Adults have long first dorsal spine.

ABUNDANCE & DISTRIBUTION: Uncommon South Florida, Bahamas, Caribbean.

HABITAT & BEHAVIOR: Inhabit burrows in mud, silty bottoms, and occasionally on sand. Live commensally with snapping shrimp that build and maintain burrows. Perch in front of burrow and warn shrimp of danger by fin movements, causing shrimp to retreat.

REACTION TO DIVERS: Wary; retreat into burrows upon approach. Very slow, nonthreatening movements will occasionally allow close view.

DISTINCTIVE FEATURES: 1. Bright yellow body stripe continues onto tail.

DESCRIPTION: Pearly white; bluish tints often on back and yellow tints often on lower head.

ABUNDANCE & DISTRIBUTION: Occasional both coasts Florida, Caribbean; also north to North Carolina. Not reported Bahamas.

HABITAT & BEHAVIOR: Hover just above burrows in the sand.

REACTION TO DIVERS: Move toward their burrows when approached; if disturbed further, they dive into burrows.

CRESTED GOBY
Lophogobius cyprinoides
FAMILY:
Goby – Gobiidae

SIZE: 1-3 in., max. 4 in.
DEPTH: 0-20 ft.

KEY LARGO, FL

ORANGESPOTTED GOBY
Nes longus
FAMILY:
Goby – Gobiidae

SIZE: 2-3 in., max. 4 in.
DEPTH: 3-30 ft.

KEY LARGO, FL

SEMINOLE GOBY
Microgobius carri
FAMILY:
Goby – Gobiidae

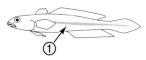

SIZE: 2-4 in., max. 5 in.
DEPTH: 20-70 ft.

ANGUILLA

DISTINCTIVE FEATURES: 1. Rounded tail. (Similar Blue Goby, *I. calliurus*, [next] distinguished by pointed tail.)

DESCRIPTION: Bluish gray; fins often yellowish. May have faint yellow and blue markings.

ABUNDANCE & DISTRIBUTION: Occasional South Florida, east and central Caribbean. Not reported Bahamas or western Caribbean.

HABITAT & BEHAVIOR: Hover just above slightly raised, "U"-shaped burrows in the sand.

REACTION TO DIVERS: Move toward their burrows when approached; if disturbed further, they dive into burrows.

NOTE: Recent evidence suggests that the genus name should be *Ptereleotris*.

DISTINCTIVE FEATURES: 1. Long, pointed tail. 2. Narrow black to red sub-marginal stripe on dorsal fin. (Similar Hovering Goby, *I. helenae*, [previous] distinguished by rounded tail and lack of stripe on dorsal fin.)

DESCRIPTION: Bluish gray to lavender.

ABUNDANCE & DISTRIBUTION: Common to occasional South Florida (both coasts). Not reported Bahamas or Caribbean.

HABITAT & BEHAVIOR: Hover just above burrows in the sand.

REACTION TO DIVERS: Move toward their burrows when approached; if disturbed further, they dive into burrows.

NOTE: Recent evidence suggests that the genus name should be *Ptereleotris*.

DISTINCTIVE FEATURES: 1. Alternating dark and light bands. 2. Diagonal bar at lower base of pectoral fin. 3. Long cirri on snout. (Similar Dwarf Blenny, *S. nanodes*, [next] has short cirri on snout.)

DESCRIPTION: Vary from brown to gray; light bands may have yellowish cast. Cirri on nape, above eyes, and on snout where they are the longest. Males have blotch on cheek [pictured].

ABUNDANCE & DISTRIBUTION: Rare Bahamas and Caribbean. Not reported Florida.

HABITAT & BEHAVIOR: Inhabit deep coral reefs.

REACTION TO DIVERS: Remain still, relying on camouflage; dart away upon close approach.

HOVERING GOBY
Ioglossus helenae
FAMILY:
Goby – Gobiidae

SIZE: 2-4 in., max. 5 in.
DEPTH: 35-130 ft.

SOUTH CAICOS

BLUE GOBY
Ioglossus calliurus
FAMILY:
Goby – Gobiidae

SIZE: 2-4 in., max. 5 in.
DEPTH: 20-155 ft.

KEY LARGO, FL

RINGED BLENNY
Starksia hassi
FAMILY:
Blenny – Clinidae

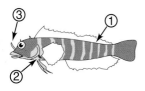

SIZE: ³/₄-1¹/₄ in.,
max. 1¹/₂ in.
DEPTH: 75-160 ft.

CAYMAN

DISTINCTIVE FEATURES: 1. White mask between eyes often runs onto snout. 2. Dark bar beneath eye. 3. Two black spots at base of tail radiate into fan-shaped markings.
DESCRIPTION: Shades of reddish brown. May have dark, wide, irregular dusky bands, especially females. Have short cirri on nape, above eyes. Short cirri on snout. (Similar Ringed Blenny, S. hassi, [previous] has long cirri on snout and does not have fan-shaped markings on tail.)
ABUNDANCE & DISTRIBUTION: Uncommon Bahamas to eastern, central and northwest Caribbean. Not reported balance of Caribbean or Florida. Often live on the outer surface of Giant Barrel Sponge *Xestospongia muta.*
HABITAT & BEHAVIOR: Inhabit patch reefs and coral heads.
REACTION TO DIVERS: Remain still, relying on camouflage; dart away upon close approach.

DISTINCTIVE FEATURES: 1. Four or five indistinct bars of even pigmentation. (Similar Palehead Blenny, *L. gobio*, [next] has bars that become darker and somewhat wider at midbody. **2. Blunt head with thick lips and large "goggle" eyes.**
DESCRIPTION: Shades of red-brown to brown or greenish brown. Numerous spots on fin rays, especially pectorals. May have indistinct pale spot on upper rear gill cover (pictured).
ABUNDANCE & DISTRIBUTION: Uncommon southeast Florida and continental coasts to Brazil. Not reported Bahamas and Caribbean islands.
HABITAT & BEHAVIOR: Inhabit coral reefs. Often live within the protective cover of fire coral branches.
REACTION TO DIVERS: Apparently feel secure within protective cover and do not move unless molested.
SIMILAR SPECIES: Puffcheek Blenny, *L. bucciferus*, distinguished by four or five body bars that are darker on the lower side.

DISTINCTIVE FEATURES: 1. Four or five irregular body bars that become darker and somewhat wider at midbody. (Similar Downy Blenny, *L.kalisherae*, [previous] distinguished by wider, indistinct bars of even pigmentation.) **2. Pale, blunt head with thick lips and large "goggle" eyes.**
DESCRIPTION: Shades of tan to brown and reddish brown.
ABUNDANCE & DISTRIBUTION: Uncommon South Florida, Bahamas, Caribbean.
HABITAT & BEHAVIOR: Prefer rocky areas, but also inhabit reefs, sand and coral rubble. Rest quietly on bottom, blending with background.
REACTION TO DIVERS: Relatively unafraid; usually allow a close approach.

DWARF BLENNY
Starksia nanodes
FAMILY:
Blenny – Clinidae

SIZE: $1/2$ - $1\,1/4$ in.,
max. $1\,3/4$ in.
DEPTH: 35 - 80 ft.

ANGUILLA

DOWNY BLENNY
Labrisomus kalisherae
FAMILY:
Blenny – Clinidae

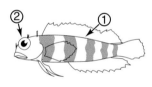

SIZE: 2-3 in., max. $3\,1/2$ in.
DEPTH: 5 - 50 ft.

DRY TORTUGAS, FL

PALEHEAD BLENNY
Labrisomus gobio
FAMILY:
Blenny – Clinidae

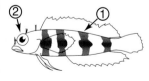

SIZE: $1\,1/2$ - $2\,1/4$ in.,
max. $2\,1/2$ in.
DEPTH: 5 - 50 ft.

CAYMAN

DISTINCTIVE FEATURES: Largest blenny in area. **1. Dark spot on upper gill cover.** (Spot may be obscure or obvious and is often ocellated especially in young). **2. Bluntish head with thick lips and large eyes. YOUNG (to over 3½ inches): 3. Dark spot on foredorsal fin that disappears with size and age.** Usually distinctly barred.

DESCRIPTION: Shades of yellow-brown to brown, red-brown or nearly black; can darken or pale dramatically to blend with background. **MALE:** Usually dark and uniformly colored with reddish tints especially on underside and fins. **FEMALE:** Spotted with vague to distinct banding.

ABUNDANCE & DISTRIBUTION: Occasional Florida, Bahamas, Caribbean; also Bermuda, Gulf of Mexico and south to Brazil. Can be locally abundant.

HABITAT & BEHAVIOR: Wide range of shallow habitats, from rocky areas mixed with sand and gravel to grass beds.

REACTION TO DIVERS: Unafraid; do not move unless closely approached.

SIMILAR SPECIES: Mimic Blenny, *L. guppyi*, is distinguished by small size (less than 3½ inches) and lack of spot on foredorsal fin.

Hairy Blenny Female

JUPITER, FL

DISTINCTIVE FEATURES: 1. Large, dark, ocellated spot on gill cover. 2. Eight or nine body bars from dorsal fin to belly.

DESCRIPTION: MALE: Bars bright orange, yellowish undercolor. **FEMALE:** Dark to medium brown bars over whitish undercolor.

ABUNDANCE & DISTRIBUTION: Occasional South Florida, Bahamas, Caribbean.

HABITAT & BEHAVIOR: Inhabit clear, shallow water from tidepools to reefs; often in areas of eroded limestone. Most abundant in water shallower than 12 feet. May seek refuge under rocks, rubble and sea urchins.

REACTION TO DIVERS: Not especially shy when near entrance of protective recesses or under sea urchins; usually allow close approach.

HAIRY BLENNY
Labrisomus nuchipinnis
Male
FAMILY:
Blenny – Clinidae

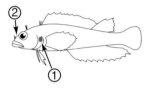

SIZE: 2¹/₂ - 6 in., max. 9 in.
DEPTH: 1 - 25 ft.

JUPITER, FL

Hairy Blenny
Young
Note ocellated spot on gill cover and dark spot on foredorsal fin.

WEST PALM BEACH, FL

SPOTCHEEK BLENNY
Labrisomus nigricinctus
Female
FAMILY:
Blenny – Clinidae

SIZE: 1¹/₄ - 2¹/₂ in.,
max. 3 in.
DEPTH: 0 - 35 ft.

ABACO, BAHAMAS

259

DISTINCTIVE FEATURES: 1. Dark, ocellated spot on gill cover. 2. Elongated foredorsal fin (male more elongated, with two or three distinct points).

DESCRIPTION: Dark tan to reddish brown. Dark brown bars on body. **MALE:** Rear dorsal fin edged with yellow.

ABUNDANCE & DISTRIBUTION: Uncommon to rare southern Bahamas and throughout Caribbean. Not reported Florida.

HABITAT & BEHAVIOR: Prefer mid-depth coral reefs. Rest on pectoral and dorsal fins, blending with background.

REACTION TO DIVERS: Not especially shy; usually allow close approach.

Diamond Blenny
Brown pattern.

CULEBRA, PR

DISTINCTIVE FEATURES: 1. Dark (black to dark blue) ocellated spot near front of dorsal fin. 2. Dusky triangular saddle markings on back and diamond markings on side. 3. Elongated ventral fins.

DESCRIPTION: Pale gray to tan; head most commonly bright yellow to gold, occasionally brown; may have red spots on head and body. Dorsal fin transparent behind area of ocellated spot.

ABUNDANCE & DISTRIBUTION: Occasional Bahamas and Caribbean. Not reported Florida.

HABITAT & BEHAVIOR: Inhabit reefs; move about bottom, and frequently stop to perch in tripod-stance, supported by long ventral fins and tail. May live in and around mats of Watercress Alga *Halimeda opuntia,* also live in association with Giant Anemones, *Condylactis gigantea* [see *Reef Creature Identification,* pg. 89]. Often take refuge in the tentacles when threatened, apparently unaffected by the anemones' stinging cells.

REACTION TO DIVERS: Relatively unafraid; allow close approach. Retreat only when molested.

QUILLFIN BLENNY
Labrisomus filamentosus
Male
FAMILY:
Blenny – Clinidae

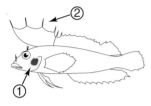

SIZE: 2-4 in., max. 5 in.
DEPTH: 40-100 ft.

CAYOS COCHINOS, HONDURAS

**Quillfin Blenny
Female**

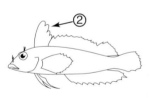

GRAND TURK

DIAMOND BLENNY
Malacoctenus boehlkei
FAMILY:
Blenny – Clinidae

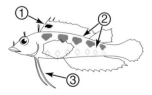

SIZE: 1½-2¼ in.,
max. 2½ in.
DEPTH: 25-80 ft.

CAYMAN

261

DISTINCTIVE FEATURES: 1. Four dark, inverted, triangular patterns form "saddles" across back (uncommonly, lower part of triangles are pale and indistinct). 2. Bar at base of tail.

DESCRIPTION: Undercolor usually white, occasionally yellow to orange. Faint, diamond-shaped patterns often on lower body; occasionally have red dots on body, especially concentrated in dark areas.

ABUNDANCE & DISTRIBUTION: Common to occasional South Florida, Bahamas, Caribbean; also south to Brazil.

HABITAT & BEHAVIOR: Inhabit reefs; move about bottom and frequently stop to perch in tripod-stance, supported by ventral fins and tail.

REACTION TO DIVERS: Not shy; often allow close approach.

DRY TORTUGAS, FL   WEST PALM BEACH, FL

DISTINCTIVE FEATURES: 1. Semicircular ocellated spot on base of spinous foredorsal fin (occasionally quite obscure). 2. Ocellated spot at middorsal fin, half on fin, half on body.

DESCRIPTION: FEMALE: Alternating light and dusky body bars; pale dots form thin stripes below midbody; banding on lower head. **MALE:** Similar, but darker with less distinct markings; occasionally totally black; distinctive white ventral fins contrast dramatically with dark body.

ABUNDANCE & DISTRIBUTION: Occasional Bahamas, Caribbean. Not reported Florida.

HABITAT & BEHAVIOR: Inhabit shallow areas of sand, gravel and rocky rubble; rarely around living coral. Occasionally associate with anemones.

REACTION TO DIVERS: Unafraid; do not move unless closely approached.

SIMILAR SPECIES: Imitator Blenny, *M. erdmani*, lacks an ocellated spot on spinous dorsal fin and has an ocellated body spot just below middorsal fin.

SADDLED BLENNY
Malacoctenus triangulatus
FAMILY:
Blenny – Clinidae

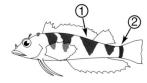

SIZE: 1 1/2 - 2 1/4 in.,
max. 2 1/2 in.
DEPTH: 6 - 50 ft.

ROATAN

Saddled Blenny
*Color and marking
variations.*

CAYMAN

DUSKY BLENNY
Malacoctenus gilli
Female
FAMILY:
Blenny – Clinidae

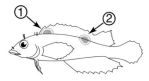

SIZE: 1 1/2 - 2 1/2 in.,
max. 3 in.
DEPTH: 1 - 15 ft.

BARBADOS

DISTINCTIVE FEATURES: 1. Pattern of dark, wide bars on dorsal fin and back lighten and change configuration at midline. (Similar female Rosy Blenny, *M. macropus*, [next], if bars are present, distinguished by dark bars that lighten or disappear at midline and do not extend onto dorsal fin.)

DESCRIPTION: Bars vary from dark brown to black and are occasionally fainter on dorsal fin.

ABUNDANCE & DISTRIBUTION: Occasional Bahamas, Caribbean. Not reported Florida.

HABITAT & BEHAVIOR: Inhabit shallow areas of sand, coral rubble and rocky shores.

REACTION TO DIVERS: Unafraid; do not move unless closely approached.

NOTE ABOUT FEMALE: Bars are much lighter and have yellowish cast. Body covered with black specks.

DISTINCTIVE FEATURES: 1. Sharply pointed snout. MALE: 2. Red spots and markings on underside of head and cheeks. FEMALE: No red spots or dependable markings.

DESCRIPTION: MALE: Vary, from wide dark bars on back becoming paler at midline [below left side, this page] to almost solid black [right]. **FEMALE:** Vary, from a few dark spots on back [below right side, this page] to wide, often indistinct, dark bars on back that lighten dramatically near midline, often disappearing completely [below right page]. (Similar Barfin Blenny, *M. versicolor*, [previous] is distinguished by wide, dark bars that extend onto dorsal fin and lighten and change pattern at midline.)

ABUNDANCE & DISTRIBUTION: Common Bahamas; occasional to uncommon Florida, Caribbean; also Bermuda.

HABITAT & BEHAVIOR: Inhabit reef tops and sand or rubble areas around reefs. Perch on bottom in tripod-stance, supported by ventral fins and tail.

REACTION TO DIVERS: Not shy; often allow close approach.

ANGUILLA

BIMINI

BARFIN BLENNY
Malacoctenus versicolor
Male
FAMILY:
Blenny – Clinidae

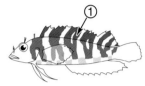

SIZE: 1½ - 2 in.,
max. 2½ in.
DEPTH: 1-15 ft.

CAYMAN

ROSY BLENNY
Malacoctenus macropus
Male
FAMILY:
Blenny – Clinidae

SIZE: 1½ - 2 in.,
max. 2¼ in.
DEPTH: 5-35 ft.

ANGUILLA

Rosy Blenny
*Female with indistinct
dark bars on back.*
[right]

Male
With barred pattern.
[far left]

Female
*With only a few
dark spots on back.*
[near left]

CAYMAN

265

DISTINCTIVE FEATURES: 1. Three dark bars on forebody, the second and third are joined near the center forming an H-shape. 2. Rear half of body yellowish with two to four darkish, often indistinct bars.

DESCRIPTION: Dark band or line markings on lips, cheeks and underside of head over pale undercolor; anal fin gold. Dark area that joins second and third bar may extend forward to first bar.

ABUNDANCE & DISTRIBUTION: Occasional Florida, Bahamas, Caribbean.

HABITAT & BEHAVIOR: Inhabit clear, shallow water, from tidepools to grass beds and reefs; often in eroded limestone areas inhabited by rock-boring urchins. Most abundant in water shallower than 20 feet. Perch on long ventral fins.

REACTION TO DIVERS: Not especially shy; usually allow close approach with slow, nonthreatening movements.

DISTINCTIVE FEATURES: 1. Blunt head, short snout. 2. Small blue spot usually present on first dorsal spine. **MALE:** Dark brown to black. 3. Foredorsal fin extremely tall. **FEMALE:** Pale and mottled in shades of brown to gray. 4. Thin, broken diagonal lines on foredorsal fin.

DESCRIPTION: Single cirri above eye, translucent or with pale banding, and may have three small branches at tip. **MALE:** Yellow-gold streak usually below blue spot on first dorsal spine; often have blue to white spots, especially on lips and throat. Although the large "sail" fin is distinctive, it is rarely seen because they seldom venture from their holes.

ABUNDANCE & DISTRIBUTION: Occasional Florida, Bahamas, Caribbean; also Gulf of Mexico. Can be locally abundant.

HABITAT & BEHAVIOR: Inhabit clear water areas of rock rubble, sand and coral. Rest in holes on long ventral fins with heads protruding. Occasionally dart from hole, repeatedly flicking sail fin up and down. Within seconds they return to their holes.

REACTION TO DIVERS: Their heads disappear into holes when closely approached. Best way to observe the Sailfins' unique behavior is to wait quietly a short distance from individual's hole. The wait can take from five to 15 minutes.

CULEBRA, PR

CAYMAN

GOLDLINE BLENNY
Malacoctenus aurolineatus
FAMILY:
Blenny – Clinidae

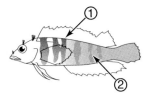

SIZE: 1-2 in., max. 2½ in.
DEPTH: 5 - 35 ft.

ABACO, BAHAMAS

SAILFIN BLENNY
Emblemaria pandionis
Male
FAMILY:
Blenny – Clinidae

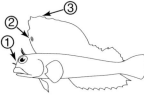

SIZE: 1½-2 in.,
max. 2½ in.
DEPTH: 3- 35 ft.

BIMINI

Sailfin Blenny
Female
*Note diagonal lines in
foredorsal fin.*
[right]

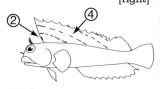

Male[far left]
*Typical resting
position in hole.*

Female [left]

WEST PALM BEACH, FL

267

DISTINCTIVE FEATURES: 1. Translucent body. 2. No cirrus above eye. MALE: 3. Dark head, occasionally with white spots. FEMALE: 4. Pale, often colorless, head.

DESCRIPTION: Some grayish to brownish or reddish markings in areas of body organs and spinal cord.

ABUNDANCE & DISTRIBUTION: Uncommon to rare Florida, Bahamas, Caribbean.

HABITAT & BEHAVIOR: Rest on pectoral and ventral fins, often on sponges and corals. Translucent to transparent bodies blend with any background. This, combined with their small size, makes them difficult to spot.

REACTION TO DIVERS: Easily approached; do not move unless molested.

NOTE: Formerly classified as genus *Emblemaria*.

BIMINI

KEY LARGO, FL

DISTINCTIVE FEATURES: 1. Cirri above eye usually branch in a single plane and in opposing pairs. (Similar Roughhead Blenny, *A. aspera*, [next] have bush-like branched cirri.) **2. Fleshy papillae on top of head and snout** (unlike similar Spinyhead Blenny, *A. spinosa*, [previous], Roughhead Blenny and Secretary Blenny, *A. maria*, [next] that have spines). **3. Iris orange.**

DESCRIPTION: Tan to yellow or orange with numerous white and brown spots.

ABUNDANCE & DISTRIBUTION: Uncommon southeastern Florida, Bahamas. Not reported Caribbean.

HABITAT & BEHAVIOR: Inhabit hard-bottom slopes extending from shore that are often dotted with patches of fire coral and small brain corals. Most often inhabit small worm holes in sea floor where they perch with heads extended.

REACTION TO DIVERS: Allow very close observation; retreat into holes only if molested.

BLACKHEAD BLENNY
Coralliozetus bahamensis
Male
FAMILY:
Blenny – Clinidae

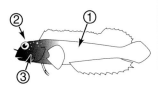

SIZE: ¹/₂ - ³/₄ in.,
max. 1 in.
DEPTH: 15 - 60 ft.

DRY TORTUGAS, FL

Blackhead Blenny
Female

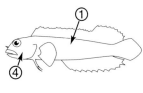

BELIZE

PAPILLOSE BLENNY
Acanthemblemaria chaplini
FAMILY:
Blenny – Clinidae

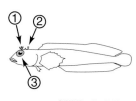

SIZE: 1 - 1¹/₂ in.,
max. 2 in.
DEPTH: 3 - 40 ft.

BIMINI

DISTINCTIVE FEATURES: 1. Cirri above eye often have only two branches, and never more than a few, toward tip. 2. Numerous tiny spines on head, including snout, give a rough appearance. 3. Yellow-green "goggle" eyes.

DESCRIPTION: Dark black to brown head and body with white speckles, and occasionally mottled or with indistinct bands. Snout and nape usually white or have greenish cast.

ABUNDANCE & DISTRIBUTION: Common Caribbean; uncommon South Florida, Bahamas.

HABITAT & BEHAVIOR: On reefs they inhabit small worm holes in white limestone rocks or pores in sponges, where they perch with heads extended. Dart out for a split second to grab suspended particles of food.

REACTION TO DIVERS: Allow a very close approach; appear curious; retreat into holes only when molested.

DISTINCTIVE FEATURES: 1. Densely branched, bush-like cirri above eye. 2. Numerous small spines on top of head give a rough appearance which, when viewed from above, form a rear pointing "V". (Similar Papillose Blenny, *A. chaplini*, [previous] have fleshy papillae rather than spines and cirri generally branch in a single plane and in opposing pairs.) 3. Iris orange.

DESCRIPTION: Vary from black to brown, tan, olive, yellow and white; often lighter toward rear. Brownish spots along dorsal and anal fin, especially toward rear; brown and white speckles over head and body. **MALE:** Ocellated black spot on foredorsal fin and usually has dark head and forebody. **FEMALE:** May have dark smudge on foredorsal fin, but never an ocellated spot, usually lighter, some nearly white.

ABUNDANCE & DISTRIBUTION: Occasional southeastern Florida, Bahamas, Caribbean.

HABITAT & BEHAVIOR: Most often inhabit small worm holes in white limestone rocks near or on reefs where they perch with heads extended. Dart out for a split second to grab suspended particles of food.

REACTION TO DIVERS: Allow very close observation; retreat into holes only if molested.

KEY LARGO, FL

BIMINI

SPINYHEAD BLENNY
Acanthemblemaria
spinosa
FAMILY:
Blenny – Clinidae

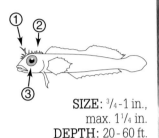

SIZE: ³/₄ - 1 in.,
max. 1¹/₄ in.
DEPTH: 20 - 60 ft.

CAYMAN

ROUGHHEAD BLENNY
Acanthemblemaria aspera
FAMILY:
Blenny – Clinidae

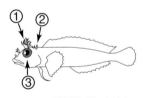

SIZE: ³/₄ - 1¹/₄ in.,
max. 1¹/₂ in.
DEPTH: 20 - 60 ft.

L CAYMAN

Roughhead Blenny

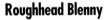

Males
[near left and right]
Note ocellated spot on
foredorsal fin.

Female [far left]

KEY LARGO, FL

DISTINCTIVE FEATURES: 1. Alternating, irregular brown and pale body bars. 2. Whitish streak behind and below eye. 3. Branched cirri above eye (less than similar Roughhead, *A. aspera*, [previous], but more than Spinyhead, *A. spinosa* [pg. 271].

DESCRIPTION: Dark black to brown head and body with white speckles, and occasionally, mottled. Large, dark spot (often navy blue) behind eye, but may not be apparent when head is a solid dark color. Snout and nape may be white or have greenish cast.

ABUNDANCE & DISTRIBUTION: Occasional Bahamas, Caribbean. Not reported Florida.

HABITAT & BEHAVIOR: On hard-bottom slopes extending from shore that are often dotted with patches of fire coral, small brain corals and small patch reefs. Most often inhabit small worm holes in white limestone rocks where they perch with heads extended. Dart out for a split second to grab suspended particles of food.

REACTION TO DIVERS: Allow a very close approach; appear curious; retreat into holes only when molested.

DISTINCTIVE FEATURES: Bright yellow, scaleless body. **1. Black dot on foredorsal fin begins behind third ray and does not extend to body. 2. Corners of mouth extend to below eyes.** (Resemble and mimic yellow phases of Blueheads, *Thalassoma bifasciatum*, [pg. 199] almost perfectly, but can be distinguished by a scaled body; black dot on foredorsal fin starts behind second ray and extends to body; and small mouth, with corners that do not extend to below eye.)

DESCRIPTION: Belly generally white. A dark stripe often runs from eye to tail. Can rapidly change color pattern to resemble any of the yellow phases of the Bluehead. Young have transparent fins and somewhat translucent body. A dark stripe runs from snout across eye to tail and has a teardrop-shaped end.

ABUNDANCE & DISTRIBUTION: Occasional Bahamas and South Florida to Central American coastal waters. Not reported Caribbean islands.

HABITAT & BEHAVIOR: Often sit on pectoral fins, in holes, with their heads protruding. This behavior is usually a clue to their identity. Similar Blueheads swim almost constantly and rarely behave in this manner. Blueheads are cleaners, and therefore, not eaten by predators or considered a threat by small prey. The mimicry of Wrasse Blennies affords the same protection from predators and allows them to get close to small fish and shrimp upon which they feed.

REACTION TO DIVERS: When swimming with Blueheads, tend to ignore divers.

Wrasse Blenny
Young mimicking yellow–back phase of Bluehead.

DRY TORTUGAS, FL

SECRETARY BLENNY
Acanthemblemaria maria
FAMILY:
Blenny – Clinidae

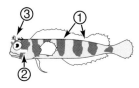

SIZE: ³/₄ - 1¹/₂ in.,
max. 2 in.
DEPTH: 6 - 25 ft.

BONAIRE

WRASSE BLENNY
Hemiemblemaria simulus
FAMILY:
Blenny – Clinidae

SIZE: 2 - 3¹/₂ in., max. 4 in.
DEPTH: 15 - 60 ft.

KEY LARGO, FL

Wrasse Blenny
*Young mimicking
white-back phase
of Bluehead.*

DRY TORTUGAS, FL

273

DISTINCTIVE FEATURES: 1. Drifts with tail "cocked." 2. Long, pointed mouth and snout.
DESCRIPTION: Reddish, with several black blotches on dorsal and anal fins near tail. Elongated body.
ABUNDANCE & DISTRIBUTION: Occasional Bahamas, Caribbean. Not reported Florida.
HABITAT & BEHAVIOR: Unlike other blennies, rarely rest on fins; usually drift inconspicuously, well off the bottom, in secluded areas. Tails are always "cocked" — ready to shoot forward and nab prey. When resting, heads protrude from small holes which they inhabit.
REACTION TO DIVERS: Generally ignore divers, but shoot away if closely approached.

DISTINCTIVE FEATURES: 1. Somewhat flattened, distinctly pointed snout. 2. Long upper jaw extends to below eye. 3. Cirri over eyes and on nape are white and have a stout base that divides into several pointed branches. 4. Dark blue spot ringed with orange usually present on rear dorsal fin.
DESCRIPTION: Highly variable, from pale shades of earthtones to almost black; anal fin often dark. Can have irregular, darkish band that extends onto fins.
ABUNDANCE & DISTRIBUTION: Occasional Florida, Bahamas, Caribbean; also Bermuda and south to Brazil.
HABITAT & BEHAVIOR: Inhabit shallow areas of eroded limestone, including tidepools and zones of rocks mixed with sea grasses and algae. Often hide in holes with only heads protruding.
REACTION TO DIVERS: Shy; hide in holes and recesses when approached.

DISTINCTIVE FEATURES: 1. Extremely tall cirri above eye, with numerous secondary branches. 2. Dark golden to brown bar extends from cirri, across eye and cheek.
DESCRIPTION: Yellow head; pale yellow-gold body; fins have yellowish cast.
ABUNDANCE & DISTRIBUTION: Uncommon Bahamas. Not reported Florida or Caribbean.
HABITAT & BEHAVIOR: Inhabit shallow, rocky, clear water areas with surge, small corals and sea fans.
REACTION TO DIVERS: Shy; scoot away upon approach.

ARROW BLENNY
Lucayablennius zingaro
FAMILY:
Blenny – Clinidae

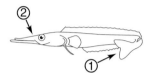

SIZE: 1 - 1½ in., max. 2 in.
DEPTH: 40 - 100 ft.

CAYMAN

BLACKFIN BLENNY
Paraclinus nigripinnis
FAMILY:
Blenny – Clinidae

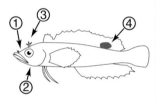

SIZE: 1 - 1¾ in., max. 2 in.
DEPTH: 0 - 20 ft.

KEY LARGO, FL

LONGHORN BLENNY
Hypsoblennius exstochilus
FAMILY:
Blenny – Blenniidae

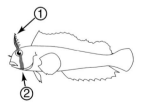

SIZE: 1 - 2 in., max. 2¼ in.
DEPTH: 0 - 20 ft.

NASSAU

275

DISTINCTIVE FEATURES: 1. Head and body covered with brilliant orange spots or polygons.
DESCRIPTION: Dark blue. Young have unbranched cirri above eyes, but adults may have up to four branches.
ABUNDANCE & DISTRIBUTION: Uncommon Florida, Caribbean; also Gulf of Mexico. Not reported Bahamas.
HABITAT & BEHAVIOR: Inhabit empty barnacle shells in shallow water. Most common in clear water on pilings, buoys, oil platforms and other similar habitats where large acorn-type barnacles attach. Generally remain within protective confines of barnacle shell with only head protruding. Dart out only to nab particles of floating food.
REACTION TO DIVERS: Shy; remain in barnacle shell. If diver remains still, however, may go about normal activities and, occasionally, dart out of shell.

DISTINCTIVE FEATURES: 1. Fringe of brush-like cirri (usually red and white banded) on top of head. 2. Cirri above each eye unbranched.
DESCRIPTION: Shades of olive-brown, can be quite pale or very dark. Variable dark markings, occasionally with pearly white spots; tail usually banded.
ABUNDANCE & DISTRIBUTION: Occasional Florida; occasional to rare Bahamas, Caribbean; also Bermuda, Gulf of Mexico and south to Brazil.
HABITAT & BEHAVIOR: Inhabit tidepools, shallow rocky reefs, jetties and areas with boulders on sand bottoms. Usually in locations with some surge and wave action. Take refuge in small holes and recesses.
REACTION TO DIVERS: Shy; rapidly retreat into protection of recess upon approach. If diver remains still, however, they often reappear and can be approached with slow, nonthreatening movements.

Molly Miller
Note unique structure of fringe of cirri on head.

FT. PIERCE, FL

TESSELATED BLENNY
Hypsoblennius invemar
FAMILY:
Blenny – Blenniidae

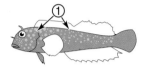

SIZE: 1-2 in., max. 2½ in.
DEPTH: 1-12 ft.

WEST PALM BEACH, FL

MOLLY MILLER
Scartella cristata
FAMILY:
Blenny – Blenniidae

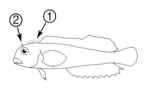

SIZE: 1½-3 in., max. 4 in.
DEPTH: 1-20 ft.

JUPITER, FL

Molly Miller
Dark phase.

PANAMA CITY, FL

277

DISTINCTIVE FEATURES: 1. Pale blue vertical line markings (occasionally net-like) down snout, over upper lip and below eyes. 2. Obscure pale spot on gill cover behind eye.

DESCRIPTION: Markings and colors vary greatly (see photos below). Usually in shades of earthtones, but can be bright yellow to gold. Series of dark spots often form broken stripes down body; stripe from eye to tail usually widest and darkest. A small, pale to brilliant blue spot occasionally on foredorsal fin. Can pale or darken and change markings to blend with background. Blunt snout. Cirri above eyes usually have three or four branches.

ABUNDANCE & DISTRIBUTION: Common Florida; uncommon Bahamas; occasional to rare Caribbean; also north to New York, Bermuda and Gulf of Mexico.

HABITAT & BEHAVIOR: Prefer shallow to mid-range reefs and hard bottoms covered with algae and gorgonians. Often inhabit small holes and recesses, but occasionally in open.

REACTION TO DIVERS: Shy; rapidly retreat into protection of recess upon approach. If diver remains still, however, they often reappear and can be approached with slow, nonthreatening movements.

JACKSONVILLE, FL   FT. LAUDERDALE, FL

DISTINCTIVE FEATURES: 1. Six solid, dark brown to black bars run across back to midline and continues onto belly in lighter shade. 2. Small orangish to bronze spots on head may continue onto body. 3. Tail lightly barred.

DESCRIPTION: Tan to yellowish or whitish undercolor. Dorsal and anal fins are lightly banded.

ABUNDANCE & DISTRIBUTION: Occasional Florida; uncommon Bahamas; also Bermuda. Not reported Caribbean.

HABITAT & BEHAVIOR: Wide range of habitats, from rocky inshore areas, jetties and shallow coral gardens to reefs of moderate depth well offshore; may inhabit areas of gravel and rubble or large stands of fire coral.

REACTION TO DIVERS: Shy; retreat into protective recesses upon close approach, but often reappear after a short, quiet wait.

SEAWEED BLENNY
Parablennius marmoreus
FAMILY:
Blenny – Blenniidae

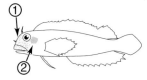

SIZE: 1¹/₂ - 3 in.,
max. 3¹/₂ in.
DEPTH: 1 - 80 ft.

JACKSONVILLE, FL

CULEBRA, PR

DRY TORTUGAS, FL

BARRED BLENNY
*Hypleurochilus
bermudensis*
FAMILY:
Blenny – Blenniidae

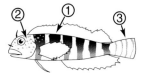

SIZE: 1 - 3 in., max. 4 in.
DEPTH: 3 - 75 ft.

SARASOTA, FL

DISTINCTIVE FEATURES: 1. Blunt, reddish brown head. 2. Large lips.

DESCRIPTION: Vary from dark reddish brown to bicolor with gray or nearly all gray, most commonly bicolor. Pectoral fins and upper border of tail may be edged and tinted with yellow to gold or red; lips often have reddish tint.

ABUNDANCE & DISTRIBUTION: Common to occasional Florida, Bahamas, Caribbean; also north to North Carolina, Bermuda and south to Brazil. Can be locally abundant.

HABITAT & BEHAVIOR: Prefer rocky inshore areas and shallow coral reefs. Rest on reef crest. Territorial; will chase away intruders.

REACTION TO DIVERS: Not shy; can be closely approached.

Redlip Blenny
Gray phase.

CAYMAN

DISTINCTIVE FEATURES: 1. White tail with black, irregular bars or spots.

DESCRIPTION: Dark brown head, body and fins. May have bluish spot on foredorsal fin (probably males).

ABUNDANCE & DISTRIBUTION: Occasional Gulf Coast of Florida. Not reported balance of Florida, Bahamas or Caribbean.

HABITAT & BEHAVIOR: Inhabit rocky and artificial reefs and areas of hard rubble.

REACTION TO DIVERS: Shy; retreat into protective recesses upon close approach, but often reappear after a short, quiet wait. Can be closely approached with slow, nonthreatening movements.

REDLIP BLENNY
Ophioblennius atlanticus

FAMILY:
Blenny – Blenniidae

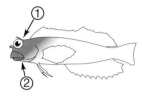

SIZE: 2¹/₂ - 4¹/₂ in.,
max. 5 in.
DEPTH: 1 - 35 ft.

GRENADINES

Redlip Blenny
*Bicolor phase -
reddish brown/gray.*

CAYMAN

ZEBRATAIL BLENNY
*Hypleurochilus
caudovettatus*

FAMILY:
Blenny – Blenniidae

SIZE: 1-2 in., max. 2¹/₂ in.
DEPTH: 5 - 75 ft.

SARASOTA, FL

DISTINCTIVE FEATURES: 1. First dorsal fin is taller than beginning of second dorsal fin.

DESCRIPTION: Head orangish brown; body pale translucent to transparent brown; three or four dusky, often somewhat indistinct, body bars appear diagonal and may fork below midline; dusky bar on base of tail, usually not much darker than body bars. (Similar triplefins normally have a distinctly darker bar on base of tail.) Snout is pointed and body elongated.

ABUNDANCE & DISTRIBUTION: Occasional to uncommon southeastern Florida, Bahamas, Caribbean.

HABITAT & BEHAVIOR: Inhabit reefs. Often perch on the surfaces of sponges or coral heads.

REACTION TO DIVERS: Generally unafraid; usually allow slow, nonthreatening, close approach.

SIMILAR SPECIES: Of the four other species of triplefins, only the Blackedge Triplefin, *E. atrorus,* has a similar tall first dorsal fin. It can be distinguished by the first dorsal spine which is longest and a black edge on the second. Known only from Bahamas.

DISTINCTIVE FEATURES: 1. First dorsal fin is shorter than beginning of second dorsal fin. 2. Three or four brownish body bars and an additional bar on base of tail are diagonal and do not contrast strongly with background.

DESCRIPTION: Head reddish or orangish brown; body pale translucent to transparent brown.

ABUNDANCE & DISTRIBUTION: Occasional to uncommon southeastern Florida, Bahamas, Caribbean.

HABITAT & BEHAVIOR: Inhabit reefs. Often perch on the surface of sponges or coral heads.

REACTION TO DIVERS: Generally unafraid; usually allow slow, nonthreatening, close approach.

SIMILAR SPECIES: Two other similar appearing species of triplefins have a short first dorsal fin, but can be distinguished by vertical body bars, short snouts and robust bodies. Redeye Triplefin, *E. pectoralis,* has bar on base of tail that is broader and darker than body bars and also has a red border behind; iris red. Mimic Triplefin, *E. jordani,* is very difficult to distinguish from the Redeye. Anal fin has six or seven bars, while that of Redeye has even pigmentation. Shallow water species, 0–15 feet, only known from Bahamas to Puerto Rico.

DISTINCTIVE FEATURES: Species best distinguished by 15–60 ft. depth range. (Similar Bluethroat Pikeblenny, *C. ocellata,* [next] inhabits 1-10 ft. depth range.) **1. Yellow to yellow-brown midbody stripe, often with dark spots or dashes. 2. Pinkish. iris.** Elongated head with flattened snout and long snake-like body. **MALE:** Foredorsal fin is quite high when extended.

DESCRIPTION: Pale tan to yellowish brown body, often yellowish snout. Rays of throat blue with yellow membrane. **MALE:** Dark, ocellated dot with a yellowish area above, located between first and second dorsal fin spines.

ABUNDANCE & DISTRIBUTION: Uncommon South Florida, Bahamas, Caribbean.

HABITAT & BEHAVIOR: Habitat is often key to identification. Inhabit small holes in areas of sand and coral rubble; often form colonies. Prefer clear water, deeper than 15 feet.

REACTION TO DIVERS: Relatively unafraid; usually allow close approach.

LOFTY TRIPLEFIN
Enneanectes altivelis
FAMILY:
Blenny – Tripterygiidae

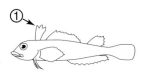

SIZE: 1-1 1/4 in.,
max. 1 1/2 in.
DEPTH: 15 - 80 ft.

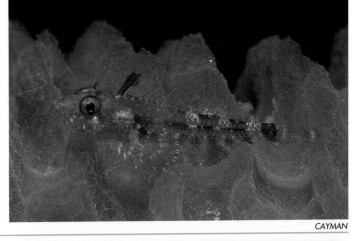

CAYMAN

ROUGHHEAD TRIPLEFIN
Enneanectes boehlkei
FAMILY:
Blenny – Tripterygiidae

SIZE: 1-1 1/4 in.,
max. 1 1/2 in.
DEPTH: 15 - 80 ft.

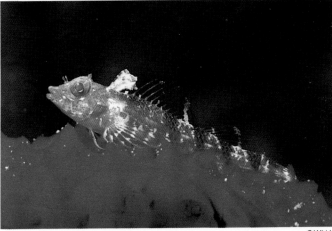

CAYMAN

YELLOWFACE PIKEBLENNY
Chaenopsis limbaughi
FAMILY:
Blenny – Clinidae

SIZE: 2-3 in., max. 3 1/2 in.
DEPTH: 15 - 60 ft.

BIMINI

DISTINCTIVE FEATURES: Species best distinguished by 1–10 ft. depth range. (Similar Yellowface Pikeblenny, *C. limbaughi*, [previous] inhabits 15-60 ft. depth range.) Elongated head with flattened snout and long, snake-like body. **1. Orange Iris.** Foredorsal fin is quite high when extended.

DESCRIPTION: MALE: Pale tan to yellowish brown body. Throat rays and occasionally membrane bright blue. Foredorsal fin with white speckles is quite high when extended. Dark blue to black markings and often yellow to orange area. **FEMALE:** Pale brown to green back, whitish underside. Usually have spots and indistinct, wide body bars.

ABUNDANCE & DISTRIBUTION: Uncommon Florida, Bahamas; uncommon to absent Caribbean.

HABITAT & BEHAVIOR: Habitat is often key to identification. Rarely found deeper than 10 feet in sandy areas mixed with sea grass and algae; may be in murky water. Solitary; often inhabit worm tubes.

REACTION TO DIVERS: Relatively unafraid; usually allow close approach.

Lancer Dragonet Female

Note blackish first dorsal fin.

KEY LARGO, FL

DISTINCTIVE FEATURES: 1. First dorsal fin elongated; yellowish in males, blackish in females. 2. Large goggle eyes extend above flattened head.

DESCRIPTION: Body mottled and marbled in shades ranging from pale whitish gray to brown and reddish brown. Can pale or darken. First dorsal fin of male [right] is longer than that of female, though length of female's is significant.

ABUNDANCE & DISTRIBUTION: Occasional South Florida, Bahamas, Caribbean; also Bermuda.

HABITAT & BEHAVIOR: Inhabit reefs and adjacent areas of mixed coral rubble and sand. Rest on bottom blending into background.

REACTION TO DIVERS: Allow a close approach, but dart away when threatened.

SIMILAR SPECIES: Spotted Dragonet, *Diplogrammus pauciradiatus*, distinguished by numerous black spots on a tan-to-white mottled background. Have unusually long first dorsal fin. Inhabit shallow grass beds.

NOTE: Formerly classified in genus *Callionymus*. Also commonly known as "Coral Dragonet."

BLUETHROAT PIKEBLENNY
Chaenopsis ocellata
Male
FAMILY:
Blenny – Clinidae

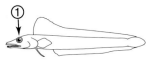

SIZE: 3-4 in., max. 5 in.
DEPTH: 1-10 ft.

BELIZE

Bluethroat Pikeblenny Female
Note typical sand, sea grass, and algae habitat.

ANGUILLA

LANCER DRAGONET
Paradiplogrammus bairdi
Male
FAMILY:
Dragonet – Callionymidae

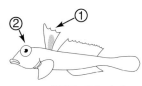

SIZE: 1 1/2 - 2 1/2 in.,
max. 4 1/2 in.
DEPTH: 6-300 ft.

CAYMAN

DISTINCTIVE FEATURES: 1. Yellowish head. Pale body. Hover vertically above burrows.

DESCRIPTION: Head varies from bright yellow to yellowish tan; body ranges from tan to bluish pearl; rear dorsal, anal and tail fins have bluish cast. Ventral fins elongated.

ABUNDANCE & DISTRIBUTION: Common South Florida, Bahamas, Caribbean.

HABITAT & BEHAVIOR: Inhabit areas of sand and coral rubble near reefs. Individuals excavate burrows in the sand by mouth. They hover above holes and, if frightened, retreat tail first. Males incubate eggs of young in their mouths.

REACTION TO DIVERS: Relatively unafraid; can be approached with slow movements.

SIMILAR SPECIES: Swordtail Jawfish, *Lonchopisthus micrognathus*, distinguished by long, pointed tail and pale bluish body bands. Generally below 90 feet; South Florida and Gulf of Mexico.

DISTINCTIVE FEATURES: Dark brown mottled head. **1. Rear gill cover rounded. 2. Blue to bluish black spot between second and fourth or fifth dorsal spines.**

DESCRIPTION: Mottled in shades of brown. Dorsal fin often has black edge, especially in larger individuals.

ABUNDANCE & DISTRIBUTION: Uncommon Florida, Bahamas, Caribbean.

HABITAT & BEHAVIOR: Inhabit areas of coral rubble, rocks and sand. Individuals excavate burrows by mouth, but do not line the hole with stones as several similar species do. Males incubate eggs in their mouths.

REACTION TO DIVERS: Somewhat shy; retreat into burrows when threatened.

SIMILAR SPECIES: Mottled Jawfish, *O. maxillosus*, is difficult to distinguish when only head protrudes from burrow. Species can be distinguished by its squared, upper rear corner of gill cover when exposed. If dorsal fin is exposed, it has several dark blotches, usually four, located low on fin; the first never starting before sixth spine.

DISTINCTIVE FEATURES: Light tan head with only indistinct, unpatterned markings. Not heavily mottled as many others.

DESCRIPTION: If body is exposed, can be distinguished by: **1. Several blotches along sides. 2. Blotch on outer half of dorsal fin starting behind sixth spine.** Common name derived from black and white bands on roof of male's mouth.

ABUNDANCE & DISTRIBUTION: Occasional South Florida, Bahamas, Caribbean.

HABITAT & BEHAVIOR: Inhabit areas of coral rubble, rocks and sand. Individuals excavate burrows by mouth and line holes with stones. Usually only the head protrudes from its hole. Males incubate eggs in their mouths (note photograph).

REACTION TO DIVERS: May allow close approach, but retreat into individual burrow when threatened.

YELLOWHEAD JAWFISH
Opistognathus aurifrons
FAMILY:
Jawfish –
Opistognathidae

SIZE: 2-3 in., max. 4 in.
DEPTH: 10-60 ft.

CAYMAN

DUSKY JAWFISH
Opistognathus whitehursti
FAMILY:
Jawfish –
Opistognathidae

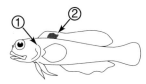

SIZE: 2 1/2 - 3 1/2 in.,
max. 4 in.
DEPTH: 3-25 ft.

WEST PALM BEACH, FL

BANDED JAWFISH
Opistognathus macrognathus
FAMILY:
Jawfish –
Opistognathidae

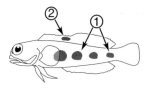

SIZE: 4-6 1/2 in., max. 8 in.
DEPTH: 3-25 ft.

BARBADOS

Odd-Shaped Bottom-Dwellers
Flounder–Batfish–Toadfish–Scorpionfish–Others

This ID Group consists of fish that normally rest on the bottom and do not have a typical fish-like shape. All are experts at camouflage.

FAMILY: Lefteye Flounder — Bothidae
10 Species Included

Flounder (typical shape)

Flounders are unique, flat fish that actually lie on their sides, not their stomachs. Those in the Family Bothidae lie on their right side with eyes up on the left side. (Members of the Family Pleuronectidae lie on their left side. Most inhabit cool to cold waters and are not found in Florida, Bahamas or Caribbean.) Within a few weeks of birth, the eye on the bottom slowly migrates to the exposed side. The eyes protrude noticeably, sometimes appearing to be raised on short, thick stalks. Their exposed pectoral fin is more like a dorsal fin, while the dorsal and anal fins almost ring the rounded body. Flounders can change, lighten or darken their colors to blend with the bottom. Many enhance their camouflage by partly burying themselves in sand or mud. They glide over the bottom with a slight wave-like motion. Many of the flounders are difficult to distinguish, but with careful attention to subtle markings, most can be identified.

FAMILY: Batfish — Ogcocephalidae
4 Species Included

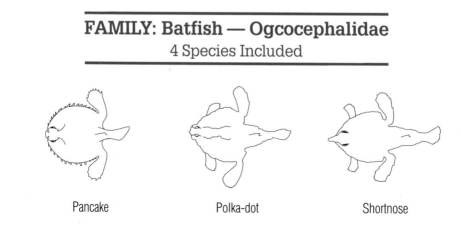

Pancake   Polka-dot   Shortnose

The pectoral and ventral fins of batfish have evolved into leg-like projections. Perched on the bottom, these strange pectoral fins give the illusion of bat wings. Camouflage of colors and markings combined with the habit of throwing sand over their body makes them difficult to locate. Lying motionless, they wait for unsuspecting prey to pass close by. Instead of swimming, they move about by "walking" on their ventral and pectoral fins. To increase speed they push off the bottom and use their tails in a sluggish, swinging motion.

FAMILY: Toadfish — Batrachoididae
10 Species Included

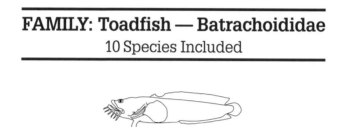

Toadfish (typical shape)

Toadfish have large, noticeably flattened heads with sizable mouths. Most species have fleshy tabs or barbels growing from the chin and head. They have tapering bodies with large, fan-like pectoral fins and a rounded tail. Most are drab, mottled shades of brown to gray, blending into the bottom background. Many toadfish are difficult to distinguish and careful attention to subtle markings is often required for identification. Because many have limited geographical distribution, the location of a sighting can be an important key to identification. They are pugnacious predators, feeding primarily on other fish and crustaceans.

FAMILY: Scorpionfish — Scorpaenidae
6 Species Included

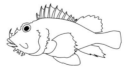

Scorpionfish (typical shape)

Fleshy appendages, or flaps, help camouflage scorpionfishes' large heads and stocky bodies. Mottled and spotted in earthtones, they are difficult to detect as they lie motionless on bottom rubble and/or algae. Spines of the foredorsal fin, which can be raised defensively, are venomous and can inflict a painful wound. Their pectoral fins are often brightly colored, but unseen unless spread. Although species are quite similar at first glance, most can easily be distinguished with attention to detail.

FAMILY: Frogfish — Antennariidae
7 Species Included

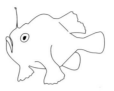

Frogfish (typical shape)

Frogfish are globular in shape with large, extremely upturned mouths which can be opened to the width of their bodies to engulf prey. Their pectoral and ventral fins have evolved into webbed, hand-like appendages which they use to grasp, perch, or "walk." The small circular gill openings are located behind and/or below the pectoral fin. The first dorsal spine is located on the snout and has evolved into a thin, stalk-like structure which is used as a lure to attract prey. Masters at camouflage, they can change to virtually any color to perfectly match the background. At rest they often look like sponges or clumps of algae. Body markings are the keys to identification.

FAMILY: Lizardfish — Synodontidae
5 Species Included

Lizardfish (typical shape)

Lizardfish have large, upturned mouths, pointed snouts and long, cylindrical bodies. Experts at camouflage, they rest motionless on the bottom, blending with their surroundings. Some bury themselves in the sand with only their heads protruding as they wait for unsuspecting prey. Because they are similar in coloration and markings, especially in their pale phases, lizardfish can be tricky to distinguish.

FAMILY: Seahorse & Pipefish — Syngnathidae
6 Species Included

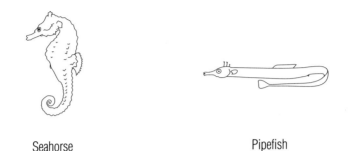

Seahorse

Pipefish

These strange little fish all have trumpet-like snouts and small mouths. Their bodies are encased in protective bony rings which are quite apparent. Seahorses are vertically oriented, and have a cocked head. Their finless, elongated tail base is often coiled around a hold-fast. Pipefish are elongated, snake-like bottom dwellers with heads that extend straight from their bodies, and small tail fins. Both are slow swimmers.

FAMILY: Others
10 Species Included

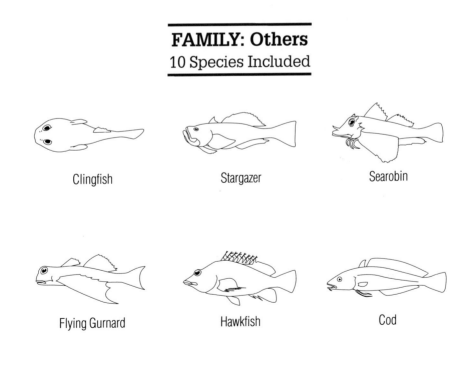

Clingfish

Stargazer

Searobin

Flying Gurnard

Hawkfish

Cod

Flounder

DISTINCTIVE FEATURES: 1. **Blue ring markings over entire body. 2. Blue spots on fins and head.** (Blue may be faint, but distinguishes the Peacock from similar Eyed Flounder, *B. ocellatus*, [next] whose ring markings are brownish, never blue.) 3. **Unusually long pectoral fin, often erect.**

DESCRIPTION: Shades of brown to tan. Can darken or pale and change color dramatically to match bottom. Eyes set on diagonal.

ABUNDANCE & DISTRIBUTION: Common Florida, Bahamas, Caribbean; also Bermuda and south to Brazil.

HABITAT & BEHAVIOR: Inhabit sand, coral rubble and sea grass areas, often near patch reefs. Rest motionless on the bottom, blending with background. When moving, glide over bottom with wave-like motion.

REACTION TO DIVERS: Apparently relying on camouflage, move only when closely approached.

SIMILAR SPECIES: Tropical Flounder, *Paralichthys tropicus*, distinguished by numerous dots and spots, rather than rings. Head more pointed. Generally larger. Common southern Caribbean; rare to absent balance of Caribbean.

DISTINCTIVE FEATURES: Body almost circular. 1. **Body covered with brown to tan rings and spots.** (Similar Peacock Flounder, *B. lunatus*, [previous] always show blue markings.) 2. **Widely spaced eyes set on diagonal. 3. Two dark, sometimes faint, tail spots near the base, one above the other.** (Similar Channel Flounder, *Syacium micrurum*, [next] easily distinguished by elongate body, close-set eyes.)

DESCRIPTION: Shades of brown to tan. Can darken or pale and change color dramatically to match bottom. Have dark, diffuse area near center of lateral line.

ABUNDANCE & DISTRIBUTION: Common Bahamas; occasional Florida, Caribbean; also north to New York, Bermuda, Gulf of Mexico and south to Brazil.

HABITAT & BEHAVIOR: Inhabit sand, coral rubble and sea grass areas, often near patch reefs. Rest motionless on bottom, blending with background. When moving, glide over bottom with wave-like motion.

REACTION TO DIVERS: Apparently relying on camouflage, move only when closely approached.

SIMILAR SPECIES: Spottail Flounder, *B. robinsi*, distinguished by a diffuse spot at midbody behind pectoral fin and two dark spots on tail, one behind the other. Occasional Florida, Bahamas, Caribbean.

DISTINCTIVE FEATURES: Elongate body. 1. **Body covered with brown to tan rings and spots.** (Similar Peacock Flounder, *B. lunatus*, [previous] always show blue markings.) 2. **Eyes close-set. 3. Several dark spots along lateral line. 4. Widely spaced, dark vertical lines in dorsal and anal fins.** (Similar Eyed Flounder, *Bothus ocellatus*, [previous] easily distinguished by almost circular body and widely spaced eyes set on a diagonal.)

DESCRIPTION: Shades of brown to tan. Can darken or pale and change color dramatically to match bottom.

ABUNDANCE & DISTRIBUTION: Occasional South Florida, Bahamas, Caribbean; also south to Brazil.

HABITAT & BEHAVIOR: Inhabit sand, coral rubble and sea grass flats; often in or near channels, bays and calm sandy beach areas. Rest motionless on bottom, blending with background. When moving, glide over bottom with wave-like motion.

REACTION TO DIVERS: Apparently relying on camouflage, move only when closely approached.

SIMILAR SPECIES: Dusky Flounder, *S. papillosum*, distinguished by banded pectoral fin and no body blotches. Florida Gulf Coast and continental coastlines to Brazil.

PEACOCK FLOUNDER
Bothus lunatus

FAMILY:
Flounder – Bothidae

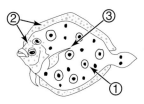

SIZE: 6 - 15 in.,
max. 18 in.
DEPTH: 2 - 40 ft.

CAYMAN

EYED FLOUNDER
Bothus ocellatus

FAMILY:
Flounder – Bothidae

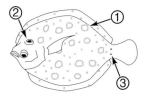

SIZE: 4 - 5 1/2 in.,
max. 7 in.
DEPTH: 2 - 60 ft.

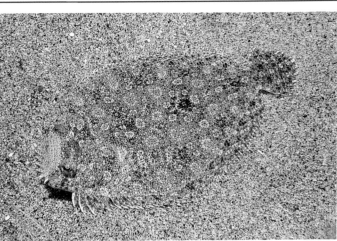

ST. LUCIA

CHANNEL FLOUNDER
Syacium micrurum

FAMILY:
Flounder – Bothidae

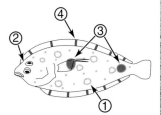

SIZE: 4 - 9 in., max. 1 ft.
DEPTH: 2 - 60 ft.

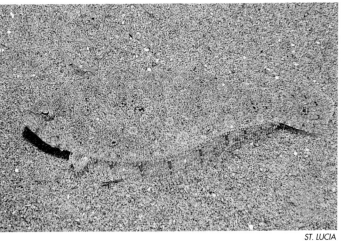

ST. LUCIA

Flounder – Clingfish

DISTINCTIVE FEATURES: 1. Three large ocellated spots with dark centers form a rear-pointing triangular pattern on back (often have several additional similar, but smaller spots).

DESCRIPTION: Tan to gray. Can darken or pale and change color dramatically to match bottom. Eyes are side by side and close-set.

ABUNDANCE & DISTRIBUTION: Common to occasional Florida; rare Bahamas; also north to North Carolina. Not reported Caribbean.

HABITAT & BEHAVIOR: Inhabit sand, coral rubble and sea grass areas, often near patch reefs. Rest motionless on the bottom, blending with background. When moving, glide over bottom with wave-like motion.

REACTION TO DIVERS: Apparently relying on camouflage, move only when closely approached.

SIMILAR SPECIES: Ocellated Flounder, *Ancylopsetta quadrocellata*, distinguished by four ocellated spots with dark centers. Three-eye Flounder, *A. dilecta*, distinguished by three ocellated spots with white centers. Both species reported only in Florida. Shrimp Flounder, *Gastropsetta frontalis*, distinguished by long ventral fin and two rear body spots, one above the other, and another spot above the pectoral fin. Uncommon Florida, Bahamas, Caribbean.

DISTINCTIVE FEATURES: Numerous, scattered, tiny black spots on upper side, especially on head. 1. Wide, flat, rounded head.

DESCRIPTION: Pale tan to brown, gray or olive. Occasionally have bands across body behind head.

ABUNDANCE & DISTRIBUTION: Occasional Bahamas, Caribbean; also western Gulf of Mexico.

HABITAT & BEHAVIOR: Inhabit shallow, clear water areas with limestone outcroppings, ledges and rocks. Often attach to undersides of ledges, recesses and rocks.

REACTION TO DIVERS: Apparently relying on camouflage and protective cover, do not move unless molested.

DISTINCTIVE FEATURES: Numerous tiny pale blue spots cover head and body. **1. Two white bands extend from lower eye across cheek. 2. Wide, flat rounded head.**

DESCRIPTION: Red-brown; occasionally has narrow red bands across rear head and body.

ABUNDANCE & DISTRIBUTION: Uncommon Bahamas, Caribbean. Not reported Florida.

HABITAT & BEHAVIOR: Inhabit shallow (rarely deeper than 30 feet), clear water areas with limestone outcroppings, ledges and rocks; occasionally around gorgonians attached to limestone bottoms. Often attach to undersides of ledges, recesses and rocks; also known to attach to sea rods and sea fans.

REACTION TO DIVERS: Apparently relying on camouflage and protective cover, do not move unless molested.

GULF FLOUNDER
Paralichthys albigutta

FAMILY:
Flounder – Bothidae

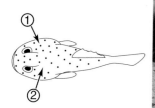

SIZE: 6 - 10 in.,
max. 15 in.
DEPTH: 1 - 60 ft.

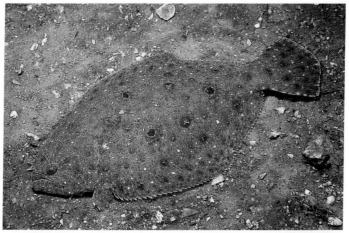

PANAMA CITY, FL

STIPPLED CLINGFISH
Gobiesox punctulatus

FAMILY:
Clingfish – Gobiesocidae

SIZE: 1 - 2 in., max. 2 ½ in.
DEPTH: 1 - 30 ft.

CAYMAN

RED CLINGFISH
Arcos rubiginosus

FAMILY:
Clingfish – Gobiesocidae

SIZE: ¾ - 1¼ in.,
max. 1½ in.
DEPTH: 1 - 100 ft.

L. CAYMAN

Batfish

DISTINCTIVE FEATURES: 1. Flat head, and forebody rounded like a "pancake." 2. Patterned network of reddish brown lines.

DESCRIPTION: Vary from reddish or yellowish brown to tan, olive or gray; may have bright yellow pectoral fins. Short projection between eyes.

ABUNDANCE & DISTRIBUTION: Rare Florida, Bahamas, Caribbean; also north to North Carolina and Gulf of Mexico.

HABITAT & BEHAVIOR: Inhabit sand, mud and rocky bottoms; occasionally found near reefs. Rest on the bottom and usually partly cover themselves with sand or mud.

REACTION TO DIVERS: Apparently relying on camouflage, do not move unless molested.

DISTINCTIVE FEATURES: 1. Light-colored body and fins covered with dark dots.

DESCRIPTION: Reddish brown to yellowish tan. Pectoral fins may be bordered in yellow. Some dots join; others are outlined in white. Short unicorn-like projection between eyes.

ABUNDANCE & DISTRIBUTION: Rare Florida and Bahamas; also Gulf of Mexico. Not reported in Caribbean.

HABITAT & BEHAVIOR: Inhabit sand, mud and rocky bottoms; occasionally found near reefs. Rest on the bottom and usually partly cover themselves with sand or mud.

REACTION TO DIVERS: Apparently relying on camouflage, do not move unless molested.

NOTE: Some ichthyologists believe the species name should be *cubifrons*.

DISTINCTIVE FEATURES: 1. Unicorn-like projection between eyes. 2. Two dark bands border pale band on tail.

DESCRIPTION: Mottled reddish brown to tan. May have dark spots edged in white along sides, but not on back. Unicorn-like projection is quite variable in length.

ABUNDANCE & DISTRIBUTION: Uncommon South Florida, Bahamas, Caribbean; also Gulf of Mexico and south to Brazil.

HABITAT & BEHAVIOR: Inhabit sand, mud and rocky bottoms; occasionally found near reefs. Rest on the bottom and usually partly cover themselves with sand or mud.

REACTION TO DIVERS: Apparently relying on camouflage, do not move unless molested.

PANCAKE BATFISH
Halieutichthys aculeatus
FAMILY:
Batfish – Ogcocephalidae

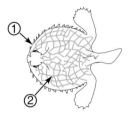

SIZE: 2 - 3 ½ in., max. 4 in.
DEPTH: 0 - 130 ft.

WEST PALM BEACH, FL

POLKA-DOT BATFISH
Ogcocephalus radiatus
FAMILY:
Batfish – Ogcocephalidae

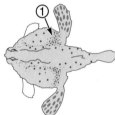

SIZE: 6 - 12 in., max. 15 in.
DEPTH: 0 - 230 ft.

WEST PALM BEACH, FL

SHORTNOSE BATFISH
Ogcocephalus nasutus
FAMILY:
Batfish – Ogcocephalidae

SIZE: 6 - 12 in., max. 15 in.
DEPTH: 0 - 1,000 ft.

CAYMAN

DISTINCTIVE FEATURES: 1. Pectoral fins light red to reddish brown, brown, tan or white with wide black band at tip. 2. Tail fin pale to white with wide, dark reddish brown to black margin.
DESCRIPTION: Mottled shades of olive to yellowish brown or reddish brown; often blotched with red and covered with white or black speckles. Numerous fleshy tabs and thread-like projections usually grow from back.
ABUNDANCE & DISTRIBUTION: Rare South Florida, Caribbean; also north to North Carolina, Gulf of Mexico and south to Brazil. Not reported Bahamas.
HABITAT & BEHAVIOR: Inhabit deep sand, mud and rocky bottoms, rarely within safe diving limits. Rest on the bottom and usually partly cover themselves with sand or mud.
REACTION TO DIVERS: Apparently relying on camouflage, do not move unless molested.

DISTINCTIVE FEATURES: 1. Zebra-striped head. 2. Wide, bright yellow border on all fins except ventrals, which are solid yellow.
DESCRIPTION: Mottled and patched in shades of brown, magenta and gray, over white. Well-developed head and unbranched chin barbels. Flattened head, fan-like pectoral fin and rounded tail.
ABUNDANCE & DISTRIBUTION: Common Cozumel. Apparently endemic, not reported elsewhere.
HABITAT & BEHAVIOR: Found in or near dark recesses. Rest on pectoral and ventral fins. Often peer out from hiding places.
REACTION TO DIVERS: Reclusive. A slow, nonthreatening approach often enables close observation.

DISTINCTIVE FEATURES: 1. Bright white lines cross head and radiate from eyes.
DESCRIPTION: Shades of gray to black. Row of small white spots runs down upper lateral line to tail; row of larger and more widely spaced spots runs down lower lateral line to tail; may have a few additional whitish markings. Well-developed unbranched barbels on head and chin. Flattened head, fan-like pectoral fins and rounded tail.
ABUNDANCE & DISTRIBUTION: Belize, including offshore atolls and islands. Not reported elsewhere.
HABITAT & BEHAVIOR: Inhabit reefs and areas of rocky rubble, in or near dark recesses. Rest on pectoral and ventral fins. Often peer out from hiding places.
REACTION TO DIVERS: Reclusive. A slow, nonthreatening approach often enables close observation.

ROUGHBACK BATFISH
Ogcocephalus parvus
FAMILY:
Batfish – Ogcocephalidae

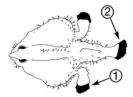

SIZE: 2 - 3 in., max. 4 in.
DEPTH: 0 - 400 ft.

CAYOS COCHINOS, HONDURAS

SPLENDID TOADFISH
Sanopus splendidus
FAMILY:
Toadfish – Batrachoididae

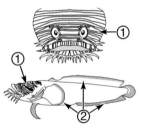

SIZE: 4 - 6 in., max. 8 in.
DEPTH: 25 - 60 ft.

COZUMEL

WHITELINED TOADFISH
Sanopus greenfieldorum
FAMILY:
Toadfish – Batrachoididae

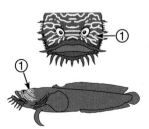

SIZE: 4 -10 in., max. 1 ft.
DEPTH: 15 -100 ft.

BELIZE

Toadfish

DISTINCTIVE FEATURES: 1. Bright white spots cover dark body.

DESCRIPTION: Shades of dark brown; fins generally darker and often have bluish cast. Well-developed unbranched barbels on head and chin. Flattened head, fan-like pectoral fin and rounded tail.

ABUNDANCE & DISTRIBUTION: Belize, including offshore atolls and islands. Not reported elsewhere.

HABITAT & BEHAVIOR: Inhabit reefs and areas of rocky rubble, in or near dark recesses. Rest on pectoral and ventral fins. Often peer out from hiding places.

REACTION TO DIVERS: Reclusive. A slow, nonthreatening approach often enables close observation.

DISTINCTIVE FEATURES: 1. Large eyes. 2. Long chin barbels that are often branched. 3. Fleshy tabs (papillae) along lateral line have fine outer points.

DESCRIPTION: Reddish brown. Diagonally streaked dorsal and anal fins; pectoral fins lightly banded. Flattened head, fan-like pectoral fins and rounded tail. Body scaled.

ABUNDANCE & DISTRIBUTION: Uncommon Caribbean coast of Central America. Not reported balance of Caribbean.

HABITAT & BEHAVIOR: Inhabit shallow waters of harbors, mangrove lagoons and entrances to creeks; occasionally inhabit reefs. Will enter fresh water. Often lie motionless with only their heads protruding from recess.

REACTION TO DIVERS: Remain still, apparently relying on camouflage; retreat into recesses only upon close approach.

SIMILAR SPECIES: Sapo, *B. surinamensis*, distinguished by smaller eyes and brown bands. Southern Caribbean. Mottled Toadfish, *Sanopus barbatus*, distinguished by fleshy tabs along lateral line that have rounded outer points, and a scaleless body. Caribbean coast of Central America.

DISTINCTIVE FEATURES: 1. Pale areas on body form rosettes, especially toward rear. 2. Brown diagonal bands on dorsal and anal fins.

DESCRIPTION: Mottled and marbled in shades of brown; head and forebody darkest and may be uniform in color. Pectoral and tail fins usually have vertical bars. Fleshy tabs below lip on lower jaw not well developed. Flattened head, fan-like pectoral fin and rounded tail.

ABUNDANCE & DISTRIBUTION: Occasional Cape Canaveral south and entire Florida Gulf Coast; rare Bahamas; also to Campeche, Mexico. Not reported Caribbean.

HABITAT & BEHAVIOR: Inhabit sea grass beds and areas of mixed sand and rocky rubble in bays, lagoons and coastal inlets.

REACTION TO DIVERS: Remain still, apparently relying on camouflage; retreat into recesses only upon close approach.

WHITESPOTTED TOADFISH
Sanopus astrifer
FAMILY:
Toadfish – Batrachoididae

SIZE: 4 - 10 in., max. 1 ft.
DEPTH: 15 - 100 ft.

BELIZE

LARGE EYE TOADFISH
Batrachoides gilberti
FAMILY:
Toadfish – Batrachoididae

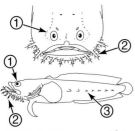

SIZE: 6 - 8 in., max. 10 in.
DEPTH: 3 - 40 ft.

BELIZE

GULF TOADFISH
Opsanus beta
FAMILY:
Toadfish – Batrachoididae

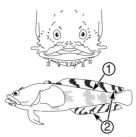

SIZE: 6 - 8 in., max. 1 ft.
DEPTH: 3 - 40 ft.

DESTIN,

30

Toadfish – Scorpionfish

DISTINCTIVE FEATURES: Tan to buff or yellow-brown with dark brown spots on head becoming more blotchy on body. **1. Well-developed fleshy tabs below lip on lower jaw.**

DESCRIPTION: Irregular markings on fins do not form bars or bands. Flattened head, fan-like pectoral fin and rounded tail. (Easily distinguished from similar Oyster Toadfish, *O. tau*, [next] by geographic location.)

ABUNDANCE & DISTRIBUTION: Common Florida Gulf Coast; also entire Gulf of Mexico. Not reported balance of Florida, Bahamas, Caribbean.

HABITAT & BEHAVIOR: Inhabit deep, rocky reefs offshore; often on and around artificial reefs. Commonly rest in entrances to recesses with only heads protruding.

REACTION TO DIVERS: Remain still, apparently relying on camouflage; retreat into recesses upon close approach.

DISTINCTIVE FEATURES: 1. Spots, dashes, blotches and other markings line up to form bars on pectoral fins and tail.

DESCRIPTION: Pale shades of brown with darker spots, blotches and other markings. Fleshy tabs below lip on lower jaw and behind mouth. Flattened head, fan-like pectoral fin and rounded tail.

ABUNDANCE & DISTRIBUTION: Common eastern coast Florida; also north to Massachusetts. Not reported balance of Florida, Bahamas or Caribbean.

HABITAT & BEHAVIOR: Prefer rocky, shallow bottoms inshore, jetties and reefs; occasionally much deeper. Often on artificial reefs and in with bottom trash. Can tolerate polluted water. Commonly rest in entrances to recesses with only heads protruding.

REACTION TO DIVERS: Remain still, apparently relying on camouflage; retreat into recesses only upon close approach.

DISTINCTIVE FEATURES: 1. Spotted pectoral, rear dorsal, anal and tail fins. 2. Dark to dusky spot on rear spinous dorsal fin.

DESCRIPTION: Mottled dark brown to red-brown. May have white area on forebody and spinous dorsal fin.

ABUNDANCE & DISTRIBUTION: Common Bahamas; occasional Florida, Caribbean.

HABITAT & BEHAVIOR: Hide on ceilings of shallow caves and under ledge overhangs and other protected spots. Also known to drift just above the bottom on reefs and areas of rocky rubble mixed with sand.

REACTION TO DIVERS: Apparently relying on camouflage, do not move unless molested.

LEOPARD TOADFISH
Opsanus pardus
FAMILY:
Toadfish – Batrachoididae

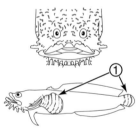

SIZE: 6-10 in., max. 15 in.
DEPTH: 35-160 ft.

PANAMA CITY, FL

OYSTER TOADFISH
Opsanus tau
FAMILY:
Toadfish – Batrachoididae

SIZE: 6-10 in., max. 15 in.
DEPTH: 3-100 ft.

JACKSONVILLE, FL

REEF SCORPIONFISH
Scorpaenodes caribbaeus
FAMILY:
Scorpionfish –
Scorpaenidae

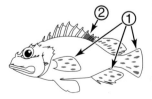

SIZE: 2-4 in., max. 5 in.
DEPTH: 3-60 ft.

DOMINICA

Scorpionfish

DISTINCTIVE FEATURES: 1. Long, large, fleshy appendage (cirri) or "plume" above each eye.

DESCRIPTION: Shades of mottled brown. Three dark bands on tail. Numerous skin flaps on body.

ABUNDANCE & DISTRIBUTION: Occasional Florida; uncommon Caribbean; rare Bahamas; also Bermuda and south to Brazil.

HABITAT & BEHAVIOR: Inhabit sand, sea grass and areas where algae is prevalent. Lie motionless, looking more like algae-covered rocks than fish.

REACTION TO DIVERS: Apparently relying on camouflage, do not move unless molested.

DISTINCTIVE FEATURES: 1. **Three dark bars on tail.** (Similar Barbfish, *S. brasiliensis*, [pg. 307] has only two.) 2. **Back side of pectoral fin, near base, has black area with brilliant white spots.**

DESCRIPTION: Mottled, in wide range of browns. Dusky band on rear body. Large appendages (cirri) or "plumes" above eyes may be absent. Often have numerous fleshy flaps (cirri) on chin and head.

ABUNDANCE & DISTRIBUTION: Occasional to common Florida, Bahamas, Caribbean; also north to New York, Bermuda, Gulf of Mexico and south to Brazil.

HABITAT & BEHAVIOR: Most common scorpionfish on coral reefs, but frequent all bottom habitats. Masters of camouflage, they lie motionless, blending with the background.

REACTION TO DIVERS: Apparently relying on camouflage, do not move unless molested.

Spotted Scorpionfish

Head view of specimen with large head plumes and numerous fleshy head flaps.

WEST PALM BEACH, FL

PLUMED SCORPIONFISH
Scorpaena grandicornis

FAMILY:
Scorpionfish –
Scorpaenidae

SIZE: 3 1/2 - 5 1/2 in.,
max. 7 in.
DEPTH: 2 - 40 ft.

CAYMAN

SPOTTED SCORPIONFISH
Scorpaena plumieri

FAMILY:
Scorpionfish –
Scorpaenidae

SIZE: 7 - 14 in.,
max. 18 in.
DEPTH: 5 - 50 ft.

ROATAN

Spotted Scorpionfish
*Rear view showing back
side of pectoral fins,
note lack of head plumes.*

CAYMAN

Scorpionfish

DISTINCTIVE FEATURES: 1. Two darkish bars on tail – center and rear margin. (Similar Spotted Scorpionfish, *S. plumieri*, [next] has three bars on tail.) **2. Dark spot above pectoral fin (and often one or more behind).**

DESCRIPTION: Shades of mottled red to red-brown, yellow-brown or yellow, often with darkish spots and blotches. Usually have long, fleshy appendage (cirri) or "plume" above each eye.

ABUNDANCE & DISTRIBUTION: Occasional Florida and continental coast to Brazil; rare Bahamas and Caribbean islands; also north to Virginia and Gulf of Mexico.

HABITAT & BEHAVIOR: Wide range of habitats, from reefs to areas of rubble and sand. Masters of camouflage, they lie motionless, blending with the background.

REACTION TO DIVERS: Apparently relying on camouflage, do not move unless molested.

Barbfish
Mottled mixture of colors.

WEST PALM BEACH, FL

DISTINCTIVE FEATURES: 1. Fleshy, upside-down mushroom-like growths extend over upper eye. 2. Two faint, thin bars mid-tail. 3. Dark margins on pectoral, soft dorsal, anal and tail fins.

DESCRIPTION: Mottled shades of red-brown to brown.

ABUNDANCE & DISTRIBUTION: Occasional Bahamas, Caribbean islands; uncommon to rare Florida, Caribbean continental coastlines.

HABITAT & BEHAVIOR: Hide under rocks, ledge overhangs and other reclusive spots. Often in areas of rocks and stone slabs mixed with sand and/or gravel.

REACTION TO DIVERS: Apparently relying on camouflage, do not move unless molested.

SIMILAR SPECIES: Smooth Scorpionfish, *S. calcarata*, distinguished by dusky upper pectoral fin, other fins unmarked; cirri above eyes small. Replace Mushroom Scorpionfish in Florida and continental coastlines of Caribbean; absent most islands.

BARBFISH
Scorpaena brasiliensis

FAMILY:
Scorpionfish –
Scorpaenidae

SIZE: 6-10 in.,
max. 14 in.
DEPTH: 5-300 ft.

JACKSONVILLE, FL

Barbfish
Yellow phase.

WEST PALM BEACH, FL

MUSHROOM SCORPIONFISH
Scorpaena inermis

FAMILY:
Scorpionfish –
Scorpaenidae

SIZE: 1½-2½ in.,
max. 3 in.
DEPTH: 1-300 ft.

CAYMAN

Frogfish

DISTINCTIVE FEATURES: Resemble sargassum weed.

DESCRIPTION: A variety of colors including brown, olive and yellow in patterns that blend with sargassum. Large mouth. Numerous fleshy tabs on body.

ABUNDANCE & DISTRIBUTION: Occasional Florida, Bahamas, Caribbean; also circumtropical and subtropical.

HABITAT & BEHAVIOR: Inhabit floating rafts of sargassum weed (a free-floating algae that drifts in open water).

REACTION TO DIVERS: Apparently relying on camouflage, do not move unless molested.

DISTINCTIVE FEATURES: Numerous dark spots over body, some of which are occasionally ringed in white. **1. Three spots on tail can usually be observed.**

DESCRIPTION: Long, undivided, whitish translucent filament, called a lure, just above lip. Large variety of color phases, including shades of deep red, pink, orange, yellow, green and tan (see examples below). Can change color, pale or darken to match background.

ABUNDANCE & DISTRIBUTION: Common to occasional Florida, Bahamas, Caribbean (but seldom seen because of excellent ability to camouflage); also Bermuda. Most common frogfish on Caribbean reefs.

HABITAT & BEHAVIOR: Inhabit reef tops. Often rest on look-alike sponges, and usually go undetected unless they move.

REACTION TO DIVERS: Apparently relying on camouflage, do not move unless molested.

SIMILAR SPECIES: Dwarf Frogfish, *A. pauciradiatus*, distinguished by small size (does not exceed two-and-a-half inches). Pale yellow and unmarked, except for a single small spot toward rear base of dorsal fin. Known only in Florida, Bahamas and Cuba.

BARBADOS

BELIZE

SARGASSUMFISH
Histrio histrio
FAMILY:
Frogfish – Antennariidae

SIZE: 2 1/2 - 4 1/2 in.,
max. 8 in.
DEPTH: Surface

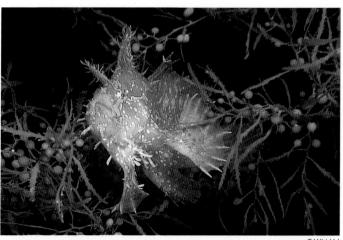

CAYMAN

LONGLURE FROGFISH
Antennarius multiocellatus
FAMILY:
Frogfish – Antennariidae

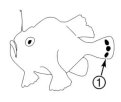

SIZE: 3 - 5 in., max. 8 in.
DEPTH: 10 - 60 ft.

BELIZE

BARBADOS

CAYMAN

Frogfish – Stargazer

DISTINCTIVE FEATURES: 1. Long, whitish, translucent filament is tipped with a boomerang-shaped "lure," just above lip.

DESCRIPTION: Irregular line and spot markings (no ringed dots), or, occasionally, dark without markings. Large variety of color phases including shades of deep red, lavender, pink, orange, yellow, tan, white and solid black. Can change color, pale or darken to match background.

ABUNDANCE & DISTRIBUTION: Uncommon Florida, Bahamas, Caribbean; also north to New Jersey, Bermuda and south to Brazil; tropical Indo-Pacific.

HABITAT & BEHAVIOR: Wide range of habitats, from reefs to sandy and even muddy bottoms. Blend with background and usually go undetected unless they move. May inflate if molested.

REACTION TO DIVERS: Apparently relying on camouflage, do not move unless molested.

NOTE: This species and the Splitlure Frogfish, *A. scaber*, were formerly considered separate species, but recent evidence indicates they are the same, so they have been united under the species name *striatus*.

DISTINCTIVE FEATURES: 1. Three large, ocellated spots with dark centers and dusky, diffuse outer rings – on dorsal fin, midbody above anus, and tail.

DESCRIPTION: Shades of red-brown to yellow-brown with numerous small, dark spots. "Lure" short with bulbous tip and numerous filaments.

ABUNDANCE & DISTRIBUTION: Uncommon Florida, Bahamas, Caribbean; also north to North Carolina and Gulf of Mexico.

HABITAT & BEHAVIOR: Wide range of habitats, from reefs to sandy and even muddy bottoms. Blend with background and usually go undetected unless they move.

REACTION TO DIVERS: Apparently relying on camouflage, do not move unless molested.

SIMILAR SPECIES: Island Frogfish, *A. bermudensis*, distinguished by small size (less than three inches). Large spot, sometimes ringed in white, toward rear base of dorsal fin. May have numerous small spots. Often rust colored, with a short lure. Known only in Bahamas.

DISTINCTIVE FEATURES: 1. Three dark stripes on tail. 2. Center stripe extends forward across base of tail and onto rear body.

DESCRIPTION: Upturned, almost vertical mouth. Dark brown upper body covered with white spots that increase in size toward rear and along sides; lower body pale.

ABUNDANCE & DISTRIBUTION: Uncommon east coast of Florida as far south as Palm Beach; also north to New York. Not reported balance of Florida, Bahamas, Caribbean.

HABITAT & BEHAVIOR: Inhabit sand, silt and rock-rubble bottoms. Able to rapidly bury themselves in sand by vibrating their bodies. Can deliver electric shock from area behind eyes.

REACTION TO DIVERS: Move only when molested. Care should be taken not to touch this fish as the shock can be painful.

SIMILAR SPECIES: Southern Stargazer, *A. y-graecum*, distinguished by central stripe on tail which does not extend forward onto body. Known from both coasts of Florida to Yucatan; not reported Bahamas, Caribbean.

STRIATED FROGFISH
Antennarius striatus
FAMILY:
Frogfish – Antennariidae

SIZE: 3-5 in., max. 7 in.
DEPTH: 10-60 ft.

BARBADOS

OCELLATED FROGFISH
Antennarius ocellatus
FAMILY:
Frogfish – Antennariidae

SIZE: 4-8 in., max. 15 in.
DEPTH: 10-70 ft.

DESTIN, FL

NORTHERN STARGAZER
Astroscopus guttatus
FAMILY:
Stargazer –
Uranoscopidae

SIZE: 8-18 in., max. 22 in.
DEPTH: 6-120 ft.

WEST PALM BEACH, FL

Searobin – Flying Gurnard – Lizardfish

DISTINCTIVE FEATURES: 1. Three reddish brown bars on tail. 2. Two long cirri on snout. 3.First three spines of pectoral fin rays are separated from remainder of fin and extend as finger-like appendages.

DESCRIPTION: Mottled and spotted, gray to reddish brown. Body and fins may exhibit bars and bands. Large head with tapered snout. Pectoral fins long, and fan-like when extended (Similar Flying Gurnard, *Dactylopterus volitans*, [next] distinguished by smaller, blunt head.)

ABUNDANCE & DISTRIBUTION: Uncommon Florida, Bahamas, Caribbean; also north to North Carolina and Gulf of Mexico.

HABITAT & BEHAVIOR: Prefer shallow areas of sea grass, sand and coral rubble. When foraging, "walk" about on modified spines of pectoral fins and also use them like hands to turn over rubble.

REACTION TO DIVERS: Shy; upon approach, spread pectoral fins and swim away.

SIMILAR SPECIES: There are about 24 species of searobins within the range of this book. They are uncommon and rarely observed by divers because of their habitats and shy behavior.

DISTINCTIVE FEATURES: 1. Huge, fan-like pectoral fins that often have brilliant, iridescent blue line and dot markings.

DESCRIPTION: Shades of gray to yellow-brown body with white spots. Can pale or darken dramatically. Blunt snout.

ABUNDANCE & DISTRIBUTION: Occasional to uncommon Florida, Bahamas, Caribbean; also north to Massachusetts, Bermuda, Gulf of Mexico, south to Argentina and eastern Atlantic.

HABITAT & BEHAVIOR: Inhabit sand, coral rubble and sea grass areas, often near shallow patch and fringe reefs. Normally fold pectoral fins against sides and perch, or "walk," on ventral fins. If alarmed, spread pectorals and swim away.

REACTION TO DIVERS: Shy; swim away when approached. Moving into their direction of travel may enable a close view.

DISTINCTIVE FEATURES: 1. Dark spot at upper end of gill cover. 2. Thin yellow-gold stripes on body. (Similar Bluestriped Lizardfish, *S. saurus*, [pg. 315] has blue stripes.)

DESCRIPTION: Reddish brown bars across back. Often show diamond-shaped patches on sides. Can pale or darken to blend with background.

ABUNDANCE & DISTRIBUTION: Common Caribbean; occasional Florida, Bahamas; also north to North Carolina, Gulf of Mexico and south to Brazil. Most common lizardfish in Caribbean.

HABITAT & BEHAVIOR: Rest on or bury themselves in sand, sometimes with only head visible; also rest on reef tops.

REACTION TO DIVERS: Apparently relying on camouflage, do not move unless closely approached.

SIMILAR SPECIES: Inshore Lizardfish, *S. foetens*, do not have dark spot at upper end of gill cover. Pectoral fins do not extend to base of ventral fins.

BANDTAIL SEAROBIN
Prionotus ophryas
FAMILY:
Searobin – Triglidae

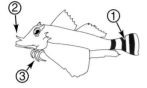

SIZE: 4 - 6 ½ in., max. 8 in.
DEPTH: 5 - 40 ft.

WEST PALM BEACH, FL

FLYING GURNARD
Dactylopterus volitans
FAMILY:
Flying Gurnard –
Dactylopteridae

SIZE: 6 - 14 in., max. 18 in.
DEPTH: 1 - 35 ft.

BARBADOS

SAND DIVER
Synodus intermedius
FAMILY:
Lizardfish – Synodontidae

SIZE: 4 - 14 in., max. 18 in.
DEPTH: 25 - 80 ft.

L. CAYMAN

313

Lizardfish

DISTINCTIVE FEATURES: 1. Tiny black spot just behind tip of snout. 2. Bars across back and onto body are distinctly reddish.

DESCRIPTION: Yellowish brown to tan; may have bluish highlights on back. Can pale or darken or change bar pattern to blend with background; occasionally, bars on back lighten and become indistinct while midline area darkens to form a prominent stripe.

ABUNDANCE & DISTRIBUTION: Occasional Florida, Bahamas, Caribbean; also Gulf of Mexico, south to Uruguay, and eastern Atlantic.

HABITAT & BEHAVIOR: Usually rest on rocks, coral and other hard surfaces, instead of sand.

REACTION TO DIVERS: Apparently relying on camouflage, do not move unless closely approached.

NOTE: Also commonly known as "Rockspear."

DISTINCTIVE FEATURES: 1. Thin blue to turquoise stripes down upper body. (Similar Sand Diver, *S. intermedius*, [next] has thin golden stripes and dark spot at upper end of gill cover.)

DESCRIPTION: Dark bars across back. Often show diamond-shaped patches on sides. Can pale or darken to blend with background.

ABUNDANCE & DISTRIBUTION: Uncommon Bahamas; rare Caribbean; also Bermuda and eastern Atlantic including the Mediterranean. Not reported Florida.

HABITAT & BEHAVIOR: Rest on bottom in shallow areas of sand and rubble. Most common in water less than 12 feet deep.

REACTION TO DIVERS: Apparently relying on camouflage, do not move unless closely approached.

DISTINCTIVE FEATURES: 1. Short, blunt snout with upturned mouth. 2. Short, dark diagonal streak at upper end of gill cover.

DESCRIPTION: Alternating stripes of pale blue and gold with narrow black borders run length of body; dusky wide bars on back.

ABUNDANCE & DISTRIBUTION: Occasional Florida, Bahamas, Caribbean; also circumtropical.

HABITAT & BEHAVIOR: Rest on or bury themselves in sand, mud or rubble, sometimes with only eyes and part of head visible.

REACTION TO DIVERS: Apparently relying on camouflage, do not move unless closely approached.

RED LIZARDFISH
Synodus synodus
FAMILY:
Lizardfish – Synodontidae

SIZE: 4-7 in., max. 13 in.
DEPTH: 2-130 ft.

CAYMAN

BLUESTRIPED LIZARDFISH
Synodus saurus
FAMILY:
Lizardfish – Synodontidae

SIZE: 4-7 in., max. 12 in.
DEPTH: 1-40 ft.

SAN SALVADOR

SNAKEFISH
Trachinocephalus myops
FAMILY:
Lizardfish – Synodontidae

SIZE: 4-12 in., max. 15 in.
DEPTH: 1-1300 ft.

ST. LUCIA

Seahorse

DISTINCTIVE FEATURES: 1. Numerous lines on head and often down neck and back.

DESCRIPTION: Vary from reddish orange to brown or even black. Markings also vary. (Never have black spots over bodies, like similar Longsnout Seahorse, *H. reidi* [next].) When living in sargassum, they often develop fleshy tabs and appendages.

ABUNDANCE & DISTRIBUTION: Uncommon to rare Florida, Bahamas, Caribbean; also north to Nova Scotia, Gulf of Mexico and south to Argentina. May be abundant in a localized area, such as under a dock.

HABITAT & BEHAVIOR: Curl base of tail around branches of gorgonians, sea grass or other holdfasts. Occasionally float free over sea grass or reefs, and in sargassum.

REACTION TO DIVERS: Allow close approach and rarely move, although they will tuck their heads down and turn away.

ST. LUCIA · CAYMAN

DISTINCTIVE FEATURES: Usually have small black spots over head and body.

DESCRIPTION: Vary greatly from yellow to reddish orange, brown or even black [see above]; may be two-toned.

ABUNDANCE & DISTRIBUTION: Uncommon Bahamas and Caribbean; rare Florida; also Bermuda. May be abundant in localized areas, such as under a dock.

HABITAT & BEHAVIOR: Curl base of tail around branches of gorgonians, sea grass or other holdfasts. Occasionally float free over sea grass or reefs, and in sargassum.

REACTION TO DIVERS: Allow close approach and rarely move, although they will tuck their heads down and turn away.

NOTE: Also commonly known as "Slender Seahorse."

LINED SEAHORSE
Hippocampus erectus
FAMILY:
Pipefish & Seahorse –
Syngnathidae

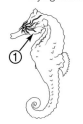

SIZE: 2 1/2 - 4 in., max. 6 in.
DEPTH: 1 - 40 ft.

KEY WEST, FL

Lined Seahorse
With fleshy tabs.
[right]

Longsnout Seahorse
Color variations.
[left]

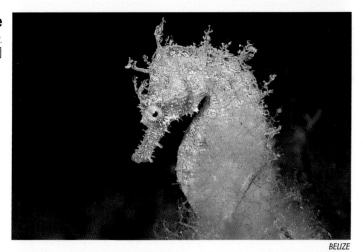

BELIZE

LONGSNOUT SEAHORSE
Hippocampus reidi
FAMILY:
Pipefish & Seahorse –
Syngnathidae

SIZE: 2 1/2 - 4 in., max. 6 in.
DEPTH: 1 - 40 ft.

L CAYMAN

317

Pipefish

DISTINCTIVE FEATURES: 1. Small tail fin on curled base of tail. 2. Clusters of fleshy tabs (papillae) on body.
DESCRIPTION: Intermediate between seahorse and pipefish. Trumpet-like snout and small mouth; head slightly cocked. Body varies from whitish, translucent and blotched to uniformly dark overall.
ABUNDANCE & DISTRIBUTION: Rare South Florida, Bahamas, Caribbean; also Bermuda and Gulf of Mexico.
HABITAT & BEHAVIOR: Considered pelagic, drift in open water or in floats of sargassum; occasionally on reefs and other bottoms, usually in clumps of algae.
REACTION TO DIVERS: Apparently relying on camouflage, do not move unless molested.

DISTINCTIVE FEATURES: 1. Two short, dark lines extend from rear of each eye. 2. Numerous pale body bands.
DESCRIPTION: Vary from dark brown to lavender. Long, slender snout.
ABUNDANCE & DISTRIBUTION: Uncommon Florida, Bahamas, Caribbean; also Bermuda.
HABITAT & BEHAVIOR: Expert at camouflage. Stay just above bottom, swimming through small holes, tunnels and recesses in reefs. In areas of grass and algae, they swim under and through tangles of vegetation and debris. Most common in shallow waters, but can be deep.
REACTION TO DIVERS: Remain still, apparently relying on camouflage, but when aware of detection they move to concealed areas.
SIMILAR SPECIES: There are at least 20 species of Pipefish within the range of this book. Because they are secretive and adept at camouflage, they are rarely observed by divers. Most are difficult to differentiate underwater because of similar shape and ability to change color.

DISTINCTIVE FEATURES: 1. White or unpigmented snout.
DESCRIPTION: Shades of brown, occasionally banded. Trumpet-like snout and small mouth. Long, snake-like body.
ABUNDANCE & DISTRIBUTION: Rare Florida, Bahamas, Caribbean.
HABITAT & BEHAVIOR: Expert at camouflage. Most common in areas of grass and algae where they stay just above the bottom, swimming under and through tangles of vegetation and debris. Occasionally around shallow patch reefs.
REACTION TO DIVERS: Remain still, apparently relying on camouflage, but when aware of detection, they move to concealed areas.

PIPEHORSE
Acentronura dendritica

FAMILY:
Pipefish & Seahorse –
Syngnathidae

SIZE: 1-2 in., max. 3 in.
DEPTH: 0-30 ft.

L. CAYMAN

SHORTFIN PIPEFISH
Cosmocampus elucens

FAMILY:
Pipefish & Seahorse –
Syngnathidae

SIZE: 3 1/2 - 5 1/2 in.,
max. 6 in.
DEPTH: 5-1135 ft.

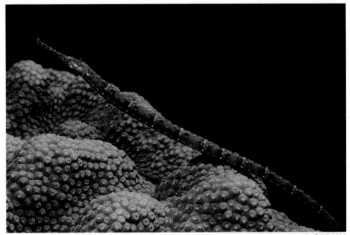

L. CAYMAN

WHITENOSE PIPEFISH
Cosmocampus albirostris

FAMILY:
Pipefish & Seahorse –
Syngnathidae

SIZE: 4-6 in., max. 8 in.
DEPTH: 3-40 ft.

CAYOS COCHINOS, HONDURAS

319

DISTINCTIVE FEATURES: 1. Bold, alternating bands of brown and yellow.

DESCRIPTION: Trumpet-like snout and small mouth. Long, thin, snake-like body. Dorsal fin clear.

ABUNDANCE & DISTRIBUTION: Rare South Florida, Bahamas, Caribbean; also Bermuda and south to Brazil.

HABITAT & BEHAVIOR: Expert at camouflage. Stay just above the bottom, swimming through small holes, tunnels and recesses in reefs. In areas of grass and algae, they swim under and through tangles of vegetation and debris.

REACTION TO DIVERS: Remain still, apparently relying on camouflage, but when aware of detection they move to concealed areas.

NOTE: Formerly classified as species *crinitus* which is now considered to be a separate species, the Banded Pipefish. It is distinguished by irregular, less conspicuous brown, tan and white (never yellow) bands.

DISTINCTIVE FEATURES: 1. Red spots over head, upper body and dorsal fin. 2. "Tassels" on tips of dorsal fin spines.

DESCRIPTION: Brown bars over whitish background; fins (except dorsal) white to clear.

ABUNDANCE & DISTRIBUTION: Common to occasional South Florida, Bahamas, Caribbean; also Gulf of Mexico.

HABITAT & BEHAVIOR: Prefer coral reefs. Perch on bottom, and occasionally flit about for short distances.

REACTION TO DIVERS: Wary; move to new perch when closely approached.

NOTE: Only member of hawkfish family in the Atlantic.

DISTINCTIVE FEATURES: 1. Scattered pale spots and small blotches. 2. Pale lateral line.

DESCRIPTION: Dark brown. Long chin barbel; ventral fins appear as a long, thin Y-shaped barbel.

ABUNDANCE & DISTRIBUTION: Common northeastern Florida; also north to North Carolina. Not reported balance of Florida, Bahamas, Caribbean.

HABITAT & BEHAVIOR: Inhabit rocky reefs. Reclusive; hide in crevices and other protective recesses.

REACTION TO DIVERS: Shy; retreat into protective recess upon approach.

SIMILAR SPECIES: Southern Hake, *U. floridana*, distinguished by a series of black spots above and behind eye; lateral line alternately black and white. Spotted Hake, *U. regia*, has two dusky lines running from eye to pectoral fin; lateral line alternately black and white. Both species in Florida including Gulf of Mexico.

HARLEQUIN PIPEFISH
Micrognathus ensenadae
FAMILY:
Pipefish & Seahorse –
Syngnathidae

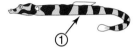

SIZE: 5-8 in., max. 9 in.
DEPTH: 5-60 ft.

CAYMAN

REDSPOTTED HAWKFISH
Amblycirrhitus pinos
FAMILY:
Hawkfish – Cirrhitidae

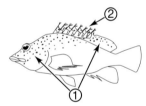

SIZE: 2-3¹/₂ in., max. 4 in.
DEPTH: 12-80 ft.

BARBADOS

CAROLINA HAKE
Urophycis earlli
FAMILY:
Cod – Gadidae

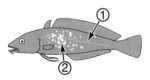

SIZE: 6-14 in., max. 17 in.
DEPTH: 20-120 ft.

JACKSONVILLE, FL

321

Odd-Shaped Swimmers
Puffer – Boxfish–Triggerfish & Filefish – Drum – Others

This ID Group consists of swimming fish that do not have a typical fish-like shape.

FAMILY: Smooth & Spiny Puffer— Tetraodontidae
12 Species Included

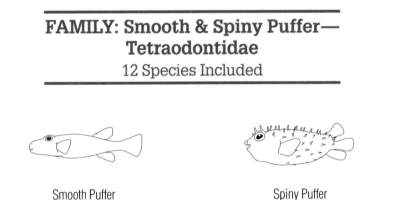

Smooth Puffer   Spiny Puffer

Puffers have the unique ability to draw in water to greatly inflate their bodies as a defense. They have fused teeth and powerful jaws which are used to crush hard-shelled invertebrates. The family is divided into two basic groups: smooth puffers–with smooth, spineless skin; and spiny puffers–with a covering of stout spines. Spiny puffers are subdivided: porcupinefish–with spines that may become erect as the body inflates; and burrfish–with spines that always remain erect. Spiny puffers were formerly classified in a separate family, Diodontidae.

FAMILY: Boxfish — Ostraciidae
5 Species Included

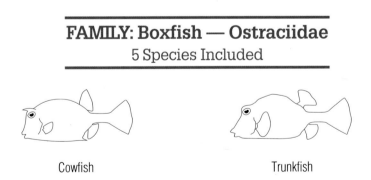

Cowfish   Trunkfish

Boxfish are protected by a triangular, bony box of armor. They have small protrusible mouths and broom-like tails. They are divided into two groups: cowfish, which have a sharp spine over each eye; and trunkfish, which do not have these spines. These relatively slow swimmers move with a sculling action of their dorsal, anal and pectoral fins. The tail fin is only brought into play when greater speed is desired.

FAMILY: Leatherjacket/Triggerfish & Filefish — Balistidae
16 Species Included

Triggerfish (typical shape)

Filefish (typical shape)

The family's common name, leatherjackets, comes from the rough, dry texture of their skin. Each member also has an elongated front dorsal spine that can be raised and lowered. The family is divided into two groups: triggerfish–that can lock their stout front dorsal fin into place with a ridged second spine; and filefish–that cannot lock their elongated spine into place. Tilefish were formerly classified in a separate family, Monacanthidae.

FAMILY: Drum & Croaker — Sciaenidae
6 Species Included

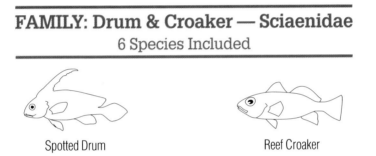

Spotted Drum

Reef Croaker

The common name of these fish is derived from their ability to vibrate their swim bladders thereby producing a low-pitched, resonant sound. Reef-dwelling drums, especially juveniles, have unusually elongated foredorsal fins, making them quite distinctive. All are similarly patterned in white and black, but are easily distinguished with attention to detail.

FAMILY: Others
14 Species Included

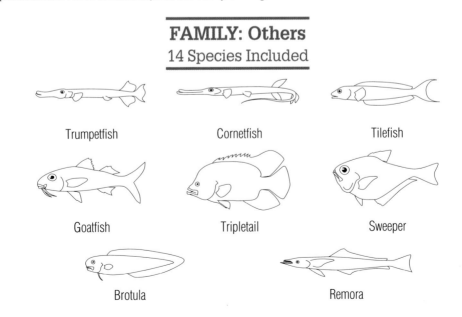

Trumpetfish

Cornetfish

Tilefish

Goatfish

Tripletail

Sweeper

Brotula

Remora

323

DISTINCTIVE FEATURES: Long, thin body. **1. Trumpet-like mouth.**

DESCRIPTION: Adept at color change. Most common phase is brown to reddish brown; can be blue-gray, bright yellow or many shades between. Have pale lines, scattered small black spots, and a black streak on upper jaw.

ABUNDANCE & DISTRIBUTION: Common Florida, Bahamas, Caribbean; also Bermuda, Gulf of Mexico and south to Brazil.

HABITAT & BEHAVIOR: Inhabit coral reefs. Change color, and position their bodies to blend with background. Often drift in vertical position, head down, paralleling stalks of sea rods. May attempt to camouflage themselves by hovering just above larger fish as they move about the reef.

REACTION TO DIVERS: Generally remain still to maintain camouflage. Move away when aware of detection or closely approached.

DISTINCTIVE FEATURES: Long, thin body. **1. Long tail filament.**

DESCRIPTION: Brownish gray to greenish brown, with blue dashes and spots. Snout and mouth shaped like a cornet. (Body length given above does not include tail filament.)

ABUNDANCE & DISTRIBUTION: Occasional southern Caribbean; uncommon Florida, Bahamas, northern Caribbean; also north to Massachusetts, Bermuda, Gulf of Mexico, south to Brazil and eastern Atlantic.

HABITAT & BEHAVIOR: Swim over shallow beds of sea grass and near patch reefs. Occasionally found on deeper reefs.

REACTION TO DIVERS: Usually wary and move away upon approach, but occasionally appear curious and swim in for a close look.

SIMILAR SPECIES: Red Cornetfish, *Fistularia petimba*, reddish with dusky saddle or wide bar markings. Rare South Florida and northwestern Caribbean.

DISTINCTIVE FEATURES: Long, white body. **1. Crescent tail. 2. Dark area on upper central tail.** Hover over sand.

DESCRIPTION: Vary from yellowish white to light bluish gray. Light yellow and bluish markings on head; tail often yellow.

ABUNDANCE & DISTRIBUTION: Common Caribbean; occasional Bahamas and Florida; also north to North Carolina, Bermuda, Gulf of Mexico and south to Brazil.

HABITAT & BEHAVIOR: Build burrows in sand and coral rubble. Hover near entrance, undulating long dorsal and anal fins.

REACTION TO DIVERS: Wary; disappear into burrows when closely approached. For a close view, try approaching from opposite side of burrow or maneuver between fish and burrow.

TRUMPETFISH
Aulostomus maculatus
FAMILY:
Trumpetfish –
Aulostomidae

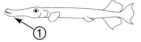

SIZE: 1 1/2 - 2 1/2 ft.,
max. 3 ft.
DEPTH: 15 - 80 ft.

CAYMAN

BLUESPOTTED CORNETFISH
Fistularia tabacaria
FAMILY:
Cornetfish – Fistulariidae

SIZE: 2 - 4 ft., max. 6 ft.
DEPTH: 5 - 30 ft.

BONAIRE

SAND TILEFISH
Malacanthus plumieri
FAMILY:
Tilefish – Malacanthidae

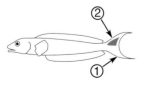

SIZE: 1 - 1 1/2 ft., max. 2 ft.
DEPTH: 20 - 70 ft.

CAYMAN

Puffer

DISTINCTIVE FEATURES: 1. Two dark bands on tail. 2. Row of dark blotches from mouth to tail.

DESCRIPTION: Olive-brown; speckled upper body, white underside. Pale or darken to blend with background. Blunt head and mouth.

ABUNDANCE & DISTRIBUTION: Common to occasional Florida, Bahamas, Caribbean; also north to Massachusetts, Bermuda, Gulf of Mexico, south to Brazil and eastern Atlantic.

HABITAT & BEHAVIOR: Inhabit sea grass, coral rubble and reefs. Hover near bottom, blending with background.

REACTION TO DIVERS: Appear unconcerned. Slow, nonthreatening approach may enable a close view.

SIMILAR SPECIES: Southern Puffer, *S. nephelus*, has tiny orange dots and olive to brown spots on back; most common in Florida. Caribbean Puffer, *S. greeleyi*, has small, dark brown spots on back; southern Caribbean only. Both prefer grass, mud bottoms or mangroves; rarely on reefs.

DISTINCTIVE FEATURES: 1. Polygon-shaped patches on back and sides are large and numerous, and range from brown to olive or gray.

DESCRIPTION: Tan to pale yellowish brown undercolor. Black spots on sides and cheeks; tail may have light bands. Whitish unmarked underside.

ABUNDANCE & DISTRIBUTION: Occasional Florida, Bahamas, Caribbean; also north to Rhode Island, Bermuda, Gulf of Mexico and south to Brazil.

HABITAT & BEHAVIOR: Inhabit shallow bays, inlets and protected inshore waters with sea grass beds and areas of sand mixed with rubble. Hover near or rest on bottom; bury in bottom material on occasion. Rarely on reefs.

REACTION TO DIVERS: Appear unconcerned. Slow, nonthreatening approach may enable a close view.

DISTINCTIVE FEATURES: 1. Pointed snout. 2. Blue lines radiate from around eye.

DESCRIPTION: Dark olive-brown upper body, white below. Blue line and dot markings over head and body. Eyes brightly colored.

ABUNDANCE & DISTRIBUTION: Common to occasional Florida, Bahamas, Caribbean; also Bermuda, Gulf of Mexico, south to Brazil and eastern Atlantic.

HABITAT & BEHAVIOR: Swim about reefs and sea grass beds. Stop to nibble on grass tips; also eat wide range of invertebrates.

REACTION TO DIVERS: Relatively unafraid; usually allow slow, close approach.

SIMILAR SPECIES: Marbled Puffer, *Sphoeroides dorsalis*, with marbled blue lines on head and snout. Distinguished by pair of small, dark, fleshy flaps on back, and banded tail. Larger than Sharpnose, and inhabit reefs deeper than 60 feet. Uncommon.

BANDTAIL PUFFER
Sphoeroides spengleri
FAMILY:
Puffer/Smooth –
Tetraodontidae

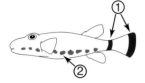

SIZE: 4 - 7 in., max. 1 ft.
DEPTH: 5 - 35 ft.

CAYMAN

CHECKERED PUFFER
Sphoeroides testudineus
FAMILY:
Puffer/Smooth –
Tetraodontidae

SIZE: 4-7 in., max. 1 ft.
DEPTH: 3 - 35 ft.

JUPITER, FL

SHARPNOSE PUFFER
Canthigaster rostrata
FAMILY:
Puffer/Smooth –
Tetraodontidae

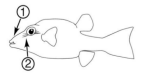

SIZE: 2-3 ¹/₂ in.,
max. 4 ¹/₂ in.
DEPTH: 5 - 45 ft.

BELIZE

Puffer

DISTINCTIVE FEATURES: 1. Reticulated pattern on back and sides.

DESCRIPTION: Light to dark brown; may have yellowish area under mouth. Three to four large black spots on body. Iris is yellow-gold; pupil has iridescent blue-green specks. Spines always erect.

ABUNDANCE & DISTRIBUTION: Occasional southern Caribbean; uncommon to rare Florida, Bahamas, northern Caribbean.

HABITAT & BEHAVIOR: Inhabit reefs and adjacent coral rubble areas. Swim slowly near bottom, blending with background.

REACTION TO DIVERS: Shy; retreat to protective recess if approached. Often peer out of entrances where they can be closely observed. Inflate if molested.

DISTINCTIVE FEATURES: 1. Irregular pattern of dark brown, more-or-less parallel stripes on back and sides.

DESCRIPTION: Yellow-brown to brown to olive-brown. Usually have large, dark, ocellated patches above and behind pectoral fins and another at base of dorsal fin. Iris is yellow-gold; pupil has iridescent blue-green specks. Spines always erect.

ABUNDANCE & DISTRIBUTION: Common Florida Gulf Coast; occasional balance of Florida and continental coasts to Brazil; rare to absent Bahamas and Caribbean islands; also north to Maine.

HABITAT & BEHAVIOR: During the summer generally inhabit grass beds, coastal bays and lagoons; in winter, more frequently inhabit natural and artificial reefs.

REACTION TO DIVERS: Shy; retreat to protective recess if approached. Often peer out of entrances where they can be closely observed. Inflate if molested.

DISTINCTIVE FEATURES: 1. Black spots on body and tail, but not on other fins. 2. Dark patch above pectoral fin.

DESCRIPTION: Olive to yellowish brown. May have more than one dark patch on back. Iris is gold with circle of black dots; pupil has iridescent blue-green specks. Spines always erect.

ABUNDANCE & DISTRIBUTION: Occasional northwestern Caribbean; uncommon to rare balance of Caribbean, Florida, Bahamas.

HABITAT & BEHAVIOR: Inhabit sea grass beds and adjacent reefs. Swim slowly near bottom, blending with background.

REACTION TO DIVERS: Shy; retreat to protective recess if approached. Often peer out of entrance where they can be closely observed. Inflate if molested.

WEB BURRFISH
Chilomycterus antillarum
FAMILY:
Puffer/Spiny –
Tetraodontidae

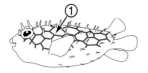

SIZE: 6-10 in., max. 1 ft.
DEPTH: 5-80 ft.

BARBADOS

STRIPED BURRFISH
Chilomycterus schoepfi
FAMILY:
Puffer/Spiny –
Tetraodontidae

SIZE: 4-8 in., max. 10 in.
DEPTH: 1-60 ft.

PANAMA CITY, FL

BRIDLED BURRFISH
Chilomycterus antennatus
FAMILY:
Puffer/Spiny –
Tetraodontidae

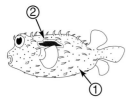

SIZE: 6-10 in., max. 1 ft.
DEPTH: 6-40 ft.

CAYMAN

329

Puffer

DISTINCTIVE FEATURES: Bright yellow body. **1. Bright white spots ringed with black cover body.**

DESCRIPTION: The post-larval stage, or "lyosphaera," of all burrfish species, *Chilomycterus,* appear the same, and it is impossible to distinguish them visually.

ABUNDANCE & DISTRIBUTION: Rare Florida, Bahamas, Caribbean.

HABITAT & BEHAVIOR: Larvae are pelagic and generally drift in open sea or sargassum floats. With age they undergo metamorphosis and settle on reefs.

REACTION TO DIVERS: Take protective cover if available.

DISTINCTIVE FEATURES: 1. Long spines on head. 2. Small dark spots on body; no spots on fins.

DESCRIPTION: Olive to brown. Dusky band runs from eye to eye; may have dusky blotches or bands on back. Iris is yellow; pupil has iridescent blue-green specks. Spines usually lowered, but may become erect without inflating body.

ABUNDANCE & DISTRIBUTION: Occasional to uncommon Florida, Bahamas, Caribbean; also Gulf of Mexico and south to Brazil; circumtropical.

HABITAT & BEHAVIOR: Inhabit grassy areas, mangroves and reefs. Swim slowly near bottom, blending with background. Occasionally swim in small schools.

REACTION TO DIVERS: Shy; retreat to protective recess if approached. Often peer out of entrance where they can be closely observed. Inflate if molested.

NOTE: Also commonly known as "Spiny Puffer."

DISTINCTIVE FEATURES: Small, dark spots over entire body. **1. Spots on fins.**

DESCRIPTION: Olive to brown back, shading to white on belly. Can pale or darken. Long spines are erect only when inflated.

ABUNDANCE & DISTRIBUTION: Occasional Florida, Bahamas, Caribbean; also north to Massachusetts, Bermuda, Gulf of Mexico, and south to Brazil; circumtropical.

HABITAT & BEHAVIOR: Lurk in or near cave openings and recesses and, occasionally, in grassy areas.

REACTION TO DIVERS: Shy; retreat to protective recess if approached. Often peer out of entrance where they can be closely observed. Inflate if molested.

SIMILAR SPECIES: Spotted Burrfish, *Chilomycterus atinga,* distinguished by short, triangular spines that are always erect.

NOTE: Also commonly known as "Spotted Spiny Puffer."

JUVENILE BURRFISH
Chilomycterus sp.
FAMILY:
Puffer/Spiny –
Tetraodontidae

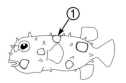

SIZE: Less than ³/₄ in.
DEPTH: 6 - 40 ft.

SAN SALVADOR, BAHAMAS

BALLOONFISH
Diodon holocanthus
FAMILY:
Puffer/Spiny –
Tetraodontidae

SIZE: 8 - 14 in.,
max. 20 in.
DEPTH: 6 - 50 ft.

CAYMAN

PORCUPINEFISH
Diodon hystrix
FAMILY:
Puffer/Spiny –
Tetraodontidae

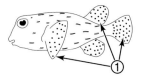

SIZE: 1 - 2 ft., max. 3 ft.
DEPTH: 10 - 60 ft.

SOUTH CAICOS

331

Boxfish

DISTINCTIVE FEATURES: 1. Honeycomb pattern on body. 2. A sharp spine above each eye (distinguishes cowfish from trunkfish).

DESCRIPTION: Vary from shades of blue to green to yellow. Reticulated or scrawled design on head. Can darken or pale and change color. Two sharp spines in front of anal fin.

ABUNDANCE & DISTRIBUTION: Occasional eastern Florida, Bahamas, Caribbean; also north to New Jersey and south to Brazil. Not reported Florida Gulf Coast.

HABITAT & BEHAVIOR: Swim about reefs, blending with background.

REACTION TO DIVERS: Extremely wary; remain motionless, apparently relying on camouflage, but when aware of detection, quickly retreat. An indirect approach is best maneuver for a close view.

DISTINCTIVE FEATURES: 1. Scrawled pattern of bluish markings covers body. 2. Blue line runs from snout to anal fin. 3. A sharp spine above each eye (distinguishes cowfish from trunkfish).

DESCRIPTION: Blue-green to yellow cast. Can darken, pale and change color. Two sharp spines in front of anal fin.

ABUNDANCE & DISTRIBUTION: Common to occasional Florida and Bahamas; occasional to uncommon Caribbean; also north to Massachusetts, Bermuda, Gulf of Mexico and south to Brazil.

HABITAT & BEHAVIOR: Live in a wide range of habitats, from grass beds to walls. Change color to blend with background.

REACTION TO DIVERS: Wary; remain motionless apparently relying on camouflage, but when aware of detection, quickly retreat. An indirect approach is the best maneuver for a close view.

DISTINCTIVE FEATURES: 1. Obvious hump on back. 2. Base of tail long. (Similar Spotted Trunkfish, *L. bicaudalis*, [pg. 335] much shorter.)

DESCRIPTION: Two sharp spines in front of anal fin (lack of spines above eyes easily distinguishes them from similar Honeycomb, *L. polygonia* and Scrawled Cowfish, *L. quadricornis* [previous]). Have three phases of markings: Young are covered with white spots; as they mature, a dark-edged honeycomb pattern develops; with growth (at about 15 inches) markings change to scrawled pattern. Vary greatly in shades of olive, green, yellow-brown, brown, blue-gray and gray. Can change color and markings.

ABUNDANCE & DISTRIBUTION: Occasional to uncommon Florida, Bahamas, Caribbean; also north to Massachusetts, Bermuda, Gulf of Mexico and south to Brazil.

HABITAT & BEHAVIOR: Generally swim in water column over sea grass beds; occasionally over reefs.

REACTION TO DIVERS: Quite wary; retreat when approached.

NOTE: Also commonly known as "Buffalo Trunkfish."

HONEYCOMB COWFISH
Lactophrys polygonia
FAMILY:
Boxfish – Ostraciidae

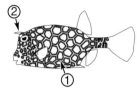

SIZE: 7-15 in., max. 18 in.
DEPTH: 20-80 ft.

BELIZE

SCRAWLED COWFISH
Lactophrys quadricornis
FAMILY:
Boxfish – Ostraciidae

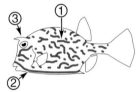

SIZE: 8-15 in.,
max. 18 in.
DEPTH: 6-80 ft.

KEY LARGO, FL

TRUNKFISH
Lactophrys trigonus
FAMILY:
Boxfish – Ostraciidae

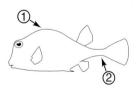

SIZE: 12-17 in.,
max. 19 in.
DEPTH: 3-35 ft.

BIMINI

333

Boxfish

DISTINCTIVE FEATURES: 1. Dark body covered with white spots. 2. Area of pale honeycomb markings on central midbody. Only member of family without a spine above eye and/or near anal fin. **JUVENILE:** 3. Dark body covered with large yellow to pale yellow spots.

DESCRIPTION: Dark around mouth and at base of pectoral fin. **JUVENILE:** As they mature, develop pale midbody area where honeycomb markings appear later.

ABUNDANCE & DISTRIBUTION: Common to occasional Florida, Bahamas, Caribbean; also north to Massachusetts, Bermuda, Gulf of Mexico and south to Brazil.

HABITAT & BEHAVIOR: Swim above reefs, occasionally over sand. Normally solitary, but occasionally swim in small groups.

REACTION TO DIVERS: Not wary; usually allow a close approach.

**Smooth Trunkfish
Intermediate Juvenile**

NORTH CAICOS

DISTINCTIVE FEATURES: 1. White, covered with black spots, including fins. 2. White around mouth.

DESCRIPTION: Two sharp spines in front of anal fin (no spines above eyes).

ABUNDANCE & DISTRIBUTION: Occasional to uncommon Florida Keys, Bahamas, Caribbean; also south to Brazil.

HABITAT & BEHAVIOR: Swim above reefs; often hover in the openings of small holes or under ledges.

REACTION TO DIVERS: Wary; retreat into protected areas when approached. Apparently curious, often return to entrance to peer out.

SMOOTH TRUNKFISH
Lactophrys triqueter
FAMILY:
Boxfish – Ostraciidae

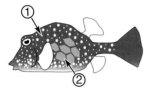

CAYMAN

SIZE: 6 - 10 in., max. 1 ft.
DEPTH: 15 - 80 ft.

Smooth Trunkfish Juvenile
About the size of a pea.

SOUTH CAICOS

SPOTTED TRUNKFISH
Lactophrys bicaudalis
FAMILY:
Boxfish – Ostraciidae

CAYMAN

SIZE: 6 -12 in., max. 16 in.
DEPTH: 15 -60 ft.

Leatherjacket

DISTINCTIVE FEATURES: 1. Streaming tips on rear dorsal and tail fin. 2. Two blue stripes on face. 3. Small lines radiate from around eye. **JUVENILE:** 4. Rows of small spots form diagonal lines on back.

DESCRIPTION: Body color in various shades of purple, blue, turquoise and green; lower half of head yellow or yellowish. Can pale or darken dramatically. **JUVENILE:** Silver to gray with yellowish tints.

ABUNDANCE & DISTRIBUTION: Common to occasional Florida, Bahamas, Caribbean; also north to Massachusetts, Bermuda, Gulf of Mexico, south to Brazil and eastern Atlantic.

HABITAT & BEHAVIOR: Swim about reef tops, coral rubble and grass beds looking for food; especially fond of sea urchins. Juveniles stay near protective recesses in areas of sand and rubble.

REACTION TO DIVERS: Relatively shy; usually difficult to approach, although on occasion they appear curious and swim around divers.

Queen Triggerfish Juvenile

BIMINI

DISTINCTIVE FEATURES: 1. Blue spots and line markings on upper body and fins. (Similar Ocean Triggerfish, *Canthidermis sufflamen*, [next] has no blue spots or line markings.)

DESCRIPTION: Color varies from light gray to olive-gray to yellowish brown. Often have white dots and lines on lower body and fins. May have faint, broad bars or blotches on upper body.

ABUNDANCE & DISTRIBUTION: Common Florida coasts; uncommon Bahamas and Florida Keys; rare Caribbean; also north to Nova Scotia, Gulf of Mexico and south to Argentina.

HABITAT & BEHAVIOR: Drift above the bottom, alone or in small groups. Juveniles, and occasionally adults, drift at the surface with sargassum.

REACTION TO DIVERS: Not shy; usually allow a close approach before retreating.

QUEEN TRIGGERFISH
Balistes vetula

FAMILY:
Triggerfish/Leatherjacket
– Balistidae

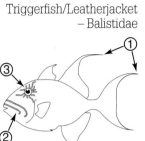

SIZE: 8 -16 in., max. 2 ft.
DEPTH: 10 - 50 ft.

CAYMAN

Queen Triggerfish
Intermediate

CAYMAN

GRAY TRIGGERFISH
Balistes capriscus

FAMILY:
Triggerfish/Leatherjacket
– Balistidae

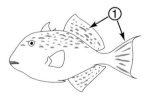

SIZE: 5 - 9 in., max. 1 ft.
DEPTH: 15 - 50 ft.

SARASOTA, FL

337

Leatherjacket

DISTINCTIVE FEATURES: Uniformly gray. **1. Black blotch at base of pectoral fin.** (Similar Gray Triggerfish, *Balistes capriscus*, [previous] lacks this blotch.)

DESCRIPTION: Vary from gray to grayish brown. Can pale or darken dramatically.

ABUNDANCE & DISTRIBUTION: Common to uncommon Florida, Bahamas, Caribbean; also north to Massachusetts, Bermuda and Gulf of Mexico.

HABITAT & BEHAVIOR: Normally swim alone or in small, loose groups in open water, well above outer reefs and near drop-offs. Most commonly observed during nesting, when the fish fan a large depression in sand patches to lay eggs. Remain near nest to guard against predators.

REACTION TO DIVERS: Generally shy and keep their distance. When guarding nest, can occasionally be closely approached.

DISTINCTIVE FEATURES: 1. Numerous white to bluish white spots, ovals and line markings cover head and body.

DESCRIPTION: Vary from olive-brown to brown, gray or bluish gray. Tail rounded and without elongated tips. Body has rough texture due to raised keel on scales.

ABUNDANCE & DISTRIBUTION: Uncommon to rare Florida, Bahamas, Caribbean; also north to North Carolina and Bermuda; circumtropical.

HABITAT & BEHAVIOR: Considered pelagic, but occasionally inhabit deep rocky slopes and reefs. Often in loose schools or aggregations.

REACTION TO DIVERS: Relatively unafraid; usually allow a close approach.

DISTINCTIVE FEATURES: 1. Three dark lines on cheek. 2. Series of dashes form thin stripes on body.

DESCRIPTION: Vary from bluish gray to brownish gray. Can pale or darken. White dot just forward of eye, with white crescent bordering upper eye. Dark line at base of dorsal and anal fins. Red to orange borders on tail.

ABUNDANCE & DISTRIBUTION: Common to occasional Caribbean; uncommon Florida and Bahamas; also north to North Carolina, Bermuda and south to Brazil.

HABITAT & BEHAVIOR: Normally inhabit low profile sections of outer reefs and offshore banks deeper than 80 feet (rarely along walls). In a few areas, however, they inhabit patch reefs as shallow as 35 feet (i.e., Turneffe Reef, Belize). Young often drift near the surface in sargassum.

REACTION TO DIVERS: Relatively unafraid; usually allow a close approach.

OCEAN TRIGGERFISH
Canthidermis sufflamen
FAMILY:
Triggerfish/Leatherjacket
– Balistidae

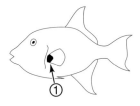

SIZE: 10-18 in., max. 2 ft.
DEPTH: 35-100 ft.

CAYMAN

ROUGH TRIGGERFISH
Canthidermis maculata
FAMILY:
Triggerfish/Leatherjacket
– Balistidae

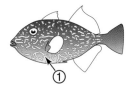

SIZE: 6-10 in., max. 13 in.
DEPTH: 0-200 ft.

JUPITER, FL

SARGASSUM TRIGGERFISH
Xanthichthys ringens
FAMILY:
Triggerfish/Leatherjacket
– Balistidae

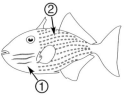

SIZE: 5-8 in., max. 10 in.
DEPTH: 35-250 ft.

CAYMAN

Leatherjacket

DISTINCTIVE FEATURES: Black body. **1. Pale blue lines along base of dorsal and anal fins.**

DESCRIPTION: May have bluish to greenish cast. Above eye, head may be blue, and below, orange or yellow. Scales have pale diamond-shaped outline. Can change color, and pale or darken.

ABUNDANCE & DISTRIBUTION: Very common to occasional Florida, Bahamas, Caribbean; also south to Brazil; circumtropical.

HABITAT & BEHAVIOR: Most commonly seen in small aggregations over reefs.

REACTION TO DIVERS: Tend to be quite shy. When approached, retreat into a small crevice and lock themselves in place by raising their trigger.

DISTINCTIVE FEATURES: 1. Covered with blue to blue-green spots, irregular lines and black dots. 2. Elongated body with long, broom-like tail.

DESCRIPTION: Vary from pale gray or tan to dark olive-brown. Can darken or pale dramatically. Tail often closed and limp.

ABUNDANCE & DISTRIBUTION: Common to uncommon Florida, Bahamas, Caribbean; also north to Massachusetts, Bermuda, Gulf of Mexico, south to Brazil; circumtropical.

HABITAT & BEHAVIOR: Drift over reefs, often in open water.

REACTION TO DIVERS: Wary; generally keep their distance. Can occasionally be approached with slow, nonthreatening movements.

SIMILAR SPECIES: Dotterel Filefish, *A. heudeloti*, has a thicker, less elongated body, nearly football-shaped in profile; rare.

DISTINCTIVE FEATURES: 1. White spot on upper base of tail, and usually, a second, smaller spot underneath. Orangish spots cover body.

DESCRIPTION: In most common color phase, they have wide, dark brown stripes and narrow, dull yellow stripes that converge near tail base. Can change to solid brown, darken or pale. May have indistinct line markings on head.

ABUNDANCE & DISTRIBUTION: Common to occasional Caribbean; occasional to uncommon Florida, Bahamas; also north to Massachusetts, Bermuda, Gulf of Mexico and south to Brazil.

HABITAT & BEHAVIOR: Stay near bottom; often hide in tangles of antler coral or gorgonians.

REACTION TO DIVERS: Tend to be shy, and hide in holes or cracks in reefs when closely approached.

BLACK DURGON
Melichthys niger
FAMILY:
Triggerfish/Leatherjacket
– Balistidae

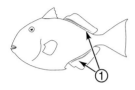

SIZE: 6 -12 in., max. 16 in.
DEPTH: 20 -100 ft.

CAYMAN

SCRAWLED FILEFISH
Aluterus scriptus
FAMILY:
Filefish/Leatherjacket –
Balistidae

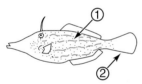

SIZE: 1- 2 ½ ft., max. 3 ft.
DEPTH: 20 - 60 ft.

ST. LUCIA

ORANGESPOTTED
FILEFISH
Cantherhines pullus
FAMILY:
Filefish/Leatherjacket –
Balistidae

SIZE: 4 -7 in.,
max. 8 ½ in.
DEPTH: 15 -60 ft.

CAYMAN

341

Leatherjacket

DISTINCTIVE FEATURES: Extremely thin. **1. Body covered with orange dots. 2. Long tail base.**

DESCRIPTION: Pale silvery gray to dark gray, orange or orangish brown; often display large, dark areas or blotches. Can pale or darken dramatically. Long, broom-like tail is often limp.

ABUNDANCE & DISTRIBUTION: Occasional Bahamas and Florida; rare Caribbean; also north to Nova Scotia, Bermuda, Gulf of Mexico and south to Brazil.

HABITAT & BEHAVIOR: Prefer sea grasses, though found over most bottoms, including reefs. Swim or drift, often in pairs or small groups.

REACTION TO DIVERS: Shy; usually keep their distance. Can occasionally be approached with slow, nonthreatening movements.

SIMILAR SPECIES: Unicorn Filefish, *A. monoceros*, is distinguished by its more elongated body which is gray to brown or silver with small, scattered, dark spots. Uncommon Florida, rare Caribbean.

Whitespotted Filefish
Orange phase.

CAYMAN

DISTINCTIVE FEATURES: 1. Noticeably extended belly appendage. 2. Orange spines at base of tail.

DESCRIPTION: Upper body shades of gray to olive or brown, with brown to orange below. Snout whitish; dorsal and anal fins are translucent yellow; tail dark. Two phases: one with large, whitish spots, the other without.

ABUNDANCE & DISTRIBUTION: Common to occasional South Florida, northwestern Caribbean; uncommon Bahamas and balance of Caribbean; also Bermuda and south to Brazil.

HABITAT & BEHAVIOR: Move about reef tops in pairs, often in both color phases.

REACTION TO DIVERS: Somewhat curious; often peer from behind gorgonians. Can be closely approached with slow, nonthreatening movements.

ORANGE FILEFISH
Aluterus schoepfi
FAMILY:
Filefish/Leatherjacket –
Balistidae

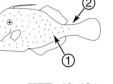

SIZE: 10 -18 in.,
max. 20 in.
DEPTH: 10 - 40 ft.

GRAND BAHAMA

Orange Filefish
*Displaying dark
blotched pattern.*

GRAND BAHAMA

WHITESPOTTED
FILEFISH
Cantherhines macrocerus
Whitespotted Phase
FAMILY:
Filefish/Leatherjacket –
Balistidae

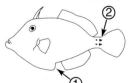

SIZE: 10 -15 in., max. 18 in.
DEPTH: 20 -70 ft.

ROATAN

Leatherjacket

DISTINCTIVE FEATURES: 1. Vague, incomplete body stripes formed by dashes and spots.

DESCRIPTION: Usually variably blotched and spotted, in shades of tan to yellow-brown or brown, but can change color to match surroundings. Males have highly extended second dorsal fin ray. Usually have 27 to 29 anal fin rays. Rarely over four inches in length. (Compare anal fin ray count and size of similar Planehead Filefish, *M. hispidus* [pg. 347].)

ABUNDANCE & DISTRIBUTION: Uncommon Florida, Bahamas, Caribbean; also north to North Carolina, Bermuda and Gulf of Mexico.

HABITAT & BEHAVIOR: Generally inhabit island reefs well offshore; also, often in floats of sargassum.

REACTION TO DIVERS: Relatively unafraid. Usually allow slow, nonthreatening approach.

DISTINCTIVE FEATURES: Slender, elongated head, snout and body. (Compare similar Fringed, *M. ciliatus,* and Planehead, *M. hispidus* [next] and Pygmy Filefish, *M. setifer* [previous].) **1. Usually have white reticulated pattern over body.**

DESCRIPTION: Variable shades of reddish brown to yellow-brown, brown or gray; upper body usually darker. Can change color, pale or darken dramatically to blend with background; reticulated markings may become indistinct. Large dewlap (extendable belly appendage) usually has yellowish edge with submarginal blue line.

ABUNDANCE & DISTRIBUTION: Occasional Florida, Bahamas, Caribbean; also north to North Carolina and Bermuda.

HABITAT & BEHAVIOR: Inhabit reefs; often drift vertically among branches of gorgonians. Their camouflage ability makes them difficult to spot.

REACTION TO DIVERS: Can be closely approached, apparently hesitant to leave the cover of gorgonian branches.

Slender Filefish
Reticulated markings indistinct, dewlap retracted.

CAYMAN

PYGMY FILEFISH
Monacanthus setifer
FAMILY:
Filefish/Leatherjacket –
Balistidae

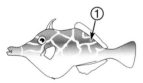

SIZE: 2-4 in.,
max. 7 ½ in.
DEPTH: 0-50 ft.

NAPLES, FL

SLENDER FILEFISH
Monacanthus tuckeri
FAMILY:
Filefish/Leatherjacket –
Balistidae

SIZE: 2-3 ½ in.,
max. 4 in.
DEPTH: 10-60 ft.

BARBADOS

Slender Filefish
*Rare color phase,
reticulated markings
absent, file retracted.*

BELIZE

Leatherjacket

DISTINCTIVE FEATURES: Thick body, and protruding, but not elongated, snout. **1. Base of dorsal fin has steep hump.**

DESCRIPTION: Highly variable shades of brown to reddish brown, yellow-brown, green or gray; usually have numerous dark and white speckles, spots and blotches. Can change color, pale or darken dramatically to blend with background. Large dewlap (extendable belly appendage) usually has large black area or submarginal band; tail often banded. Small fleshy tabs often on body. Males have two recurved spines on base of tail [right], absent in females [below right].

ABUNDANCE & DISTRIBUTION: Occasional Florida, Bahamas, Caribbean; also north to Newfoundland, Bermuda, Gulf of Mexico, south to Argentina and eastern Atlantic.

HABITAT & BEHAVIOR: Generally inhabit sandy or rubble-strewn bottoms with sea grasses or algae growth. Often green when over sea grasses and green algae. Often drift vertically in clumps of algae. Their camouflage ability makes them difficult to spot.

REACTION TO DIVERS: Can be closely approached, apparently hesitant to leave their cover.

Planehead Filefish
Female

Note lack of long second dorsal fin ray.

JACKSONVILLE, FL

DISTINCTIVE FEATURES: Thick, blotched body. **1. Snout and nape profile nearly straight, at about a 45-degree angle.**

DESCRIPTION: Usually blotched in variable shades of tan to brown or gray, occasionally greenish. Males have highly extended second dorsal fin ray. Usually have 31 to 33 anal fin rays. Normally more than four inches in length. (Compare anal fin ray count and size of similar Pygmy Filefish, *M. setifer* [pg. 345].)

ABUNDANCE & DISTRIBUTION: Uncommon Florida; also north to Nova Scotia, Bermuda, Gulf of Mexico and Brazil. Not reported Bahamas, Caribbean.

HABITAT & BEHAVIOR: Generally inhabit rocky reefs or rubble-strewn bottoms, occasionally with sea grasses or algae.

REACTION TO DIVERS: Relatively unafraid. Usually allow slow, nonthreatening approach.

FRINGED FILEFISH
Monacanthus ciliatus

FAMILY:
Filefish/Leatherjacket –
Balistidae

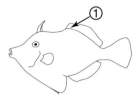

SIZE: 3-5 in., max. 8 in.
DEPTH: 10-60 ft.

BARBADOS

Fringed Filefish

*Green color phase
blends with sea
grasses and algae.*

CONCEPTION IS., BAHAMAS

PLANEHEAD FILEFISH
Monacanthus hispidus
Male
FAMILY:
Filefish/Leatherjacket –
Balistidae

SIZE: 4-8 in., max. 10 in.
DEPTH: 10-160 ft.

JACKSONVILLE, FL

Goatfish

DISTINCTIVE FEATURES: 1. A row of three dark, rectangular body blotches is normally visible when fish are active (when resting, change to blotched or mottled reddish brown). 2. Two barbels under tip of chin.

DESCRIPTION: Rapidly and dramatically change color from white to blotched and mottled red to reddish brown when becoming inactive. Light bluish lines often on head and, occasionally, upper body.

ABUNDANCE & DISTRIBUTION: Common Florida; occasional Bahamas, Caribbean; also north to Massachusetts, Bermuda, Gulf of Mexico and south to Brazil.

HABITAT & BEHAVIOR: Use barbels to dig in sand and around areas of rubble for food. Often congregate in small groups of four to six. When not searching for food, often rest on bottom and match color to blend with background.

REACTION TO DIVERS: Unconcerned; move away only when threatened.

SIMILAR SPECIES: Red Goatfish, *Mullus auratus*, distinguished by reddish brown stripes across both dorsal fins. Reddish brown body with two yellowish stripes.

Yellow Goatfish
*Non-feeding,
schooling behavior.*

CAYMAN

DISTINCTIVE FEATURES: 1. Yellow tail and midbody stripe. 2. Two barbels under tip of chin.

DESCRIPTION: White; upper body may have shadings ranging from blue to olive or red. Fins, other than tail, may be white or yellowish.

ABUNDANCE & DISTRIBUTION: Abundant to common Florida, Bahamas, Caribbean; also Bermuda, Gulf of Mexico and south to Brazil.

HABITAT & BEHAVIOR: Use barbels to dig in sand and around areas of rubble for food. Feed alone or congregate in small groups; when not feeding, often swim lazily in large schools or aggregations over nearby reefs.

REACTION TO DIVERS: Unconcerned; move away only when threatened.

SPOTTED GOATFISH
Pseudupeneus maculatus
Active Color Phase
FAMILY:
Goatfish – Mullidae

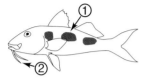

SIZE: 5 - 8 in., max. 11 in.
DEPTH: 5 - 60 ft.

WEST PALM BEACH, FL

Spotted Goatfish
Inactive color phase.

CAYMAN

YELLOW GOATFISH
Mulloidichthys martinicus
FAMILY:
Goatfish – Mullidae

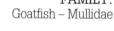

SIZE: 6 - 12 in.,
max. 15 ½ in.
DEPTH: 5 - 200 ft.

CAYMAN

349

DISTINCTIVE FEATURES: 1. Two orangish to bronze stripes on first dorsal fin. 2. Dusky bands or lines on lobes of tail. 3. Two barbels under tip of chin.

DESCRIPTION: Upper body usually shades of red; pale below, often with yellow stripes or lines between; may have wider yellow or red stripe on midbody. Can rapidly and dramatically lighten, darken or change color.

ABUNDANCE & DISTRIBUTION: Occasional North Florida; uncommon to absent Caribbean; also north to North Carolina and south to Brazil. Not reported Bahamas.

HABITAT & BEHAVIOR: Use barbels to dig in sand and around areas of rubble for food. Often congregate in small groups of four to six.

REACTION TO DIVERS: Unconcerned; move away only when threatened.

DISTINCTIVE FEATURES: 1. Rear dorsal and tail fins black with white spots. JUVENILE: 2. Black spot on nose. (Similar Jackknife Fish, *E. lanceolatus* [next] has vertical black dash on nose.) 3. Extremely long dorsal fin.

DESCRIPTION: Front dorsal fin unusually long. Black and white bars on head, and multiple stripes on body. **JUVENILE:** Black and white bars on head and long black stripe from dorsal fin to tail.

ABUNDANCE & DISTRIBUTION: Occasional South Florida, Bahamas, Caribbean.

HABITAT & BEHAVIOR: Inhabit secluded areas of reefs, often under ledges or near the entrances to small caves. Usually swim in established circuitous patterns. Feed in open at night.

REACTION TO DIVERS: Unafraid. Can be closely approached with slow, nonthreatening movements.

**Spotted Drum
Intermediate,
Juvenile/Adult**

ROATAN

DWARF GOATFISH
Upeneus parvus
FAMILY:
Goatfish – Mullidae

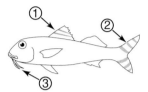

SIZE: 5 - 8 in., max. 8 in.
DEPTH: 60 - 240 ft.

JACKSONVILLE, FL

SPOTTED DRUM
Equetus punctatus
FAMILY:
Drum – Sciaenidae

SIZE: 6 - 9 in., max. 11 in.
DEPTH: 15 - 100 ft.

CAYMAN

Spotted Drum Juvenile

SIZE: ³/₄ - 1 ¹/₂ in.

CAYMAN

Drum

DISTINCTIVE FEATURES: 1. Fins white with no spots. ADULT & JUVENILE: 2. Single black band runs from top of front dorsal fin to and along midbody line to tip of tail. JUVENILE: 3. Vertical black dash on nose. (Similar Spotted Drum, *E. punctatus*, [previous] has black dot on nose.)

DESCRIPTION: Elongated front dorsal fin. Black and white bars on head. **JUVENILE:** Very young are yellow-gold. With maturity, color fades to a yellowish cast in white areas, with yellow-gold borders on black stripes; eventually may lose all yellow-gold coloration [below far right].

ABUNDANCE & DISTRIBUTION: Occasional Florida, Bahamas; uncommon to rare Caribbean; also north to South Carolina, Bermuda and south to Brazil.

HABITAT & BEHAVIOR: Inhabit secluded areas of reefs, often under ledges or near the entrances to small caves. Generally feed in open at night, although large groups occasionally forage in open sandy areas during day. Generally found deeper than similar Spotted Drum and Highhat.

REACTION TO DIVERS: Unafraid; can be closely approached with slow, nonthreatening movements.

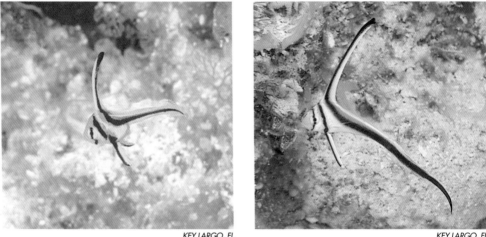

KEY LARGO, FL   *KEY LARGO, FL*

DISTINCTIVE FEATURES: 1. Black and white striped body. JUVENILE: 2. Very young have extremely long dorsal fin. 3. Older juveniles have band between eyes. (Similar Cubbyu, *Equetus umbrosus*, distinguished by very young having short dorsal fin, and older juveniles having oval marking between eyes.)

DESCRIPTION: Elongated front dorsal fin. Black band on dorsal fin ends at base; all other fins dark. (Both the adult and juvenile are distinguished from similar Spotted Drum and Jackknife by the lack of bars on head.) **JUVENILE:** Develop spot in dorsal fin.

ABUNDANCE & DISTRIBUTION: Common Florida; occasional to uncommon Bahamas, Caribbean; also Bermuda and south to Brazil.

HABITAT & BEHAVIOR: Inhabit secluded areas of reefs, often under ledges or near the entrances to small caves. Drift in pairs or small groups. May mix with similar Cubbyu, *E. umbrosus*, [next]. Feed in open at night.

REACTION TO DIVERS: Apparently feel secure in protected reef openings where they can be closely approached.

JACKKNIFE FISH
Equetus lanceolatus
FAMILY:
Drum – Sciaenidae

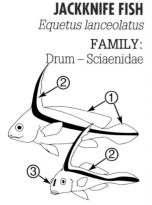

SIZE: 5 - 8 in., max. 9 in.
DEPTH: 40 - 140 ft.

PANAMA CITY, FL

JACKSONVILLE, FL

ANGUILLA

HIGHHAT
Equetus acuminatus
FAMILY:
Drum – Sciaenidae

SIZE: 5 - 8 in., max. 9 in.
DEPTH: 15 - 60 ft.

CAYMAN

continued next page **353**

Drum

ANGUILLA ANGUILLA

DISTINCTIVE FEATURES: Dark brownish gray to black. Thin, indistinct body stripes. **JUVENILE: 1. Have relatively short dorsal fin compared to other juveniles of genus *Equetus*. 2. Black oval marking between eyes.** (Similar Highhat, *E. acuminatus*, [previous] distinguished by band between eyes.)

DESCRIPTION: Body shape virtually identical to Highhat, but never have bold black and white stripes. Intermediates between juvenile and adult may have thin black and white stripes. (Highhat is distinguished by thicker stripes.)

ABUNDANCE & DISTRIBUTION: Common Florida; also north to North Carolina and Gulf of Mexico. Not reported Bahamas, Caribbean.

HABITAT & BEHAVIOR: Inhabit secluded areas of reefs, often under ledges or near the entrances to small caves. Drift in pairs or small groups. May mix with similar Highhat, *E. acuminatus*, [previous].

REACTION TO DIVERS: Apparently feel secure in protection of reef openings, where they can be closely approached.

PANAMA CITY, FL

PANAMA CITY, FL

354

Highhat Juveniles

continued from previous page

Note long dorsal fin in very young. [far left]

With maturity, develop bar between eyes and spot in dorsal fin [left and right].

WEST PALM BEACH, FL

CUBBYU
Equetus umbrosus
FAMILY:
Drum – Sciaenidae

SIZE: 5 - 8 in., max. 10 in.
DEPTH: 15 - 300 ft.

WEST PALM BEACH, FL

Cubbyu Juveniles

Note relatively short dorsal fin of very young.
[far left]

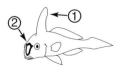

With maturity, develop oval marking between eyes.
[left]

PANAMA CITY, FL

Drum

DISTINCTIVE FEATURES: 1. Black spot at base of pectoral fin.
DESCRIPTION: Pale reddish brown to gray, silvery cast. Large eyes and somewhat elongated body.
ABUNDANCE & DISTRIBUTION: Occasional South Florida; uncommon eastern Caribbean; rare to absent balance of Caribbean; also south to Brazil. Not reported Bahamas.
HABITAT & BEHAVIOR: Reclusive; hide during day in crevices, caves and holes in reefs. Often gather in small aggregations.
REACTION TO DIVERS: Wary; tend to remain hidden. Can occasionally be closely approached with slow, nonthreatening movements.

DISTINCTIVE FEATURES: 1. Brownish spots on scale rows form body stripes that, above the midline, diagonal distinctly upward below the rear spinous dorsal fin and toward the fore soft dorsal fin.
DESCRIPTION: Pale reddish brown to gray, silvery cast. Large eyes and somewhat elongated body.
ABUNDANCE & DISTRIBUTION: Occasional east-central Florida, Caribbean; also Gulf of Campeche and south to Guyana. Not reported balance of Florida or Bahamas.
HABITAT & BEHAVIOR: Inhabit areas around rocky outcroppings and patch reefs, especially those with abundant algal growth. Often hover over accumulations of loose vegetation and debris where they retreat if disturbed. Young usually in less than 30 feet, while adults can range to nearly 100 feet.
REACTION TO DIVERS: Wary; keep their distance and retreat into protective cover if rapidly approached. Can occasionally be closely approached with slow, nonthreatening movements.

DISTINCTIVE FEATURES: Deep, heavy body. 1. Long, dangling chin barbels (about 12).
DESCRIPTION: Dark gray to silvery or brassy with large, noticeable scales; fins blackish. Usually have four to five broad dark bars which they can pale or darken.
ABUNDANCE & DISTRIBUTION: Occasional Florida and Central American coastlines to southeastern Caribbean; also north to Nova Scotia, north Gulf of Mexico and south to Brazil. Not reported Bahamas or balance of Caribbean.
HABITAT & BEHAVIOR: Inhabit sand, mud, gravel and rocky, rubble-strewn bottoms. Often near shoreline and under bridges, piers or docks. Bottom feeders; dig in bottom material with barbels.
REACTION TO DIVERS: Wary; keep their distance and retreat rapidly when approached. Apparently curious; if diver remains still, will often make several close passes.

REEF CROAKER
Odontoscion dentex
FAMILY:
Drum – Sciaenidae

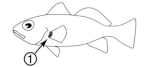

SIZE: 4 - 7 ¹/₂ in., max. 1 ft.
DEPTH: 15 - 80 ft.

MIAMI, FL

STRIPED CROAKER
Bairdiella sanctaeluciae
FAMILY:
Drum – Sciaenidae

SIZE: 4-6 in., max. 8 in.
DEPTH: 10-100 ft.

JUPITER, FL

BLACK DRUM
Pogonias cromis
FAMILY:
Drum – Sciaenidae

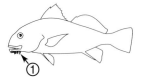

SIZE: 1 - 3 ft., max. 5 ¹/₂ ft.
DEPTH: 1 - 60 ft.

FT. PIERCE, FL

Tripletail – Sweeper – Brotula

DISTINCTIVE FEATURES: 1. Rear dorsal and anal fins large (giving the impression of three tail fins). 2. Nape profile concave.

DESCRIPTION: Lightly mottled; vary from cream to yellow-brown, greenish brown, gray and black.

ABUNDANCE & DISTRIBUTION: Occasional Florida, Bahamas, Caribbean; also north to Massachusetts, Bermuda, Gulf of Mexico, and south to Argentina; circumtropical.

HABITAT & BEHAVIOR: Sluggish; often float on their sides near surface. Prefer shaded areas under floats of sargassum, docks, buoys and anchored boats.

REACTION TO DIVERS: Somewhat wary; slowly move away upon approach. Slow, nonthreatening movements may allow close observation.

DISTINCTIVE FEATURES: 1. Dark band at base of anal fin.

DESCRIPTION: Shiny copper color. Large eyes, deep belly profile, and very thin body. Common name derives from juvenile which is almost transparent.

ABUNDANCE & DISTRIBUTION: Common to occasional Florida, Bahamas, Caribbean; also Bermuda and south to Brazil.

HABITAT & BEHAVIOR: Drift in caves, dark areas of reefs, under docks and interiors of shipwrecks by day. Usually congregate in small groups to large schools.

REACTION TO DIVERS: Appear unconcerned; allow a slow, close approach.

NOTE: Also commonly known as "Copper Sweeper" and "Hatchetfish."

SIMILAR SPECIES: Shortfin Sweeper, *P. poeyi*, distinguished by lack of dark band at base of anal fin. Slightly smaller, reaching a maximum length of four inches. Light yellowish brown; may have dark upper body. Reported only in Caribbean.

DISTINCTIVE FEATURES: Blackish brown to black elongated body becoming ribbon-like toward rear. (Note: pictured specimen is bearing young and, consequently, has an abnormally enlarged abdomen.) 1. Continuous dorsal and anal fins end with pointed tail.

DESCRIPTION: Fins dusky. Long, barbel-like, Y-shaped ventral fins; single lateral line. No distinctive markings.

ABUNDANCE & DISTRIBUTION: Occasional southern Caribbean; uncommon balance of Caribbean, South Florida and Bahamas.

HABITAT & BEHAVIOR: Reclusive; inhabit deep crevices, recesses and caves in reefs, virtually never coming completely into open. Viviparous (bear young alive) rather than oviparous (egg-laying), like most fish.

REACTION TO DIVERS: Very shy; retreat deep into dark recesses upon approach. With much patience and quiet waiting, may reappear in opening of recess.

TRIPLETAIL
Lobotes surinamensis
FAMILY:
Tripletail – Lobotidae

SIZE: 1½-2½ ft.,
max. 3½ ft.
DEPTH: 0-20 ft.

MIAMI, FL

GLASSY SWEEPER
Pempheris schomburgki
FAMILY:
Sweeper – Pempheridae

SIZE: 3-5 in., max. 6 in.
DEPTH: 15-80 ft.

BARBADOS

BLACK BROTULA
Stygnobrotula latebricola
FAMILY:
Viviparous Brotula –
Bythitidae

SIZE: 1½-2½ in.,
max. 3 in.
DEPTH: 4-70 ft.

WEST PALM BEACH, FL

Remora

DISTINCTIVE FEATURES: 1. Wide white borders on dark tail.

DESCRIPTION: Disc-shaped sucker on top of head. Black midbody stripe bordered with wide white stripes; white border on dorsal and anal fins.

ABUNDANCE & DISTRIBUTION: Uncommon Florida, Bahamas, Caribbean; also north to Massachusetts, Bermuda and Gulf of Mexico.

HABITAT & BEHAVIOR: Attach to sharks, rays, large fish, turtles – even boats or divers!

REACTION TO DIVERS: Unafraid. Occasionally approach divers in an attempt to attach. If this occurs, the grip may be firm, but harmless. Detach easily if pushed forward.

DISTINCTIVE FEATURES: 1. Thin white borders on dark tail.

DESCRIPTION: Disc-shaped sucker on top of head. Black midbody stripe bordered with white stripes; thin white border on dorsal and anal fins. **LARGER ADULT:** Stripe confined to head; white edge on dorsal, anal and tail fins become narrow and almost indistinct with age.

ABUNDANCE & DISTRIBUTION: Occasional Florida, Bahamas, Caribbean; also north to Massachusetts, Bermuda, Gulf of Mexico and south to Uruguay; circumtropical.

HABITAT & BEHAVIOR: Attach to sharks [note photo], rays, large fish, turtles – even boats or divers! Adult Sharksuckers are the most common free-swimming remora.

REACTION TO DIVERS: Unafraid. Occasionally approach divers in an attempt to attach. If this occurs, the grip may be firm, but harmless. Detach easily if pushed forward.

SIMILAR SPECIES: Juvenile Cobia, *Rachycentron canadum*, [pg. 79] distinguished by lack of white borders on fins, and white stripe on center of tail.

WHITEFIN SHARKSUCKER
Echeneis neucratoides
FAMILY:
Remora – Echeneidae

SIZE: 10-18 in.,
max. 30 in.
DEPTH: 0-150 ft.

CAYMAN

SHARKSUCKER
Echeneis naucrates
FAMILY:
Remora – Echeneidae

SIZE: 10-18 in.,
max. 3½ ft.
DEPTH: 0-150 ft.

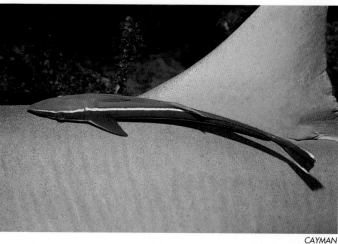

CAYMAN

Sharksucker Larger Adult

CAYMAN

361

Eels
Moray—Conger Eel—Snake Eel

This ID Group consists of fish with long, snake-like bodies. They are generally found on the bottom in dark reef recesses, or in sand.

FAMILY: Moray — Muraenidae
12 Species Included

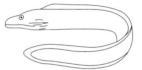

Moray
(typical shape)

Morays have no pectoral or ventral fins; their dorsal, tail and anal fins form a single, long continuous fin that begins behind the head, encircles the tail and extends midway down the belly. Their heavy, scaleless bodies are coated with a clear, protective mucus layer.

Morays constantly open and close their mouths, which is often perceived as a threat, but in reality this behavior is necessary to move water through their gills for respiration. They are not aggressive, although they can inflict a nasty bite if molested. During the day, they are reclusive and tend to hide in dark recesses. Occasionally they are seen with their heads extended from holes. They forage in the open, on the reefs, at night. Colors and markings make identification easy.

FAMILY: Conger — Congridae
3 Species Included

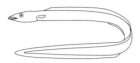

Conger Eel
(typical shape)

Conger eels' dorsal, anal and tail fins are continuous, but unlike morays, they also have pectoral fins. They are thin and elongated, with dull colors and few markings. Because they live deep within recesses in the reef structure, they are rarely seen by divers. An exception is the Garden Eel, which lives in colonies in sand around reefs.

FAMILY: Snake Eel — Ophichthidae
5 Species Included

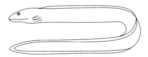

Snake Eel
(typical shape)

Most species of snake eels are virtually without fins and strongly resemble snakes. In fact, when first encountered, uninformed divers think they are seeing a sea snake, although none inhabit the waters of Florida, the Caribbean or the Bahamas. Generally snake eels are shy, reclusive fish that hide in dark recesses or burrow under sand during the day with their heads occasionally exposed. Although they normally hunt at night, at times they are sighted foraging in the open during daylight hours. Distinctive spots are the key to their identification.

DISTINCTIVE FEATURES: Uniform green to brown.

DESCRIPTION: Heavy body with no markings.

ABUNDANCE & DISTRIBUTION: Common Bahamas, Caribbean, Florida Keys; occasional Florida; also north to Massachusetts, Bermuda, Gulf of Mexico and south to Brazil.

HABITAT & BEHAVIOR: Wide range of habitats, from murky bays to clear-water reefs. Hide during the day in recesses; heads often extend from openings. Forage in open at night. Constantly open and close mouth, an action required for respiration — not a threat.

REACTION TO DIVERS: Appear unconcerned; usually allow close approach before they withdraw into reef.

DISTINCTIVE FEATURES: 1. Speckling of dark spots and blotches cover body.

DESCRIPTION: Heavy to medium body. Pale undercolor from white to yellow.

ABUNDANCE & DISTRIBUTION: Common Caribbean; occasional Bahamas and Florida; also north to North Carolina, Bermuda, Gulf of Mexico, south to Brazil and eastern Atlantic.

HABITAT & BEHAVIOR: Inhabit shallow reefs, areas of rocky rubble and grass beds. Hide during the day in recesses; heads often extend from openings. Forage in open at night. Constantly open and close mouth, an action required for respiration — not a threat.

REACTION TO DIVERS: Appear unconcerned; usually allow close approach before they withdraw into reef.

DISTINCTIVE FEATURES: 1. Pale, often yellowish, spots or rosettes cover head and body. 2. Dark spot around gill opening.

DESCRIPTION: Dark brown undercolor. Medium body. Nostrils have tubular extensions.

ABUNDANCE & DISTRIBUTION: Occasional Florida; also north to New England and Gulf of Mexico. Not reported Bahamas or Caribbean.

HABITAT & BEHAVIOR: Inhabit reefs, ledges and rocky areas in moderate depths well offshore. Hide during the day in recesses with only heads extended from openings. Forage in open at night. Constantly open and close mouth, an action required for respiration — not a threat.

REACTION TO DIVERS: Shy; occasionally allow slow, nonthreatening approach before they withdraw into reef.

GREEN MORAY
Gymnothorax funebris
FAMILY:
Moray - Muraenidae

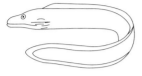

SIZE: 3 - 5 ft., max. 8 ft.
DEPTH: 10 - 100 ft.

CAYMAN

SPOTTED MORAY
Gymnothorax moringa
FAMILY:
Moray - Muraenidae

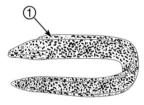

SIZE: 1 ½ - 3 ft., max. 4 ft.
DEPTH: 6 - 40 ft.

CAYMAN

RETICULATE MORAY
Muraena retifera
FAMILY:
Moray - Muraenidae

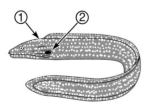

SIZE: 8 - 18 in., max. 2 ft.
DEPTH: 50 - 250 ft.

JACKSONVILLE, FL

DISTINCTIVE FEATURES: Mottled body. **1. Brilliant yellow-gold eyes. 2. Dark stripe or edge on dorsal fin.**

DESCRIPTION: Heavy to medium body. Densely mottled in shades of brown over yellowish undercolor. Inside of mouth is lavender and purple.

ABUNDANCE & DISTRIBUTION: Occasional Caribbean; uncommon Florida, Bahamas; also Bermuda and south to Brazil.

HABITAT & BEHAVIOR: Inhabit shallow reefs and rocky areas. Prefer clear water. Hide during the day in recesses; heads often extend from openings. Forage in open at night. Constantly open and close mouth, an action required for respiration — not a threat.

REACTION TO DIVERS: Appear unconcerned; usually allow close approach before they withdraw into reef.

DISTINCTIVE FEATURES: 1. Jaws arched, with only tips making contact when closed; numerous sharp, pointed teeth visible.

DESCRIPTION: Dark brown to maroon, often lightly mottled. **JUVENILE:** Light brown with dark, bold reticulated markings.

ABUNDANCE & DISTRIBUTION: Uncommon Florida, Bahamas, Caribbean; also Bermuda and eastern Atlantic.

HABITAT & BEHAVIOR: Prefer shallow water, often around patch reefs and sand areas, but may be found much deeper. Hide during the day in recesses; heads may extend from openings. Forage in open at night. Constantly open and close mouth, an action required for respiration — not a threat.

REACTION TO DIVERS: Shy; retreat upon approach. Occasionally allow slow, nonthreatening approach before they withdraw into reef.

DISTINCTIVE FEATURES: 1. Series of white spots along edges of jaws. 2. Jaws arched, with only tips making contact when closed; numerous sharp, pointed teeth visible.

DESCRIPTION: Reddish brown. Black line markings in area of gill openings; dark ring around eye.

ABUNDANCE & DISTRIBUTION: Uncommon Florida, Bahamas, Caribbean; also Bermuda, Gulf of Mexico, south to Brazil and eastern Atlantic.

HABITAT & BEHAVIOR: Inhabit coral reefs, patch reefs and shallow rocky areas. Hide during the day in recesses; heads may extend from openings. Forage in open at night. Constantly open and close mouth, an action required for respiration — not a threat.

REACTION TO DIVERS: Shy; retreat upon approach. Occasionally allow slow, nonthreatening approach before they withdraw into reef.

PURPLEMOUTH MORAY
Gymnothorax vicinus
FAMILY:
Moray - Muraenidae

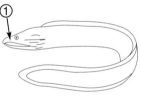

SIZE: 1 1/2 - 3 ft., max. 4 ft.
DEPTH: 5 - 35 ft.

CAYMAN

VIPER MORAY
Enchelycore nigricans
FAMILY:
Moray - Muraenidae

SIZE: 1 - 2 ft., max. 2 1/2 ft.
DEPTH: 4 - 100 ft.

ST. LUCIA

CHESTNUT MORAY
Enchelycore carychroa
FAMILY:
Moray - Muraenidae

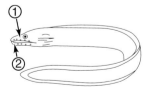

SIZE: 8 - 10 in., max. 13 in.
DEPTH: 4 - 100 ft.

BIMINI

367

DISTINCTIVE FEATURES: 1. Shades of brown covered with small yellow spots (size of spots can vary considerably between individuals and, on rare occasions, are reversed, with yellow undercolor and brown spots, or a net-like pattern).

DESCRIPTION: Tip of tail yellow to gold. Ring of yellow around pupil.

ABUNDANCE & DISTRIBUTION: Common to occasional Caribbean; occasional Bahamas; uncommon Florida; also Bermuda.

HABITAT & BEHAVIOR: Prefer shallow to mid-range coral reefs. Hide during the day in recesses; heads often extend from openings. Forage in open at night. Constantly open and close mouth, an action required for respiration — not a threat.

REACTION TO DIVERS: Appear unconcerned; usually allow close approach before they withdraw into reef.

NOTE: Formerly classified in the genus *Muraena*.

DISTINCTIVE FEATURES: 1. Semicircular black spots, outlined in white, along upper edge of dorsal fin. 2. Numerous pale spots form net-like pattern on body.

DESCRIPTION: Shades of cream to yellow, yellow-brown and brown.

ABUNDANCE & DISTRIBUTION: Occasional both coasts of Florida (may be locally abundant, especially in grass beds); also north to New Jersey and Bermuda. Not reported Bahamas, Caribbean.

HABITAT & BEHAVIOR: Inhabit grass beds to offshore banks, but not coral reefs. Forage in open at night. Constantly open and close mouth, an action required for respiration — not a threat.

REACTION TO DIVERS: Appear unconcerned; usually allow close approach before they withdraw into reef.

NOTE: Also commonly known as "Ocellated Moray."

SIMILAR SPECIES: Blackedge Moray, *G. nigromarginatus*, distinguished by black spots on upper edge of dorsal fin that join to form a black border. Gulf of Mexico.

DISTINCTIVE FEATURES: 1. Pale yellowish to bright yellow chain-like markings.

DESCRIPTION: Heavy body. Dark brown to black, with irregular, often interconnected, bright yellow bars. Yellow eyes.

ABUNDANCE & DISTRIBUTION: Common many eastern Caribbean islands; occasional Bahamas and Florida; rare Cayman and western Caribbean; also Bermuda and south to Brazil.

HABITAT & BEHAVIOR: Prefer shallow, clear-water reefs and rocky shores. Hide during the day in recesses; heads often extend from openings. Forage in open at night; occasionally in tidal zones where they feed on crabs. Constantly open and close mouth, an action required for respiration — not a threat.

REACTION TO DIVERS: Appear unconcerned; usually allow close approach before they withdraw into reef.

GOLDENTAIL MORAY
Gymnothorax miliaris
FAMILY:
Moray - Muraenidae

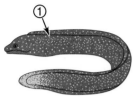

SIZE: 1 - 1 ½ ft., max. 2 ft.
DEPTH: 5 - 50 ft.

CAYMAN

HONEYCOMB MORAY
Gymnothorax saxicola
FAMILY:
Moray - Muraenidae

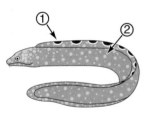

SIZE: 14 - 20 in., max. 2 ft.
DEPTH: 30 - 300 ft.

JACKSONVILLE, FL

CHAIN MORAY
Echidna catenata
FAMILY:
Moray - Muraenidae

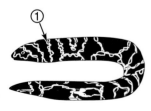

SIZE: 1 - 1 ½ ft.,
max. 2 ½ ft.
DEPTH: 0 - 40 ft.

BIMINI

DISTINCTIVE FEATURES: 1. Interior of mouth bright to pale orange. 2. Dusky spot around gill opening. 3. Large dark spots cover body and fins.

DESCRIPTION: Shades of brown. Dark spots are bold and highly contrasting on young, smaller specimens, but with age and size undercolor darkens, making spots less conspicuous, and becoming barely discernible on old, large individuals. Head enlarges abruptly behind short, "pug" snout; small eye set far forward, near tip of snout; body heavy. Nostrils have tubular extensions.

ABUNDANCE & DISTRIBUTION: Rare eastern Florida and Caribbean coastline of Central America; also north to North Carolina and eastern Africa. Not reported Bahamas or balance of Caribbean.

HABITAT & BEHAVIOR: Inhabit clear-water reefs. Usually hide during the day in recesses with only heads extended from openings. Constantly open and close mouth, an action required for respiration — not a threat.

REACTION TO DIVERS: Appear unconcerned; usually allow close approach before they withdraw into reef.

DISTINCTIVE FEATURES: 1. Numerous wide, dark and pale bands ring body.

DESCRIPTION: Shades of gray to tan or olive, often with bluish overtones; bands may be reddish brown to brown or cream. Head enlarges abruptly behind short snout; small eye set far forward, near tip of snout; loose, flabby or wrinkled skin on head and body; body heavy.

ABUNDANCE & DISTRIBUTION: Occasional Bahamas, eastern Caribbean; rare balance of Caribbean; also Bermuda, eastern Atlantic, and Indian Ocean to western Pacific. Not reported Florida.

HABITAT & BEHAVIOR: Inhabit clear-water reefs. Usually hide during the day in recesses with only heads extended from openings, but occasionally lie in the open on reefs. Forage in open at night. Constantly open and close mouth, an action required for respiration — not a threat. When disturbed or threatened, puff up loose skin on head and forebody to appear larger.

REACTION TO DIVERS: Appear unconcerned; usually allow close approach before they withdraw into reef.

DISTINCTIVE FEATURES: Head and body extend from sand. Live in colonies.

DESCRIPTION: Thin body. Dark brown to gray. Jutting lower jaw.

ABUNDANCE & DISTRIBUTION: Common to occasional South Florida, Bahamas, Caribbean.

HABITAT & BEHAVIOR: Found in colonies on sand near coral reefs. Extend head and upper body from burrow. Continuously move in graceful, wave-like motions to catch plankton.

REACTION TO DIVERS: Extremely shy; withdraw into burrows when approached. Even slow movements fail to help because exhaled bubbles frighten them.

NOTE: Formerly classified in the genus *Nystactichthys*.

STOUT MORAY
Muraena robusta
FAMILY:
Moray - Muraenidae

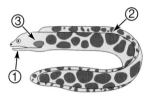

SIZE: 1 ¹/₂ - 4 ft.,
max. 5 ¹/₂ ft.
DEPTH: 50 - 200 ft.

DAYTONA BEACH, FL

BROADBANDED MORAY
Channomuraena vittata
FAMILY:
Moray - Muraenidae

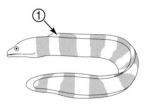

SIZE: 1 ¹/₂ - 4 ft., max. 5 ft.
DEPTH: 15 - 80 ft.

ST. LUCIA

BROWN GARDEN EEL
Heteroconger halis
FAMILY:
Conger - Congridae

SIZE: 8 -15 in., max. 20 in.
DEPTH: 15 - 200 ft.

CAYMAN

DISTINCTIVE FEATURES: 1. Dark border on dorsal, tail and anal fins. 2. Upper and lower jaws of equal length.
DESCRIPTION: Usually bluish gray to gray, occasionally shades of brown.
ABUNDANCE & DISTRIBUTION: Occasional to uncommon Bahamas, Caribbean (primarily near islands); rare Florida; also Bermuda and south to Brazil.
HABITAT & BEHAVIOR: Wide range of habitats from reefs to areas of rocky rubble. Reclusive; hide in deep, dark recesses of reefs during day. Forage in open at night.
REACTION TO DIVERS: Extremely shy; rapidly retreat into recesses when approached.
SIMILAR SPECIES: Conger Eel, *C. oceanicus*, distinguished by upper jaw that is longer than lower. Virginia to northeast Florida and northern Gulf of Mexico.

DISTINCTIVE FEATURES: 1. Small yellow spots on head. 2. Large, diffuse, pale spots on body.
DESCRIPTION: Thin body. Often grayish, but can be olive to purplish brown. Body spots often have pale yellow centers.
ABUNDANCE & DISTRIBUTION: Occasional to uncommon Florida and continental coasts of Caribbean; uncommon to rare Bahamas, Caribbean islands; also Bermuda.
HABITAT & BEHAVIOR: Wide range of habitats, from shallow grass beds to areas of rocky rubble to reefs. Usually hide during day and forage in open at night. Can move about beneath the sand.
REACTION TO DIVERS: Relatively unafraid; allow close approach before disappearing into the sand or a hole.
NOTE: Formerly classified as species *acuminatus*.

DISTINCTIVE FEATURES: 1. Bright yellow-gold spots with diffuse black borders on body and head.
DESCRIPTION: Thin body. Tan, may have yellow to green cast.
ABUNDANCE & DISTRIBUTION: Occasional to uncommon Bahamas, Caribbean islands; uncommon to rare Florida and continental coasts of Caribbean; also Bermuda and south to Brazil.
HABITAT & BEHAVIOR: Usually hide during day in sand or on shallow patch reefs, but occasionally out in open. Generally come out to forage at night. Can move about beneath sand.
REACTION TO DIVERS: Relatively unafraid; allow a close approach before disappearing into sand or a hole.
NOTE: Formerly classified as species *oculatus*.
SIMILAR SPECIES: Blackspotted Snake Eel, *Quassiremus productus*, distinguished by rust-colored spots with black centers.

MANYTOOTH CONGER
Conger triporiceps
FAMILY:
Conger - Congridae

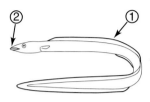

SIZE: 1 - 2 ½ ft.,
max. 3 ½ ft.
DEPTH: 6 - 250 ft.

ST. LUCIA

SHARPTAIL EEL
Myrichthys breviceps
FAMILY:
Snake Eels – Ophichthidae

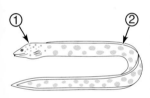

SIZE: 1 - 2 ½ ft.,
max. 3 ½ ft.
DEPTH: 5 - 40 ft.

L. CAYMAN

GOLDSPOTTED EEL
Myrichthys ocellatus
FAMILY:
Snake Eels - Ophichthidae

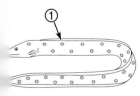

SIZE: 1 - 2 ½ ft.,
max. 3 ½ ft.
DEPTH: 5 - 40 ft.

ST. LUCIA

DISTINCTIVE FEATURES: 1. Broad, dark bar across top of head may extend down onto cheeks. (Similar Spotted Spoon-nose, *Echiophis intertinctus*, [next] lacks this band.) **2. Dark spots on head and body.**

DESCRIPTION: Vary from white to gray, cream or tan; often have yellowish cast. Thin body.

ABUNDANCE & DISTRIBUTION: Uncommon to rare Florida, Bahamas, Caribbean; also Bermuda and south to Brazil.

HABITAT & BEHAVIOR: Inhabit sand flats or areas of mixed sand, gravel and coral rubble; often extend only their heads. Most common in shallow water. May forage out in open at night. Can move about beneath the sand.

REACTION TO DIVERS: Relatively unafraid; allow close approach before disappearing into their burrows or sand.

Spotted Spoon-nose Eel

Head detail: note pointed canine teeth along jaw edge and single protruding tooth from roof of mouth.

BARBADOS

DISTINCTIVE FEATURES: 1. Short, pointed, V-shaped snout. 2. Numerous large, irregular spots on back. 3. Small spots on head.

DESCRIPTION: Cream to pale yellowish. Two to four large, pointed canine teeth near front on each side of jaw and one or two long, pointed teeth on roof of mouth [above left].

ABUNDANCE & DISTRIBUTION: Rare Florida, Bahamas, Caribbean; also north to North Carolina, Gulf of Mexico and south to Brazil.

HABITAT & BEHAVIOR: Usually hide during day in sand that is often adjacent to shallow patch reefs, but occasionally out in open. Generally come out to forage at night. Can move about beneath sand.

REACTION TO DIVERS: Relatively unafraid; allow close approach before retreating into sand. May bite if molested.

SPOTTED SNAKE EEL
Ophichthus ophis
FAMILY:
Snake Eels - Ophichthidae

SIZE: 1 - 2 ½ ft., max. 4 ft.
DEPTH: 3 - 35 ft.

BARBADOS

Spotted Snake Eel
Head detail:
note broad, dark bar.

BARBADOS

SPOTTED SPOON-NOSE EEL
Echiophis intertinctus
FAMILY:
Snake Eels - Ophichthidae

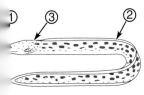

SIZE: 2 - 3 ft., max. 3 ½ ft.
DEPTH: 3 - 75 ft.

BARBADOS

375

Sharks & Rays
Carpet Shark–Hammerhead–Pointed-Nose Shark–Ray

This ID Group consists of fish whose skeletons are composed of cartilage rather than bone, and therefore called cartilaginous fishes. All have small, hard scales that give them a rough, sandpapery feel. Sharks and rays are classified into numerous families which are often difficult to distinguish and remember. Consequently, they will be discussed more by general appearance than by family.

FAMILY: Carpet Shark — Rhincodontidae
2 Species Included

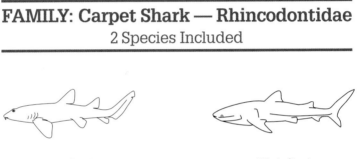

Nurse Shark   Whale Shark

Carpet sharks, which include Nurse and Whale Sharks, are distinguished by small eyes set behind the mouth's termination; dorsal fins well back on the body with the first dorsal fin starting beyond the halfway point of head and body; a large and extended upper tail lobe and small to indistinct lower lobe. Whale sharks are the largest fish in the world.

FAMILY: Pointed-Nose Shark — Requiem & Mackerel
12 Species Included

Pointed-Nose Shark (typical shape)

Sharks with more-or-less pointed noses are represented by at least eight families within our area. Generally, they are rarely observed by divers and, when sighted, are extremely difficult to distinguish. Important clues for underwater identification are the general shape of the snout, placement of the dorsal fin in relation to the pectoral fin, and the shape and size of fins. On a few sharks (Tiger, Blacktip and Whitetip), markings are distinctive, while in others (Lemon and Mako), color is important.

FAMILY: Hammerhead Shark — Sphyrnidae
4 Species Included

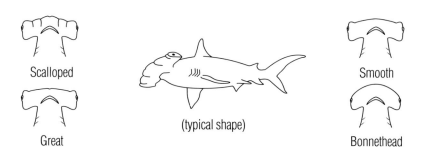

Scalloped

Great

(typical shape)

Smooth

Bonnethead

Hammerheads are a distinctive family of sharks because of the dramatic shape of their heads. The head is flattened and extended to either side, with the eyes set on the outer edges. Species can be determined by observing the shape of the head's leading edge.

ORDER: Ray — Rajiformes
11 Species Included

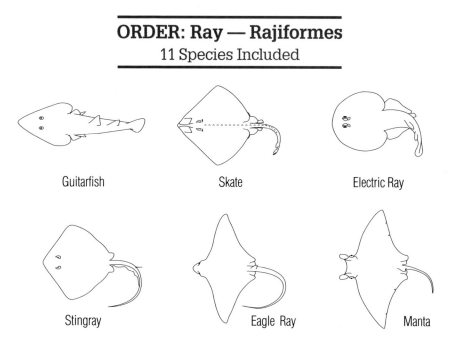

Guitarfish

Skate

Electric Ray

Stingray

Eagle Ray

Manta

Rays are represented by seven families within our area. Their greatly enlarged pectoral fins, which give them a disc-like shape, are used for swimming much like birds use their wings for flight.

Members of five families are bottom-dwellers. These include the sawfishes, guitarfishes, electric rays, skates and stingrays. All have mouths on their undersides. Electric rays are distinguished by their circular shape and thick, short tails. As the common family name implies, these fish have the ability to discharge an electrical shock. Skates and stingrays generally have more pointed snouts and "wing-tips." Stingrays have sharp spines in their elongated tails, while skates do not.

There are two families of "flying" rays — Eagle Rays and Mantas. Most of their time spent swimming. Keys to identification are body shape and back markings.

DISTINCTIVE FEATURES: 1. Bold pattern of large, white spots cover body.

DESCRIPTION: Gray to gray-brown, fading to white underside; thin whitish lines join spots on back. Three ridges run along sides from head to base of tail; first dorsal fin more than halfway back on body. World's largest fish.

ABUNDANCE & DISTRIBUTION: Rare Florida, Bahamas, Caribbean; also circumtropical.

HABITAT & BEHAVIOR: Considered open-water oceanic. Occasionally cruise along walls and steep slopes. Feed on plankton, baitfish, tuna, squid and pelagic crustaceans that are sieved from the water.

REACTION TO DIVERS: Ignore divers. Do not overtly react to being ridden; however, apparently are irritated. Usually dive and disappear shortly after such activities, but often remain in area, making numerous passes if unmolested.

DISTINCTIVE FEATURES: 1. Two barbels on upper lip. 2. Two dorsal fins, of nearly equal size, are set far back. 3. Small mouth.

DESCRIPTION: Vary from gray to yellow-brown. Tail fin has no distinct lower lobe.

ABUNDANCE & DISTRIBUTION: Occasional Florida, Bahamas, Caribbean; also north to Rhode Island, Bermuda, Gulf of Mexico, south to Brazil and eastern Atlantic.

HABITAT & BEHAVIOR: In all habitats, from shallow water to outer reefs. Often lie on sand, under ledges and overhangs.

REACTION TO DIVERS: Usually lie motionless unless molested. May bite if provoked.

DISTINCTIVE FEATURES: Back commonly yellowish brown, but can be brown or gray. **1. Second dorsal fin nearly equal in size to first. 2. Short, blunt, rounded snout.**

DESCRIPTION: Underside pale. Upper lobe of tail much larger than lower.

ABUNDANCE & DISTRIBUTION: Occasional Florida and continental waters to northern South America; uncommon to rare Bahamas, Caribbean islands; also north to North Carolina, south to Brazil and eastern Atlantic.

HABITAT & BEHAVIOR: Cruise inshore waters; may rest on bottom. Often school in Florida during winter.

REACTION TO DIVERS: Appear unafraid; often swim away, but may make close pass. Can often be closely approached when resting on bottom. Considered dangerous; can be aggressive especially in the vicinity of spearfishing activities.

WHALE SHARK
Rhincodon typus
FAMILY:
Carpet Shark –
Rhincodontidae

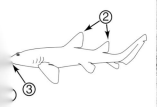

SIZE: 20 - 45 ft., max. 55 ft.
DEPTH: 0 - 100 ft.

CURACAO

NURSE SHARK
Ginglymostoma cirratum
FAMILY:
Carpet Shark –
Rhincodontidae

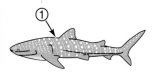

SIZE: 5 - 9 ft., max. 14 ft.
DEPTH: 12 - 100 ft.

BELIZE

LEMON SHARK
Negaprion brevirostris
FAMILY:
Requiem Shark –
Carcharhinidae

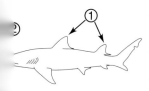

SIZE: 5 - 8 ft., max. 11 ft.
DEPTH: 3 - 100 ft.

BIMINI

Requiem Shark

DISTINCTIVE FEATURES: 1. Dark bars and blotches on body.

DESCRIPTION: Bluish to brownish gray with pale underside. Short, broad snout; upper lobe of tail long.

ABUNDANCE & DISTRIBUTION: Uncommon Florida, Bahamas, Caribbean; also north to Massachusetts, Bermuda, Gulf of Mexico, south to Uruguay; circumtropical.

HABITAT & BEHAVIOR: Cruise all waters; usually solitary. Voracious predator.

REACTION TO DIVERS: Appear unafraid, but usually shy and swim away; occasionally make close pass. Considered quite dangerous; can be aggressive, especially in the vicinity of spearfishing activities.

DISTINCTIVE FEATURES: 1. Long, flattened snout. 2. Second dorsal fin begins above middle of anal fin. 3. Adults usually have a few scattered pale spots on back.

DESCRIPTION: Olive-gray to brown with pale underside. Often have a few scattered pale spots. Dorsal and tail fins may be edged in black.

ABUNDANCE & DISTRIBUTION: Uncommon Florida, Bahamas, Caribbean; also north to North Carolina, Gulf of Mexico and south to Uruguay.

HABITAT & BEHAVIOR: Inhabit shallow coastal waters, including bays and estuaries.

REACTION TO DIVERS: Wary; generally move away upon approach, but may make a close pass Not considered especially dangerous.

SIMILAR SPECIES: Some ichthyologists believe there are two or three species of Sharpnose Shark instead of one. Since all have an identical external appearance (the differences are based on vertebral counts) they are considered as one in this text.

DISTINCTIVE FEATURES: Heavy body; no markings on fins. **1. Short snout. 2. Small eyes. Dorsal fin begins above mid-pectoral fin.**

DESCRIPTION: Gray to brown with pale underside. Upper lobe of tail much larger than lower. Fin not marked.

ABUNDANCE & DISTRIBUTION: Occasional Florida and continental waters to northern Sout America; rare Bahamas, Caribbean Islands; also north to New York and south to Braz circumtropical.

HABITAT & BEHAVIOR: Cruise inshore waters and reefs, occasionally in small groups.

REACTION TO DIVERS: Wary; generally move away when approached, but may make close pa Considered dangerous, especially in the vicinity of spearfishing activities.

TIGER SHARK
Galeocerdo cuvier

FAMILY:
Requiem Shark –
Carcharhinidae

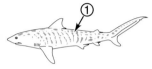

SIZE: 7 - 12 ft., max. 24 ft.
DEPTH: 10 - 200 ft.

WEST PALM BEACH, FL

ATLANTIC SHARPNOSE SHARK
Rhizoprionodon terraenovae

FAMILY:
Requiem Shark –
Carcharhinidae

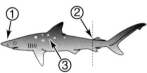

SIZE: 2 - 3 ft., max. 3½ ft.
DEPTH: 3 - 40 ft.

BIMINI

BULL SHARK
Carcharhinus leucas

FAMILY:
Requiem Shark –
Carcharhinidae

SIZE: 6 - 9 ft., max. 12 ft.
DEPTH: 10 - 200 ft.

BIMINI

DISTINCTIVE FEATURES: 1. Inside tips of pectoral fins and tips of ventral fins, anal fins and lower lobe of tail are dusky. (Similar Blacktip Shark, *C. limbatus*, [next] distinguished by pale to white anal fin; similar Spinner Shark, *C. brevipinna*, distinguished by solid black tips on fins, not dusky.) **2. First dorsal fin relatively small and starts behind pectoral fin. 3. Gill slits relatively small and start above plane of pectoral fin.**

DESCRIPTION: Silvery-gray with white underside. Heavy body.

ABUNDANCE & DISTRIBUTION: Occasional Bahamas, Caribbean; uncommon Florida; also northeast Gulf of Mexico and south to Brazil.

HABITAT & BEHAVIOR: Cruise reefs and shallows. Most common shark on coral reefs. Often have a dark leach attached to dorsal fin (note photograph).

REACTION TO DIVERS: Wary; generally keep their distance, but may make close pass. Considered dangerous, especially in the vicinity of spearfishing activities.

SIMILAR SPECIES: Dusky Shark, *C. obscurus*, distinguished by relatively slender body and larger gill openings.

DISTINCTIVE FEATURES: 1. Anal fin pale to white. 2. Black tips and edging on pectoral, ventral and dorsal fins and lower lobe of tail fade to diffuse inner edge. 3. Silver white streak on flank.

DESCRIPTION: Black tips and edging fade with age and may be indistinct, especially on first dorsal. Bluish silver-gray on back fading to white underside.

ABUNDANCE & DISTRIBUTION: Uncommon Florida, Bahamas, Caribbean; also north to New York and south to Brazil; circumtropical.

HABITAT & BEHAVIOR: Cruise reefs and shallows, occasionally in lagoons.

REACTION TO DIVERS: Wary; generally keep their distance, but may make close pass. Considered dangerous, especially in the vicinity of spearfishing activities.

SIMILAR SPECIES: Spinner Shark, *C. brevipinna*, distinguished by solid black tips (as if dipped in ink) on second dorsal, pectoral and anal fins and lower lobe of tail. (Remaining fins are occasionally also black tipped.) A circumtropical coastal shark, but not common in shallow water.

DISTINCTIVE FEATURES: 1. Ridge on back between first and second dorsal fins. 2. Dorsal fin is rounded, relatively small and starts behind pectoral. 3. Second dorsal fin has long trailing edge. 4. Older adults have long pectoral fins.

DESCRIPTION: Silvery-gray with white underside; dusky edge often on pectoral, second dorsal, anal and upper tail fins. Relatively slender. Skin smooth to the touch.

ABUNDANCE & DISTRIBUTION: Uncommon Florida, Bahamas, Caribbean; also north to North Carolina; eastern Atlantic.

HABITAT & BEHAVIOR: Generally an open-water shark, rarely inshore.

REACTION TO DIVERS: Wary; generally move away upon approach, but may make close pass. Considered dangerous, especially in the vicinity of spearfishing activities.

REEF SHARK
Carcharhinus perezi
FAMILY:
Requiem Shark –
Carcharhinidae

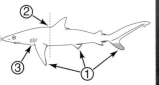

SIZE: 5 - 8 ft., max. 10 ft.
DEPTH: 0 - 150 ft.

NASSAU

BLACKTIP SHARK
Carcharhinus limbatus
FAMILY:
Requiem Shark –
Carcharhinidae

SIZE: 5 - 6 ½ ft.,
max. 8 ½ ft.
DEPTH: 0 - 150 ft.

WALKER'S CAY, BAHAMAS

SILKY SHARK
Carcharhinus falciformis
FAMILY:
Requiem Shark –
Carcharhinidae

SIZE: 5 - 7 ft., max. 10 ft.
DEPTH: 0 - 150 ft.

NASSAU

383

Requiem Shark–Mackerel Shark

DISTINCTIVE FEATURES: No markings on fins. **1. Ridge on back between first and second dorsal fins. 2. Dorsal fin pointed, large and tall (about twice the length of the snout), and starts over mid-pectoral fin. 3. Relatively short snout (shorter than width of mouth).**

DESCRIPTION: Bluish gray to brownish gray, brown or bronze with pale to white underside. Relatively heavy body.

ABUNDANCE & DISTRIBUTION: Common northeastern and Gulf Coast of Florida (summers); uncommon balance of Florida; rare Bahamas, Caribbean; also north to New England and Gulf of Mexico.

HABITAT & BEHAVIOR: Inhabit shallow coastal waters and estuaries during summer; young are generally in shallow water while large adults are more common at depths of 60 to 180 feet. During winter, move offshore to depths over 300 feet.

REACTION TO DIVERS: Wary; generally move away upon approach, but may make close pass. Considered dangerous, especially in the vicinity of spearfishing activities.

DISTINCTIVE FEATURES: 1. Large rounded foredorsal fin with large white tip. 2. Long pectoral fins, usually with white tips.

DESCRIPTION: Medium brown to gray brown upper body, yellowish white underside. Rounded snout.

ABUNDANCE & DISTRIBUTION: Uncommon Florida, Bahamas, Caribbean; also north to New York, Gulf of Mexico and south to Uruguay; circumtropical and temperate.

HABITAT & BEHAVIOR: Pelagic; not over reefs. Occasionally pass near oceanic islets and rocks. Voracious predator that often feeds on tuna.

REACTION TO DIVERS: Appear unafraid; often make close passes, circle and may bump. Considered dangerous, but usually do not attack unless chum or fish blood is in water.

DISTINCTIVE FEATURES: Distinctly bluish with white underside. **1. Slender, conical snout. 2. Large dorsal fin begins above and just behind pectoral fin. 3. Lobes of tail nearly equal in size.**

DESCRIPTION: Front teeth slender and curved back.

ABUNDANCE & DISTRIBUTION: Rare Florida, Bahamas, Caribbean; circumtropical.

HABITAT & BEHAVIOR: Cruise oceanic waters; rarely venture over reefs. Occasionally pass near oceanic islets and rocks.

REACTION TO DIVERS: Appear unafraid; often make close passes, circle and may bump. Considered quite dangerous, but usually do not attack unless chum or fish blood is in water.

SANDBAR SHARK
Carcharhinus plumbeus
FAMILY:
Requiem Shark –
Carcharhinidae

SIZE: 5 - 7 ft., max. 8 ft.
DEPTH: 20 - 800 ft.

SARASOTA, FL

OCEANIC WHITETIP SHARK
Carcharhinus longimanus
FAMILY:
Requiem Shark –
Carcharhinidae

SIZE: 7 - 10 ft., max. 12 ft.
DEPTH: 0 - 200 ft.

NASSAU

SHORTFIN MAKO
Isurus oxyrinchus
FAMILY:
Mackerel Shark –
Lamnidae

SIZE: 5 - 9 ft., max. 12 1/2 ft.
DEPTH: 0 - 200 ft.

SWAN IS.

DISTINCTIVE FEATURES: 1. Front edge of "hammer" slightly rounded and scalloped. 2. Inside tip of pectoral fin dark. 3. Rear edge of ventral fin straight.

DESCRIPTION: Gray with pale underside.

ABUNDANCE & DISTRIBUTION: Uncommon Florida, Bahamas, Caribbean; also north to New Jersey, Bermuda, Gulf of Mexico, and south to Brazil; circumtropical.

HABITAT & BEHAVIOR: Considered oceanic, though occasionally cruise reefs, walls and shallows.

REACTION TO DIVERS: Wary; generally move away when approached, but occasionally make a close pass. Considered dangerous, especially in the vicinity of spearfishing activities.

SIMILAR SPECIES: Great Hammerhead, S. mokarran, distinguished by a relatively flat front edge of "hammer"; inside tip of pectoral fin not dark; rear edge of ventral fin curved. Smooth Hammerhead, S. zygaena, distinguished by a slightly rounded front edge of "hammer" that is smooth and not scalloped. Inhabit shallow coastal waters of Florida in winter only.

DISTINCTIVE FEATURES: 1. Smooth, "spade-shaped" head.

DESCRIPTION: Gray with pale underside.

ABUNDANCE & DISTRIBUTION: Occasional Florida and continental waters to northern South America, western Bahamas and Cuba; also north to North Carolina and south to Argentina. Not reported Caribbean islands.

HABITAT & BEHAVIOR: Inhabit shallow bays, sounds and estuaries, where they feed primarily on crabs.

REACTION TO DIVERS: Wary; usually move away. Not considered a threat to divers.

DISTINCTIVE FEATURES: 1. Head and pectoral fins form a triangular ray-like forebody. 2. Thick, tapered, shark-like rear body.

DESCRIPTION: Vary from gray to brown, with many pale spots. Have rectangular area on each side of pointed snout. (Clearnose Skate, Raja eglanteria, [next] has similar appearing snout, but is easily distinguished by overall body shape.)

ABUNDANCE & DISTRIBUTION: Uncommon Florida and Yucatan; also north to North Carolina and Gulf of Mexico. Not reported Bahamas, Caribbean.

HABITAT & BEHAVIOR: Inhabit shallow inshore areas of sand, sea grass and mud, and occasionally near shallow patch reefs. Often lie half buried, in mud or sand. Feed on small mollusks and crustaceans.

REACTION TO DIVERS: Appear unconcerned; lie still on bottom unless molested.

SIMILAR SPECIES: Southern Guitarfish, R. percellens, is virtually indistinguishable, but inhabits Caribbean waters instead; rare.

SCALLOPED HAMMERHEAD
Sphyrna lewini

FAMILY:
Hammerhead Shark –
Sphyrnidae

SIZE: 5 - 9 ft., max. 14 ft.
DEPTH: 20 - 160 ft.

CAYMAN

BONNETHEAD
Sphyrna tiburo

FAMILY:
Hammerhead Shark –
Sphyrnidae

SIZE: 3 - 4 ft., max. 5 ft.
DEPTH: 3 - 40 ft.

FLORIDA BAY

ATLANTIC GUITARFISH
Rhinobatos lentiginosus

FAMILY:
Guitarfish – Rhinobatidae

SIZE: 1 - 2 ft., max. 2 1/2 ft.
DEPTH: 0 - 45 ft.

WEST PALM BEACH, FL

387

Skate–Electric Ray

DISTINCTIVE FEATURES: 1. Clear rectangular area on each side of pointed snout. (Atlantic Guitarfish, *Rhinobatos lentiginosus*, [previous] have similar appearing snout, but are easily distinguished by overall body shape.) **2. Single row of spines down back and tail. 3. Row of spines down each side of tail.**

DESCRIPTION: "Wing" tips pointed, with leading edges straight or slightly concave. Shades of brown with darker brown patterns of spots, streaks and blotches.

ABUNDANCE & DISTRIBUTION: Common Florida Gulf Coast; occasional Florida northeastern coast; uncommon Florida southeastern coast; also north to Massachusetts. Not reported Bahamas, Caribbean.

HABITAT & BEHAVIOR: Prefer water temperatures between 50-70 degrees and seasonally move inshore or offshore to stay within that range. Inhabit flat areas of sand and gravel. Often lie half buried in bottom material.

REACTION TO DIVERS: Appear unconcerned; lie still on bottom unless molested.

SIMILAR SPECIES: Roundel Skate, *R. texana*, distinguished by a blue spot on each "wing" with a black inner ring and yellow outer ring. Shallow bays to 300 feet, both Florida coasts and Gulf of Mexico.

DISTINCTIVE FEATURES: Tan with light brown blotches. **1. Front of broad, circular forebody is squared. 2. First dorsal fin is tall, pointed and much larger than second.**

DESCRIPTION: Front edge of disc is scalloped.

ABUNDANCE & DISTRIBUTION: Rare northeastern Caribbean. Not reported balance of Caribbean, Florida or Bahamas.

HABITAT & BEHAVIOR: Inhabit shallow reefs. Can shock if molested.

REACTION TO DIVERS: Not aggressive; remain motionless unless disturbed. If touched, can deliver electric shock!

NOTE: Virtually nothing is known about this species. The only known specimen [pictured] was photographed by Captain Wayne Hasson in Grand Cayman. The author is very interested in information about additional sightings.

SIMILAR SPECIES: Atlantic Torpedo, *Torpedo nobiliana*, is uniformly dark olive to brown or black, occasionally with black blotches and small white spots. Nova Scotia to Florida Keys.

DISTINCTIVE FEATURES: 1. Nearly circular forebody. 2. Relatively short tail with thick base; appears as a tall, thin pyramid when viewed from above. 3. Two dorsal fins on tail.

DESCRIPTION: Shades of gray to brown. Color may be uniform or with dark blotches and circles outlined with small black spots.

ABUNDANCE & DISTRIBUTION: Common southeastern and southern Caribbean; uncommon Florida; rare to absent Bahamas and balance of Caribbean; also north to North Carolina and south to Argentina.

HABITAT & BEHAVIOR: Inhabit sand bottoms, areas of gravel/rubble, and sea grass beds; often in lagoons and bays.

REACTION TO DIVERS: Appear unconcerned; do not move unless molested. If touched, can deliver mild (14- to 37-volt) electric shock.

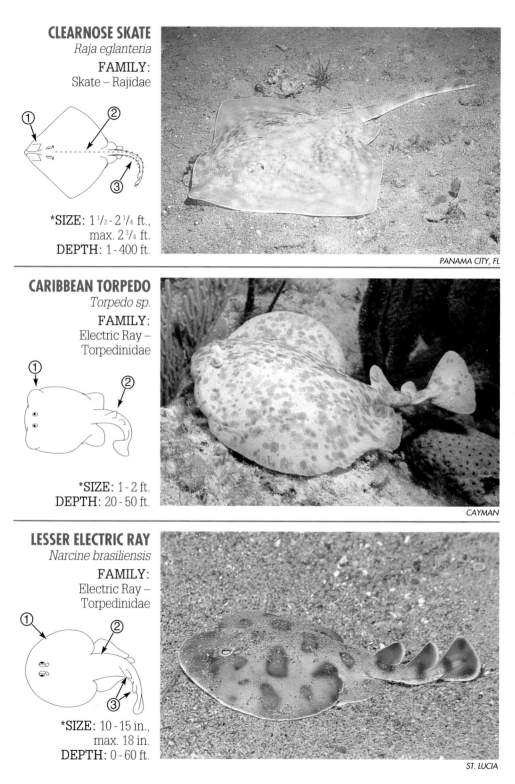

CLEARNOSE SKATE
Raja eglanteria
FAMILY:
Skate – Rajidae

*SIZE: 1 1/2 - 2 1/4 ft.,
max. 2 3/4 ft.
DEPTH: 1 - 400 ft.

PANAMA CITY, FL

CARIBBEAN TORPEDO
Torpedo sp.
FAMILY:
Electric Ray –
Torpedinidae

*SIZE: 1 - 2 ft.
DEPTH: 20 - 50 ft.

CAYMAN

LESSER ELECTRIC RAY
Narcine brasiliensis
FAMILY:
Electric Ray –
Torpedinidae

*SIZE: 10 - 15 in.,
max. 18 in.
DEPTH: 0 - 60 ft.

ST. LUCIA

Stingray

DISTINCTIVE FEATURES: 1. Snout and tips of "wings" pointed.

DESCRIPTION: Vary from brown to gray and black; underside white. Whip-like tail, with one or two venomous spines at base. *Size refers to diameter of disk, excluding tail.

ABUNDANCE & DISTRIBUTION: Common Caribbean; occasional Bahamas and Florida; also north to New Jersey, Bermuda, Gulf of Mexico and south to Brazil.

HABITAT & BEHAVIOR: Inhabit sandy areas. Lie on bottom, often covered with sand.

REACTION TO DIVERS: Appear unconcerned; lie motionless unless closely approached or molested.

SIMILAR SPECIES: Caribbean Stingray, *Himantura schmardae*, distinguished by circular-shaped disk. Caribbean only, primarily southern.

DISTINCTIVE FEATURES: 1. Irregular row of spines and bumps down midback and onto tail. 2. Numerous rows of spines on tail. 3. Snout and tips of "wings" pointed.

DESCRIPTION: Vary from brown to gray and black; underside white. Whip-like tail, with one or two venomous spines at base. *Size refers to diameter of disk, excluding tail.

ABUNDANCE & DISTRIBUTION: Occasional Central and North Florida; rare South Florida; also north to New England. Absent balance of Florida, Bahamas, Caribbean.

HABITAT & BEHAVIOR: Inhabit sandy areas. Lie on bottom, often covered with sand.

REACTION TO DIVERS: Appear unconcerned; lie motionless unless closely approached or molested.

DISTINCTIVE FEATURES: 1. Numerous spots. 2. Snout and tips of "wings" rounded.

DESCRIPTION: Yellowish brown with numerous pale and dark spots and blotches; can change color and pale or darken dramatically. Stout tail with venomous spine near end. *Size refers to diameter of disk, excluding tail.

ABUNDANCE & DISTRIBUTION: Common Florida; occasional Bahamas, Caribbean; also north to North Carolina and Gulf of Mexico.

HABITAT & BEHAVIOR: Inhabit sandy areas, especially around reefs. Lie on bottom, often covered with sand.

REACTION TO DIVERS: Appear unconcerned; lie motionless unless closely approached or molested.

SOUTHERN STINGRAY
Dasyatis americana
FAMILY:
Stingray – Dasyatidae

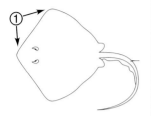

*SIZE: 3-4 ft., max. 5 1/2 ft.
DEPTH: 1-80 ft.

CAYMAN

ROUGHTAIL STINGRAY
Dasyatis centroura
FAMILY:
Stingray – Dasyatidae

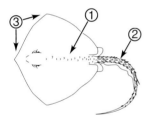

*SIZE: 4-6 ft., max. 7 ft.
DEPTH: 1-80 ft.

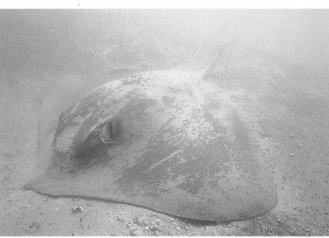

FT. PIERCE, FL

YELLOW STINGRAY
Urolophus jamaicensis
FAMILY:
Round Stingray –
Urolophidae

*SIZE: 8-12 in.,
max. 15 in.
DEPTH: 1-80 ft.

MIAMI, FL

391

DISTINCTIVE FEATURES: "Wings" extend much further from body than their width. **1. Short, relatively thin tail without spine.**

DESCRIPTION: Shades of brown to gray, often with purplish overtones, pale underside. Covered with numerous dark or pale spots and markings.

ABUNDANCE & DISTRIBUTION: Occasional central and northeast coast Florida; rare South Florida, Caribbean; also north to New England and south to Brazil. Not reported Bahamas.

HABITAT & BEHAVIOR: Inhabit sandy areas, especially bays and inlets. Lie on bottom, often covered with sand.

REACTION TO DIVERS: Appear unconcerned; lie motionless unless closely approached or molested.

SIMILAR SPECIES: Spiny Butterfly Ray, *G. altavela*, distinguished by spine at base of tail. Rare.

DISTINCTIVE FEATURES: 1. Numerous white spots and circular markings over dark back.

DESCRIPTION: White underside. Pronounced head with flattened, tapered snout. Long, thin tail with one to five venomous spines at base. *Size refers to measurement from wing-tip to wing-tip.

ABUNDANCE & DISTRIBUTION: Common to occasional Florida, Bahamas, Caribbean; also north to Virginia, Bermuda, Gulf of Mexico, south to Brazil; circumtropical.

HABITAT & BEHAVIOR: Cruise walls and sandy areas. Occasionally pair and, on rare occasion, school. Stop to dig in sand for mollusks, upon which they feed.

REACTION TO DIVERS: Wary; veer away upon sighting divers.

DISTINCTIVE FEATURES: 1. Large mouth on leading edge of head.

DESCRIPTION: Dark back, often with whitish patches on shoulder and, occasionally, other areas. White underside, often with grayish areas and blotches. *Size refers to measurement from wing-tip to wing-tip.

ABUNDANCE & DISTRIBUTION: Uncommon Florida, Bahamas, Caribbean; also north to Massachusetts, Bermuda, Gulf of Mexico and south to Brazil.

HABITAT & BEHAVIOR: Considered oceanic. Cruise near surface, filtering plankton from water. Occasionally they pass along walls and over reefs.

REACTION TO DIVERS: Tend to ignore divers and may remain in area unless rapidly approached, which may cause them to move away.

SIMILAR SPECIES: Devil Ray, *Mobula hypostoma*, distinguished by location of mouth below leading edge of head, and by unmarked, dark back. Do not exceed four feet in width. Cruise open water, often in large schools. Primarily Caribbean.

SMOOTH BUTTERFLY RAY
Gymnura micrura

FAMILY:
Stingray – Dasyatidae

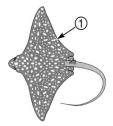

*SIZE: 1 ½ - 3 ft., max. 4 ft.
DEPTH: 1 - 60 ft.

FT. PIERCE, FL

SPOTTED EAGLE RAY
Aetobatus narinari

FAMILY:
Eagle Ray – Myliobatidae

*SIZE: 4 - 6 ½ ft., max. 8 ft.
DEPTH: 6 - 80 ft.

CAYMAN

MANTA
Manta birostris

FAMILY:
Manta – Mobulidae

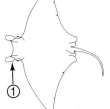

*SIZE: 6 - 14 ft., max. 22 ft.
DEPTH: 0 - 40 ft.

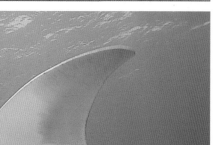

CAYMAN

Marine Reptiles and Mammals

Several species of marine reptiles and mammals inhabit the waters of Florida, the Bahamas and Caribbean. Sea turtles are marine reptiles that only come ashore to lay eggs. All species of turtles are endangered because of overharvesting of both adults and their eggs, and the loss of nesting habitats. Three species, Loggerheads, Hawksbills and Green turtles, are encountered on occasion by divers. Two additional species, the Leatherback and the Atlantic Ridley, are rarely sighted.

The most accurate clues for turtle identification are the patterns on the tops of shells which are formed by three sets of plates: a. **central plates** - large plates running down the center of the shell; b. **costal plates** - a single row paralleling each side of the central plates; c. **bordering plates** - small plates on the shell's edge. The front center bordering plate is known as the **nuchal**.

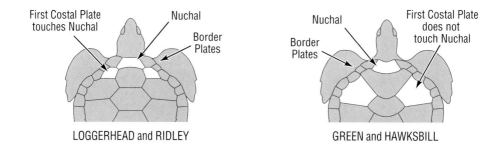

LOGGERHEAD and RIDLEY · GREEN and HAWKSBILL

WEST PALM BEACH, FL

Loggerheads, *Caretta caretta*, are relatively common along both Florida coastlines in the late fall, winter and early spring when they inhabit the region to mate, and lay their eggs. They are often sighted sleeping on the reef. Identification can usually be made by noting their large bulbous heads, and massive, somewhat humped, reddish brown shells. Identification can be confirmed by observing the five or more costal plates; the first touching the nuchal. Atlantic Ridleys have a similar shell pattern, but can be distinguished by their nearly circular olive-green to gray shell and smaller size.

Atlantic Ridleys, *Lepidochelys kempii*, are most common in the Gulf of Mexico. They are the only sea turtles to have nearly circular shells. This, coupled with their small size (rarely much larger than two feet in diameter and weighing between 80 and 100 pounds) and the olive-green to gray back and yellow undershell, can usually confirm identification. The first of their five costal plates touches the nuchal.

Two pairs of plates between eyes.

HAWKSBILL

One pair of plates between eyes.

GREEN

Hawksbills, *Eretmochelys imbriocota*, are most common in the Caribbean and are occasionally encountered by divers on reefs. They can usually be distinguished by their beautiful brown shells with yellow-brown, fan-like markings and overlapping shell plates. (This is the only species with overlapping plates.) Because Greens and Loggerheads can appear quite similar, these distinctions alone are not always reliable. Additional clues include an overhanging upper beak

resembling a "hawk's bill," and rear border plates that usually have a serrated edge. Four costal plates, the first of which does not touch the nuchal, further distinguish them from Loggerheads. They also have two pairs of plates between the eyes. This distinguishes them from similar appearing Greens which have only a single pair of plates between the eyes. Hawksbills are medium sized, usually two and a half to three feet in length, and weigh between 95 and 165 pounds.

Green Turtles, *Chelonia mydas*, were once abundant in the Caribbean, but today, because of overharvesting, their numbers have greatly declined. Their common name does not come from their shell color, but, instead, from the color of their fatty tissue. They have brown to dark brown shells with occasional shades of olive that are generally unmarked, but on occasion, have a mottled

or wave-like pattern similar in appearance to both the Hawksbill and Loggerhead. Shell plates lie side by side (not over-lapping). They have only two plates between the eyes, where Hawksbills have two pairs . The first of their four costal plates does not touch the nuchal, which helps to distinguish them from Loggerheads and Ridleys. Like Loggerheads, Greens

can be quite large, usually between three and four feet in length and weighing between 250 and 450 pounds. The largest Green recorded weighed a whopping 650 pounds!

Leatherbacks, *Dermochelys coriacea*, the largest of all living turtles, are easily distinguished by their lack of shell plates. Instead, their back is covered with a tough, leather-like, slate-black to bluish black skin. Seven prominent ridges run down the back. This generally pelagic species,that feeds on jellyfish, is rarely encountered by divers. They are usually between four and five and a half feet in length and weigh between 650 and 1200 pounds.

Aquatic mammals, called cetaceans, include whales and dolphins. About 12 species of whales and 12 species of dolphins inhabit Florida, Caribbean and Bahamian waters. Because whales prefer deep waters well offshore, they are seldom sighted by divers. Encounters with Humpbacks may occur on special expeditions designed for that purpose. Two dolphin species, the Bottlenosed and the Atlantic Spotted, are occasionally observed by divers.

GRAND BAHAMA

Atlantic Spotted Dolphins, *Stenella plagiodon*, are pelagic, but occasionally venture into shallow water near shore. They appear to be quite curious about humans and have been known to cavort with snorkelers for hours. Atlantic Spotted Dolphins can be distinguished by a dark gray color on the back that shades to white on the belly. White spots on the back change to black on the belly. They have a prominent, medium length beak, and a distinct groove running between the snout and forehead.

Bottlenosed Dolphins, *Tursiops truncatus*, are the most familiar dolphin species. They are famed for their habit of jumping and cavorting in the bow wakes of boats and ships. They can be

distinguished by a lack of markings, dark gray back that gradually shades to white on the belly, and a short but prominent beak. If a boat stops when followed by a pod of Bottlenosed Dolphins, the playful mammals may remain nearby while snorkelers enter the water, but they seldom interact when scuba is used. On rare occasions, they swim near reefs.

BELIZE

396

SCIENTIFIC NAME INDEX

COMMON NAME INDEX

Ja

ADDITIONAL REFERENCES

A Field Guide to Atlantic Coast Fishes of North America,
C. Richard Robbins and G. Carleton Ray, The Peterson Field Guide Series,
Houghton Mifflin Company, Boston.

An Illustrated Field Guide to the Fishes of Gray's Reef
National Marine Sanctuary,
Matthew R. Gilliagan, U. S. Department of Commerce, N.O.A.A., NOS MEMD 25.

Caribbean Reef Fishes,
John E. Randall, T. F. H. Publications.

Dr. Bob Shipp's Guide to Fishes in the Gulf of Mexico,
KME Seabrooks, Mobile.

Fishes of the Bahamas and Adjacent Tropical Waters,
Second Edition, James E. Bohlke and Charles C. G. Chaplin,
University of Texas Press, Austin.

Fishes of the Gulf Of Mexico – Texas, Louisiana, and Adjacent Waters,
H. Dickson Hoese and Richard H. Moore, Texas A&M University Press,
College Station.

Handguide to the Coral Reef Fishes of the Caribbean,
F. Joseph Stokes, Lippincott & Crowell, Publishers.

Reef Fish,
Ronald E. Thresher, The Palmetto Publishing Company, St. Petersburg.

The Sharks of North American Waters,
Jose I. Castro, Texas A&M University Press, College Station.

PERSONAL RECORD OF FISH SIGHTINGS

1. DISKS & OVALS/COLORFUL
Butterfly—Angelfish—Surgeonfish

No.	Name	Page	Date	Location	Notes
	Banded Butterflyfish *Chaetodon striatus*	21			
	Foureye Butterflyfish *Chaetodon capistratus*	21			
	Spotfin Butterflyfish *Chaetodon ocellatus*	23			
	Reef Butterflyfish *Chaetodon sedentarius*	23			
	Longsnout Butterflyfish *Chaetodon aculeatus*	25			
	Cherubfish *Centropyge argi*	25			
	Flameback Angelfish *Centropyge aurantonotus*	25			
	Queen Angelfish *Holacanthus ciliaris*	27			
	Blue Angelfish *Holacanthus bermudensis*	27			
	Townsend Angelfish Hybrid	29			
	French Angelfish *Pomacanthus paru*	29			
	Gray Angelfish *Pomacanthus arcuatus*	31			
	Rock Beauty *Holacanthus tricolor*	31			
	Blue Tang *Acanthurus coeruleus*	33			
	Ocean Surgeonfish *Acanthurus bahianus*	35			
	Doctorfish *Acanthurus chirurgus*	35			

2 SILVERY
Dolphin—Jack—Mackerel—Needlefish—Halfbeak/Flyingfish—Barracuda—Bonnetmouth—Bonefish
Snook—Mullet—Porgy—Chub—Mojarra—Tarpon—Cobia—Flyingfish—Spadefish—Silverside

Name	Page	Date	Location	Notes
Dolphin *Coryphaena hippurus*	41			
Pompano Dolphin *Coryphaena equisietis*	40			
Rainbow Runner *Elagatis bipinnulata*	41			
Bar Jack *Caranx ruber*	43			
Blue Runner *Caranx crysos*	43			
Yellow Jack *Caranx bartholomaei*	43			
Horse-eye Jack *Caranx latus*	45			
Crevalle Jack *Caranx hippos*	45			

No.	Name	Page	Date	Location	Notes
	Black Jack *Caranx lugubris*	45			
	Almaco Jack *Seriola rivoliana*	47			
	Greater Amberjack *Seriola dumerili*	47			
	Cottonmouth Jack *Uraspis secunda*	47			
	African Pompano *Alectis ciliaris*	49			
	Permit *Trachinotus falcatus*	49			
	Florida Pompano *Trachinotus carolinus*	48			
	Palometa *Trachinotus goodei*	51			
	Lookdown *Selene vomer*	51			
	Atlantic Bumper *Chloroscombrus chrysurus*	51			
	Atlantic Leatherjacket *Oligoplites saurus*	50			
	Bigeye Scad *Selar crumenophthalmus*	53			
	Rough Scad *Trachurus lathami*	52			
	Mackerel Scad *Decapterus macarellus*	53			
	Redtail Scad *Decapterus tabl*	52			
	Round Scad *Decapterus punctatus*	53			
	Cero *Scomberomorus regalis*	55			
	Spanish Mackerel *Scomberomorus maculatus*	55			
	King Mackerel *Scomberomorus cavalla*	55			
	Wahoo *Acanthocybium solandri*	57			
	Flat Needlefish *Ablennes hians*	57			
	Keeltail Needlefish *Playbelone argalus*	57			
	Redfin Needlefish *Strongylura notata*	56			
	Houndfish *Tylosurus crocodilus*	59			
	Timucu *Strongylura timucu*	58			
	Atlantic Needlefish *Strongylura marina*	58			
	Ballyhoo *Hemiramphus brasiliensis*	59			
	Balao *Hemiramphus balao*	59			
	Halfbeak *Hyporhamphus unifasciatus*	58			
	Great Barracuda *Sphyraena barracuda*	61			

No.	Name	Page	Date	Location	Notes
	Southern Sennet *Sphyraena picudilla*	61			
	Guaguanche *Sphyraena guachancho*	61			
	Boga *Inermia vittata*	63			
	Bonnetmouth *Emmelichthyops atlanticus*	63			
	Bonefish *Albula vulpes*	63			
	Ladyfish *Elops saurus*	62			
	Common Snook *Centropomus undecimalis*	65			
	Striped Mullet *Mugil cephalus*	65			
	White Mullet *Mugil curema*	65			
	Silver Porgy *Diplodus argenteus*	67			
	Spottail Pinfish *Diplodus holbrooki*	67			
	Sea Bream *Archosargus rhomboidalis*	67			
	Pinfish *Lagodon rhomboides*	69			
	Red Porgy *Pagrus pagrus*	69			
	Sheepshead *Archosargus probatocephalus*	69			
	Sheepshead Porgy *Calamus penna*	71			
	Saucereye Porgy *Calamus calamus*	71			
	Jolthead Porgy *Calamus bajonado*	73			
	Whitebone Porgy *Calamus leucosteus*	72			
	Pluma *Calamus pennatula*	73			
	Littlehead Porgy *Calamus proridens*	73			
	Knobbed Porgy *Calamus nodosus*	72			
	Chub, Bermuda/Yellow *Kyphosus sectatrix/incisor*	75			
	Yellowfin Mojarra *Gerres cinereus*	75			
	Flagfin Mojarra *Eucinostomus melanopterus*	75			
	Slender Mojarra *Eucinostomus jonesi*	77			
	Mottled Mojarra *Eucinostomus lefroyi*	77			
	Silver Jenny *Eucinostomus gula*	77			
	Bigeye Mojarra *Eucinostomus havana*	76			
	Tarpon *Megalops atlanticus*	79			

No.	Name	Page	Date	Location	Notes
	Cobia *Rachycentron canadum*	79		.	
	Mirrorwing Flyingfish *Hirundichthys speculiger*	79			
	Atlantic Spadefish *Chaetodipterus faber*	81			
	Pilot Fish *Naucrates ductor*	81			
	Silversides, Herrings, Anchovies	81			

3. SLOPING HEAD/TAPERED BODY
Grunt—Snapper

No.	Name	Page	Date	Location	Notes
	French Grunt *Haemulon flavolineatum*	85			
	Striped Grunt *Haemulon striatum*	85			
	Smallmouth Grunt *Haemulon chrysargyreum*	85			
	White Grunt *Haemulon plumieri*	87			
	Bluestriped Grunt *Haemulon sciurus*	87			
	Caesar Grunt *Haemulon carbonarium*	87			
	Tomtate *Haemulon aurolineatum*	89			
	Cottonwick *Haemulon melanurum*	89			
	Spanish Grunt *Haemulon macrostomum*	91			
	Sailors Choice *Haemulon parra*	91			
	Black Grunt *Haemulon bonariense*	90			
	Margate (white) *Haemulon album*	91			
	Pigfish *Orthopristis chrysoptera*	97			
	Porkfish *Anisotremus virginicus*	97			
	Black Margate *Anisotremus surinamensis*	99			
	Mutton Snapper *Lutjanus analis*	99			
	Gray Snapper *Lutjanus griseus*	101			
	Cubera Snapper *Lutjanus cyanopterus*	101			
	Dog Snapper *Lutjanus jocu*	103			
	Mahogany Snapper *Lutjanus mahogoni*	103			
	Schoolmaster *Lutjanus apodus*	105			
	Lane Snapper *Lutjanus synagris*	105			
	Yellowtail Snapper *Ocyurus chrysurus*	107			
	Blackfin Snapper *Lutjanus buccanella*	107			

No.	Name	Page	Date	Location	Notes
	Red Snapper *Lutjanus campechanus*	109			
	Caribbean Red Snapper *Lutjanus purpureus*	108			
	Vermillion Snapper *Rhomboplites aurorubens*	109			

4. SMALL OVALS
Damselfish—Chromis/Damselfish—Hamlet/Seabass

No.	Name	Page	Date	Location	Notes
	Longfin Damselfish *Pomacentrus diencaeus*	113			
	Dusky Damselfish *Pomacentrus fuscus*	113			
	Threespot Damselfish *Pomacentrus planifrons*	115			
	Cocoa Damselfish *Pomacentrus variabilis*	115			
	Beaugregory *Pomacentrus leucostictus*	117			
	Bicolor Damselfish *Pomacentrus partitus*	119			
	Yellowtail Damselfish *Microspathodon chrysurus*	119			
	Sergeant Major *Abudefduf saxatilis*	121			
	Night Sergeant *Abudefduf taurus*	123			
	Yellowtail Reeffish *Chromis enchrysurus*	123			
	Blue Chromis *Chromis cyanea*	123			
	Purple Reeffish *Chromis scotti*	125			
	Brown Chromis *Chromis multilineata*	125			
	Sunshinefish *Chromis insolata*	127			
	Butter Hamlet *Hypoplectrus unicolor*	127			
	Barred Hamlet *Hypoplectrus puella*	129			
	Indigo Hamlet *Hypoplectrus indigo*	129			
	Shy Hamlet *Hypoplectrus guttavarius*	129			
	Yellowbelly Hamlet *Hypoplectrus aberrans*	131			
	Golden Hamlet *Hypoplectrus gummigutta*	131			
	Yellowtail Hamlet *Hypoplectrus chlorurus*	131			
	Black Hamlet *Hypoplectrus nigricans*	133			
	Blue Hamlet *Hypoplectrus gemma*	133			
	Masked Hamlet *Hypoplectrus sp.*	133			
	Tan Hamlet *Hypoplectrus sp.*	135			

5. HEAVY BODY/LARGE LIPS
Grouper/Seabass—Seabass—Basslet

No.	Name	Page	Date	Location	Notes
	Jewfish *Epinephelus itajara*	139			
	Warsaw Grouper *Epinephelus nigritus*	138			
	Nassau Grouper *Epinephelus striatus*	139			
	Red Grouper *Epinephelus morio*	139			
	Yellowfin Grouper *Mycteroperca venenosa*	141			
	Black Grouper *Mycteroperca bonaci*	143			
	Scamp *Mycteroperca phenax*	143			
	Tiger Grouper *Mycteroperca tigris*	145			
	Misty Grouper *Epinephelus mystacinus*	147			
	Yellowmouth Grouper *Mycteroperca interstitialis*	147			
	Gag *Mycteroperca microlepis*	149			
	Comb Grouper *Mycteroperca rubra*	149			
	Mutton Hamlet *Alphestes afer*	149			
	Marbled Grouper *Epinephelus inermis*	151			
	Graysby *Epinephelus cruentatus*	151			
	Red Hind *Epinephelus guttatus*	153			
	Rock Hind *Epinephelus adscensionis*	153			
	Coney *Epinephelus fulvus*	155			
	Bank Sea Bass *Centropristis ocyurus*	157			
	Black Sea Bass *Centropristis striata*	157			
	Pygmy Sea Bass *Serraniculus pumilio*	157			
	Sand Perch *Diplectrum formosum*	159			
	Dwarf Sand Perch *Diplectrum bivittatum*	158			
	Aquavina *Diplectrum radiale*	158			
	Harlequin Bass *Serranus tigrinus*	159			
	Snow Bass *Serranus chionaraia*	158			
	Two-spot Bass *Serranus flaviventris*	158			
	Lantern Bass *Serranus baldwini*	161			
	Orangeback Bass *Serranus annularis*	161			

No.	Name	Page	Date	Location	Notes
	Tobacco *Serranus tabacarius*	161			
	School Bass *Schultzea beta*	160			
	Belted Sandfish *Serranus subligarius*	163			
	Tattler Bass *Serranus phoebe*	163			
	Chalk Bass *Serranus tortugarum*	163			
	Peppermint Bass *Liopropoma rubre*	165			
	Candy Basslet *Liopropoma carmabi*	165			
	Cave Bass *Liopropoma mowbrayi*	165			
	Wrasse Bass *Liopropoma eukrines*	167			
	Creole-fish *Paranthias furcifer*	167			
	Greater Soapfish *Rypticus saponaceus*	167			
	Freckled Soapfish *Rypticus bistrispinus*	168			
	Whitespotted Soapfish *Rypticus maculatus*	169			
	Spotted Soapfish *Rypticus subbifrenatus*	169			
	Yellowcheek Basslet *Gramma linki*	169			
	Fairy Basslet *Gramma loreto*	171			
	Heliotrope Basslet *Gramma klayi*	170			
	Blackcap Basslet *Gramma melacara*	171			
	Threeline Basslet *Lipogramma trilineatum*	171			

6. SWIM WITH PECTORAL FINS/OBVIOUS SCALES
Parrotfish—Hogfish/Wrasse—Wrasse—Razorfish/Wrasse

No.	Name	Page	Date	Location	Notes
	Blue Parrotfish *Scarus coeruleus*	175			
	Midnight Parrotfish *Scarus coelestinus*	175			
	Rainbow Parrotfish *Scarus guacamaia*	177			
	Queen Parrotfish *Scarus vetula*	177			
	Stoplight Parrotfish *Sparisoma viride*	179			
	Princess Parrotfish *Scarus taeniopterus*	179			
	Striped Parrotfish *Scarus croicensis*	181			
	Redband Parrotfish *Sparisoma aurofrenatum*	183			

No.	Name	Page	Date	Location	Notes
	Redtail Parrotfish *Sparisoma chrysopterum*	185			
	Redfin Parrotfish *Sparisoma rubripinne*	185			
	Greenblotch Parrotfish *Sparisoma atomarium*	187			
	Bucktooth Parrotfish *Sparisoma radians*	187			
	Bluelip Parrotfish *Cryptotomus roseus*	189			
	Hogfish *Lachnolaimus maximus*	191			
	Spanish Hogfish *Bodianus rufus*	191			
	Spotfin Hogfish *Bodianus pulchellus*	193			
	Creole Wrasse *Clepticus parrae*	193			
	Puddingwife *Halichoeres radiatus*	195			
	Yellowhead Wrasse *Halichoeres garnoti*	197			
	Bluehead *Thalassoma bifasciatum*	199			
	Slippery Dick *Halichoeres bivittatus*	201			
	Clown Wrasse *Halichoeres maculipinna*	203			
	Blackear Wrasse *Halichoeres poeyi*	205			
	Rainbow Wrasse *Halichoeres pictus*	205			
	Yellowcheek Wrasse *Halichoeres cyanocephalus*	207			
	Dwarf Wrasse *Doratonotus megalepis*	209			
	Green Razorfish *Hemipteronotus splendens*	209			
	Rosy Razorfish *Hemipteronotus martinicensis*	211			
	Pearly Razorfish *Hemipteronotus novacula*	211			

7. REDDISH/BIG EYES
Squirrelfish—Bigeye—Cardinalfish

No.	Name	Page	Date	Location	Notes
	Squirrelfish *Holocentrus adscensionis*	215			
	Longspine Squirrelfish *Holocentrus rufus*	215			
	Reef Squirrelfish *Holocentrus coruscum*	215			
	Dusky Squirrelfish *Holocentrus vexillarius*	217			
	Longjaw Squirrelfish *Holocentrus marianus*	217			
	Deepwater Squirrelfish *Holocentrus bullisi*	219			
	Cardinal Soldierfish *Plectrypops retrospinis*	219			

No.	Name	Page	Date	Location	Notes
	Blackbar Soldierfish *Myripristis jacobus*	219			
	Short Bigeye *Pristigenys alta*	221			
	Glasseye Snapper *Priacanthus cruentatus*	221			
	Bigeye *Priacanthus arenatus*	223			
	Belted Cardinalfish *Apogon townsendi*	223			
	Broadsaddle Cardinalfish *Apogon pillionatus*	222			
	Barred Cardinalfish *Apogon binotatus*	223			
	Roughlip Cardinalfish *Apogon robinsi*	225			
	Pale Cardinalfish *Apogon planifrons*	225			
	Mimic Cardinalfish *Apogon phenax*	224			
	Whitestar Cardinalfish *Apogon lachneri*	225			
	Oddscale Cardinalfish *Apogon anisolepis*	224			
	Flamefish *Apogon maculatus*	227			
	Twospot Cardinalfish *Apogon pseudomaculatus*	227			
	Bridle Cardinalfish *Apogon aurolineatus*	229			
	Sawcheek Cardinalfish *Apogon quadrisquamatus*	229			
	Bigtooth Cardinalfish *Apogon affinis*	229			
	Dusky Cardinalfish *Phaeoptyx pigmentaria*	231			
	Freckled Cardinalfish *Phaeoptyx conklini*	230			
	Sponge Cardinalfish *Phaeoptyx xenus*	230			
	Blackfin Cardinalfish *Astrapogon puncticulatus*	231			
	Bronze Cardinalfish *Astrapogon alutus*	230			
	Conchfish *Astrapogon stellatus*	231			

8. SMALL, ELONGATED BOTTOM-DWELLERS
Goby—Blenny—Dragonet—Jawfish

No.	Name	Page	Date	Location	Notes
	Neon Goby *Gobiosoma oceanops*	235			
	Yellowline Goby *Gobiosoma horsti*	235			
	Spotlight Goby *Gobiosoma louisae*	235			
	Yellowprow Goby *Gobiosoma xanthiprora*	237			
	Slaty Goby *Gobiosoma tenox*	236			

No.	Name	Page	Date	Location	Notes
	Yellownose Goby *Gobiosoma randalli*	237			
	Barsnout Goby *Gobiosoma illecebrosum*	237			
	Cleaning Goby *Gobiosoma genie*	239			
	Sharknose Goby *Gobiosoma evelynae*	239			
	Broadstripe Goby *Gobiosoma prochilos*	241			
	Shortstripe Goby *Gobiosoma chancei*	241			
	Greenbanded Goby *Gobiosoma multifasciatum*	241			
	Nineline Goby *Ginsburgellus novemlineatus*	240			
	Tiger Goby *Gobiosoma macrodon*	243			
	Rockcut Goby *Gobiosoma grosvenori*	243			
	Orangesided Goby *Gobiosoma dilepsis*	243			
	Leopard Goby *Gobiosoma saucrum*	245			
	White-eye Goby *Bollmannia boqueronensis*	245			
	Spotfin Goby *Gobionellus stigmalophius*	244			
	Dash Goby *Gobionellus saepepallens*	245			
	Goldspot Goby *Gnatholepis thompsoni*	247			
	Colon Goby *Coryphopterus dicrus*	247			
	Bartail Goby *Coryphopterus thrix*	246			
	Spotted Goby *Coryphopterus punctipectophorus*	247			
	Pallid Goby *Coryphopterus eidolon*	249			
	Bridled Goby *Coryphopterus glaucofraenum*	249			
	Masked Goby *Coryphopterus personatus*	251			
	Glass Goby *Coryphopterus hyalinus*	251			
	Peppermint Goby *Coryphopterus lipernes*	251			
	Rusty Goby *Priolepis hipoliti*	251			
	Crested Goby *Lophogobius cyprinoides*	253			
	Orangespotted Goby *Nes longus*	253			
	Seminole Goby *Microgobius carri*	253			
	Hovering Goby *Ioglossus helenae*	255			
	Blue Goby *Ioglossus calliurus*	255			
	Ringed Blenny *Starksia hassi*	255			

No.	Name	Page	Date	Location	Notes
	Dwarf Blenny *Starksia nanodes*	257			
	Downy Blenny *Labrisomus kalisherae*	257			
	Puffcheek Blenny *Labrisomus bucciferus*	256			
	Palehead Blenny *Labrisomus gobio*	257			
	Hairy Blenny *Labrisomus nuchipinnis*	259			
	Mimic Blenny *Labrisomus guppyi*	258			
	Spotcheek Blenny *Labrisomus nigricinctus*	259			
	Quillfin Blenny *Labrisomus filamentosus*	261			
	Diamond Blenny *Malacoctenus boehlkei*	261			
	Saddled Blenny *Malacoctenus triangulatus*	263			
	Dusky Blenny *Malacoctenus gilli*	263			
	Imitator Blenny *Malacoctenus erdmani*	262			
	Barfin Blenny *Malacoctenus versicolor*	265			
	Rosy Blenny *Malacoctenus macropus*	265			
	Goldline Blenny *Malacoctenus aurolineatus*	267			
	Sailfin Blenny *Emblemaria pandionis*	267			
	Blackhead Blenny *Emblemaria bahamensis*	269			
	Spinyhead Blenny *Acanthemblemaria spinosa*	269			
	Papillose Blenny *Acanthemblemaria chaplini*	271			
	Roughhead Blenny *Acanthemblemaria aspera*	271			
	Secretary Blenny *Acanthemblemaria maria*	273			
	Wrasse Blenny *Hemiemblemaria simulus*	273			
	Arrow Blenny *Lucayablennius zingaro*	275			
	Blackfin Blenny *Paraclinus nigripinnis*	275			
	Longhorn Blenny *Hypsoblennius exstochilus*	275			
	Tesselated Blenny *Hypsoblennius invemar*	277			
	Molly Miller *Scartella cristata*	277			
	Seaweed Blenny *Parablennius marmoreus*	279			
	Barred Blenny *Hypleurochilus bermudensis*	279			
	Redlip Blenny *Ophioblennius atlanticus*	281			
	Zebratail Blenny *Hypleurochilus sp.*	281			

No.	Name	Page	Date	Location	Notes
	Lofty Triplefin *Enneanectes altivelis*	283			
	Blackedge Triplefin *Enneanectes atrorus*	282			
	Roughhead Triplefin *Enneanectes boehlkei*	283			
	Redeye Triplefin *Enneanectes pectoralis*	282			
	Mimic Triplefin *Enneanectes jordani*	282			
	Yellowface Pikeblenny *Chaenopsis limbaughi*	283			
	Bluethroat Pikeblenny *Chaenopsis ocellata*	285			
	Lancer Dragonet *Paradiplogrammus bairdi*	285			
	Yellowhead Jawfish *Opistognathus aurifrons*	287			
	Dusky Jawfish *Opistognathus whitehursti*	287			
	Banded Jawfish *Opistognathus macrognathus*	287			

9. ODD-SHAPED BOTTOM-DWELLERS

Flounder—Clingfish—Batfish—Toadfish—Scorpionfish—Frogfish—Stargazer—Searobin
Gurnard—Lizardfish—Seahorse—Pipefish—Hawkfish—Hake/Cod

No.	Name	Page	Date	Location	Notes
	Peacock Flounder *Bothus lunatus*	293			
	Tropical Flounder *Paralichthys tropicus*	292			
	Eyed Flounder *Bothus ocellatus*	293			
	Spottail Flounder *Bothus robinsi*	292			
	Channel Flounder *Syacium micrurum*	293			
	Dusky Flounder *Syacium papillosum*	292			
	Gulf Flounder *Paralichthys albigutta*	295			
	Ocellated Flounder *Ancylopsetta quadrocellata*	294			
	Three-eye Flounder *Ancylopsetta dilecta*	294			
	Shrimp Flounder *Gastropsetta frontalis*	294			
	Stippled Clingfish *Gobiesox punctulatus*	295			
	Red Clingfish *Arcos rubiginosus*	295			
	Pancake Batfish *Halieutichthys aculeatus*	297			
	Polka-dot Batfish *Ogcocephalus radiatus*	297			
	Shortnose Batfish *Ogcocephalus nasutus*	297			
	Roughback Batfish *Ogcocephalus parvus*	299			
	Splendid Toadfish *Sanopus splendidus*	299			

No.	Name	Page	Date	Location	Notes
	Pipehorse *Acentronura dendritica*	319			
	Shortfin Pipefish *Cosmocampus elucens*	319			
	Whitenose Pipefish *Cosmocampus albirostris*	319			
	Harlequin Pipefish *Micrognathus ensenadae*	321			
	Banded Pipefish *Micrognathus crinitus*	320			
	Redspotted Hawkfish *Amblycirrhitus pinos*	321			
	Carolina Hake *Urophycis earlli*	321			
	Southern Hake *Urophycis floridana*	320			

10. ODD-SHAPED SWIMMERS
Trumpetfish—Cornetfish—Tilefish—Puffers/Smooth—Puffers/Spiny—Boxfish
Triggerfish/Leatherjacket—Filefish/Leatherjacket—Goatfish—Drum—Croaker/Drum
Tripletail—Sweeper—Viviparous Brotula—Remora

	Name	Page			
	Trumpetfish *Aulostomus maculatus*	325			
	Bluespotted Cornetfish *Fistularia tabacaria*	325			
	Red Spotted Cornetfish *Fistularia petimba*	324			
	Sand Tilefish *Malacanthus plumieri*	325			
	Bandtail Puffer *Sphoeroides spengleri*	327			
	Southern Puffer *Sphoeroides nephelus*	326			
	Caribbean Puffer *Sphoeroides greeleyi*	326			
	Checkered Puffer *Sphoeroides testudineus*	237			
	Sharpnose Puffer *Canthigaster rostrata*	327			
	Marbled Puffer *Sphoeroides dorsalis*	326			
	Web Burrfish *Chilomycterus antillarum*	329			
	Striped Burrfish *Chilomycterus schoepfi*	329			
	Bridled Burrfish *Chilomycterus antennatus*	329			
	Balloonfish *Diodon holocanthus*	331			
	Porcupinefish *Diodon hystrix*	331			
	Spotted Burrfish *Chilomycterus atinga*	330			
	Honeycomb Cowfish *Lactophrys polygonia*	333			
	Scrawled Cowfish *Lactophrys quadricornis*	333			
	Trunkfish *Lactophrys trigonus*	333			

No.	Name	Page	Date	Location	Notes
	Smooth Trunkfish _Lactophrys triqueter_	335			
	Spotted Trunkfish _Lactophrys bicaudalis_	335			
	Queen Triggerfish _Balistes vetula_	337			
	Gray Triggerfish _Balistes capriscus_	337			
	Ocean Triggerfish _Canthidermis sufflamen_	339			
	Rough Triggerfish _Canthidermis maculata_	339			
	Sargassum Triggerfish _Xanthichthys ringens_	339			
	Black Durgon _Melichthys niger_	341			
	Scrawled Filefish _Aluterus scriptus_	341			
	Dotterel Filefish _Aluterus heudeloti_	340			
	Orangespotted Filefish _Cantherhines pullus_	341			
	Orange Filefish _Aluterus schoepfi_	343			
	Unicorn Filefish _Aluterus monoceros_	342			
	Whitespotted Filefish _Cantherhines macrocerus_	343			
	Pygmy Filefish _Monacanthus setifer_	345			
	Slender Filefish _Monacanthus tuckeri_	345			
	Fringed Filefish _Monaanthus ciliatus_	347			
	Planehead Filefish _Monacanthus hispidus_	347			
	Spotted Goatfish _Pseudupeneus maculatus_	349			
	Red Goatfish _Mullus auratus_	348			
	Yellow Goatfish _Mulloidichthys martinicus_	349			
	Dwarf Goatfish _Upeneus parvus_	351			
	Spotted Drum _Equetus punctatus_	351			
	Jackknife Fish _Equetus lanceolatus_	353			
	Highhat _Equetus acuminatus_	353			
	Cubbyu _Equetus umbrosus_	355			
	Reef Croaker _Odontoscion dentex_	357			
	Striped Croaker _Bairdiella sanctaeluciae_	357			
	Black Drum _Pogonias cromis_	357			
	Tripletail _Lobotes surinamensis_	359			
	Glassy Sweeper _Pempheris schomburgki_	359			

No.	Name	Page	Date	Location	Notes
	Shortfin Sweeper *Pempheris poeyi*	358			
	Black Brotula *Stygnobrotula latebricola*	359			
	Whitefin Sharksucker *Echeneis neucratoides*	361			
	Sharksucker *Echeneis naucrates*	361			

11. EELS
Moray—Conger Eel—Snake Eel

	Name	Page	Date	Location	Notes
	Green Moray *Gymnothorax funebris*	365			
	Spotted Moray *Gymnothorax moringa*	365			
	Reticulate Moray *Muraena retifera*	365			
	Purplemouth Moray *Gymnothorax vicinus*	367			
	Viper Moray *Enchelycore nigricans*	367			
	Chestnut Moray *Enchelycore carychroa*	367			
	Goldentail Moray *Gymnothorax miliaris*	369			
	Honeycomb Moray *Gymnothorax saxicola*	369			
	Blackedge Moray *Gymnothorax nigromarginatus*	368			
	Chain Moray *Echidna catenata*	369			
	Stout Moray *Muraena robusta*	371			
	Broadbanded Moray *Channomuraena vittata*	371			
	Brown Garden Eel *Heteroconger halis*	371			
	Manytooth Conger *Conger triporiceps*	373			
	Conger Eel *Conger oceanicus*	370			
	Sharptail Eel *Myrichthys breviceps*	373			
	Goldspotted Eel *Myrichthys ocellatus*	373			
	Blackspotted Snake Eel *Quassiremus productus*	372			
	Spotted Snake Eel *Ophichthus ophis*	375			
	Spotted Spoon-nose Eel *Echiophis intertinctus*	375			

12 SHARKS & RAYS
Carpet Shark—Requiem Shark—Mackerel Shark—Hammerhead Shark
Guitarfish-Skate—Electric Ray—Stingray—Round Stingray—Eagle Ray—Manta

	Name	Page	Date	Location	Notes
	Whale Shark *Rhincodon typus*	379			
	Nurse Shark *Ginglymostoma cirratum*	379			
	Lemon Shark *Negaprion brevirostris*	379			

No.	Name	Page	Date	Location	Notes
	Tiger Shark *Galeocerdo cuvier*	381			
	Atlantic Sharpnose Shark *Rhizoprionodon terraenovae*	381			
	Bull Shark *Carcharhinus leucas*	381			
	Reef Shark *Carcharhinus perezi*	383			
	Dusky Shark *Carcharhinus obscurus*	382			
	Blacktip Shark *Carcharhinus limbatus*	383			
	Spinner Shark *Carcharhinus brevipinna*	382			
	Silky Shark *Carcharhinus falciformis*	383			
	Sandbar Shark *Carcharhinus plumbeus*	385			
	Oceanic Whitetip Shark *Carcharhinus longimanus*	385			
	Shortfin Mako *Isurus oxyrinchus*	385			
	Scalloped Hammerhead *Sphyrna lewini*	387			
	Great Hammerhead *Sphyrna mokarran*	386			
	Smooth Hammerhead *Sphyrna zygaena*	386			
	Bonnethead *Sphyrna tiburo*	387			
	Atlantic Guitarfish *Rhinobatos lentiginosus*	387			
	Southern Guitarfish *Rhinobatos percellens*	386			
	Clearnose Skate *Raja eglanteria*	389			
	Roundel Skate *Raja texana*	388			
	Caribbean Torpedo *Torpedo sp.*	389			
	Atlantic Torpedo *Torpedo nobiliana*	388			
	Lesser Electric Ray *Narcine brasiliensis*	389			
	Southern Stingray *Dasyatis americana*	391			
	Caribbean Stingray *Himantura schmardae*	390			
	Roughtail Stingray *Dasyatis centroura*	391			
	Yellow Stingray *Urolophus jamaicensis*	391			
	Smooth Butterfly Ray *Gymnura micrura*	393			
	Spiny Butterfly Ray *Gymnura altavela*	392			
	Spotted Eagle Ray *Aetobatus narinari*	393			
	Manta *Manta birostris*	393			
	Devil Ray *Mobula hypostoma*	392			

ADDITIONAL SPECIES

No.	Name	Page	Date	Location	Notes

NOTES

THE REEF SET

by
Paul Humann

REEF FISH IDENTIFICATION FLORIDA-CARIBBEAN-BAHAMAS
The book that revolutionized fishwatching! Enlarged 2nd edition.
392 pp, over 500 color plates. **$39.95**

REEF CREATURE IDENTIFICATION FLORIDA-CARIBBEAN-BAHAMAS
More than 30 marine life scientists from eight nations collaborated with the
author to compile the most comprehensive and accurate visual identification
guide of reef invertebrates ever published.
344 pp, 478 color plates. **$37.95**

REEF CORAL IDENTIFICATION FLORIDA-CARIBBEAN-BAHAMAS
252 pp, 475 color plates. **$32.95**

Shelf Case for the Three Volume Set $10.00
Three Volume REEF SET with free Shelf Case $115.00

REEF FISH IDENTIFICATION– Galápagos
Finally, a comprehensive fish identification guide for the Galápagos Islands – the
world's most spectacular natural aquarium. 260 beautiful color plates display the
famous archipelago's fabulous fish life in an easy-to-use, quick reference format.
Comb binding, 200 pp, 6"x 9". **$34.95**

FISH-IN-A-POCKET WATERPROOF MINI-BOOKS!
Have you ever wished you could take your ID books with you underwater? Now
you can! Our new waterproof mini-books (4 3/4" x 6") are the perfect size for your
BC pocket. Each 24-page booklet contains 132 color photographs of the most
commonly sighted reef animals. Brief ID tips, size of each species and arrows
pointing to distinguishing marks make this the perfect underwater reference.

FISH-IN-A-POCKET FLORIDA-CARIBBEAN-BAHAMAS. **$9.95**
CREATURE-IN-A-POCKET FLORIDA-CARIBBEAN-BAHAMAS. **$9.95**
FISH-IN-A-POCKET INDO-PACIFIC. **$9.95**

To order any of the above products, contact:

NEW WORLD PUBLICATIONS
1861 Cornell Rd, Dept. M, Jacksonville, Florida 32207
1-800-737-6558   http://www.fishid.com
Please allow 2 to 3 weeks for delivery.